Using Norton Utilities® 7

ALAN C. ELLIOTT
RON HOLMES

que

Using Norton Utilities 7.

Copyright © 1993 by Que® Corporation.

Library of Congress Catalog No.: 92-84095

ISBN: 1-56529-079-8

95 94 93   4 3 2 1

Interpretation of the printing code: the rightmost double-digit number is the year of the book's printing; the rightmost single-digit number is the number of the book's printing. For example, a printing code of 93-1 shows that the first printing of the book occurred in 1993.

Screens reproduced in this book were created using Collage Plus from Inner Media, Inc., Hollis, NH.

This book is based on Norton Utilities 7.0 but can be used with other versions in which the commands apply.

Publisher: David P. Ewing

Associate Publisher: Rick Ranucci

Operations Manager: Sheila Cunningham

Publishing Plan Manager: Thomas H. Bennett

Marketing Manager: Ray Robinson

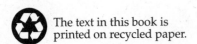

The text in this book is printed on recycled paper.

To Leslie, Mary, and Evelyn.

CREDITS

Title Manager
Shelley O'Hara

Acquisitions Editor
Sherri Morningstar

Product Development Specialist
Joyce Nielsen

Technical Editors
Ron Holmes
Robert Smith
David A. Wolfe

Production Editor
Virginia Noble

Editors
Sara Allaei
William A. Barton
Elsa M. Bell
Barb Colter
Jane A. Cramer
Susan M. Dunn
Bryan Gambrel
Philip Kitchel
Heather Northrup
Kathy Simpson
Colleen Totz

Book Designer
Scott Cook

Production Team
Jeff Baker
Claudia Bell
Julie Brown
Brad Chinn
Brook Farling
Carla Hall-Batton
Heather Kaufman
Bob LaRoche
Joy Dean Lee
Jay Lesandrini
Caroline Roop
Linda Seifert
Sandra Shay

Composed in *Cheltenham* and *MCPdigital* by Que Corporation

Alan C. Elliott is an assistant director of Academic Computing Services at the University of Texas Southwestern Medical Center in Dallas. He holds a master's degree (M.A.S.) in statistics from Southern Methodist University and an M.B.A. from the University of Texas at Arlington. He has written several books, including *Introduction to Microcomputing with Applications*, *A Daily Dose of the American Dream*, *PC Programming Techniques*, *Using Norton Utilities 6*, and *Using PROCOMM PLUS for Windows*. He is the revision author of *Using PROCOMM PLUS*, 2nd Edition, and is coauthor of the 1985 and 1988 editions of the *Directory of Statistical Microcomputing Software*. He is also author of the software packages Kwikstat (data analysis), PC-CAI (computer-assisted instruction) and Information Please (free-form database), all published by TexaSoft. His articles have appeared in professional and popular periodicals, including *PC Week*, *Collegiate Microcomputer Journal*, *Communications in Statistics*, and *American Statistician*.

Ron Holmes, a computer technician for the Metropolitan School District of Wayne Township in Indianapolis, Indiana, assists in the acquisition, installation, and maintenance of all hardware within the school district. He teaches dBASE and PC operating systems for a local college, as well as runs a consulting business that provides custom programming, database management, and preventive maintenance services. Since 1985, Ron has served as a technical editor for Que Corporation, providing technical editing and support on more than 20 books. He is also coauthor of *Using Norton Desktop for DOS* and *Using Microsoft Works 3 for DOS*.

ACKNOWLEDGMENTS

I want to thank Sherri Morningstar for the opportunity to work on this book. The entire staff was very professional, helpful, and supportive throughout the project. Special thanks go to Robin Drake, Ginny Noble, Jane Cramer, Elsa Bell, and Kathy Simpson for their help in editing the manuscript and asking insightful questions to make the presentation better. Ron Holmes deserves thanks for his careful technical review of the manuscript.

This project could not have been finished without the support of my wife, Annette, and without some patience from my kids, Mary and William.

Trademarks

All terms mentioned in this book that are known to be trademarks or service marks have been appropriately capitalized. Que cannot attest to the accuracy of this information. Use of a term in this book should not be regarded as affecting the validity of any trademark or service mark.

CONTENTS AT A GLANCE

TABLE OF CONTENTS

I Taking Charge of Your Computer

II Protecting Your Files

III Basic Recovery Techniques

IV Advanced Recovery Techniques

V Making Your Computer Work More Efficiently

VI Managing Your Computer's Resources

xxix

Introduction

Think of your PC as an automobile. A fine roadster can take you a lot of places in style. It can also occasionally get a flat tire or need a carburetor adjustment. There is nothing more frustrating than chugging down the highway bellowing smoke and overheating. If you depend on that roadster to get you where you want to go, you will spend a little time tuning it and checking the tires for potential problems. You will also want to keep a fully inflated spare tire in your trunk, just in case.

Your PC is much like that roadster. You don't want to go too long without a checkup, and if something does go wrong, you want a tool set that can help you quickly fix that flat tire or remedy other problems that might crop up from time to time. The PC's tune-up involves disk access; a flat tire is a lost file or an accidentally formatted disk. Norton Utilities is the toolbox that can fix (and prevent) many disk-related problems. The backup you create using the Norton Backup program is your spare tire. This book shows you how to use these tools effectively. Then you can drive your PC with confidence—and take a trip around the world of computing as if you were in a finely tuned and polished touring sedan.

Norton Utilities, Norton Backup, and Norton Commander are the best-known data-recovery and disk-management programs available for the IBM PC and compatible computers. This book has two goals:

- To help beginners understand and learn how to use these programs

- To help new and seasoned users gain insights into making information storage more reliable, safer, and better organized

Hard disks can be a blessing and a curse. They are a blessing because they can store a great deal of information. They are a curse when you have hundreds of unorganized files and can't find the one you need. The Norton Utilities programs for file management and computer management can help you manage your hard disk. This book shows you how to use these programs to organize your disk, find lost files, navigate through a maze of directories, and be more productive in the use of your hard disk.

Who Should Read *Using Norton Utilities 7*?

Computer users with some experience will tell you, "It's not *if* you will lose information on your computer—it's *when!*" You should read this book if you want to prevent that inevitable *when*, or if you have already experienced it and are looking for a way to make sure that it doesn't happen again. Perhaps you are in the middle of a crisis and are looking for some way to recover information that may be lost. This book contains the information that, along with Norton Utilities, can give you the best chance of data recovery and help you prevent many kinds of data loss in the future.

Using Norton Utilities 7 is for anyone who uses an IBM PC or a compatible computer with the PC DOS or MS-DOS operating system. Norton Utilities 7 and the companion program, Norton Backup, give you capabilities to protect, recover, and manage your computer's resources beyond what is available from standard DOS commands. This comprehensive book will help you get the most out of your computer and the Norton programs, whether you are a novice in using computers or you have used PCs for many years.

What Is Covered in This Book?

This book covers Norton Utilities 7.0, with references to Norton Utilities 6.0 and 5.0 and Norton Advanced Utilities 4.5. Covered also are Norton Backup 2.0 and Norton Commander 3.0.

The book is divided into seven parts and contains a Command Reference and four appendixes. The following sections describe the book's contents in detail.

Part I: Taking Charge of Your Computer

Part I provides an overview of Norton Utilities. Chapter 1 introduces the Norton main screen and shows you how to access Norton programs, interact with Norton dialog boxes, and access Help. Chapter 2 describes the Norton configuration program, accessed from the Norton main screen or the DOS prompt. The configuration program allows you to customize the Norton Utilities programs for your computer. Chapter 3 introduces disk drive concepts and terms that are used throughout the rest of the book. If you are new to computer use or data recovery, you may want to pay particular attention to Chapter 3 to learn about the workings of the disk drive.

Part II: Protecting Your Files

Part II describes how to use the Norton programs that are designed to protect your files from disaster. Although you may have been attracted to Norton Utilities because its programs can help you *recover* from information loss, it is perhaps more important to pay close attention to how the utilities can help you *prevent* loss. Your goal should be to use the recovery techniques rarely and use the prevention techniques consistently. Chapter 4 covers the Safe Format and Image utilities. These fundamental components of Norton Utilities enable you to protect floppy disks and hard disks against accidental formatting by storing on your disk a duplicate copy of important disk information that you can use to reconstruct a formatted disk.

Chapter 5 describes the SmartCan utility. The SmartCan name is a shortened version of a concept of a "smart" trash can. When you are using SmartCan to monitor your disk as files are erased, you can imagine the files being thrown into a nearby trash can. Actually, the files are still on disk, but the SmartCan program protects that area on disk to prevent the erased files from being overwritten. The files can be recovered (unerased) for a period of time (you can choose that period of time) just as you can pull a sheet of paper out of the nearby trash can. Finally, when the trash can is hauled off to the dump, the files are permanently lost. Thus, the SmartCan utility enables you to manage your erased files.

Chapter 6 describes the Disk Monitor utility. This program takes a different approach to protecting files against erasure. Unlike SmartCan, which allows files to be erased but "protects" them for a period of time, Disk Monitor watches the activity of the computer and will not let certain files be erased unless permission is granted. For example, a slip of the fingers could cause you to type DEL *.EXE instead of DIR *.EXE.

Without Disk Monitor, the files would be erased. If, for some reason, you did not discover the accident (maybe your eight-year-old did this and didn't know what had happened), the erased files could go undiscovered until it was too late for them to be unerased. With Disk Monitor in place and watching for this kind of erasure, the disaster could have been prevented. Disk Monitor contains two additional features: Disk Light and Disk Park. Disk Light enables you to simulate a hard disk access light on your monitor so that you can monitor disk access. Disk Park causes your disk drive components to "park" in a safe position, enabling you to move your computer with less chance of hard disk damage.

The Diskreet utility is covered in Chapter 7. With Diskreet, you can protect files by encrypting them (changing them into an unreadable code). You then can decrypt the files (recover them to their original state) with a password. Because most computers can be accessed by anyone (there is little or no built-in protection from DOS), Diskreet gives you the ability to store highly confidential files on your computer without fear that they will be read on purpose or accidentally by someone not authorized to view their contents. Diskreet lets you protect files in two ways. First, you can protect individual files or groups of files by encrypting each file. Second, you can create an NDisk, which is like a new disk on your computer (a logical disk, not physically a new drive). This new NDisk can be used just like a normal disk drive to store and retrieve files (from any program). To use the NDisk, however, you must open it with a password. If the drive is not opened, the files stored on the NDisk are encrypted and unreadable. When you close the NDisk, you have protected all files contained in the NDisk. Thus, Diskreet protects your files by keeping them away from unauthorized eyes.

Another utility to prevent files from being accessed by unauthorized users is WipeInfo, covered in Chapter 8. Normally, when you erase a file, its contents remain on disk for a time, until they are overwritten by another file. This means that confidential files, even though they are erased, can possibly be unerased from your disk drive and read by an unauthorized user. The WipeInfo utility erases a file (or a disk) more thoroughly than DOS erases it; WipeInfo overwrites the actual contents of the file or disk with other data. When you want to get rid of information for good, WipeInfo is the command to use.

Chapter 9 covers two Norton Commands—File Attributes and File Find—that can be used to set file attributes. These attributes control how a file can be accessed by users. By setting file attributes, you can cause a file to be read-only or hidden. A read-only file cannot be erased or overwritten. Thus, setting a file to read-only gives some protection against the file being accidentally erased or changed. The hidden attribute allows you to hide a file from normal view. The name of a hidden file will not show up on a directory listing (when you use the DIR command) even though the file is on disk. Setting attributes for some files is a simple way to give those files some measure of protection against accidental destruction while still allowing them to be accessed by the user.

Part III: Basic Recovery Techniques

The chapters in Part III discuss how to use the automated Norton Utilities programs to recover lost information on your disks. (See Part IV for advanced recovery techniques.) This part of the book helps you recover from most types of disk disasters; you learn how to recover erased files, unformat disks, and correct file access problems on a disk. You should use the techniques in Part III before you attempt to use those in Part IV. For the most part, the techniques in Part III are automated. You need to know little about disk construction, sectors, clusters, and so on, because the smart people at Symantec have programmed their knowledge about data recovery into the programs. If the techniques covered in these chapters cannot recover your information, proceed to Part IV.

Chapter 10 describes how to unerase file and directories. The UnErase command is probably the most well known of the Norton Utilities programs. The recovery of one file can easily pay for the software program itself (as well as for this book) in terms of saved time and effort to reconstruct an important file.

Chapter 11 describes how to unformat a disk. The techniques discussed include recovery of formatted disks that contain Image (see Chapter 4) or MIRROR (DOS 5 and later) recovery information, as well as recovery of disks that do not contain this information.

Norton Disk Doctor (NDD), covered in Chapter 12, is a diagnostic tool for your disk. NDD examines the disk for defects and checks files for integrity. When a problem is found with the disk, NDD can often fix the problem on the spot. If the problem cannot be fixed, NDD will usually be able to tell you what files are affected by the disk defect. Although disks are very reliable, they can lose information over time and develop errors in file storage. Periodic use of NDD can locate and correct minor disk problems before they develop into major disasters.

Disk Tools, described in Chapter 13, can help you recover from four specific problems. The Make a Disk Bootable option enables you to place the needed files on a disk to make it a boot disk, whether or not the disk was originally a boot disk. The Recover from DOS's RECOVER option enables you to recover files that have been "lost" during use of the DOS RECOVER command. With the Revive a Defective Disk option, you can place a fresh copy of the system information on a disk, enabling you to correct problems caused by damaged system information. The Mark a Cluster option allows you to mark as good or bad any cluster on a disk. Marking the cluster as bad means that it will no longer be used to store file information. Marking a cluster as good means that the cluster will be available to store file information.

A key component of your data recovery toolbox is Rescue Disk. Chapter 14 describes how to create a rescue disk and how to use it to perform a rescue on your hard disk. Basically, a rescue disk is an emergency boot disk that can be used to boot your computer if it will not boot from the hard drive. This disk also contains key Norton data-recovery programs (such as NDD, UnErase, and UnFormat) that can help you correct problems on your hard disk. It is essential that you create a rescue disk for your computer.

With the File Fix utility, described in Chapter 15, you can reconstruct some specific kinds of application program files, including database, spreadsheet, and word processing files. Occasionally, these kinds of files can sustain damage caused by the application program, power outages, or disk-related problems. File Fix can often reconstruct a file according to the application's specifications and recover some, if not all, of the lost information.

Part IV: Advanced Recovery Techniques

When possible, the automated recovery techniques covered in Part III should be used to recover data or fix problems with your disk. Some problems, however, require more advanced techniques. Part IV covers two features of Norton Utilities—Manual UnErase and Disk Editor—that allow you to examine and recover specific locations on a disk.

Chapter 16 describes the UnErase utility's Manual UnErase feature. This should be used when the automated UnErase technique cannot recover an erased file. Often the contents of the file are on disk, but the UnErase program cannot locate all the clusters that make up the file. With Manual UnErase, you can search the disk for the clusters needed to reconstruct the file, and recover as much of the file as you can locate.

Chapter 17 covers Norton Disk Editor. This set of routines enables you to explore the information on the disk down to the level of examining each individual byte. With Disk Editor, you can display and edit information on a disk. This utility allows you to fix problems in programs and files and to recover all or portions of erased files.

Part V: Making Your Computer Work More Efficiently

Part V describes a number of Norton Utilities that can be used to fine-tune your computer so that it runs more efficiently. These utilities allow you to display important information about your system, rearrange files on your hard disk for quick access, calibrate your hard disk for optimal use, and optimize disk and memory access.

Chapter 18 describes the Norton System Info program. Although this program does not in itself change anything about your computer's setup, System Info is a valuable tool for comparing your computer's disk and processor speed with that of other computers, and for discovering what components are being used on your computer (such as monitor type, disk types, and BIOS date).

Chapter 19 describes the Speed Disk utility. Through constant use, your hard disk writes files to disk, erases files, copies files, and so on. Eventually, the files on your disk are no longer stored in contiguous areas—that is, the files become fragmented. Part of a file is stored in one place on disk, and another part of the file is stored on another part of the disk. DOS is usually able to keep track of the various parts of the files, but fragmentation can eventually cause the disk to have slower file access and may even cause loss of file information for extremely fragmented files. Speed Disk rearranges the location of files on your disk to unfragment the files, making disk access faster.

The Calibrate utility, described in Chapter 20, is used to analyze and optionally reset the way your hard disk stores data. Calibrate enables you to optimize the storage method for your disk type. Calibrate also is capable of performing a nondestructive low-level format on some disks, which allows you to check your disk's reliability without destroying any information on the disk.

The Norton Cache utility, covered in Chapter 21, allows you to use a disk cache to make disk access faster. A disk cache is a method of intelligently storing in your computer's RAM any information you are likely to read from disk. Reading information from RAM is much faster than reading directly from the disk, so disk access time is improved.

Part VI: Managing Your Computer's Resources

The chapters in Part VI describe the Norton programs that are designed to help you manage the resources on your computer. This includes setting certain computer features such as cursor size, colors, mouse options, time and date, and more. These chapters also include managing your directories (creating, changing, removing, and renaming them), creating batch files and menus, finding files on disk, diagnosing hardware problems, and other utilities.

Chapter 22 describes Norton Control Center. Using this program, you can change a number of settings on your computer, such as the size of the cursor, the monitor's colors, the number of lines displayed, and the date and time.

Chapter 23 describes the Norton Change Directory command (NCD). This command is an enhanced version of the DOS CD, MD, and RD directory commands, with additional features for renaming and deleting directories and for moving quickly between directories. With NCD, you can view your computer's directory structure on-screen and use several methods, including a mouse, to switch directories.

Norton Batch Enhancer is described in Chapter 24. This utility enables you to create batch files with more options than DOS batch files. Batch Enhancer includes the creation of custom menus; drawing borders on the screen; and executing commands according to dates, times, days of the week, and user input.

The Norton File Find command, described in Chapter 25, is helpful in locating files anywhere on any disk according to a file specification or the contents of the file. For example, if you remember creating a report about Alabama some time ago but forgot where the report was stored, you can search your disk for all files with a TXT extension that contain the word ALABAMA. Also described in Chapter 25 are the related commands Text Search (TS) and File Locate (FL).

Chapter 26 describes the command-line utilities File Date (FD), Duplicate Disk (DUPDISK), File Size (FS), Line Print (LP), and Directory Sort (DS). With File Date, you can change the date and time on files. You use Duplicate Disk to copy disks. With File Size, you can show the amount of file space taken up by one file or a group of files and determine whether the file can be copied to a target disk. You use Line Print to print files to the printer. Finally, Directory Sort enables you to sort a disk directory listing.

Chapter 27 describes the Norton Diagnostics utility. Using Norton Diagnostics, you can run your computer through a battery of tests that will help you determine whether there are any problems with your computer's memory, video, serial or parallel ports, disks, keyboard, or mouse. Each of these components is examined by the program to see whether they are working properly.

Part VII: Using NDOS, Norton Backup, and Norton Commander

Part VII introduces NDOS and the Norton Utilities companion programs Norton Backup and Norton Commander. NDOS is a program that replaces many DOS commands with enhanced versions of the commands and introduces over 40 new commands. You continue to use DOS commands just as you have always used them, but with NDOS, you suddenly have a more powerful operating system. Chapter 28 introduces you to the power of NDOS and contains a reference to its commands, including the enhanced DOS commands and the new NDOS commands.

Chapter 29 covers the Norton Backup program. This program enables you to copy information from your hard disk to floppy disks or other backup media. Then, if your hard disk is damaged or you lose files that cannot be recovered, you can use the backup copies of your hard disk to retrieve that information. This chapter covers Version 2.0 of Norton Backup.

Chapter 30 describes Norton Commander 3.0. Commander enables you to customize your DOS environment so that you can enter commands from the DOS prompt or select DOS-like commands from pull-down menus. The Commander disk-management features assist you in copying, renaming, erasing, and finding files. Its viewing features enable you to view popular kinds of spreadsheet, database, and word processing programs and graphics at any time—without your having to use the program that created these special files. With Commander, you can link two computers so that you can share and transfer files; and you can use MCI Mail, which enables you to send and receive electronic mail, paper mail, and faxes.

Command Reference

The Norton Utilities 7 Command Reference is an alphabetical list of Norton Utilities 7 commands. Commands from previous versions of Norton Utilities (Versions 4.5, 5.0, and 6.0) are also listed, with reference to the current command that contains the function of the old command. Included in the list is the syntax to use when you type the command from the DOS prompt. For many of the commands, additional notes and examples of use are given. This reference section will be helpful to you if you are comfortable in using a command but simply need a reminder about its syntax. Browsing through this reference will give you an overview of the capabilities of Norton Utilities 7.

Appendixes

The four appendixes give you additional information and tips about using Norton Utilities, Norton Backup, and Norton Commander. If you are a computer beginner, be sure to read the review of PC DOS and MS-DOS in Appendix A. This appendix contains information about the basic DOS commands referred to in this book.

Appendix B provides a comparison of DOS and Norton commands. If you already know and use some of these DOS commands, this comparison shows you which Norton commands you can substitute for DOS commands and what additional features the Norton commands offer.

Appendix C includes installation instructions for Norton Utilities, Norton Backup, and Norton Commander. You may have already installed these programs, using the information in the original program manual. If not, Appendix C leads you through the installation process. It also gives you some information not covered in the Norton program manuals.

If you have a problem with your disk and don't know which Norton command to use, see Appendix D. This troubleshooting guide is divided into two parts. The first part offers solutions to common disk problems, including the following:

- The computer no longer boots from the hard disk.

- You cannot format the hard disk as a system disk.

- The computer is infected by a virus.

- You have continuing read and write problems on your hard disk that you can solve only with a low-level format.

The second part of Appendix D discusses responses to common DOS error messages that deal with disk problems. The appendix refers to DOS and Norton commands that can help you solve these problems.

What You Need To Know To Use This Book

To use this book, you need to have a PC-compatible computer that uses the MS-DOS or PC DOS operating system, Version 2.0 or later. Although many of the commands covered in this book will work on floppy disk systems, a significant amount of the book discusses hard disk management. You need a copy of Norton Utilities 7.0, Norton Backup 2.0, or Norton Commander 3.0. Because the book covers these programs separately, you can use this book for information on one or more of these programs. Some examples require you to attach a printer to your computer. You may also need a blank floppy disk for some examples.

Before you read this book, you should familiarize yourself with a text-editing program like DOS's Edlin editor or the DOS Editor, available in DOS 5.0 and 6.0. Any editor or word processor that can save files in text mode will do. If you already use a text-editing program or word processing program that can save files in text mode, you can use that program for the small amount of editing used in the examples in this book.

How To Use This Book

This book explains how to use Norton Utilities from a topical viewpoint and on a command-by-command basis.

Chapter 2 is a discussion of the Norton configuration procedures. This chapter explains how to set up options for running Norton Utilities. Depending on what options you chose to install during the installation, you may want to refer to Chapter 2 from time to time to change your Norton setup options.

If you are familiar with such terms as sectors, tracks, clusters and cylinders, you may want to skip Chapter 3. However, if you are interested in getting an overview of how disks work, Chapter 3 provides you with information that will be useful in understanding the workings of many of the Norton Utilities programs.

If you are a new user of Norton Utilities (or you want to refresh your knowledge of the Norton programs), read Parts II, III, V, and VI carefully. These parts cover the use of Norton commands. New users should pay particular attention to Part II because it covers features that can help you protect your data and eliminate the need to use some of the more difficult recovery procedures.

If you already know how to use a Norton command but need a reminder about the command syntax or options, refer to the Command Reference. This reference lists the commands alphabetically and briefly explains all options. You may want to look at this reference often, even after you learn the basics of Norton commands. To learn about using NDOS, refer to Chapter 28. You can use NDOS with or independent of the other Norton Utilities commands.

If you have a problem with a floppy disk or hard disk and you don't know which commands are appropriate for fixing the problem, refer to the troubleshooting guide in Appendix D. This appendix is useful also when you encounter a disk-related DOS error message. Appendix D contains a selection of alphabetically listed DOS error messages. Each message is described with possible causes and solutions.

What Is Not Covered in This Book?

Some problems related to information on your computer are beyond the scope of this book. If, for example, you lose information by accidentally erasing a range of cells in a Lotus 1-2-3 spreadsheet before saving it, this book (and Norton Utilities) cannot help you recover from the mistake. If you turn off the computer or lose power before saving a file to disk, the information is lost. These are instances when information is stored in the electronic memory of the computer and has not been placed on disk.

At times, software programs may contain bugs that make the information in a file useless. The logical nature of the file may be fine—that is, the file is OK according to DOS, but the information in the file has been scrambled or overwritten by the program. This kind of problem cannot be solved with Norton programs. If you overwrite a file on disk with a file having the same name, the original file cannot be recovered because its space on disk is now being used by different information. These are cases in which the file is stored properly on disk, but the information in the file is wrong.

Although Norton Utilities may be helpful for recovering from damage caused by some computer virus programs, these dangerous programs are getting more and more sophisticated in their capability to destroy data on a computer. There are simply too many ways that a virus can destroy data for all of them to be covered in this book. Appendix D gives you some help on this topic, however.

Physical damage to a hard disk or floppy disk can make data unrecoverable by the methods described in this book. In some cases, professional disk repair technicians can extract information from a physically damaged disk. Mechanical problems with a disk drive also can cause loss of information. These problems must be corrected by a technician before you can recover any information.

Conventions Used in This Book

Certain conventions are used in *Using Norton Utilities 7* to help you understand the techniques and features described in the text. This section provides examples of these conventions.

Words printed in uppercase include DOS commands (CHKDSK), Norton commands (DUPDISK), and file names (STATUS.DOC). Case is not important when you are actually entering commands, file names, or command options because DOS is not case-sensitive.

Note the special formatting used in this book:

Format	Use
Italics	Variables; emphasized text; new terms
Boldface	Hot keys for menu options; text the reader types
Special typeface	On-screen prompts and messages

In most cases, keys are represented as they appear on the keyboard. The arrow keys are indicated by name (for example, the up-arrow key) and occasionally with an arrow symbol (for example, ↑). The Print Screen key is abbreviated as PrtSc, Page Up is PgUp, Insert is Ins, and so on. On your keyboard, these key names may be spelled out or abbreviated differently.

Throughout the text, the term *Enter* instead of *Return* is used for the Enter key.

Alt+C indicates that you press the Alt key and hold it down while you press the C key. Other key combinations (such as Alt+Esc) are performed in the same manner. If key combinations are not indicated with a plus sign (+), don't hold down any of the keys; just press each key once in the order listed (for example, End Home).

When the word *type* is used in a phrase, such as "type C," it means that you should type the character *C* but not press the Enter key. When the word *enter* is used in a phrase, such as "enter **NORTON**," it means that you should type the word *norton* and press the Enter key.

When the word *choose* is used, it usually refers to choosing an option from a dialog box or menu. Often the names of these options include a highlighted character, such as **OK**. The phrase "choose **OK**" means that you should press Alt+O (press and hold down the Alt key and then press the O key) or click the **OK** option with the mouse pointer. You also may be able to highlight the specified option (by pressing the arrow keys or the Tab key) and then press Enter. The word *select* usually means to choose some item from a list, such as a list of file names. You select an item by using the arrow keys to highlight the item, or by pointing to the list with the mouse pointer and clicking.

Throughout this book, various Norton commands are also referred to as programs. Both descriptions are common usage.

Taking Charge of Your Computer

PART

1

OUTLINE

Norton Utilities Basics
Configuring Norton Utilities
Understanding How Disks Work

Norton Utilities Basics

There is a big difference between driving a finely tuned car and one that's coughing, spewing smoke, and not firing on all cylinders. Which would you rather drive? You get farther and faster when your machine is tuned for maximum performance.

With periodic visits to the Norton Utilities "Tune-Up Shop," you will be able to keep your PC running like a finely tuned sports car. In this program, you will find a number of tools available to help you keep your machine running at peak performance and protecting your data from loss. And you don't have to be a master mechanic to be able to use these tools. With this book as a guideline, you will be able to use all the Norton Utilities programs—just like a pro.

This chapter provides an overview of the Norton Utilities 7 programs and refers you to the chapters in which you can find more specific information about these programs. If you are new to Norton Utilities, be sure to read through this chapter to get a bird's-eye view of the whole Norton Utilities 7 family of commands and programs and to gain a basic understanding of the Norton interface, keys, and dialog boxes.

Understanding Norton Utilities 7

Norton Utilities 7 consists of a number of utility programs (often called *Norton commands*) that provide you with tools to manage information on disk. These tools include programs to protect information, recover information, make your hard disk work more efficiently, and manage your computer resources.

If you have been using Norton Utilities 4.5, you will find that some of the Version 4.5 commands have been incorporated into the newer Versions 5.0, 6.0, and 7.0 commands. Some commands originally included in 4.5 were absent from 5.0, but have been reincorporated into 6.0 and 7.0. The Command Reference, which gives you an alphabetical listing of Norton commands, lists 4.5, 5.0, 6.0, and 7.0 commands.

The Norton Utilities 7.0 commands fall into six basic categories, which are reflected in the divisions of this book. Here are the categories:

Category	Function
Configuration	Enables you to configure Norton Utilities for use on your computer
Security	Protects the information on your disk
Recovery	Helps you automatically recover lost information
Advanced Recovery	Helps you recover lost information, using advanced procedures
Efficiency	Helps you fine-tune and manage the resources on your hard disk
Productivity	Helps you manage the information on your hard disk to make your work more efficient and productive

A new set of commands was introduced to the Norton family with the introduction of NDOS in Version 6.0 and has been enhanced in Version 7.0. NDOS is a Norton Utilities replacement program for the normal DOS command processor COMMAND.COM. NDOS transforms your command prompt (for example, C:\>) into a much more powerful command processor containing more commands than you normally have available with DOS. NDOS is described in Chapter 28, "Using NDOS."

The enhancements found in each new Norton Utilities version reflect changes in the MS-DOS operating system. Beginning with MS-DOS 5.0, the operating system contains several commands related to information recovery. The relationships between the Norton commands and the new DOS commands—particularly MIRROR, UNDELETE, and UNFORMAT—are covered as part of the descriptions of the Norton commands Image (Chapter 4), UnFormat (Chapter 11), and UnErase (Chapter 10). Norton Utilities 7.0 is compatible with new features in DOS 6.0. Appendix B, "Comparing DOS and Norton Utilities Commands," compares some DOS commands with similar commands in Norton Utilities.

If you are already familiar with DOS commands, you will find that many of the Norton commands have a similar syntax and are therefore simple to learn and use. You can use some of the Norton commands as replacements for DOS commands. The replacement commands generally contain significant improvements over the normal DOS commands. The Norton Safe Format command, for example, not only formats a disk but also is designed to prevent you from accidentally formatting a disk. Moreover, you can use Norton commands by selecting options from a master command menu, so you don't have to remember all the options to include in the command given at the DOS prompt. (Later sections of this chapter provide details on how to issue Norton commands.)

The following sections describe categories of tools provided by the Norton Utilities commands and programs. Each category is broken into additional sections that briefly discuss the specific Norton tools applicable to that topic and indicate the chapters where you can find detailed information about that program or command.

File Protection

The Norton Utilities programs probably are most famous for recovering lost information, but they also are useful for *preventing* the loss of information—safeguarding your information on disk from damage.

A number of bad things can happen to information on your disk. *Physical problems* involve damage to the storage media and the mechanics of the disk drive. *Logical damage* involves the loss of magnetically stored information on disk. Norton Utilities cannot help you recover from physical damage to disks, but can help you prevent and recover from logical damage. Chapter 3, "Understanding How Disks Work," discusses the makeup, use, and care of disks.

Because information on a disk is stored as a magnetic image, this image can weaken until information is difficult or impossible to read. Loss of information on disk often results from accidental deletion of files or accidental formatting of the disk. Logical damage to a disk occurs when DOS loses information about where the data is stored—that is, DOS "forgets" where a file is located on disk. With Norton Utilities, you may be able to fix (or prevent) damage related to logical problems, magnetic weaknesses, or accidental erasure or formatting of the disk. The following sections briefly describe specific Norton utilities that provide protection for data. For details on these utilities, see the referenced chapters.

Safe Format and Image

Probably the first thing you should do with Norton Utilities is to make sure that you are safe from the prospect of someone accidentally formatting your hard disk. Otherwise, you could lose weeks, months, or years of work in a matter of minutes. Prevent this disaster by using Safe Format (SFORMAT or SF), a Norton replacement for the DOS FORMAT command. Safe Format gives you an added layer of protection against accidental formatting because the user must go through a few more steps to initiate a format.

If you load Norton Utilities with the Install program that comes on disk, you can replace the DOS FORMAT command with the Norton Safe Format command (see Appendix C, "Installing Norton Programs"). If you do not choose this option during the installation, you still can perform that task manually (see Chapter 4, "Using Safe Format and Image").

Implementing the Image procedure protects you from accidental formatting of your disk (see Chapter 4). Each time you boot your computer, the Image program stores information about your files (a duplicate copy of DOS directory information) on disk. Then, if your disk is formatted accidentally, the UnFormat program can use this duplicate information to restore the formatted disk. Chapter 11, "Unformatting Disks," describes the UnFormat utility.

Disk Monitor, SmartCan, File Find, and File Attributes

Individual files on disk can be lost if you accidentally erase them or overwrite them with other files. The Norton Disk Monitor program enables you to protect information on your disk from being erased. If you have a number of files that you want to protect from accidental change, the Disk Monitor program can help. For more information, see Chapter 6, "Using Disk Monitor."

SmartCan also can be used to prevent accidental data loss. This program intercepts any command that erases files on your disk and places those files in a special place on disk so that they can be reliably unerased. Chapter 5, "Using SmartCan," covers this capability.

Finally, the Norton File Find (FILEFIND or FF) and File Attributes (FA) commands can help you use some of the features of DOS file storage to protect files from being erased or altered. With these commands, you can set a file to a read-only mode so that the file can be used but not altered. Also you can hide files and cause them to be backed up more often. These commands are described in Chapter 9, "Setting File Attributes."

Diskreet

Another way to protect information is to make sure that it does not fall into the wrong hands. One way to protect files is to encrypt the files (turn them into a secret code) so that they cannot be read by unauthorized persons. The Diskreet program was designed to perform this task. For details, see Chapter 7, "Using Diskreet."

WipeInfo

Formatting a disk does not *destroy* the information on the disk—it simply erases some of the file information. If you erase a file or format a disk, someone else can use a program such as Norton Utilities to recover that information; therefore, the data is not safely destroyed. This is a potential problem for anyone who places financial, personal, corporate, secret, or other valuable information on a disk. Norton provides alternatives to the DOS ERASE (DEL) and FORMAT commands. You can use the WipeInfo command to completely destroy information on a disk. Chapter 8, "Destroying Files Permanently with WipeInfo," provides complete details on this utility program.

Recovery Techniques

Files can be lost or damaged in a number of ways. You can format your disk accidentally. You can use the DEL or ERASE command and erase a whole batch of important files. Perhaps you erase a file because you think you have another copy of it elsewhere—only to find that the erased file was your only copy after all. Or you may intentionally format your disk because you have a backup and then discover that the backup is no good.

Loss of information can also occur when the power shuts off for some reason before you save a file to your disk. Perhaps your program freezes, forcing you to perform a *warm boot* (pressing Ctrl+Alt+Del) before all information is written to a file. Your disk may become so full that DOS loses information about where the contents of a file are located. Bugs in software, hardware failures, and human errors are potential causes of damaged files.

In many cases, Norton Utilities can help you recover all or portions of damaged or lost files. The primary programs for recovery include UnErase, UnFormat, Norton Disk Doctor (NDD), Disk Tools, Rescue Disk, and File Fix. If you are an advanced user or you want to recover files that cannot be recovered with the automatic recovery techniques, you can use Manual UnErase and Disk Editor.

The following sections describe the Norton Utilities programs for recovering data automatically and for advanced (manual) recovery of data.

UnFormat and UnErase

When a disk is formatted, the actual data on the disk is not disturbed. The format clears out the file information in the disk's directory. With a duplicate copy of the information on disk, the UnFormat program can reconstruct the information needed to unformat the disk and get all the files back. Chapter 11, "Unformatting Disks," describes the UnFormat command, and Appendix B compares the Norton UnFormat command with the DOS UNFORMAT command (Versions 5.0 and later).

The UnErase program is useful for recovering files or directories you have erased (see Chapter 10, "Unerasing Files and Directories").

Norton Disk Doctor (NDD)

Problems relating to your hard disk can mount before you even realize that a problem exists. Norton Disk Doctor (NDD) closely examines all the information on your disk and determines whether problems exist that could cause information in a file to become lost. Examples are fragmented files and unclosed files from power outages. NDD optionally attempts to correct such problems when they are found. Chapter 12, "Diagnosing and Treating Disks with Disk Doctor," provides details on using this utility.

Disk Tools, Rescue Disk, and File Fix

Disk Tools is a collection of utilities that can help you restore a disk and make a disk bootable. Chapter 13, "Using Disk Tools," describes these utilities.

The Rescue Disk program enables you to create a rescue disk—a disk containing the key DOS and Norton programs you may need for recovering information from a logically damaged or formatted hard disk. Chapter 14, "Creating and Using a Rescue Disk," describes the process.

The File Fix program allows you to repair damaged database, spreadsheet, or word processing files created by major application programs such as dBASE, Lotus 1-2-3, and WordPerfect. Chapter 15, "Restoring Files with File Fix," provides details on this program.

Manual UnErase and Disk Editor

When the automatic recovery techniques cannot restore lost files, you can use other—more advanced—Norton techniques for file recovery. The Manual UnErase command allows you to search your disk for pieces of a file and put the pieces back together. Chapter 16, "Recovering Files with Manual UnErase," describes this process.

Norton Disk Editor enables you to "perform surgery" on the information on disk. By directly editing the inner workings of the disk, you can remove or replace bad or damaged information with good information. If, for example, the disk information that contains the addresses of files on disk is damaged, you may be able to transplant a new copy of this information to disk—making the information usable again. See Chapter 17, "Using Disk Editor," for details on using this program.

CAUTION: Disk Editor is powerful *and* dangerous. Like the knife of a surgeon, Disk Editor can be helpful in the hands of someone who uses it with care and knowledge. If you accidentally change important disk information, you can destroy access to all the data on your disk.

Computer Efficiency

Keeping information on your disk safe is vital. As with an automobile, a few maintenance tasks can keep your machine running smoothly and at top speed. You can use several Norton Utilities commands to perform these maintenance procedures, as described in the following sections.

System Info

The System Info (SYSINFO) command allows you to take a look into the inner workings of your computer to discover what components (microprocessor, BIOS, and so on) it uses and how fast it runs when compared to other standard computers. Chapter 18, "Using System Info," provides details.

Speed Disk

One of the problems with disks is that, after much use, files become overly entangled or fragmented. When DOS runs out of enough space for storing a file in one contiguous area on the disk, the operating system resorts to storing part of a file here, part there, and so on. This problem can become bad enough to cause DOS to lose information on some files. Furthermore, because DOS must look here and there to find a file, your access to the hard disk can be slowed considerably. The Norton Speed Disk (SPEEDISK) program can rearrange the files on your hard disk in such a way as to remove fragmentation and restore maximum speed to the disk. If you hear your disk grinding when a file is being read or saved, or if your disk seems to be slowing down, you may be able to regain speed with Speed Disk. See Chapter 19, "Making Your Disk Run Faster with Speed Disk," for more information.

Calibrate

Another command that can help your hard disk work more efficiently is Calibrate, described in Chapter 20, "Using Calibrate." You can use this command (entered as CALIBRAT) to adjust how much information DOS reads from your hard disk in one pass. Fine-tuning this adjustment can give your hard disk more speed. Calibrate can also perform a nondestructive low-level format of your hard disk to check the disk for reliability—without disturbing the information already on disk.

Norton Cache

The Norton Cache program can help you access your hard disk more efficiently, with the result of making many programs run faster. See Chapter 21, "Using Norton Cache," for details.

Resource Management

A number of commands in Norton Utilities can give you more control over your computer than you can have by using DOS commands alone. These Norton commands help you manage your hard disk more efficiently and enable you to choose certain setup parameters for your computer. The following sections describe the Norton commands for managing computer resources.

Norton Control Center

Norton Control Center (NCC) is a utility that enables you to make your computer do things you may never have thought possible. You can change the size of your cursor, for example. If you use a laptop with a hard-to-read monitor, making the cursor bigger makes it easier to find on-screen. Some PCs require that you use the DOS Setup program on the diagnostic disk to permanently set the date and time on the computer. You can now do that with Norton Control Center. Other settings available include monitor colors, how fast characters repeat when you hold down a key for more than a few seconds, how many lines are displayed on-screen, and settings for serial ports. Chapter 22, "Using Norton Control Center," provides details on using this program.

Norton Change Directory

As newer and more advanced hard disks come on the market, users must deal with keeping track of more information on disk. The Norton Change Directory (NCD) command enables you to navigate between directories much more easily than having to remember the full name of each directory on disk (see Chapter 23, "Using Norton Change Directory"). The NCD command replaces the functions of the DOS commands Change Directory (CD), Remove Directory (RD), and Make Directory (MD)—and offers more. With NCD, you can display the directory on-screen in a treelike graph that shows various relationships among the directories. Using the arrow keys or the mouse, you can highlight the directory you want to access. Not only can you make, change to, and remove directories as in DOS, but you can also rename directories and perform other directory management tasks.

Batch Enhancer

Batch files contain series of commands that you use repetitively. DOS has a number of commands that are used in batch files, such as the

PAUSE command and the ECHO command. Norton Utilities supplies some additional commands, called the Batch Enhancer commands, that enable you to create more sophisticated batch files. With these commands, you can do such tasks as draw boxes, prompt the user for input, and branch according to the user's answer. Read Chapter 24, "Creating and Using Batch Files," to learn more about this useful program.

File Find, File Locate, and Text Search

Within each directory on disk, you may have hundreds of files. Finding a particular file can be a nightmare. Often you know that you have a file on disk, but you cannot remember where you saw it. The Norton File Find, File Locate, and Text Search commands enable you to find a specific file no matter which directory holds it. The File Find and Text Search commands also can perform a text search to find a file by searching the text *inside* the file. File Find and Text Search can even search files you have erased. Chapter 25, "Finding Files," describes these utilities.

Command-Line Utilities

A series of command-line utilities have been a popular part of the Norton Utilities package for many years; Version 7 retains these utilities and adds another. The original utilities include Directory Sort (DS), File Size (FS), Line Print (LP), and File Date (FD). The added utility is Duplicate Disk (DUPDISK).

The following sections describe these command-line utilities. For details on using these programs, see Chapter 26, "Using Norton Command-Line Utilities."

Directory Sort (DS)

Have you ever spent time looking through a directory listing to find a particular file? Being able to list the files by the date they were created (or by size, name, or extension) would undoubtedly be helpful. With the Directory Sort (DS) command, you can sort files in a number of ways and then use the DIR command to list the sorted directories.

File Size (FS)

The File Size (FS) command allows you to find out how much disk space is taken by one or more files, and to determine whether there is enough space on a disk to copy a group of files (such as those in a directory) to a disk. You can also use FS to determine how much of the disk is being used to store files and how much of the space is allocated for use but is not used.

Line Print (LP)

The Line Print (LP) command enables you to print an ASCII file to the printer without having to use a word processor. This command is more powerful and has more options than the DOS PRINT command. With Line Print, you can specify margins, type of printer, page numbering, and more.

Duplicate Disk (DUPDISK)

The Duplicate Disk (DUPDISK) program gives you a better alternative to the DOS DISKCOPY command. Not only can you copy from one disk to another with this command, but also you can use the command to quickly make multiple copies of the same disk.

File Date (FD)

With the File Date (FD) command, you can change the date and time for any or all files on a disk. For example, for support and identification purposes, you can change the dates and times of a group of files to specify when they were distributed to other users.

Norton Diagnostics

The Norton Diagnostics program allows you to put your computer through a treadmill of tests to check specific hardware components of your machine, such as memory, video, disk drives, and communication ports. See Chapter 27, "Using Norton Diagnostics," for more information.

The NDOS Command Processor

Norton's NDOS replaces the DOS command processor COMMAND.COM, giving you a larger number of "DOS" commands and enhancing the current set of DOS commands (such as DIR and COPY). For example, with NDOS you can include multiple commands on one line and recall commands that you have previously entered. The NDOS command processor is described in Chapter 28, "Using NDOS."

Norton Backup

The Norton Backup program, although not a part of the Norton Utilities Package, is a powerful backup routine that enables you to design backup procedures that you can store, use, and reuse to back up particular files on your hard disk. For example, you can design a series of backup procedures to be used daily, weekly, and monthly—allowing you to automate a complete backup protection plan for your computer. Devising and using a backup strategy is described in Chapter 29, "Backing Up and Restoring Files with Norton Backup."

Norton Commander

Norton Commander is an additional program that complements Norton Utilities. Commander is particularly helpful for working with directory structures; creating custom menus; using MCI Mail; and copying, moving, renaming, and deleting groups of files.

Running Norton Commands from the DOS Prompt

You can use most Norton Utilities commands as if they were DOS commands. In fact, Norton designed commands so that they operate with a syntax similar to DOS commands. To format a disk in drive A with the system switch (make the disk a bootable disk), you can enter the following familiar DOS command:

FORMAT A:/S

To format a disk in drive A with the Norton Safe Format command and the same option, enter this command:

SFORMAT A:/S

Notice that the syntax of the two commands is identical; only the names of the commands are different. Notice also that a command consists of distinct parts: the command (in this example, SFORMAT), any parameters (here, the disk drive), and switches. In the discussion of each command in this book, the appropriate syntax is explained.

Using the Norton Interface

If you do not remember how to enter a Norton command at the DOS prompt, you have another option. Norton Utilities provides you with an easy-to-use interface with which you can access the Norton commands. To use the Norton interface, you need to remember only one command: **NORTON**. The following sections describe how to use the Norton interface.

Specifying the Path

If you are not in the Norton directory, DOS cannot execute the NORTON command unless you have given a PATH command that includes the Norton directory (usually \NORTON or \NU7) in the DOS search path. The DOS search path typically is set up in the AUTOEXEC.BAT file, in a line similar to this:

PATH C:\;C:\DOS;C:\NORTON

With the \NORTON directory included in the path (in this example, the directory is on drive C), you can access the Norton interface and commands from any directory and drive on your computer. The Installation program optionally includes the proper command in the PATH statement in your AUTOEXEC.BAT file. However, if you did not allow this change, you can still change the path statement later by choosing the **S**tartup Programs option from the Norton **C**onfiguration menu, as described in Chapter 2.

Understanding the Norton Main Screen

After you type **NORTON** at the DOS prompt and press Enter, you see a screen similar to the one in figure 1.1.

At the top of the screen is the *menu bar*, listing the pull-down menus. On the left side of the screen is a *list box* containing the available Norton commands. In figure 1.1, Disk Doctor is highlighted in the list, and the command NDD (for Norton Disk Doctor) appears on the *input line*. To the right of the Commands list is a brief description of the highlighted command. In this case, the screen displays a description of Norton Disk Doctor, including the syntax of the NDD command and available switches.

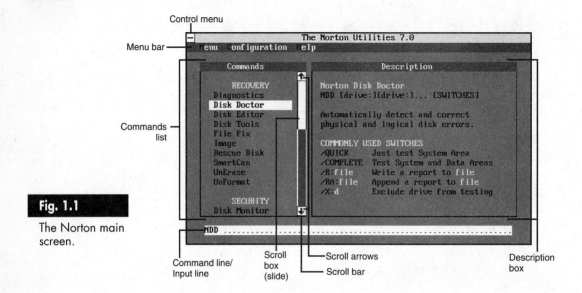

Fig. 1.1

The Norton main screen.

Not all commands are visible at one time in the Commands list. To see other commands, you can use the up- and down-arrow keys to display the commands. You can also press Home to go to the top of the list, and End to go to the bottom of the list.

You can list the commands by topic or alphabetically. For more information, see the section "The Menu Menu" later in this chapter.

To end Norton Utilities and return to the DOS prompt, press Esc or double-click the Control menu in the upper-left corner of the screen.

Choosing Commands

On the Norton main screen, you can point to the name of a command by using the direction keys on the cursor keypad to move the highlight up or down in the Commands list. After you *highlight* (point to) the command you want to use, press Enter to *run* (shoot) the command. This point-and-shoot method enables you to choose and run a command easily without having to remember the exact command name or options.

If your computer has a mouse attached, you will see a *pointer* (a block or an arrow) in the Norton screen. To choose a command with the mouse, move the mouse pointer to point to the command; then click the left or right mouse button once. The command appears at the bottom of the screen, and you can type any appropriate switches or options and then press Enter to run the command.

To reveal commands not shown in the list, use one of the following methods:

■ Place the mouse pointer on the up or down *scroll arrow* at the upper right or lower right of the Commands list. Press the mouse button to move the Commands list up or down.

■ Point to the highlighted rectangle (*scroll box* or *slide*) in the *scroll bar* on the right side of the Commands list. Press and hold down a mouse button, and move the mouse pointer up or down to scroll through the list.

■ Click the top, middle, or bottom of the scroll bar to move to the top, middle, or bottom of the list.

On a two-button mouse, pressing both buttons together is the same as pressing Esc on the keyboard.

Editing the Command Line

The input line at the bottom of the Norton main screen displays the *selected* command—the one to which you pointed. Your cursor is positioned after the command on the input line. Here you can type any options or switches before you press Enter to run the command.

Some command lines get complicated, and you may get to the end of a line before you realize that you have made an error at the beginning. You can use the Backspace key to erase all your work and start over, of course. If you use the built-in editing keys, however, you can save yourself some work. Table 1.1 lists these editing keys.

Table 1.1 Norton Command-Line Editing Keys	
Key	**Action**
→	Moves cursor to the right
←	Moves cursor to the left
Ctrl+D	Moves cursor right one character
Ctrl+S	Moves cursor left one character
Ctrl+→ or Ctrl+F	Moves cursor right one word

continues

Table 1.1 Continued

Key	Action
Ctrl+← or Ctrl+A	Moves cursor left one word
Backspace	Deletes character to the left
Del or Ctrl+G	Deletes character at cursor
Ctrl+T	Deletes word to the right
Ctrl+W	Deletes word to the left
Ctrl+Y	Deletes the line

Using the Menus

The menu bar displays the **M**enu, **C**onfiguration, and **H**elp options. **M**enu, **C**onfiguration, and **H**elp are *pull-down menus*. To open one of these menus, use one of the following methods:

- Press F10 to access the menu, and highlight the first menu item. Use the right- or left-arrow key to move the highlight to the menu you want to open; then press Enter.

- Hold down the Alt key and press the first letter of the menu name (for example, press Alt+M to select **M**enu). In this book, the highlighted letter of the menu name appears in boldface.

- Point to the menu item with the mouse and click once.

After you open one of the menus, you can move to another menu by pressing the right- or left-arrow key or by pointing to the menu bar, pressing and holding down the mouse button, and dragging the mouse to the left or right. To close a pulled-down menu, press Esc, click a blank area outside the menu, or click both mouse buttons.

Figure 1.2 shows the **M**enu pull-down menu.

To choose an item on a pull-down menu, use one of the following methods:

- Use the up- and down-arrow keys to highlight your choice; then press Enter.

- Point to your choice with the mouse and click.

■ Use the *shortcut key* (or key combination) listed next to the menu item on the menu. The shortcut for Sort by Name is Alt+N, and the shortcut for Sort by Topic is Alt+T. When you see shortcut keys like these listed in a pull-down menu, you can access those commands (without pulling down the menu) by pressing the key combination listed. For example, to sort commands by name even when the **M**enu menu is not pulled down, you just press Alt+N.

■ Press the *hot key*. The hot key in a menu item is designated by a letter that is different in color from the rest of the letters in the item. When a menu is open, pressing the hot key selects that menu option.

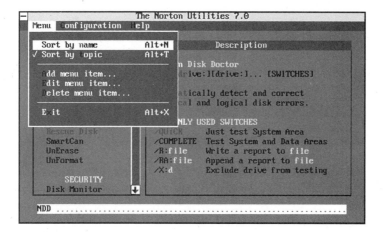

Fig. 1.2

The **M**enu menu.

The Menu Menu

The **M**enu menu contains six options. The first set of options includes Sort by **N**ame and Sort by **T**opic. These two options affect how commands are listed in the Commands list. By default, the commands in the Commands list are listed by topic. The topics are Recovery, Security, Speed, and Tools. Because the Commands list is longer than the box containing it, you can see only the Recovery and Security topics at the beginning of the Commands list. Within the topics, the commands are listed alphabetically. If you choose the Sort by **N**ame option from the **M**enu menu, the program immediately lists the commands together in alphabetical order by name (instead of by topic).

The next three options on the menu are **A**dd Menu Item, **E**dit Menu Item, and **D**elete Menu Item. You can use these three commands to customize the Commands list; for example, you can add your own commands, edit how the commands are presented, or delete items from the list.

 NOTE Each of these menu options is followed by an *ellipsis* (...). When you choose a menu option followed by an ellipsis, you will need to select or enter additional information before the command performs a task.

The Configuration Menu

When you choose the Configuration menu, it presents the following six options (see fig. 1.3):

- Video and Mouse enables you to control video and mouse options, including screen colors and mouse sensitivity.

- Printer Setup adds, deletes, and configures printer options.

- Startup Programs specifies which Norton programs are started automatically when you boot your computer.

- Alternate Names enables you to select alternative names for certain Norton programs. For example, you can choose either SYSINFO or SI for the System Info command.

- Passwords allows you to limit the use of certain programs (such as WipeInfo) by requiring that a password be given before the program will execute.

- Menu Editing controls which commands appear in the Norton menu.

The Configuration menu and the program NUCONFIG are discussed in detail in Chapter 2, "Configuring Norton Utilities."

The Help Menu

By selecting the Help option from the Norton main screen, you can access a series of Norton Help screens that function like a minimanual for Norton Utilities. When you choose the Help menu, you see the pull-down menu illustrated in figure 1.4.

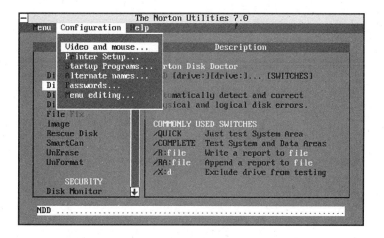

Fig. 1.3

The **C**onfiguration menu.

You also can select **Help** by pressing the F1 key on your keyboard.

T I P

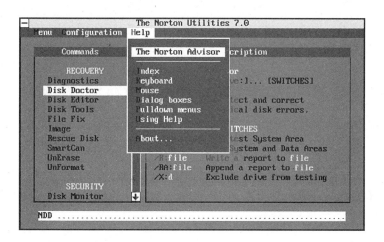

Fig. 1.4

The **H**elp menu.

When you choose The Norton Advisor from the **Help** menu, seven options are revealed:

Option	Description
About the Norton Advisor	Describes the purpose of the remaining six options on the Advisor menu.
How to Use Advisor	Describes how to use the remaining five options on the Advisor menu.

continues

Option	Description
Common Disk Problems	Lists problems that commonly occur with disks. This option covers such problems as the computer no longer booting from a disk, problems in copying files, and other topics related to accessing information on your disk. See Appendix D, "Dealing with Disk-Related Problems," for a discussion of some common problems.
DOS Error Messages	Lists common DOS error messages and recommends solutions. For example, Norton Advisor recommends an action when you encounter the message Bad command or file name.
CHKDSK Error Messages	Lists messages displayed by the DOS CHKDSK command, such as errors in the file allocation table (FAT), and recommends an action for each message. See Appendix A, "A DOS Review," for more information about CHKDSK.
Application Error Messages	Lists common messages in popular application programs (such as WordPerfect, Lotus 1-2-3, and dBASE) and recommends an action for each message.
Search	Allows you to search for the meaning of an error message. You enter all or part of the error message, and the search will find error messages that match. If an error message is found, advice is displayed concerning what action might be taken.

The second part of the **Help** menu enables you to display an **Index** to the Help system or to display information about these topics:

Keyboard

Mouse

Dialog Boxes

Pulldown Menus

Using Help

About displays copyright information about the Norton Utilities program.

If you choose the Index option, you will see the screen shown in figure 1.5. This screen describes how to use the Index. Choose the Index button at the bottom of the screen to see the main index for the Norton Help system.

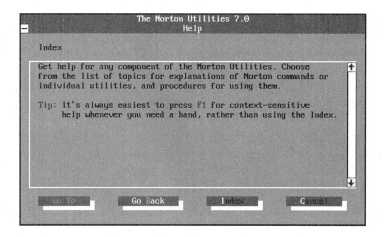

Fig. 1.5

The Norton Help Index screen.

To display more help on one of the topics in the Index listing, use the up- and down-arrow keys to highlight the topic and then choose **G**o To. Alternatively, double-click the topic. At the bottom of the Help screen, notice two other options: Go **B**ack and **C**ancel. After you have used **G**o To to see several screens, you can backtrack by choosing the Go **B**ack option. The **C**ancel option causes the Help program to end, and the Norton main screen appears again.

If, for example, you choose the How to Use Help option and then choose **G**o To, a screen like that shown in figure 1.6 is displayed.

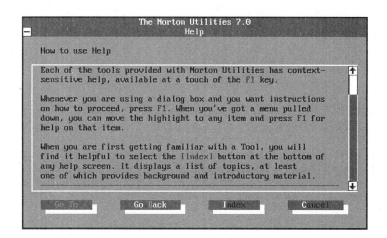

Fig. 1.6

A Norton Help screen.

When the information in the Help screen is too large for the screen, you can scroll the information by pressing the up- and down-arrow keys or by using the mouse and the scroll bar. The information in figure 1.6, for example, continues beyond the bottom line shown on the screen.

The Norton Help system is extensive and thorough. However, sometimes you just want to know what options are available for a particular command-line utility. For this kind of help, see the section "Getting Instant Help," later in this chapter.

Choosing Options from Dialog Boxes

In addition to using the keyboard or mouse to select options from the Norton main screen, you often need to choose options from other kinds of Norton menus, called *dialog boxes*. Basically, a dialog box is a screen that contains several options. You "dialogue" with this box by "telling" it what options you want to choose. To choose options, you can use the keyboard or the mouse, or both. Figure 1.7 shows the dialog box that appears when you choose **Configuration** and then choose Video and Mouse. This dialog box includes several kinds of options, as described in the following sections.

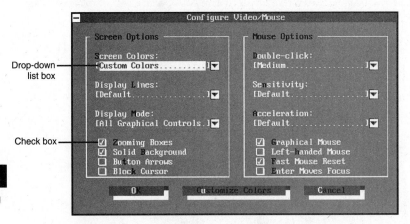

Fig. 1.7

A Norton dialog box.

Using a Drop-Down List Box

Notice the six options that have a triangle pointing down at the right of the option. These are called *drop-down list boxes*. The purpose of this kind of box is to enable you to choose from a list of options. The currently selected option is listed in the *option field*. After you open a *drop-down list*, the down triangle at the right of the option field changes to an up triangle. Figure 1.8 shows the Custom Colors drop-down list box opened.

Table 1.2 lists the keyboard commands that you can use to access and work with a drop-down list.

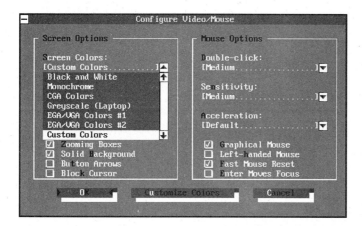

Table 1.2 Drop-Down List Keys

Key	Action
Alt+highlighted letter	Highlights the list box. For example, press Alt+S to highlight the Screen Colors drop-down list box.
Ctrl+↓	Opens the drop-down list, displaying the list of options.
Ctrl+↑	Closes the drop-down list.
Arrow keys	Selects an option in the list.
Home	Moves to the first option in the list.
End	Moves to the last option in the list.
PgUp	Moves the list up one screen.
PgDn	Moves the list down one screen.
Space bar	Selects the currently highlighted item in the list.

To use a mouse with a drop-down list box, click the triangle to open the box. If the list box has a scroll bar, use the scroll bar or scroll arrows to move the list up or down. To select an item on the list, point to it with the mouse pointer and click. To close the list box, click the triangle next to the option field or click elsewhere in the dialog box.

After you choose an item, the drop-down list box contracts, leaving only the item you have chosen displayed in the list box.

Using Check Boxes

Figure 1.8 contains a number of check boxes at the bottom of the dialog box. When an item is selected, a check mark appears in the box. When the item is not selected (*deselected*), no check mark appears. To select or deselect an item, press Alt plus the highlighted character of the option. In figure 1.8, for example, Alt+Z selects or deselects the **Z**ooming Boxes option. If you prefer, you can press Tab to move the highlight to the check box, and then press the space bar to select or deselect the option. If you are using a mouse, point to the option and click to select or deselect.

Using Radio Buttons

Another kind of selection item is the radio button. Figure 1.9 shows the Surface Test dialog box from Norton Disk Doctor. This dialog box contains a number of radio button options. A *radio button* appears as an empty circle if the option is deselected or as a circle enclosing a dot if the option is selected.

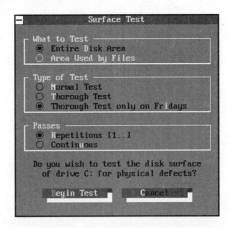

Fig. 1.9

A dialog box that includes radio buttons.

The name *radio button* came from the old-style car radios that allowed you to press a button to choose a radio station. When one button is pressed, it turns off any other currently selected button. Thus, only one button (option) can be selected at any time. Figure 1.9 contains three sets of radio buttons. Notice that only one option is chosen in each of the three boxes. In the top box are two options. However, one of the buttons (Area Used by Files) is grayed, which means that the option cannot be selected at the present time. Sometimes radio buttons are unavailable, such as a network option when your computer is not on a network.

To select or deselect a radio button option, press Alt plus the letter of the option. If you prefer, you can use the Tab or arrow keys to move to an option, and press the space bar to select or deselect the option. If you are using a mouse, point to the radio button you want to select or deselect and then click.

Getting Instant Help

In addition to the information provided about commands in the Norton menu screen, you have another way to get on-screen help about Norton commands. If you enter at the DOS prompt a Norton command followed by a question mark, a Help screen appears. This screen lists the command's possible options and switches, and may give some sample uses of the command. For example, to get information on the File Date (FD) command, enter the following at the DOS prompt:

FD ?

Remember to include a space between the command (FD) and the question mark (?). Figure 1.10 shows the help information that appears on-screen for this example.

```
C:\NU7>fd ?

Change the file time and date information.

FD pathname [/D[date]] [/T[time]] [/P] [/S]

    /D[mm-dd-yy]   Set the date to [mm-dd-yy].
    /T[hh:mm:ss]   Set the time to [hour:minute:second].
    /P             Pause after each screen.
    /S             Include Subdirectories.

Running FD without /D and /T will stamp the current
date and time on all files matching the file specified.

C:\NU7>
```

Fig. 1.10

Help information for the FD command.

Summary

The information on your computer disk may not be safe. Accidental erasures, unintentional disk formatting, problems with computer programs, power outages, and other difficulties can compromise your data. Although DOS has a few options that can help you protect your data, more are needed. Norton Utilities gives you additional ways to build in preventive measures and protect the information on your computer disk. Then, if a loss occurs, you still may be able to recover some or all of your information by using Norton Utilities' recovery techniques.

This chapter provided an overview of the Norton Utilities 7 programs. In the next chapter, you continue your exploration of Norton Utilities by learning how to configure it for your computer.

Configuring Norton Utilities

A utomobiles come in a variety of colors and shapes and with different levels of power and finesse. Differences in people's tastes and in their ideas about how a car should perform account for this variety. A utility program should have no fewer options. In fact, Norton Utilities provides a number of options that enable you to customize the program so that it meets your expectations about color, power, speed, and ease of use.

As indicated in Chapter 1, you can access configuration options from the Norton main screen. You can also enter the NUCONFIG command from the DOS prompt to access the same Norton configuration options. This chapter shows you how to make choices from the Configuration menu and how to access the same configuration choices with the NUCONFIG command.

Setting Video and Mouse Options

You learned in Chapter 1 that the Norton Utilities main screen is displayed when you start Norton Utilities by entering **NORTON** at the DOS prompt (see fig. 2.1). To open the Configuration menu, press Alt+C (the hot key for this option) or point to the **C**onfiguration menu with the mouse pointer and click. Figure 2.2 shows the **C**onfiguration menu options.

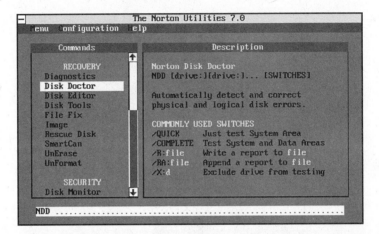

Fig. 2.1

The Norton Utilities main screen.

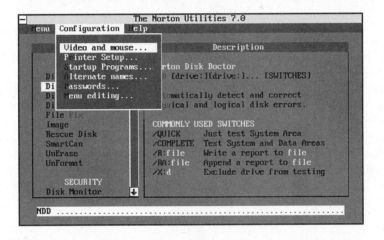

Fig. 2.2

The **C**onfiguration menu options.

The Video and Mouse option enables you to choose how the Norton main menu (and other Norton menus) appears on your monitor. After you choose this option, a screen similar to the one in figure 2.3 appears, showing the Configure Video/Mouse dialog box. With this dialog box, you can set the color, number of lines on-screen, video mode, and sensitivity for your mouse.

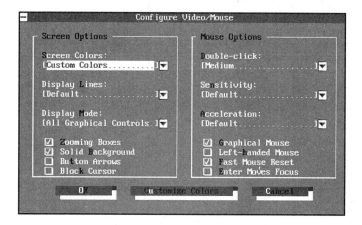

Fig. 2.3

The Configure Video/Mouse dialog box.

The Configure Video/Mouse dialog box is divided into two parts: one for screen settings (Screen Options) and one for mouse settings (Mouse Options). The following sections discuss the options available in both parts of this dialog box.

The first three options in each half of the Configure Video/Mouse dialog box are pull-down list boxes. To pull down a list box, click the triangle, press Tab to move the highlight to the option and then press PgDn, or press Alt plus the option's hot key (highlighted key). To choose an item in the list box, click the item you want and then press Enter, or use the arrow keys to choose the item and then press Enter. The pull-down list box contracts, leaving only the option you have chosen displayed in the list box.

For the rest of the options in the dialog box, press Tab to highlight the option, and then press the space bar to select or deselect the option. Alternatively, you can press Alt plus the appropriate hot key to choose an option, or you can just click the option.

Setting Screen Options

The first option in the Screen Options section is Screen Colors. The following color settings are available:

Option	Description
Black and White	Sets colors for composite black-and-white (often black-and-amber) monitors
Monochrome	Sets colors for monochrome monitors

continues

Option	Description
Grayscale (Laptop)	Sets colors for grayscale monitors and LCD (laptop) monitors
CGA Colors	Sets blue, yellow, and green colors for CGA monitors (sometimes called RGB monitors)
EGA/VGA Colors #1	Sets a blue background with red and yellow highlights
EGA/VGA Colors #2	Sets a gray background with blue and green highlights
Custom Colors	Enables you to choose the color combination

If you choose the **C**ustomize Colors option (button at bottom of screen), the Customize Colors dialog box appears (see fig. 2.4). From this dialog box, you can choose the color combination you want. The list box at the left enables you to choose items to color; the box at the right shows you an example of how the new color settings look.

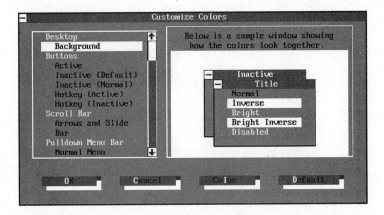

Fig. 2.4

The Customize Colors dialog box.

To set colors from the Customize Colors dialog box, follow these steps:

1. From the list box, highlight the item you want to color.

2. Choose the Color button at the bottom of the dialog box. The Colors dialog box appears (see fig. 2.5). The dialog box's title bar reflects the item that you selected to color in the Customize Colors dialog box.

3. Move back and forth between the **B**ackground and **F**oreground color bars by using the up- and down-arrow keys, the mouse, or the appropriate hot key. Use the left- and right-arrow keys to choose text colors, or simply click your color choices.

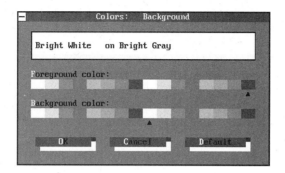

Fig. 2.5

The Colors
dialog box.

4. Choose **OK** to save your changes and return to the Customize Colors dialog box.

   If you choose **C**ancel, you return to the Customize Colors dialog box without saving any color changes; if you choose **D**efault, the color settings return to their original default combinations.

5. Repeat steps 1 through 4 to color other items. Then choose **OK** in the Customize Colors dialog box to lock in your color choices and return to the Configure Video/Mouse dialog box.

   If you choose **C**ancel in the Customize Colors dialog box, you return to the Configure Video/Mouse dialog box without making any changes. If you choose **D**efault, all color choices revert to the default colors.

You can also specify in the Configure Video/Mouse dialog box how many lines of characters to display on your monitor. Choose the Display **L**ines option and then choose one of the following options (the default setting for this option is 25):

Option	Description
Default	Setting that defaults to the standard setup for your monitor
25	Setting most common for PC monitors
28	Setting for EGA- or VGA-compatible monitors only
43	Setting for VGA-compatible monitors only
50	Setting for VGA-compatible monitors only

The Display **M**ode option determines whether certain utilities use standard screen text characters or graphical symbols. The following options are available:

Standard

Some Graphical Controls

All Graphical Controls

You must have a graphics monitor (EGA or VGA) to use the Some Graphical Controls and All Graphical Controls options. Using the Standard option can make the program display information faster, but graphical displays are more aesthetic and more Windows-like.

At the bottom of the Screen Options section are four check boxes:

■ The Zooming Boxes option causes dialog boxes to appear to zoom (grow from small to large) into place on-screen. If you are using a slow computer, you may want to deselect this option in order to speed the display of dialog boxes. This option is selected by default.

■ The Solid Background option causes the screen background to be a solid color rather than a textured pattern. This option is selected by default.

■ The Button Arrows option turns on or off the triangles that appear on both sides of the selected command button. These triangles appear by default in grayscale (Laptop), black-and-white, and monochrome modes because no color exists to indicate which of the command buttons is active—that is, which button executes if you press Enter. If you are using a color setting, you can opt to turn the triangles off.

■ The Block Cursor option changes the underline cursor to a block. You may want to use this option on a laptop or when you have a hard time seeing the cursor on-screen. The cursor is present whenever you type text on-screen. By default, this option isn't selected.

Setting Mouse Options

From the Mouse Options section of the Configure Video/Mouse dialog box, you can choose settings to configure your mouse (refer to fig. 2.3).

The Double-Click setting regulates how fast you must click successively for the program to recognize two clicks as separate commands or as one command. You can choose Slow, Medium (default), or Fast. Choose the speed that is best for you.

The Sensitivity setting controls the sensitivity of the mouse's movement. You can choose Default, Low, Medium, or High. If you choose

High sensitivity, moving the mouse a shorter distance on the mouse pad causes greater movement on-screen. Low sensitivity means you must move the mouse farther on the mouse pad to get the same movement on-screen. The sensitivity of your mouse depends on its type. You must experiment with these settings to see which is most comfortable for you to use.

The Acceleration setting controls the speed of the mouse—the faster you move the mouse, the greater the speed of the mouse pointer. You can choose Default, Low, Medium, or Fast acceleration. With acceleration set to Fast, moving the mouse quickly moves the pointer a greater distance than moving the mouse slowly over the same distance. The default acceleration for your mouse depends on the mouse type. You must experiment with these settings to see which is the most comfortable for you to use.

At the bottom of the Mouse Options section are four more check boxes:

- The Graphical Mouse option enables you to make the mouse pointer an arrow rather than a rectangle.

- The Left-Handed Mouse option reverses the function of the right and left buttons on the mouse.

- The Fast Mouse Reset option is provided for serial mouse users and for computers using PS/2 or COMPAQ mouse ports. To get optimal speed from your mouse, choose this option if your computer uses one of these ports.

- The Enter Moves Focus option enables you to decide how pressing Enter will be interpreted in a dialog box. When this option is checked, pressing Enter in a dialog box causes the highlight (focus) to move to the next option in the dialog box. When this option is unchecked, pressing Enter causes the same action as choosing the active button. For example, if the active button is OK (as in most cases), pressing Enter accepts the settings in the dialog box and closes it.

Setting Printer Options

The Printer Setup option in the Configuration menu enables you to specify what kind of printer you are using and to choose other options, such as type of print (compressed or normal), margins, and header page size. When you choose the Printer Setup option, the Configure Printer dialog box appears (see fig. 2.6). To exit the Configure Printer dialog box, choose Close.

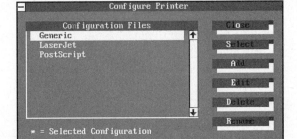

Fig. 2.6

The Configure
Printer dialog
box.

NOTE The options in the Configure Printer dialog box do not affect
your printer settings or capabilities in other programs, such
as WordPerfect or PageMaker.

The following sections describe how to select, add, edit, rename, and
delete printer information.

Selecting a Printer

The Configure Printer dialog box contains a list of predefined printers
from which to choose settings for generic printers, HP LaserJets, and
PostScript printers. To specify which printer to use when printing information, highlight the name of the appropriate printer in the Configuration Files list box and then choose **S**elect. You can also double-click the
printer name to select it. An asterisk appears next to the name of the
selected printer.

Adding a Printer

To enter information about a printer, choose **A**dd. You are then
prompted to enter a brief description of your printer. This description
is only a personal description to help you remember information about
the printer. For example, you could type **MYLaser**. The Printer Settings
dialog box then appears, displaying in the title bar the name you typed
for the printer (see fig. 2.7). This dialog box enables you to select a
printer from the Printer Type drop-down list box and add it to the list
of predefined printers. You may also specify several settings for a new
printer you are adding.

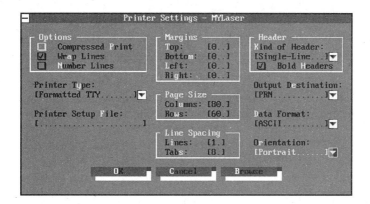

Fig. 2.7

The Printer
Settings dialog
box.

Usually, you must choose the kind of printer you have from the Printer
Type drop-down list box. If you have a Hewlett-Packard LaserJet model,
for example, choose the HP LaserJet option. The default type is Formatted TTY, a generic printer type.

If your printer isn't listed in the Printer Type drop-down list box, the
printer may *emulate* one of the listed printers. In other words, it may
use some of the same printer commands. For example, almost all dot-
matrix printers emulate an Epson printer. Almost all laser printers emulate either an HP LaserJet printer or a PostScript printer. Look in your
printer's manual for information on which common printers it may
emulate. If you choose a printer type that is incorrect, your printer
may print strange characters in a document or eject too many pages.
Choosing incorrectly can even cause the printer to jam or freeze.

In the Options section of the dialog box, you can choose from Compressed Print, Wrap Lines, and Number Lines. Compressed Print instructs the printer to use a small type font when printing. Wrap Lines
causes the printer to wrap long lines of text to the next line; otherwise,
a long line is truncated. Number Lines causes the printout to have each
line numbered, starting with a 1 for the first line.

The Printer Setup File text box enables you to specify the name of a file
containing printer commands that are used to set up your printer. If
your printer supports color printing, for example, you may want to
place information in the setup file that will send a setup command to
the printer to cause it to print in color. The setup file contains lines of
setup commands. Each line contains information that is sent to the
printer. For example, a file may contain this single line:

\027A

This line sends the command consisting of the Esc character (ASCII character number 27) followed by a capital A. Use the following formats for creating the command lines in the setup file:

Character	Description
\nnn	nnn represents an ASCII code, such as 027 for the Esc character.
\C	C is a control character you want to send. For example, \A stands for Ctrl+A.
C	C is a keyboard character you want to send. The line \027\015 in the setup file, for example, sends an Esc character followed by the ASCII character 15. The line \027A in the setup file sends an Esc character followed by the keyboard character A.

Printer control commands vary for different printers and usually appear in the appendix of printer manuals. Consult your printer manual to determine what commands you can or must use. Under normal circumstances, you do not have to use any commands; the printer will work fine with its default settings.

T I P   If you don't remember the name of the printer setup file or the directory where it is located, choose the **B**rowse command button at the bottom of the dialog box. This command displays **D**irectories and **F**iles list boxes that you can use to locate the file name.

The Margins, Page Size, and Line Spacing sections in the middle of the Printer Settings dialog box enable you to choose settings for the top, bottom, left, and right margins; the number of columns and rows to put on a page; the line spacing to use; and the number of characters for a tab marker to represent. The defaults for these settings are shown in figure 2.7. To specify a setting, highlight the appropriate option and then type the value.

The options in the Header section of the dialog box enable you to choose the kind of header that appears on the printed page. The **K**ind of Header options include None, Single-Line (default), and Two-Line. You can print the heading in boldface type by choosing the Bold Headers check box, which is checked by default.

With the Output **D**estination option, you can direct the output of the printer to a particular port. By default, the setting is PRN, but you can choose LPT1, LPT2, LPT3, COM1, COM2, COM3, COM4, or Disk File. The Disk File option sends the printout to a file on your disk, rather than to the printer. The LPT options are for parallel (line printer) ports, and the COM options are for serial (communications) ports. Choose the port to which your printer is attached.

In the **D**ata Format area of the Printer Settings dialog box, you can specify the type of format to be used when printing to the printer. The following three options are available:

Option	Description
ASCII	Tells the program you are printing ASCII files
WordStar	Tells the program you are printing files formatted as a WordStar word processing file
EBCDIC	Refers to a mainframe format type that is different from the PC ASCII standard

The Orientation drop-down list box, which is available for some printers, contains options to choose Portrait (upright) orientation or Landscape (sideways) orientation.

After you set all printer options, choose **OK** to lock in the information. When you return to the Configure Printer dialog box, the name of the printer you added appears on the menu. If you choose **C**ancel, you return to the Configure Printer dialog box, canceling all printer changes.

Editing Printer Information

If something about your printer has changed, such as the output destination, you can edit the printer settings for that printer. In the Configuration Files list box in the Configure Printer dialog box, highlight the name of the printer you want to edit and then choose **E**dit.

The Printer Settings dialog box appears. This dialog box contains the information for the selected printer (refer to fig. 2.7). Edit the information in the dialog box, using the procedures described in the preceding section.

Renaming or Deleting a Printer

To rename one of the printer selections, highlight the name in the Configuration Files list box in the Configure Printer dialog box. Then choose **R**ename. Type the new name at the prompt and choose **OK** to lock in the new name.

If you no longer have access to a printer, you can remove it from the printer list. To delete a printer from the Configure Printer dialog box, highlight the name of the printer you want to omit. Then choose **D**elete. The printer name is removed from the printer list.

Setting Startup Program Options

Each time your computer is turned on or rebooted, you must initialize several of the Norton Utilities programs that are designed to protect the information on your computer (such as Image or SmartCan). The purpose of the **S**tartup Programs option on the **C**onfiguration menu is to allow you to choose which Norton programs you want to place in your computer's startup file (AUTOEXEC.BAT). If a program is in the startup file, the program executes every time you turn on your computer or reboot. When you choose the **S**tartup Programs option, the Startup Programs dialog box appears (see fig. 2.8).

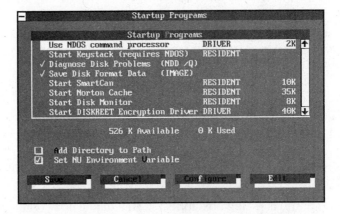

Fig. 2.8

The Startup Programs dialog box.

The options in the dialog box refer to Norton Utilities programs. (All of these programs are described in detail later in this book.) Each option in the dialog box and the chapter that covers the program for that option are listed in the following table:

Option	Description
Use NDOS Command Processor	Installs the NDOS command processor (see Chapter 28).
Start Keystack (requires NDOS)	Installs the NDOS Keystack program, which is used to create keystroke macros for DOS programs (see Chapter 28).
Diagnose Disk Problems (NDD/Q)	Installs the Norton Disk Doctor (NDD) in quick mode. This program provides a quick check for problems related to your disk drive (see Chapter 12).
Save Disk Format Data (IMAGE)	Installs the Image program, which saves a "snapshot" of your disk's system and directory areas. Use this snapshot to repair or unformat your disk (see Chapter 4).
Start SmartCan	Installs the SmartCan program, which protects deleted files from being overwritten. This program allows you to undelete more reliably any recently erased files (see Chapter 5).
Start Norton Cache	Installs the Norton Cache2 program, which gives you faster disk access (see Chapter 21).
Start Disk Monitor	Installs the Disk Monitor program, which provides you with an on-screen disk light and disk protection (see Chapter 6).
Start DISKREET Encryption Driver	Installs the Diskreet program, which provides a file encryption procedure to secure confidential files (see Chapter 7).

To choose a startup program, highlight the program and then press the space bar to select it. When a program is selected, a check mark appears to the left of the name (refer to fig. 2.8).

Several of the programs are *memory resident*, which means that they take up some of your computer's RAM (random-access memory) when loaded. To the right of the option name is the word DRIVER or RESIDENT. If no word is listed, the command is a program that is loaded (for example, NDD), performs a function, and is then released from memory. A *driver*, however, is a set of instructions that remains on disk until needed by a program. A *resident program* (short for *terminate-and-stay-resident* or *TSR*) is loaded into RAM and remains there until you turn off the computer or until the program is unloaded. An option that is resident also displays a number indicating the program's memory requirement. For example, the SmartCan program requires 10K (10 kilobytes) of RAM. Below the Startup **P**rograms list box is a line indicating the current amount of memory on your computer (526K in fig. 2.8) and the amount of memory that will be used by the selected resident programs (0 K in fig. 2.8). When you select a resident program from the list, the K Used item indicates the total amount of memory required to run the selected program.

CAUTION: If you frequently run programs that require a large amount of memory, using resident programs may cause your application program to be unable to run. You must be careful not to choose so many resident programs that your other programs cannot function.

NOTE   Many TSR programs are on the market. The amount of memory reported in the Startup Programs dialog box is only the amount of RAM that will be taken up by the Norton programs you have selected. If you are using other TSR programs, you must also add their memory requirements to find out the total amount of RAM used for your memory-resident programs.

After you have selected the programs you want installed at startup (and deselected the programs you don't want), choose the **S**ave button to place the required commands in your AUTOEXEC.BAT or CONFIG.SYS file. Depending on what option you have chosen, you may be prompted to enter additional information:

Program	Information Needed
Diagnose Disk Problems (NDD/Q)	Specify the appropriate disk drive
Save Disk Format Data (IMAGE)	Specify the appropriate disk drive
Start Norton Cache	Specify various options (see Chapter 21 for details)
Start Disk Monitor	Specify whether you want to monitor disk access or display disk light (or both)

If you choose to include the Norton Cache program, any current cache program in your AUTOEXEC.BAT or CONFIG.SYS file will be disabled.

You do not have to choose the Save option in order to enter the information needed by a startup program. Instead, you can highlight the program option and then choose the Configure button. If additional information is needed, the appropriate dialog boxes appear.

To leave the Startup Programs dialog box without making any changes, choose Cancel.

If you choose the Edit option in the Startup Programs dialog box, you are able to edit manually your AUTOEXEC.BAT and CONFIG.SYS programs. Use this option only if you are familiar with the contents of these files and are comfortable editing this information.

If you check the Add Directory to Path check box in the Startup Programs dialog box, the path to your Norton program is added to your PATH statement in your AUTOEXEC.BAT file. Usually, this addition was made when you ran the installation procedure.

You use the Set NU Environment Variable check box to place a SET command in your AUTOEXEC.BAT file that allows DOS to find NU (Norton Utilities) files even when you are not running Norton programs from the Norton directory.

Selecting Alternate Names

The Alternate Names option in the Configuration menu displays the Alternate Program Names dialog box. In this dialog box, you can choose between two names for several Norton programs: a longer name and an abbreviated name (see fig. 2.9). If you have used Norton Utilities for a number of years, you may be more comfortable with the original short names (such as SI instead of SYSINFO). The length of the name, however, does not affect the way the program runs. You may prefer the short name for a program because it saves keystrokes, or the long name because it is easier to remember.

Here are the options in the Alternate Program Names dialog box:

Option/Program	Long Name	Short Name
Disk Editor	DISKEDIT	DE
File Find	FILEFIND	FF

continues

Option/Program	Long Name	Short Name
Safe Format	SFORMAT	SF or FORMAT
System Information	SYSINFO	SI
Disk Duplication	DUPDISK	DD or DISKCOPY
Speed Disk	SPEEDISK	SD

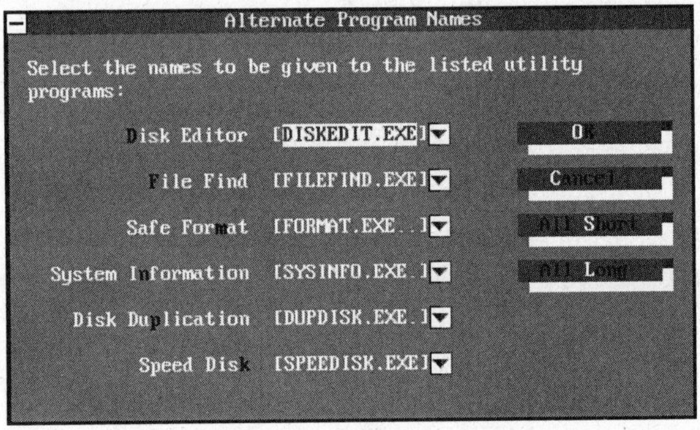

Fig. 2.9

The Alternate Program Names dialog box.

If you substitute FORMAT for SFORMAT or DISKCOPY for DUPDISK, when you execute a FORMAT or DISKCOPY command in the Norton Utilities directory, DOS uses the Norton Utilities versions of those commands. In other words, executing the FORMAT command runs a Safe Format operation instead of a DOS FORMAT operation.

The lists for each program are contained in the drop-down list boxes. You can choose names one at a time, or you can choose the All Short button to make all the names short. Choose All Long if you want all the names to be the original long names. When you have specified the names you want to use, choose OK to lock in your choices. If you want to exit the dialog box and cancel any changes you have made, choose Cancel.

Setting Passwords

Norton Utilities enables you to place password protection on several Norton programs to prevent their unauthorized use. When you choose the Passwords option from the Configuration menu, you can then specify or remove the password for any of the following programs (see fig. 2.10):

Calibrate
Disk Editor
Disk Tools
File Fix
Norton Disk Doctor
Diagnostics
Configuration
Safe Format
Speed Disk
UnErase
UnFormat
Wipe Information

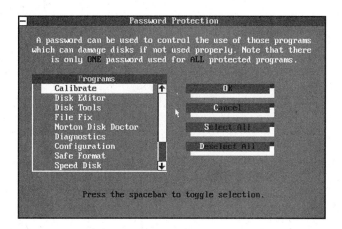

Fig. 2.10

The Password Protection dialog box.

To specify that a program is to be password-protected, highlight the command name and press the space bar, or double-click the command name to turn a check mark on or off to the left of the command name. When you have checked all programs you want to protect, press Enter or choose OK. To protect all programs in the list, choose Select All. To remove protection from all programs, choose Deselect All. Finally, to exit the dialog box without changing any of the settings, choose Cancel.

The password you specify applies to all programs you choose to password-protect. After you choose the programs to be protected and specify a password, you are able to run those programs only after entering the password. When you set the password, you must enter it a second time as a verification.

> **CAUTION:** Do not forget the password. You cannot run the protected program without it.

To set a new password, follow these steps:

1. In the Password Protection dialog box, select the programs for which you want to specify or change the password. (Remember that one password applies to all selected programs.) A check mark appears beside each selected program.

2. Choose **OK** or press **Enter**. The Password dialog box appears with the **New Password** text box highlighted (see fig. 2.11).

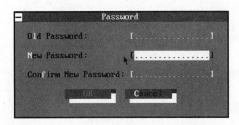

Fig. 2.11

The Password
dialog box.

3. Type a password (up to 15 characters) in the **New Password** text box. Norton displays asterisks, rather than characters, as you type the password.

   After you finish typing the password, press Enter. The highlight moves to the Confirm New Password text box.

4. In the Confirm New Password text box, retype the password and press Enter. This step verifies the password.

   The password you type must be the same in both the **New Password** and the Confirm New Password text boxes. When the passwords are identical, the **OK** button becomes active. Until the passwords match, the **OK** button is inactive, and the **Cancel** button is active. If you press Enter and the passwords don't match, Norton displays a dialog box with an error message and prompts you to retype the confirmation password.

5. Choose **OK** or press **Enter**.

To change the existing password to a new password, choose the **Pass-**words option from the **Configuration** menu. Norton displays a dialog box that prompts you to enter the existing password.

 **NOTE** If you press Enter or choose **OK** in this dialog box, the program just beeps. If you type the password incorrectly, the program displays an error box with the message Incorrect. From this message box, you return to the Norton main screen. Then you must enter the password correctly to continue with this procedure.

After you enter the password correctly, the Configure Password dialog box appears with the Old Password text box highlighted. Type the old password and press Enter. Then proceed as if you were entering a new password (see the preceding steps). To remove the password, press Enter in the **N**ew Password text box. The program prompts you to confirm that you want to remove the password.

For another method of removing the password, follow these steps in the Password Protection dialog box:

1. Deselect checked programs that you want to remove from password protection. Highlight the name and press the space bar, or double-click the name with the mouse pointer.

2. Choose **OK**.

Choosing Menu Editing

The **M**enu Editing option in the Configuration menu displays the Norton Menu Editing dialog box. In this dialog box, you can enable or disable the editing of the Norton menu (see fig. 2.12). Normally, you can add, delete, or change the contents of the Norton main menu. If you are not careful, however, you can alter the menu so that you can no longer access Norton programs from it. To prevent the menu from being changed, choose the **D**isable Editing option. To restore the default setting, choose **E**nable Editing.

Using the NUCONFIG Command

The previous sections describe how to use the configuration options from the Configuration menu in the Norton main screen. However, you do not have to be in the Norton main screen to set these configuration options. You can enter the NUCONFIG command at the DOS prompt, enabling you to choose Norton configuration options without having to go through the NORTON main screen.

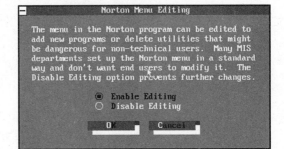

Fig. 2.12

The Norton Menu
Editing dialog
box.

At the DOS prompt, just enter the command **NUCONFIG**. The Configure
Norton Utilities menu is displayed (see fig. 2.13). This menu contains
the same options as the **C**onfiguration pull-down menu. To choose
one of the options from the Configure Norton Utilities menu, press Alt
plus the hot key for the appropriate menu item. You can also point to
the menu item with the mouse pointer and click. To exit the menu,
choose **Q**uit.

When you choose options from the Configure Norton Utilities menu, the dialog boxes for those options are exactly the
same as the dialog boxes you access with the **C**onfiguration
menu in the Norton main screen.

You also can access the Configure Norton Utilities menu
from the Norton main screen. Choose Configuration from
the Commands list.

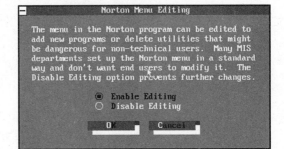

Fig. 2.13

The Configure
Norton Utilities
menu.

Summary

Norton Utilities 7 is an extremely flexible program. You can specify a number of options by using the Configuration menu in the Norton main screen or the NUCONFIG command from the DOS prompt. If you don't like an option you have chosen, you can access the option again and change it to your liking. This chapter described all the configuration options, giving you an idea of which ones you might use in customizing the Norton Utilities programs for your needs.

In the next chapter, you learn some basic information about how disks work. An understanding of this process is essential to using Norton Utilities with your computer.

Understanding How Disks Work

When you drive your car, you can certainly do it without knowing where the carburetor is located. A little knowledge about your car, though, might help you notice and understand the noises and grinds your car develops. You can then take the car to a mechanic before something really goes wrong.

Norton Utilities enables you to perform a number of preventive, diagnostic, and corrective procedures on disks, and you don't even have to know all the ins and outs of how disks work. However, when you understand more about how disks work, you will be able to understand better how problems can arise, the symptoms of potential problems, and the terms used by DOS and Norton when they diagnose and fix problems associated with your disk. This chapter provides an overview of how disks work. It introduces you to terms you will see over and over again, such as *sectors*, *clusters*, and *tracks*. If you already understand how disks work and are comfortable with computing terms, you may want to skip this chapter.

Disks lose information in two basic ways: physical loss and logical loss. *Physical damage* to a floppy disk can result from spilled coffee, a bent disk, a disk left in a car on a hot day, or any number of other misuses. You should always store a floppy disk in its protective envelope and never expose the disk to heat, dust, or liquids. A hard disk can sustain physical damage if you move or bump the computer while it is operating. Even if you drop it only an inch, you can damage the hard disk.

Logical damage to a disk occurs when DOS loses information about where data is stored—that is, DOS "forgets" where a file is located. The data on a disk that is stored as a magnetic image can also weaken just by the process of aging, until that data is difficult or impossible to read. Logical data loss can result also from accidental deletion of files or accidental formatting of the disk, from sudden loss of power, or from a problem caused by a bug in a computer program (including bugs in DOS itself).

Usually, only a technician can repair physical damage to a disk or disk drive—and the technician may not always succeed. With Norton Utilities, you may be able to fix damage relating to logical problems, magnetic weaknesses, or accidental erasure or formatting of the disk.

Your goal, however, should be to safeguard your data on disk from the beginning. In fact, the adage "A stitch in time saves nine" is relevant. A little prevention now can save you much time later. Understanding how DOS manages the information on disk can give you a better understanding of what is happening in your computer, and you will be better prepared to protect the information on your computer by using Norton Utilities.

This chapter covers the fundamentals of data storage and should be sufficient knowledge for using competently most of the programs in the Norton arsenal. Additional information about data storage is covered in the discussions of Manual UnErase and Disk Editor in Chapters 16 and 17, respectively.

How Memory Works

Computers have a *binary* memory pattern. That is, the computer's memory consists of 0s (zeros) and 1s (ones). Each 0 or 1 in the computer's memory is called a *bit*. Information in the computer's RAM (random-access memory) is stored on this chip as an on or off signal; the on signal is 1, and the off signal is 0. Each RAM chip stores thousands of these 0s and 1s. When you create a word processing document, for example, RAM stores the entire document as a series of 0s and 1s. You don't really see the 0s and 1s when you use the word processor because the computer interprets the patterns of 0s and 1s into information we can read. For example, the pattern 01000001 is the uppercase A.

To store computer information, therefore, you must have a way to store these 0s and 1s. Early computers used *punch cards*. A hole punched in the card was interpreted as a 1; no hole meant 0. Today, the popular way to store computer information is on magnetic media.

You may recall from elementary school when your science teacher placed some steel shavings on a sheet of paper and put a magnet under the paper. The shavings all pointed in one direction or another, according to the poles of the magnet. Recording media—such as that on a cassette tape, a VCR tape, or a floppy disk—is covered with a coat of iron oxide, which reacts to magnetism in a way similar to those steel shavings. On a cassette recorder, the recording head is an electric magnet that magnetizes the iron oxide on the tape as the tape goes by. The stronger the signal, the more the iron oxide reacts.

To store computer information on magnetic media, only two signals are needed: one strong and one weak. The computer interprets a strong magnetic signal as a 1 and a weak signal as a 0. Thus, a pattern of 1s and 0s can be written to and then read from magnetic media.

A computer disk is sort of a cross between a record and a cassette tape. Information on the disk is stored on magnetic tracks, which work like the magnetic coating on a cassette tape and the grooves on a record, except that you cannot see the tracks.

The magnetic media is coated on the top and bottom of floppy and hard disks. A small head similar to the recording head on a tape recorder rides just above the surface of the disk. This head places magnetic signals on the disk (patterns of 0s and 1s) and reads them back. The work of reading and writing to disk, however, is not done haphazardly but is a precise bit of mechanical and software engineering.

How Floppy and Hard Disks Evolved

Disk media has improved over time. When the IBM PC first appeared, the disk drive had a read/write head for only one side of the floppy disk. Thus, the only disk media was a single-sided floppy disk.

Shortly afterward, double-sided disks appeared in which the drive had a read/write head on both sides of the disk. This improvement to the drive was relatively straightforward. No new housing or motor was needed. The addition of a second head and some electronics doubled the disk's storage capacity.

Most improvements to disk storage have involved the storing of more information with great precision. The mechanical and electrical improvements have given disks this capability, and DOS has responded with the capability to handle the added capacity.

One problem in reading and writing data to a floppy disk is dust particles. Dust in the air can get on the disk, make the disk "dirty" (even though we cannot see the dirt), and limit the precision (smallness) of the information storage area on the disk. Another problem with floppy disks is that they are just that—floppy. (Even though 3 1/2-inch disks have a hard plastic cover, the actual disk inside the housing is "floppy.") When they spin around in the disk drive, some up-and-down movement occurs. Because of this movement, keeping the read/write head close enough to work but not close enough to scratch the surface of the disk is difficult. In fact, some floppy disks wear out because of contact with the read/write head.

Hard disks are housed in a dust-free compartment, and the magnetic media is coated onto a hard metal platter. These factors solved many of the problems of dust and movement associated with floppy disk drives, as well as the problem of not having enough room on a disk to store information. In summary, the hard disk has three important advantages:

■ The hard disk has a greater storage capacity than the floppy disk.

■ The hard disk is housed in a dust-free compartment, so dust is not a problem.

■ The magnetic media is coated on a hard platter (hence the name *hard disk*), so there is less up-and-down movement as the disk turns.

These improvements enable the read/write head to be placed closer to the disk, to read and write with more precision, and to rotate faster, enabling data to be stored and retrieved more quickly than on a floppy disk.

How Disks Are Organized

A formatted floppy or hard disk contains specific areas on the disk where data is stored. Each disk contains a number of circular areas called *tracks*. A standard 360K floppy disk (double-sided/double-density) has 40 tracks, numbered 0 to 39. The 1.2M 5 1/4-inch disks, the 720K 3 1/2-inch disks, and the 1.44M high-density disks all use 80 tracks. Each track consists of a number of pieces called *sectors*. On a 360K disk, each track has 9 sectors, numbered 1 through 9. Figure 3.1 illustrates the tracks and sectors on a typical 360K disk.

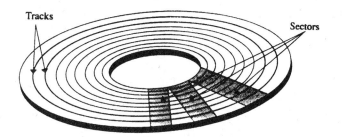

Fig. 3.1

A disk's tracks and sectors.

A pair of matching tracks, one on the top of the disk and the other on the bottom of the disk, is called a *cylinder*. Each track on a disk is divided into a number of sectors, and each sector holds 512 bytes of information. A *byte* is eight 0 and 1 signals. As noted earlier, each 0 or 1 signal is called a *bit*. Usually, each character stored on disk requires one byte of space. Thus, a byte often is referred to as one character of information. (The byte 01000011 is the character C.)

Although it may seem complicated at first, using this relationship for sides, tracks, clusters, sectors, bytes, and bits, DOS can keep track of the information on the disk. The next few sections explain in more detail how these pieces come together on the disk to make information storage possible.

Tracks

Tracks are concentric rings encoded onto a disk during the formatting process to which data can be written or from which data can be read. Floppy disks usually contain 40 or 80 tracks on each side, and hard disks contain from 100 to more than 1,000 tracks on each side. When the disk drive is manufactured, it is designed so that the reading and writing heads can move in and out across the surface of the disk as it rotates. The head assembly can stop at given places along the path of movement, and as the disk rotates under the head, it reads or writes information to the disk.

Each head assembly is designed so that the head stops at predetermined places on the disk. For example, a 360K 5 1/4-inch disk is designed to permit only 40 stopping points (tracks). These 40 stopping points are numbered from 0 to 39, as illustrated in figure 3.2. The track at the outer portion of the disk's recording area is assigned the number 0, and the track nearest the center of the disk is track number 39.

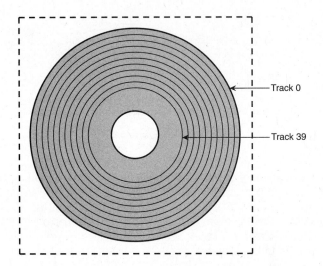

Track 0

Track 39

Fig. 3.2

Tracks on a 360K 5 1/4-inch disk.

These tracks are circular, concentric, and not connected in any way. A disk is not like a phonograph record, which has a single, spiraling groove. In a disk, the tracks are perfectly circular and do not touch each other.

NOTE Data can sometimes become unreadable on a disk if the read/write head on the disk drive becomes misaligned. This prevents the head from riding directly over the track where the data on the disk resides. When this occurs, it is a physical problem that must be corrected by a hardware technician. It is not generally correctable by a user.

Cylinders

A *cylinder* is a set of tracks that occupies one head position. A standard floppy disk drive has two heads: one head reads and writes to the top of the disk, and the other head reads and writes to the bottom. A hard disk may have 2, 4, 8, or more heads. Each head is mounted on the same movement mechanism known as an *actuator*. The head actuator can move the heads to any given track position for reading and writing.

NOTE The "seek" test performed by the Norton program System Info graphically shows the actuator moving in and out between tracks on the disk as it performs a speed test to determine how fast data can be written and read from the disk (see Chapter 18). The term *seek time* is the amount of time it takes for the disk head to move to the proper track (cylinder) that you want the disk head to read. *Average access time* is a measure of time (based on an average of seeks) that it takes to move the head to the position on disk where you want to read.

This multiple-head movement can cause confusion about the term *track*; track 35, for example, exists on the top as well as the bottom of a floppy disk. On a floppy disk, the term *cylinder* describes both tracks at a given position on the top and bottom of the disk. For example, cylinder 25 refers to the top and bottom surface at the 26th position from the outside of the disk. Thus, instead of discussing two track numbers 25, you can discuss the single cylinder 25 (and mean the same thing). On a hard disk, cylinder 25 refers to position 26 for all heads on the actuator.

On a floppy disk, the bottom track of the disk is called side 0, and the top track is called side 1. Cylinder 1 consists of both track 1, side 0 and track 1, side 1. Some hard disks have more than one platter, or disk. When two disks are included (as on a hard disk), the sides are numbered 0 and 1 on the first disk, and 2 and 3 on the second disk. The set of four matching tracks on the two disks is the cylinder.

Sectors

A *sector* is a portion of one of the concentric tracks on a disk. A disk's track is too large to be managed as a single piece of information. Therefore, each track is divided into a number of sectors. These sectors can be described as slices of a track. Different types of disks and disk drives split a track into different numbers of sectors. Floppy disk formats, for example, currently use between 8 and 18 sectors per track. Hard disks store data at a higher density and can use between 17 and 64 sectors per track. Sectors created by standard formatting procedures always have a 512-byte capacity. Figure 3.1, shown earlier, shows how a track is divided into sectors.

Sectors are numbered beginning with 1, unlike tracks or cylinders, which begin with 0. A 1.2M floppy disk, for example, contains 80 cylinders numbered from 0 to 79, and each track on each cylinder has 15 sectors numbered from 1 to 15.

Sectors are numbered sequentially (1 through 15) on floppy disks. On hard disks, however, sectors are often interleaved. *Interleaved* sectors are not numbered sequentially but in some intertwining manner. The interleaving is usually required because the disk spins so fast that after reading one sector, the disk controller is not yet ready to read the next sector that immediately follows. Thus, the next sector to be read is spaced several sectors away so that the controller can catch up.

NOTE The Norton utility called Calibrate can reset a hard disk's interleave to maximize the hard disk's access time (see Chapter 20).

When a disk is formatted, additional areas are created on the disk so that the disk controller can number sectors and identify the beginning and end of each sector. These areas precede and trail each sector's data area. This process accounts for some discrepancy in the differences between a disk's unformatted capacity and its formatted capacity. For example, an unformatted 2M 3 1/2-inch disk has a formatted capacity of only 1.44M. The "lost" space is used mostly for sector record keeping. Thus, although each sector stores 512K of data, the sector actually takes up 571K on the disk. To visualize how this works, examine the illustration in figure 3.3.

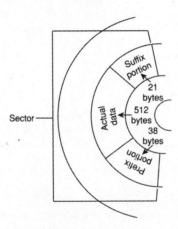

Fig. 3.3

Divisions of a sector.

You can think of a sector as being a book. The contents of the book are in the middle, but there is a table of contents at the beginning of the book and an index at the end of the book. When a disk is formatted, sectors are laid out on the magnetic media in this way. When information is written to a file (which uses the sector), data is written to the data portion of the sector. The information before and after the data in the sector is not altered. This information contains the sector number and a checksum code, which is a number used to check the integrity of the sector.

Clusters

A *cluster* is the amount of space that the disk can read or write at one time. This usually consists of several sectors. Thus, a cluster is a collection of two or more sectors. Although the disk is divided into sectors (usually 512 bytes each), keeping track of each sector is often too much overhead for the disk, so DOS often reads and writes multisector units (clusters) at a time. The number of sectors taken by disks are summarized in table 3.1.

Table 3.1 Cluster Sizes

Disk Size	Disk Type	Number of Sectors	Cluster Size
160K	5 1/4" single-sided/single-density	1	512K
180K	5 1/4" single-sided/double-density	1	512K
320K	5 1/4" double-sided/single-density	2	1024K
360K	5 1/4" double-sided/double-density	2	1024K
720K	3 1/2" double-sided/double-density	2	1024K
1.2M	5 1/4" high-density	1	512K
1.44M	3 1/2" high-density	1	512K
10M	Hard disk	8	4096K
Most other hard disks	Hard disk	4	2048K

Note: If a 20M or greater hard disk is formatted under DOS 2.x, the cluster size is 8,192 (16 sectors).

A file is stored in one or more clusters. Thus, if a cluster is 1024K, then even the smallest file will take up at least 1024K of disk space. (Even though a directory listing may say that the file is smaller, it still takes a minimum of a cluster to store.) For more information about how files and clusters are related, see the section "The File Allocation Table (FAT)" later in this chapter.

Because many files are longer than one cluster, portions of the file must be stored on a number of clusters. Often, these clusters are not stored on disk one after the other, but may be scattered all over the disk. How is all of this information managed? Keeping the information about where files are stored is one of the primary jobs of the Disk Operating System (DOS).

How DOS Manages Data

When a disk is formatted, the disk is divided into two major areas called the system area and the data area. Each area has a role to play in storing and managing the data on the disk.

The *system area* contains the boot record, the file allocation table (FAT), and the root directory. The system area is stored on track 0, the outermost track of the disk. Whenever DOS needs to know information about the files stored on a disk, DOS reads this information from the system area of the disk. When you enter a DIR command, for example, DOS first looks at the directory to get information on the files and displays this information on-screen. Every formatted disk contains a system area.

The *data area*, where the actual information in files is stored, immediately follows the system information on disk. The system area controls the contents of this data area. DOS references the information in the system area when it needs to know where to read and write the data.

The Boot Record

DOS reserves as the DOS boot record the first sector of the first track (track 0) of a disk. The *boot record* contains characteristics about the disk, such as the DOS version used to format the disk, the number of bytes per sector on disk, the number of heads, and other information. The boot record is written to every formatted disk, even if the disk does not have booting capabilities. When a computer is booted, it looks at the boot record of the startup disk (usually disk A: or C:). If the disk is a bootable disk, this record gives the computer information on where to find the startup system information. When you access a disk in a disk drive (such as doing a directory listing on a floppy disk in drive A), DOS first looks at the boot record to determine what kind of disk is being accessed. This information tells DOS how to access file information for the disk.

The File Allocation Table (FAT)

The *file allocation table (FAT)* contains information about the status of each sector on the disk. The FAT tells DOS which clusters on the disk are in use, contain files, are available for use, or are bad and should not be used. When you must write a file to disk, DOS consults the FAT to find out where to store the information. If a file is large and cannot fit in one contiguous space on disk, DOS uses the FAT to find the next available space. If DOS cannot store a file in contiguous clusters, the result is a *fragmented file*—a file that is stored in pieces on disk.

Furthermore, because the FAT deals in clusters, a file may be allocated to a cluster that is not fully used. For example, if a cluster is 1,024 bytes, and a 200-byte file is stored, 824 bytes of unused space remain in the cluster. This space cannot be used by other files at the same time, so this area of disk space within this cluster is "wasted." This unused disk space is called *slack*. (You can determine the amount of slack on disk by using the Norton File Size utility, discussed in Chapter 26.)

Cluster sizes differ, so the slack space for a particular file on a floppy disk may be different from the slack for the same file on a hard disk. Although a floppy disk may have a 1,024-byte cluster, many hard disks have 2,048-byte clusters. The same 200-byte file has a slack space of 1,848 bytes on such a hard disk.

Slack space is of particular interest when you are protecting information on disk. If a cluster was previously used for a top secret file and is now only partially used to store a current file, the slack space may contain secret information that could be read with a program like Norton Disk Editor, discussed in Chapter 17. The Norton WipeInfo program, discussed in Chapter 8, gives you a way to erase the slack space on a disk to prevent these leftover pieces of files from being read or recovered.

Another consideration of slack space occurs when you have a bad sector that must be fixed. For example, when you run the Norton Disk Doctor (see Chapter 12), it may find a bad sector on disk. However, even though part of the cluster is bad, the file might be completely recovered if it is contained in a good portion of the cluster and if the bad sector is in the slack space. When NDD finds a bad sector, it will attempt to copy the data from the associated cluster to a different unused cluster; and NDD may be able to make the file usable again if the data from the file can be recovered from the good portion of the cluster.

The Root Directory

The third part of the system information on disk is the *root directory*—the main directory (\) on any formatted disk. This disk space is allocated for storing information about the root directory's files. Subdirectories have their own areas where file information is stored. Subdirectories, like files, can be stored in the data area in no particular location. Table 3.2 shows the information that a directory reports for each file the directory contains.

Table 3.2 File Information Stored in the Root Directory		
Item	**Size in bytes**	**Stored As**
File name	8	ASCII characters
Extension	3	ASCII characters
Attributes	1	Bit values
Time	2	Coded time
Date	2	Coded date
Starting FAT entry	2	Word (a binary coded number)
File size	4	Long integer (size in bytes)

NOTE The root directory reserves 10 bytes for future use in case something else about a file must be stored.

Notice that the file name size is eight characters—the maximum length for a file name. The extension is allocated three characters. Attributes include read-only, archive, hidden, and system. (You can control the attributes with Norton File Find, discussed in Chapters 9 and 25.) The starting FAT entry tells DOS where to look in the FAT to find where the file is stored on disk. The date and time entries tell DOS when this file was last changed, and the file size entry tells DOS how much space the file takes in bytes. The information in the Stored As column of table 3.2 specifies the method used to store this information.

How Files Are Erased

When you store a file on disk, the information that the file contains is written to the disk's data area. The root directory (or a similar subdirectory) and the FAT store the information about where the file data is. When you erase a file with the DOS ERASE or DEL command, the first character of the entry in the directory that contains the file name is replaced with the ASCII sigma character number 229 (σ), the lowercase Greek letter sigma, and related entries in the FAT are zeroed out. DOS does not overwrite (unless you use WipeInfo, as explained in Chapters 4 and 8) or remove the information from the file. The ASCII character number 229 that DOS adds to the erased file's directory tells DOS that the file and the space the file occupied are now free to be used by other files.

If, for example, you erase a file named MYFILE, the "erased" name becomes σYFILE in the DOS directory. The erased name does not appear when you use the DIR command, but you can view the name with the Norton UnErase utility.

Because the ERASE and DEL commands do not touch the real information in the file, you may be able to recover an erased file if you have written no other files (or few files) to disk since erasing the file. The rest of this chapter discusses ways to recover files.

How Disks Are Formatted

The formatting process prepares disks to store information. The earlier portion of the chapter describes the specific areas of the disk—the system area, the data area, and how DOS manages data on a formatted disk. This section describes the process of formatting a new disk and reformatting a disk that already contains information.

Actually, there are two ways to format a disk: a physical format (also called low-level format) and a logical format (called high-level format). A low-level format divides the disk's tracks into a specific number of sectors. The sector header and trailer information is recorded, as well as other information. Each sector is filled with a 512-byte dummy value, usually the value F6 (in hexadecimal).

A high-level format places the disk structure needed by DOS for managing files and data. During this process, DOS places on the disk a volume boot sector, a file allocation table (FAT), and a root directory. DOS also checks the disk for integrity. Thus, to prepare a disk to hold data, both types of formatting (low and high) must be performed. For a new, out-of-the-box floppy disk, DOS FORMAT (or Norton Safe Format) will perform both kinds of formatting at the same time—what is usually called formatting a disk. For a hard disk, the low-level format is a separate procedure (and usually not performed by the casual user). When a hard disk is formatted with DOS FORMAT or Norton Safe Format, a high-level format is performed. For a hard disk, an additional procedure is performed after the low-level format and before the high-level format (using the DOS FDISK command) to prepare a disk. This procedure is called *partitioning*.

The way a disk is formatted is important for data recovery. Because there are different kinds of formatting, and because floppy and hard disk formatting can be quite different, it is important to understand what is happening when you format a disk. The next two sections explain how the formatting process works for floppy disks and hard disks, and discusses how differences in formatting affect data recovery.

Formatting a Floppy Disk

The FORMAT command in early versions of DOS (before DOS 5.0) formats a floppy disk with both low- and high-level formats simultaneously. This means that when you format a disk, the sector information is reset to a dummy value (usually F6 in hexadecimal). When a floppy disk is formatted in this way, you cannot recover any information from the disk with an unformatting technique.

Beginning with DOS 5.0, DOS's default format for a floppy disk is a high-level format, enabling you to recover from the format, if needed. To perform a format that includes both low- and high-level formats, you can use the DOS FORMAT command with the /U (unconditional) switch.

Norton Utilities allows you to format a floppy disk with the Safe Format procedure. When you use this, a high-level format is performed on the floppy disk, and recovery information is stored on the disk. Because the data in the sectors is not overwritten in a high-level format, you may be able to recover the information from the disk by unformatting it with Norton UnFormat (see Chapter 11). Norton's Safe Format also allows two other format options. The Quick Format option, like the safe (high-level format) option, places new system information on the disk but does not perform byte-by-byte integrity testing. Therefore, Quick Format is much quicker than the normal format procedure. The Safe Format DOS option causes the disk to be formatted with the standard DOS-type format used in versions of DOS before 5.0. Use of this option completely erases all data, and you cannot recover information from a disk formatted in this way.

Formatting a Hard Disk

The complete formatting process for a hard disk consists of three steps:

1. A low-level format, usually performed at the factory

2. Partitioning with FDISK, usually performed only once on a new hard disk

3. A high-level format with FORMAT or Norton Safe Format

Usually, when you hear someone talk about formatting a hard disk, the person is referring to a high-level format with the DOS FORMAT command. For most computers that you purchase today, the hard disk is already formatted and normally contains a number of programs already copied to the disk. Therefore, it is possible that you will never have the opportunity (or the need) to format or partition a hard disk. For some occasions, however, you may still need to perform one or more of the formatting steps for a hard disk.

A low-level format, as described earlier, prepares a hard disk by laying out the sectors on the disk and filling them with dummy information. The process also performs an integrity test and places information in the headers of bad sectors, telling DOS not to use these sectors to store information. It is not uncommon to have some bad sectors on a hard disk. Usually, a low-level format is performed on a disk at the factory, and it may never need to be performed again on the disk. On rare occasions, your disk may develop problems that can be solved only by performing a low-level format. This cannot be performed by the normal FORMAT or Norton Safe Format command. Some hard disks have a built-in program that allows you to run a low-level format. See Appendix D for information on when and how to use this built-in low-level format program. When you run this low-level format, all information on your disk is destroyed. An alternative to this destructive low-level format is found in the Norton Calibrate program. Calibrate can perform a nondestructive low-level integrity check of your hard disk.

When you install a new hard disk in a computer, a low-level format has usually been performed on the drive. Some people go ahead and perform their own low-level format just to make sure that the disk is properly checked.

The next step after performing a low-level format is to partition the disk. In the DOS world, you can install more than one type of operating system on a drive. Thus, you may have both DOS and OS/2 (or some other operating system) on your drive. The DOS FDISK program allows you to prepare your hard disk to accept one or more operating systems. For information on using FDISK, see your DOS manual or *Using MS-DOS 6*, Special Edition from Que Corporation.

After a hard disk has been prepared by a low-level format and partitioned by FDISK, the disk is ready to receive a high-level format. When you format a hard disk with DOS FORMAT or Norton Safe Format, a new system area is written to the disk, and an integrity test is performed on the disk. The actual data in the disk sectors is not affected, however. Thus, it is possible for you to reconstruct the system information by using IMAGE or MIRROR information (see Chapter 4) and recover the information from the disk with an unformatting procedure.

Avoiding Problems Associated with Formatting Floppy Disks

As the PC has evolved, the disk types available have grown. Today, there are four common disk types: the 360K and 1.2M 5 1/4-inch disks, and the 720K and 1.44M 3 1/2-inch disks. The 360K and 720K disks are called "double-density," and the 1.2M and 1.44M disks are called "high-density." The way that each disk drive physically writes and reads information to and from the floppy disk is designed to work with a specific kind of disk. You can have severe data loss problems when using low-density disks formatted as high-density disks or when using high-density disks formatted as low-density disks. In each case, the improper format causes problems, as described in this section.

It has become popular with some computer users to save money by formatting 720K disks as 1.44M disks. The process is simple. On some machines (PS/2s, for example), you can easily format a 720K disk as 1.44M—in fact, just using the normal DOS FORMAT command will do it. For other computers, you must first punch a hole in the upper-left corner (looking at the disk with the label in front and the write-protect hole at the upper right). Some commercial tools allow you to punch this hole. When you format a disk in this way, you can store more information on the less-expensive 720K disk. However, this practice is a time bomb.

The 1.44M and 720K disks are constructed differently; the actual disk media that stores the magnetic image is made of different kinds of material. The recording heads for low- and high-density drives are also different. High-density drives use a higher current (signal strength) to write the magnetic image to the disk. The media used in a 720K disk is not designed to handle this signal permanently. Although the disk may work for a period of time (usually months), eventually the magnetic signal on the 720K disk formatted as a 1.44M will begin to fade, resulting in data loss. Many people who have placed important backup information on these kinds of disk are sorely disappointed when they go back to them a year later to find that the disks are unreadable and unrecoverable.

Another common problem is the interchange of 360K disks and 1.2M disks. Although you may have some success in using 360K and 1.2M disks interchangeably in 360K and 1.2M drives, incompatibilities exist that may eventually result in data loss. Always use 360K disks in 360K drives and use 1.2M disks in 1.2M drives. You can read 360K disks from a 1.2M drive with no problem, but problems can occur if you write to a 360K disk on a 1.2M drive and then try to read it later on a 360K drive.

You can format a 360K disk in a 1.2M drive with DOS FORMAT or even Norton Safe Format. If the disk is a "virgin" disk (freshly formatted out of the box), you may then be able to use that disk in a 360K drive. However, a 360K drive and a 1.2M drive have read and write heads of different widths. The 1.2M drive's heads are smaller. Therefore, if you write to a 360K disk on a 1.2M drive, you may not completely overwrite any information already in a sector. When a 360K drive tries to read the information on the disk, it will be reading a wider path than was written by the 1.2M drive. This may result in the 360K drive reading unintentioned information and often means data loss on the disk.

> **CAUTION:** Always use the correct disk size for the drive you are using. Although you may get by with using a wrong-density disk for a while, the ultimate result will be data loss.

Summary

This chapter introduced you to a number of terms and concepts in computer data storage, which are mentioned throughout the remaining chapters. You will see these concepts used by DOS and other programs. Although this chapter is not intended to make you a computer engineer, it should give you enough of a feel for how disks work. You can then use Norton Utilities more effectively and understand more easily the messages and other information displayed by various Norton and DOS programs.

The next chapter begins Part II of this book, in which you learn how to use several Norton utilities to protect your valuable data.

Protecting
Your Files

Using Safe Format and Image

Using SmartCan

Using Disk Monitor

Using Diskreet

Destroying Files Permanently with
  WipeInfo

Setting File Attributes

Using Safe Format and Image

Taking a little time to lock your car doors when you are out shopping can save you a lot of grief. Likewise, taking the added measure of using Norton's file-protection utilities will cost you little time but is well worth the effort. Although versions of DOS since 5.0 provide some protection commands for your files, the power of Norton Utilities can give you an extra measure of safety.

The information stored on your disk is subject to many potential dangers. You can accidentally erase a file; you (or a "friend") can accidentally format a disk containing valuable information; or a "foe" can search your disk and read private information in files, even if they have been erased. In large mainframe environments, operators and systems managers take great care in protecting the data stored on the computer. Usually, a PC owner must be both an operator and a systems manager. In those roles, you must take the initiative to protect your information in the following ways:

- Prevent information from being lost as a result of accidental formatting

- Prepare for possible accidental formatting

■ Prevent important files from being erased or overwritten

■ Permanently dispose of valuable or secret information

Part II of this book discusses the Norton Utilities 7 programs that can help you protect information on your disk in these ways. This chapter explains Safe Format (SFORMAT or SF) and Image (IMAGE). Chapter 5 covers SmartCan (SMARTCAN), which protects erased files. Disk Monitor (DISKMON), covered in Chapter 6, protects files from being erased. Chapter 7 explains Diskreet (DISKREET), which encrypts files. WipeInfo, covered in Chapter 8, gets rid of information for good. Finally, File Attributes (FA), which prevents files from being changed or erased, is discussed in Chapter 9.

Although you may not want to use all of these protection programs at once, each has its own special purpose and features. Begin with this chapter to find out about Safe Format and Image. These programs should be used by *every* computer user. The Safe Format (SFORMAT) program gives you protection against accidental formatting and provides protection and speed beyond that available with the DOS FORMAT command. Just in case your disk is reformatted accidentally, Norton provides the Image and UnFormat commands. (UnFormat is covered is Chapter 11.) After you have learned how to use Safe Format and Image, continue with Chapters 5 through 9 to determine which of the utilities in those chapters provide the kinds of data protection you need.

Using Safe Format

Formatting is the procedure that prepares a disk (a floppy disk or hard disk) to store information. If you format a disk that contains information (files), the information on the disk is often erased. This loss can be devastating if the disk contained important data that is hard to recover.

 NOTE If you have not already done so, refer to Chapter 3 for specific information about how formatting prepares a disk to store data.

Computers are often so reliable that they are taken for granted. Even when important information is being stored on a computer, the user often gives no thought about losing the information—until it happens! Suppose, for example, that a new employee simply entered FORMAT at the C:\> prompt and then wondered what was happening. By the time you were called to look at the computer, the hard disk was fully formatted, and the damage was done. Just like all the king's horses and all the king's men, you or your support staff must try to put the pieces back together again. The hard disk may have contained important research, financial, or organizational information—and it was not backed up regularly. You may have to reconstruct the information that had been on disk from letters, papers, and records dating back several years. This process may cost thousands of dollars in personnel time. In some cases, the original source of the information cannot be recovered. Few people are prepared in any way for this expensive problem. Presumably, because you are reading this now, you are interested in protecting your data. If you also supervise other people, you should take the responsibility to see that they also use data-protection procedures.

 **NOTE** Although Norton Utilities does not provide a backup procedure, backing up information on disk should be a standard practice, and the first step in protecting your data. DOS provides the BACKUP command for making backup copies of your hard disk. You also can buy a backup program called Norton Backup, and a number of other software programs enable you to back up your hard disk onto floppy disks, tapes, or other media. The DOS BACKUP procedure is covered in Appendix A. See Chapter 29 for more information on using the Norton Backup program.

Depending on your version of DOS, it is easy to reformat a disk accidentally. Versions of DOS before 3.3 enable you to format the hard disk (drive C) simply by entering the following command:

FORMAT C:

(If you are at the C:\> prompt, you just enter **FORMAT**.) Then you press Enter in response to a prompt asking whether you are sure that your disk is in place. If you control any computers that are still using a version of DOS earlier than 3.3, one measure of protection you can take is to upgrade those computers to a new version of DOS.

Beginning with DOS 3.3, you must specify the volume name for the disk before the format proceeds if you are formatting a hard disk. This provides some added protection against accidental format. Whatever the cause, accidental formatting is a problem that continues to occur, even with the recent DOS safeguard of requiring a volume label with the FORMAT command. Norton Safe Format gives you additional levels of protection against accidental formatting. For example, Safe Format displays information about the impending format. Even after entering the Safe Format command, you must specifically choose an option that allows you to perform a hard disk format. To help prevent accidental formatting of floppy disks, Safe Format gives you a warning message if the disk (either hard disk or floppy disk) that you are about to format already contains files.

Furthermore, even if you choose to proceed with the format, Safe Format saves a copy of the old file information to a place on disk that can be recovered (unless you specifically choose an option not to save the unformat information). Because the formatting procedure essentially just erases all information about where files are stored on disk (but does not actually erase the contents of the files), you can use the file information saved by Safe Format to recover information on a formatted disk. Refer to Chapter 11 for a discussion of format recovery.

Starting Safe Format

You can begin the Safe Format program from either the Norton main screen or the DOS prompt. To begin Safe Format from the Norton main screen, begin Norton Utilities by typing **NORTON** at the DOS prompt and pressing Enter. The Norton Utilities main screen appears, as shown in figure 4.1. Use the down-arrow key or the mouse to scroll through the commands on the left until the Safe Format option is highlighted. Then press Enter or double-click the mouse to begin the Safe Format program.

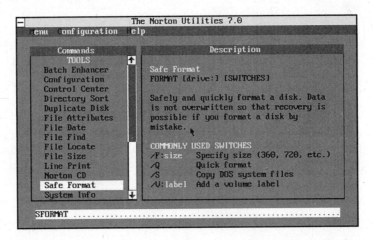

Fig. 4.1

The Norton Utilities main screen.

If you don't want to use this screen to run the command, you can start Safe Format from the DOS prompt by typing **SFORMAT** and pressing Enter.

With either method, you can begin Safe Format with one or more switches. If you enter the SFORMAT command without any switches, the Safe Format dialog box is displayed so that you can select options to use for the format process.

Using the Safe Format Dialog Box

Whether you use the Norton main screen or the SFORMAT command to start Safe Format, the Safe Format dialog box appears (see fig. 4.2). This dialog box enables you to choose a variety of formatting options. It contains all the options you could choose by using the DOS FORMAT command, and more. The following sections describe the Safe Format dialog box options.

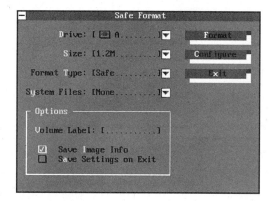

Fig. 4.2

The Safe Format dialog box.

Specifying the Drive

The **Drive** option in the Safe Format dialog box specifies which disk is to be formatted. Depending on how you installed Norton Utilities, hard disk names may not appear in the list of drives to format. You cannot format network drives with Safe Format.

Indicating the Disk Size

You use the **S**ize option to indicate the size of the disk, such as 360K or 1.2M, to be formatted. The program detects the disk sizes that your computer supports, and lists them in the Size box. Norton Utilities 7 supports 2.88M disks, which are supported also by DOS 5.0 and 6.0. Note that even though your 3 1/2-inch disk is read by the program as a 1.44M disk, you can choose to format a 720K disk in that drive. You can choose also to format a 360K disk in a 1.2M 5 1/4-inch drive. Be aware, however, of potential problems in formatting a 360K disk in a 1.2M drive (for detailed information, see Chapter 3 on understanding how disks work).

Choosing the Format Type

The Format Type option sets the format type that will be used: Safe, Quick, or DOS. (These settings relate to the /Q and /D switches that you use when entering the command at the DOS prompt.) Here are the format types:

Format Type	Description
Safe	Formats the disk information but keeps file information on disk (similar to the Image information described later in this chapter) so that you can recover files.
Quick	Creates a new system area and does not overwrite any data areas. This mode is useful for formatting previously formatted floppy disks. By erasing the system area that contains the addresses of all files and directories on disk, this format is simply a quick way to erase all files and remove all directories from a disk. A Quick format can take about 5 seconds, whereas a normal format takes about 45 seconds. However, see the following caution about a potential danger in using this option.
DOS	Formats a disk, using the regular DOS procedure (before DOS 5.0). No recovery information is written to disk, and an UnFormat may not be able to recover any files.

CAUTION: You should be careful when using the Quick format option (or the /Q switch when using Safe format from the DOS prompt) to perform a format. Certain viruses (such as the pervasive "Stoned" virus) can attach themselves to the system area of a disk. Quick format does not clear out that area of the disk. Thus, if you format a disk infected with Stoned or a similar virus, the virus will remain on disk. If you format the disk by using the Safe or DOS format type, this kind of virus is overwritten and destroyed. Therefore, if you know the history of the disk (you know that it has not been subjected to any virus), you can use the Quick format without any problem. But if the disk you are about to format is from an unknown source, you should format it by using the Safe or DOS format.

Setting the System Files Option

The System Files option specifies whether the disk to be formatted will contain the system files or whether space will be reserved for system files. (These settings relate to the /S and /B switches used when you enter the command from the DOS prompt.) The options available in this drop-down list are None (the default), Put on Disk, and Leave Space. When you put the system files on a disk, the disk becomes a bootable disk. You would want to format a disk in this way if you intend to use the disk as a boot disk for a computer.

If you choose the None option, the system files are not placed on the disk, and no room is reserved for them. If you choose the Put on Disk option, all system files necessary to create a boot disk are placed on the newly formatted disk. If you choose the Leave Space option, the system files are not placed on the disk, but room is reserved on the disk to allow the system files to be put on the disk with the DOS SYS command. The Leave Space option is a relic of old DOS versions in which this was the only way to create a disk that could later have the DOS system files loaded. Using Norton's Disk Tools (see Chapter 13), you can easily place system files on a formatted disk even if it was not previously formatted with the Leave Space option. Usually, you want to choose the None option. This allows the disk to have the maximum amount of space available to store files.

Entering the Volume Label

The Volume Label option near the bottom of the Safe Format dialog box specifies which, if any, label will be given to the disk. A *volume label* is the name of the disk that appears at the top of a directory listing. Volume labels are a way to identify disks. For example, to establish ownership of the disk, you may want to use your name or initials as the volume label. You are not required to have a volume label on a disk (except recently for hard disks). To provide a volume label, press the Tab key until the Volume Label option is highlighted (or point to the option with the mouse pointer and click once). Then enter the label (maximum of 11 characters) you want to place on the formatted disk. (You can set this option also with the /V:*label* switch when you use Safe Format from the DOS prompt.)

Using the Save Image Info Option

The Save Image Info option, when checked, causes Safe Format to take a "snapshot" of the disk's system area so that you can unformat the disk if you discover that you formatted the wrong one. This is what the Image program does for your hard disk (see "Preparing for an Accidental Format" later in this chapter).

Saving the Safe Format Settings

The Save Settings on Exit option, when checked, causes Safe Format to remember all the changes you have made in the option boxes so that they will contain the same settings the next time you use the program. If the settings are not saved (that is, if this option is not checked), the options will return to the default state the next time you enter the Safe Format dialog box.

Specifying the Configuration To Format

The Configure button at the upper right of the Safe Format dialog box enables you to set additional options for Safe Format. If you choose Configure, the Configuration dialog box shown in figure 4.3 appears. You use the options on the left to choose the disk drive to configure. In this case, drive B is currently selected. You use the list on the right to indicate what kind of disk is normally used in the specified disk drive. (For a 3 1/2-inch disk, the disk size could be 720K, 1.44M, or 2.88M.) The headings of both lists change depending on the drive selected.

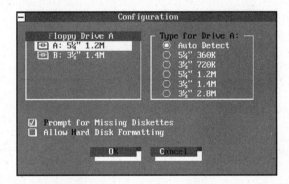

Fig. 4.3

The Configuration dialog box.

If you don't specify the disk configuration, Safe Format uses your computer's autodetect feature to determine the disk type automatically. (For example, it knows the difference between a 720K disk and a 1.44M disk because the 720K has only one hole at the bottom left of the disk casing, and the 1.44M disk has an additional hole at the bottom right of the disk casing.)

T I P   If you choose Save Settings on Exit in the Safe Format dialog box, Safe Format will remember the drive type.

CAUTION: On some computers, primarily IBM PS/2 models, the autodetect feature will not detect the correct disk type. This is a hardware design problem. The specification for the 1.44M disk detect was established too late for the PS/2 design to take advantage of it. For example, if you place a 720K (double-density) disk into a PS/2 1.44M (high-density) drive, the computer will not be able to detect that the disk should be formatted as a 720K disk. Therefore, it is quite easy to format a 720K disk as a 1.44M disk on this machine. (See Chapter 3 concerning physical problems in formatting a 720K disk as a 1.44K disk.) Furthermore, if you attempt to read the resulting 1.44M formatted disk in a machine that *does* detect the correct disk capacity, it will try to read the disk as a 720K disk, and you will likely get an error message saying that the disk is unreadable.

The following sections describe the other options in the Configuration dialog box. After you finish setting the options in this dialog box, choose **OK** to return to the Safe Format dialog box. If you do not want to change the configuration settings, choose **C**ancel.

Prompting for Missing Disks

At the bottom of the Configuration dialog box are two check boxes. The **P**rompt for Missing Diskettes option causes Safe Format to display the following prompt when it finds no disk in the drive that has been chosen to be formatted:

```
The disk is missing from the drive
Please insert a disk
```

If you don't choose this option, Norton will try to begin formatting even if no disk is in the drive. If there is no disk in the drive, an error message is displayed.

Allowing Hard Disk Formatting

The Allow **H**ard Disk Formatting option is a safety feature. To format a hard disk, you have to choose this option. It is best to leave this option unchosen so that it is not possible to format your hard disk accidentally. If the option to allow hard disk formatting is not chosen, drive names for hard disks will not appear in the drive selection list.

Starting the Format Process

The Format option in the Safe Format dialog box initiates formatting with all the option settings you have chosen. After you choose this option, the Safe Format command attempts to read the disk to see whether you are attempting to format a disk that already contains data.

Figure 4.4 shows the warning that is given if information is found on a disk to be formatted. This safeguard prevents you from formatting a disk that contains important data. When you see this dialog box, pay attention to the list of files displayed. This list is a double check for you, telling you the names of the files on the disk about to be format-ted. If you recognize the file names as files on a disk that you do *not* want to format, choose No to cancel the format. If you choose not to proceed, you are returned to the Safe Format screen with the menu selections offered. If you choose Yes on the warning screen, the format process begins.

Fig. 4.4

The warning box that appears if you try to format a disk containing data.

After the format process begins, statistics and a display of progress appear on-screen (see fig. 4.5). The top section of the dialog box sum-marizes the choices, such as drive and disk size, that you made before the format operation began. The horizontal bar tells you how much of the disk has been formatted. During the format process, you will see the Cylinder count increase to the number of cylinders on the disk. The Head count will swap back and forth from 0 to 1. Heads and cylinders are explained in Chapter 3.

The section to the right of the horizontal bar contains statistics with which you can track the progress of the format. This box shows (in kilobytes) how much total space is available on disk, how much system space is used, and whether any bad spaces were found. Total Space is the total number of kilobytes available on the formatted disk. If you have not requested that the system be placed on the disk, the System Space needed will be 0. If there are any flaws on the disk, they will appear as Bad Space. The Usable Space is the Total Space *minus* the System Space and Bad Space.

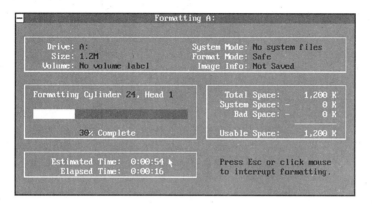

Fig. 4.5

Safe Format in progress.

If you press Esc during the format process, another dialog box appears, asking whether you want to cancel the current operation. If you selected the Save Image Info option or the Safe format type in the Safe Format dialog box, you may as well let the format finish, even if you mistakenly format the wrong disk. Then you can recover the information with the UnFormat command. If you are using the DOS format mode and discover that you are formatting the wrong disk, interrupt the format immediately and attempt to recover the original information on disk with the UnFormat command (see Chapter 11 for details).

T I P

Most floppy disks should have 0 (zero) bad spaces found during the formatting process. When a bad space is found, the format program marks that space (in the FAT) as unusable space, and DOS will not attempt to write information to the disk in that space. Therefore, even if the disk contains some bad spaces, it is still a usable disk. It simply has less space than a normal disk. However, many disk experts recommend that if bad spaces are found on a floppy disk during the format, it may be a signal that other spots on the disk are potentially "weak." That is, they may lose their magnetic signal. These experts will tell you to trash any floppy disk that does not format perfectly. You will have to judge for yourself whether your data is worth the small risk of using a not-so-perfect disk.

At the bottom of the screen shown in figure 4.5 is a box displaying estimated and elapsed time for the format process. Estimated Time shows about how long the total format will take. For the disk being formatted in this example, the time is about 54 seconds. Elapsed Time tells you how much actual time has elapsed during the format. These two numbers together (in this case, 54 seconds minus 16 seconds) tell you about how much time remains in the format process.

After the Safe Format procedure is complete, Norton displays a message telling you that the format was successful (see fig. 4.6). You can also read from the Safe Format dialog box how many, if any, bad sectors were found during the format. If the format is unsuccessful, a message telling you that the disk could not be formatted appears. When you choose **OK** in the successful or unsuccessful format message box, you return to the Safe Format dialog box. You can begin to format another disk, or choose E**x**it to return to the Norton main screen. If you began Safe Format from DOS, the DOS prompt appears when you end the program.

Fig. 4.6

A message telling you that the format was successful.

> Drive A: has been
> successfully formatted.
>
> OK

T I P   Many people format an entire box of disks at once. This saves you some time and allows you to have formatted disks ready to be used without having to perform a format each time you need to use a new disk.

Replacing the DOS Format with Safe Format

Norton's Safe Format is safer and more intuitive to use than the DOS FORMAT command. For this reason, you may want to replace the FORMAT command on your hard disk with Safe Format. Then, when you or someone else tries to enter the DOS FORMAT command, the Norton Safe Format command will run.

> **CAUTION:** When replacing the FORMAT command with the Safe Format command, make sure that you don't have another copy of FORMAT.COM or FORMAT.EXE located somewhere on a disk or directory that could be accessed before your Safe Format command. Use the File Find or File Locate command (see Chapter 25) to search your disk for any file named FORMAT.*. Erase or rename any version of FORMAT that you do not want accessed.

You can use one of three methods to change SFORMAT to FORMAT:

- The simplest way is to choose the **C**onfiguration option in the Norton main screen, as described in Chapter 2. From the **C**onfiguration menu, choose **A**lternate Names. In the Alternate Program Names dialog box, choose Safe For**m**at; then specify FORMAT.EXE as the name you want to use for the Safe Format command.

- Enter the NUCONFIG command at the DOS prompt. In the Configure Norton Utilities dialog box, choose **A**lternate Names. In the Alternate Program Names dialog box, choose Safe For**m**at and specify FORMAT.EXE as the new name for the Safe Format command.

- To replace your DOS FORMAT command manually, rename the DOS FORMAT.EXE file to something else (for example, XXFORMAT.EXE) and rename the Norton Safe Format SFORMAT.EXE file to FORMAT.EXE. For example, you can use the following commands:

      REN FORMAT.EXE XXFORMAT.EXE

      REN SFORMAT.EXE FORMAT.EXE

  Make sure that the new FORMAT program is located in a directory that is in the DOS path.

Using the Safe Format Switches

Whether you start the Safe Format command from the DOS prompt or the Norton main screen, you can use a number of switches to make the command more specific. If you are starting Safe Format from the command line in the Norton main screen, the switches that you type appear in the command line, just as if you were entering the command at the DOS prompt. Notice that the description of the command in the Norton main screen lists the syntax of the command and some of the commonly used switches (see fig. 4.7).

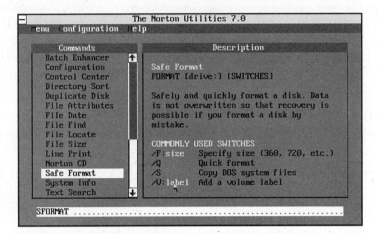

Fig. 4.7

The Norton main screen showing the switches you can use with the Safe Format command.

The syntax of the SFORMAT command (depending on which command name you have chosen) is one of the following:

SFORMAT [*d*:][*switches*]

FORMAT [*d*:][*switches*]

SF [*d*:][*switches*]

The *d*: option is the letter of the drive you want to format, and *switches* are the available switches you can use with Safe Format.

Use the SFORMAT syntax line if you have not chosen SF or FORMAT as an alternative name for Safe Format (see the preceding section for details on using alternative names for Safe Format). After you enter the options you want to use, press Enter to begin the Safe Format program.

NOTE   Throughout this book, when the syntax of a command is described, *optional parameters* are listed in brackets ([ ]). In the FORMAT command, the drive letter shown as [*d*:] is an optional parameter. It does not have to appear when you use the command. When you use items listed in brackets in the description, do not type the brackets on the DOS command line. If parameters are included in the description of a command and are not enclosed in brackets, those parameters are required.

Norton Safe Format has the same switches as the DOS FORMAT command, in addition to a few added by Norton. The Safe Format switches that are similar to DOS FORMAT switches are listed in table 4.1. The Safe Format switches unique to Norton are listed in table 4.2.

Table 4.1 Safe Format Switches Similar to DOS FORMAT Switches

Switch	Description
/B	Leaves space for system files
/S	Places system files on disk
/V:*label*	Places a volume label on disk
/1	Formats as single-sided
/4	Formats as 360K (in a 1.2M drive)
/8	Formats 8 sectors per track
/N:*n*	Specifies the number of sectors per track (*n* = 8, 9, 15, or 18)
/T:*n*	Specifies the number of tracks (*n* = 40 or 80)
/F:*size*	Specifies the size of floppy disk (*size* = 360, 720, 1.2, 1.44, or 2.88)

Table 4.2 Unique Safe Format Switches

Switch	Description
/A	Enables you to bypass choosing Format from the Norton Safe Format dialog box. The format begins without any response required from you. This switch is primarily for use in batch files, where you perform the same kind of format repetitively and you want to avoid having to answer prompts. Be careful when using this switch because it defeats some of the purposes of the Safe Format command. If you are sure, however, that the format you want to perform is selected properly, the /A switch can save you some time.
/D	Enables you to revert to the DOS FORMAT procedure. With this switch, the format is performed as if it were performed by the DOS FORMAT command—the system information is not saved for possible recovery. You may want to use the DOS version of FORMAT if the disk contains files that you do not want to be recovered easily (such as personnel records).
/Q	Enables you to perform a Quick format. This switch is useful for formatting disks you have formatted previously. Instead of checking the entire disk for bad sectors, as in a normal format, the command in Quick format mode merely replaces the system area of the disk with a new system area. This process is essentially the same as erasing all the files on the disk.
/*size*	Specifies the size of a floppy disk (*size* = 360, 720, 1.2, 1.44, or 2.88).

To format a disk in drive B as a system disk (for copying system files to the disk) and to place the volume label MYDISK on the disk, use this command:

FORMAT B:/S/V:MYDISK

Notice in this command that the drive name is represented as a single letter followed by a colon. If you provide no drive name, you must choose from the **Drive** list box (in the Safe Format dialog box) the drive letter of the disk to format.

If you have an old formatted floppy disk that you want to reformat, you don't have to wait 45 seconds (which is what a normal 360K disk takes). Entering the command

FORMAT B:/Q

performs a Quick format that takes only 10 to 15 seconds. This version of FORMAT is usable only on previously formatted disks.

Using the Image (IMAGE) Program

No matter how many precautions you take, you (or someone else) still may find a way to accidentally format a disk containing important information. With a little preventive medicine, however, you can handle this problem. The medicine is the Norton Image (IMAGE) program. The Image program allows you to prepare for the possibility of an accidental format; Image stores file information to a safe location on disk each time you boot.

The Image program creates a file named IMAGE.DAT on your hard disk. This file contains system and directory information about the files on your hard disk drive. When a hard disk is formatted, the system and directory information is changed to tell DOS that all file space is available on your disk. The actual contents of the files on disk are not changed. Therefore, the IMAGE.DAT file is able to provide an alternative copy of the information that DOS needs in order to "find" your files on disk—that same information which was destroyed with the hard disk format. Norton's UnFormat utility (see Chapter 11) can use this information to recover your system and directory information to its previous state, giving back to DOS the information needed to access your files on disk and thus performing an unformat.

Preparing for an Accidental Format

Norton Utilities does its best to help you recover from a hard disk format. Before Norton Utilities became available, an accidental format was an almost insurmountable disaster. Now, with Norton Utilities, you have a real chance of a full recovery.

The thoroughness of the recovery that Norton Utilities can perform, however, depends on how well you prepare your computer for this potential problem. There are three ways to protect your computer (and yourself) against accidental format of your hard disk:

- Perform a periodic backup of your hard disk. (Then you can recover by using the backup.)

- Use the Norton Safe Format command on your computer rather than the standard DOS FORMAT command (as described in the previous sections) to give you protection against accidental format.

- Use the Norton Image command, preferably from within your AUTOEXEC.BAT file, so that a backup image of your important system and directory information will be stored each time you boot your computer.

Because UnFormat can help recover only the files that were present the last time the Image command was run, you need to use Image periodically. For most people, a convenient method is to issue the command each time the computer is booted. The next section describes how to do that.

Running Image from the AUTOEXEC.BAT File

To run the Image command each time you boot your computer, you need to place that command in your AUTOEXEC.BAT file. (The AUTOEXEC.BAT file is a batch file containing a series of commands that executes each time you boot your computer.)

If you are familiar with the AUTOEXEC.BAT file and are comfortable using an ASCII editor, you can simply add the Image command to your existing AUTOEXEC.BAT file. If you stored Norton Utilities in a directory other than the root directory (such as NORTON), make sure that a PATH command precedes the IMAGE command in the AUTOEXEC.BAT file. Your AUTOEXEC.BAT file, for example, may contain the lines

PATH C:\;C:\DOS;C:\NORTON
IMAGE

or

PATH C:\;C:DOS
C:\NORTON\IMAGE

The first version (PATH) sets up the DOS search path to look for commands first in the root directory, then in the DOS directory, and finally in the NORTON directory. The next line issues the Norton IMAGE command, which DOS now is able to find in the NORTON directory. In the second version, the NORTON directory is not in the path, so the IMAGE command must contain the C:\NORTON\ prefix to tell DOS where to find the IMAGE command. Now when you boot your computer, Norton issues the IMAGE command and creates the file IMAGE.DAT.

NOTE If you are not familiar with your AUTOEXEC.BAT file or you don't know how to use an ASCII editor to change the file, you can use the Configuration menu from the Norton main screen, or use the NUCONFIG command from the DOS prompt to place IMAGE in your AUTOEXEC.BAT file. (Chapter 2 discusses the Norton configuration procedure.)

If the IMAGE.DAT file is present, other Norton commands (for example, Disk Edit and UnErase) use that file automatically. These programs do not need the IMAGE.DAT file in order to work, but if the file is there, the programs work faster and more effectively.

NOTE When the IMAGE.DAT file is created, its read-only attribute is set on. This means that the information in the file can be read, but you cannot erase or change the file (without resetting the read-only attribute). This is a safety feature to help prevent accidental erasure of this file. For example, even if you perform an ERASE *.* in your root directory, the IMAGE.DAT file will not be erased. See Chapter 9 for more information about file attributes.

Running Image from the DOS Prompt

You do not have to run the Image program from the AUTOEXEC.BAT file. You can run the program at any time by entering the command at the DOS prompt. The syntax is

IMAGE [*switch*]

If IMAGE.DAT already exists, the old IMAGE.DAT is renamed IMAGE.BAK. The only switch for this command is /NOBACK. If you use the /NOBACK switch, the file IMAGE.BAK, which contains information from the preceding use of the IMAGE command, is not created.

If you enter the IMAGE command with no switches, the program creates a new copy of the IMAGE.DAT file on disk.

NOTE As an added safety measure, in case you accidentally format your hard disk, make sure that you have a bootable floppy disk—a rescue disk—that contains the UnFormat program. See Chapter 14 for information on creating and using this important disk.

NOTE Beginning with Version 5.0, DOS contains a command called MIRROR that is similar in function to the NORTON Image command. When you enter the MIRROR command at the DOS prompt, information is written to a file that contains a duplicate copy of your disk's system and file directory. If you have used the MIRROR command and your disk has been formatted, the Norton UnFormat command can read that information and use it to restore the formatted disk.

Running Image from the Norton Main Screen

You can also run the Image program from the Norton main screen. From this screen, scroll the Commands list until the Image option is highlighted; then press Enter or double-click with the mouse. The Image program will run just as it did when it was executed from the DOS prompt (see the preceding section).

Summary

Norton Utilities offers you a number of ways to protect your information on disk. Most of these safety measures, however, require that you do a little planning. Make sure that you set up your AUTOEXEC.BAT file to issue the Image command each time you boot. Make sure also that you are using the Safe Format command rather than the original DOS FORMAT command. If you accidentally format a disk, you can recover it if you have taken these precautions.

After you have made sure that you have taken the two primary precautions outlined in this chapter, read the remaining chapters in Part II to learn about other Norton programs that can help you safeguard your data. The next chapter, "Using SmartCan," describes a special Norton utility that helps you recover from accidentally deleting files you need to keep.

Using SmartCan

When you erase a file, DOS does not actually destroy the contents of the file. DOS erases only some of the file's directory information. With the directory information erased, the disk space that the file occupied can now be used by other files. However, until that space is used, the contents of the erased file are actually still on disk. Thus, the Norton UnErase command can often find and unerase a file. When you erase a file, however, and DOS gets a message that the disk space used by that file is now available, a new file can overwrite the erased file at any time. As a result, you are not able to unerase the file that occupied that space.

The SmartCan command (called File Save and Erase Protect in earlier versions of Norton Utilities) moves the contents of unerased files to disk space that is not commonly used. Relocating the files reduces the chance of them being overwritten, and they remain unerasable longer. SmartCan is able to manage this erased space on disk. Using SmartCan options, you can tell the command how long to protect files, what kinds of files to protect, and when to stop protecting files (based on a set number of days and a set amount of space to use for the erased information). You must use the SmartCan command *before* erasing files so that it can keep the erased space from becoming lost.

Understanding SmartCan

Using SmartCan is like throwing something into a trash can (a "smart" trash can); you know that, for a while, you can retrieve the tossed-out item if you need to. After you empty the trash can and the garbage person hauls it away, however, you no longer have access to the tossed-out item. In the same way, you can unerase an erased file for a while. But when SmartCan stops protecting the file, it is likely to be lost forever.

SmartCan is a memory-resident program. After you begin this type of program, it stays in the computer's memory, monitoring requests to erase files by other programs. You can run the SmartCan program interactively (in menu mode) or as a DOS-type command. At first, you need to run the program interactively in order to set the options you want, such as which drives to protect and how long to save files. Then you can activate the SmartCan command by placing it in your AUTOEXEC.BAT file so that the protection is turned on each time you boot your computer.

The following sections describe how to set up SmartCan's options and how to activate the program so that it protects your erased files.

Specifying the SmartCan Settings

To use SmartCan interactively, choose the SmartCan option from the Norton main screen or type **SMARTCAN** at the DOS prompt. The Configure SmartCan dialog box appears (see fig. 5.1). Using this dialog box, you can choose SmartCan options and activate the program to begin protecting files. You can specify which files and drives to protect, set limits to protecting files, and purge protected files from the protection list.

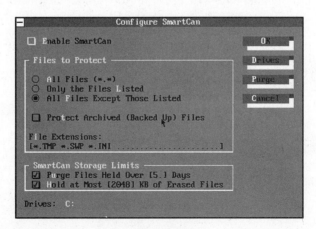

Fig. 5.1

The Configure SmartCan dialog box.

Selecting the Drives To Protect

The **D**rives option at the right of the dialog box enables you to specify which drives to protect. If you choose the **D**rives option, you are
prompted to choose the appropriate disk drives (see fig. 5.2). Smart-
Can monitors files being erased on only the disks you specify.

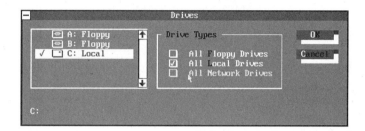

Fig. 5.2

The Drives dialog
box.

In the Drives dialog box, you can choose one or more of the drives from
the Drive list box on the left. A selected drive is designated by a check
mark to the left of its name. In figure 5.2, drive C (the hard disk) is the
only drive selected. To choose a drive, press Tab or the arrow keys to
move the highlight to the Drive list box; then use the up- and down-
arrow keys to highlight the drive you want to mark for protection.
Press the space bar to select or deselect a drive. You also can double-
click the drive name with the mouse to select or deselect that drive.

You use the Drive Types section to specify what drive types to protect.
Drive types include floppy, local (hard disks), and network drives. To
choose one of the three options in the Drive Types section, press Alt
plus the highlighted letter for the appropriate drive type (for example,
Alt+F for All **F**loppy Drives). Or point to the option with the mouse
pointer and click to select or deselect the check box. If you chose the
All **F**loppy Drives option, all floppy drives in the Drive list are selected.
The All **N**etwork Drives option is usable only when you have network
drives available.

After you make your selections, choose **O**K to exit the dialog box and
save your changes; choose **C**ancel to exit without saving changes.

Selecting the Files To Protect

In the Configure SmartCan dialog box (refer to fig. 5.1), you use the
Files to Protect section to specify which files to protect when they are
erased. You can choose one of the following options: **A**ll Files (*.*),

Only the Files Listed (in the File Extensions text box), or All Files Except Those Listed (in the File Extensions text box). Because these options are presented as radio buttons, you can choose only one of them at a time. For example, you can choose to protect the files listed in the File Extensions text box or to protect all files *except* those listed in that text box—but not both.

You can choose also whether to protect archived files. These are files that have been backed up. Because they have been backed up, they should have copies of themselves to recover if you need them. Therefore, you may choose not to protect those files. Usually, a limited amount of space is available on your disk to protect erased files; eliminating the protection of archived files allows more unarchived files to be protected before this space becomes too full. Choose or click Protect Archived (Backed Up) Files to select or deselect this option.

 NOTE The computer knows that a file has been archived because the archive attribute is set when the file is backed up. See Chapter 9 concerning setting file attributes.

Whether you choose to protect or exclude listed files, you must first make a list, of course. Type your list in the File Extensions text box at the bottom of the Files to Protect section. Notice that this text box lists the *.TMP, *.SWP, and *.INI files by default. Norton uses these files to store temporary information. Because the All Files Except Those Listed option is chosen in figure 5.1, all files except the *.TMP, *.SWP, and *.INI files are protected.

To add more files to the list, use the Tab key, the arrow keys, or the mouse to highlight the File Extensions text box. Then type the extensions of the files you want to exclude or include. You may choose to exclude *.EXE and *.COM files, for example, because you probably have copies of these files on original disks. However, you may want to include *.DBF and *.WK3 files because they are important data files. You can choose to exclude or include, but you cannot do both.

Here are the common files that you may want to exclude from protection:

File Extension	File Type
*.TMP	A temporary file used by Norton Utilities
*.SWP	A temporary file used by Norton Utilities
*.INI	A temporary file used by Norton Utilities
*.EXE	Program files that you should have on original disks

File Extension	File Type
*.COM	Program files that you should have on original disks
*.SYS	Program support files that you should have on original disks
*.OVL	Program overlay files that you should have on original disks

Here are the common files that you may want to include for protection:

File Extension	File Type
.WP	Word processing files
.WK	Spreadsheet files
*.DBF	Database data files

You may want to exclude or include other file types depending on the program applications you use.

Specifying Storage Limits

The SmartCan Storage Limits options are located at the bottom of the Configure SmartCan dialog box. These options enable you to choose how long SmartCan holds a file before that file is no longer protected and how much disk space is allocated to hold erased files.

As you can see in figure 5.1, the Purge Files Held option holds files five days by default before the files are no longer protected. To choose this option, press Alt+U or click the option to select or deselect it. If you want to change the default setting, press Tab or use the mouse to move to the number-of-days field (maximum of 99 days); then type the number of days you want.

The Hold at Most option enables you to specify how much disk space to use to protect erased files. Its default value depends on how much space is available on your disk. In figure 5.1, you can see that the amount listed is 2,048 kilobytes. Press Alt+H to choose the Hold at Most option, or click the option to select or deselect it. If you choose the option, press Tab or use the mouse to move to the amount-of-space field; then type a new value.

Enabling SmartCan

SmartCan does not begin protecting files until it is enabled. You can enable SmartCan from the Configure SmartCan dialog box by choosing the Enable SmartCan option at the top of the dialog box (refer to fig. 5.1).

After you choose OK to quit SmartCan, the options you chose are saved, and you return to DOS (or the Norton menu). If you chose Enable SmartCan, the SmartCan program is then active. At this time, whether you begin the program from the DOS prompt or from your AUTOEXEC.BAT file, SmartCan uses the settings you chose in the Configure SmartCan dialog box to protect the files you specified. If, however, you choose the Cancel option in the dialog box, all settings that you changed are lost, and you return to DOS or the Norton menu. To set up your AUTOEXEC.BAT file to run SmartCan each time you boot, use the Configuration option in the Norton main screen (see Chapter 2).

Purging Protected Files

As you create and erase files, SmartCan (when enabled) is protecting the erased files by holding them on disk. This storage takes up some of your disk's space. If you need more disk space on your computer, you can choose to *purge* (stop protecting) currently protected files.

To purge files, you must display the Configure SmartCan dialog box by choosing the SmartCan option from the Norton main screen or by typing **SMARTCAN** at the DOS prompt. The Configure SmartCan dialog box appears (refer to fig. 5.1). Choose the Purge button to display the Purge Deleted Files dialog box (see fig. 5.3). This dialog box contains a list of the files that have been erased and are currently being protected. This list is called the *held list*.

You can use the arrow keys or the mouse to move up and down the held list. Below the list box is additional information about the file currently highlighted, including the deleted file's full path name (which shows the directory where the file was located) and the date and time the file was deleted. This information may be helpful if you have more than one erased file by the same name.

If SmartCan is protecting more than one drive, you can display the appropriate drive's held files by choosing the Drive button at the bottom of the dialog box. When you choose Drive, Norton displays the Select Drive dialog box, which you can use to specify which drive's protected files to list (see fig. 5.4). Select the drive you want; then choose OK.

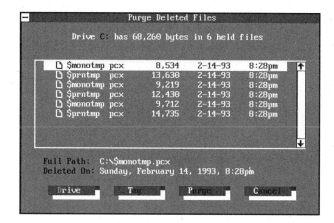

Fig. 5.3

The Purge
Deleted Files
dialog box.

Fig. 5.4

The Smartcan
Select Drive
dialog box.

Before you can purge files, you must mark them. You can mark files in two ways: by file type (such as all DBF files) or as individual files.

To mark a group of files according to a file specification, choose the **T**ag button. A dialog box like the one in figure 5.5 appears. This screen contains the prompt Tag the files and a text box where you can type a file specification. Enter a file specification (such as *.WKS) indicating which file names you want to remove from the held list. After you type the specification, choose **O**K. To exit this box without specifying a tag, choose **C**ancel. When you exit the Tag dialog box, all files that match the specification are tagged with a triangle on each side of the file's description line. You can repeat the tag option to tag other kinds of files.

You can use the standard DOS wild-card characters—the question mark (?) and the asterisk (*)—in the text box after the Tag the files prompt. The file specification *.WPW, for example, indicates that you want to mark all files that have a WPW extension. You can use *.* to mark *all* the file names.

T   I   P

Fig. 5.5

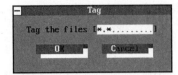

The Tag dialog
box.

You can also tag (or untag) files one at a time. Highlight the file name in
the held list; then press the space bar to tag or untag the file. Alternatively, point to a file name with the mouse pointer and double-click.
The Purge Deleted Files dialog box may have more files than those you
see listed. To see more file names, press the up- and down-arrow keys
to scroll the held list, or use the scroll bar and the mouse to move the
list up and down.

T I P   To tag most of the files that meet a certain file specification, use the
tag option to mark all the files (such as all *.WKS files). Then untag
individually the few you do not want removed from the held list.

After you mark the individual files to purge, a triangle appears on both
sides of the file's description in the held list in the Purge Deleted Files
dialog box.

After you have marked all the files you want to remove from the held
list, choose the **P**urge button. The marked files are removed from the
purge list. Choose **O**K to close the Purge Deleted Files dialog box and
return to the Configure SmartCan dialog box.

Using SMARTCAN from the DOS Prompt

The SMARTCAN command is usually included in the AUTOEXEC.BAT
file so that it is in effect when any files are deleted. The Norton configure procedure can place the correct command in your AUTOEXEC.BAT
file (see the section "Setting Startup Program Options" in Chapter 2).
You also can place the SMARTCAN command in the AUTOEXEC.BAT
file yourself; choose the command from the Norton main screen or type
the command at the DOS prompt. Note the syntax of this command:

SMARTCAN [*switches*]

Here are the available switches for the SMARTCAN command:

Switch	Description
/OFF	Disables the SMARTCAN command so that deleted files are not affected. SMARTCAN remains in memory but does not function unless it is turned on by the /ON switch.
/ON	Enables SMARTCAN to move deleted files to a safe area.
/SKIPHIGH	Stores the SmartCan program in low memory. (SmartCan is stored in high memory by default.)
/STATUS	Displays the status of the SMARTCAN command.
/UNINSTALL	Removes the SMARTCAN command from memory if the command was the last memory-resident (TSR) command loaded.
/CONVERT	Converts information from old Erase Protect trash cans.

The /OFF switch allows you to temporarily suspend SmartCan's protection. The SmartCan program remains in memory but no longer protects erased files. If you want to erase some files and do not want SmartCan to hold these files for protection, enter **SMARTCAN /OFF** at the DOS prompt, erase the files, and then enter **SMARTCAN /ON** to turn file protection back on.

The /SKIPHIGH switch refers to the use of your computer's RAM memory. The initial 640K RAM memory in your computer is referred to as low memory. Memory above 640K is called high memory. When a program is stored in high memory (as SmartCan is by default, if high memory is available), you have more low memory to be used by your applications programs. If you are using a memory manager (or DOS 5.0 or later) that uses your high memory, use the /SKIPHIGH option to store the SmartCan program in low memory.

The /STATUS switch displays a brief report about the current status of the SmartCan program on-screen. The report may contain information similar to this:

```
SmartCan Status:        Enabled
Drives Protected:       C: (SmartCan contains 528K
                        in 21 files)
Files Protected:        All files except those
                        with these extensions
                        TMP, SWP, INI
Archive Files:          Not protected
Files Deleted After:    5 days
```

The /UNINSTALL switch removes the SmartCan program from memory, deactivating file erase protection. When you end SmartCan with this option, you must reactivate the program by typing **SMARTCAN** again. If you attempt to run a program and receive a message indicating that not enough memory is available, you might try uninstalling SmartCan (or other TSR programs) to free up enough memory so that the application program does run.

The /CONVERT switch converts old trash cans created under the Erase Protect program into SmartCan trash cans. Usually, this conversion is performed when you install the Norton Utilities program. If it was not, you can enter **SMARTCAN /CONVERT** to perform the conversion on your old trash cans.

Using SmartCan on a Network

SmartCan enables you to protect erased files on a network. When you run the command the first time on a network, SmartCan creates a directory, TRASHCAN, that branches off the root directory. The network manager should make this directory available to all users of the network.

To run SmartCan properly on a network, initiate the command after the network driver and shell are loaded.

Summary

You learned in this chapter that the SmartCan program is like a "smart" trash can. When you erase a file (throw it away), the file remains in the trash can for a few days, depending on the amount of time you specify. As long as the trash collector has not emptied the trash can, you can retrieve (unerase) the file. SmartCan is also selective about what erased files it protects. You can choose to exclude or include certain types of files.

SmartCan allows you to erase files, but it protects those erased files for a period of time. The next chapter describes Disk Monitor, which takes a different approach to file protection. Disk Monitor provides protection that prevents certain kinds of files from being erased in the first place.

Using Disk Monitor

The preceding chapter discussed Norton Utilities SmartCan. SmartCan protects files that have been erased for a period of time, giving them a better chance of being unerased if needed. Another aspect of protecting files, however, is to make sure that they don't get erased in the first place. This task is the primary responsibility of Norton Disk Monitor. You can use Disk Monitor to protect information on disk from accidental or unauthorized destruction, including a measure of protection against a virus infection.

Understanding Disk Monitor

Files can be erased in a number of ways. You can use the DOS DEL or ERASE command to erase a file, or you can erase a file by overwriting it with another file (such as copying one file to another file whose name already exists). Programs can also erase files "in the background" without your knowing what is being done. Most normal programs do not erase or overwrite files without your permission, but some malicious or unstable programs can do this kind of damage. To stop important files from being erased or overwritten, you need a file monitor that carefully watches DOS to see whether it is getting ready to overwrite an important file. This program is Norton Disk Monitor.

Before you or another user can access a protected file (including writing to, changing, or erasing it), Disk Monitor checks to see whether you have given permission for the file to be altered in this way. If the file is protected from change, Disk Monitor does not allow you or another user (or program) to alter the file. When a program that tries to alter a protected file is run—a spreadsheet program, for example—a message appears telling you that a protected file is about to be altered. You can choose to allow the change to proceed, stop the change from happening, or cancel the protection.

Disk Monitor can also save your important files from virus programs. These programs may try to alter critical files such as COMMAND.COM, AUTOEXEC.BAT, and CONFIG.SYS—the ones most often attacked by a virus program.

Another form of disk protection offered by Disk Monitor is given to you in the form of visual help—the Disk Light. Some computers have a hard disk light at the front of the computer. This light flashes when the disk is being accessed. If you notice that the disk is being accessed excessively, even when nothing is supposed to be happening to the disk, it may be a warning that a malicious program is doing something to your disk. Seeing such access might help you put a stop to it before all your data is scrambled.

However, some hard disks do not have such a light (usually add-on hard disks that are not factory installed). Also, if you are attached to a network, you have no light to tell you when you are accessing the network's drive. The Disk Monitor Disk Light allows you to place a "disk light" on your monitor. When the disk is being accessed, a blinking light appears on the screen, enabling you to monitor the activity of the drive.

Finally, Disk Monitor allows you to park your disk. *Parking* the disk is a safety measure that is important to perform before you move your computer. If the hard disk is not parked, the disk read and write heads may be stationed over a critical area of the disk. Then, if the computer is moved, a bump could cause serious damage to the disk platter, and files stored on the disk could be permanently lost.

You can use Disk Monitor interactively or like a DOS command. The next few sections cover the use of Disk Monitor for file protection. They also discuss how to set up Disk Light and how to park the disk using both the interactive and DOS prompt methods.

Setting Up Disk Monitor

The Disk Monitor command is a memory-resident program. Thus, when you begin the program, Disk Monitor stays in the computer's memory to monitor what is going on while you run other programs. You can use the Disk Monitor command interactively or from the DOS prompt. The first time you use Disk Monitor, however, you must use it interactively to choose its initial settings. To begin Disk Monitor, choose Disk Monitor from the Norton main screen or type **DISKMON** at the DOS prompt. A dialog box similar to the one in figure 6.1 appears.

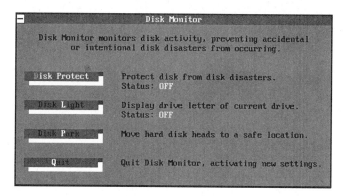

Fig. 6.1

The Disk Monitor dialog box.

You can choose an option in the dialog box by pressing Alt plus the highlighted character in the option's name or by clicking the option name. When you choose **Q**uit, the settings you chose are stored in a file named DISKMON.INI.

After you have saved initial settings for Disk Monitor, the settings in the DISKMON.INI file are activated when you enter the DISKMON command at the DOS prompt, as discussed later in this chapter.

The next few sections explain the options in the Disk Monitor dialog box.

Protecting the Disk

The **Disk Protect** option in the Disk Monitor dialog box enables you to turn protection on and off and to specify which files you want to protect. After you choose the **Disk Protect** option, a dialog box similar to the one in figure 6.2 appears.

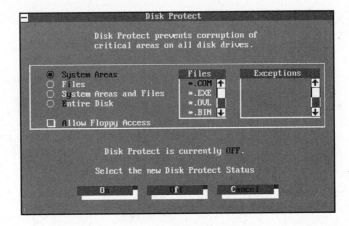

Fig. 6.2

The Disk Protect
dialog box.

In the Disk Protect dialog box, you can choose one of the following
radio button options:

Option	Description
System Areas	Specifies protection for the system area on your disk. This area includes the partition table, the boot record, and the system files.
Files	Specifies protection for files listed in the Files box. This protection excludes all files listed in the Exceptions box.
System Areas and Files	Specifies protection of system files and other files as indicated in the Files and Exceptions list boxes.
Entire Disk	Specifies protection for the entire disk.

In a group of radio button options, you can use only one of the options
at a time. To choose an option, press Alt plus the highlighted option
key or just click the option name.

The **S**ystem Areas option provides protection for the areas of the disk
that contain the partition table, the boot record, and the system files.
These areas are of critical importance to the health of your computer
and are often the target of malicious programs.

NOTE   The data area of your disk is where your files are stored.
Chapter 3 discusses the difference between the system area
and the data area.

If you are using the computer with programs that might contain a virus or other malicious program, you need to protect your system area. Programs that are being developed and are unstable may also require you to protect your system area. For instance, they might write to the disk unexpectedly or incorrectly.

When an attempt is made to write information to the disk in a protected area, you are warned with an on-screen message (except for some instances described later in this chapter). You can then respond to the message to allow write access or prevent it. If you choose too much protection, normal use of the computer could become bothersome because of the constant need to respond to warning messages. For that reason, choose the combination of system and file protection that gives you the level of safety you want for your disk. You might want to experiment with levels of protection to see which level makes you feel secure without being too stringent.

Below the radio buttons in the Disk Protect dialog box is a check box option called **Allow Floppy Access**. If you check this option, Disk Monitor enables you (or a program) to format floppy disks without asking for your permission. If your work involves a lot of floppy disk formatting, you might want to select this option. However, if you have had an experience of formatting the wrong floppy disk, you may want to leave this option deselected as a warning to double check the disk before formatting. To select this option, press Alt+A or click the check box.

The two list boxes at the right side of the Disk Protect dialog box are used to specify the kinds of files to protect and not to protect. The Files list box specifies the kinds of files (according to file extension) that you want to protect (assuming that you have chosen to protect files). To change, add to, or delete file specifications from this list, press Tab until the highlight is in the list box, or click a file specification in the list. To add to the list, scroll to the end of it. A blank field is at the end of the list, where you can type a new specification (such as *.CAD). Press the down-arrow key, and another blank field opens. Add as many specifications as you need. To delete a specification, place the highlight on the appropriate specification and then press the space bar.

Working with the Exceptions list is similar to working with the Files list. When you change, add to, or delete from the Exceptions list, however, you must use full file names. You cannot use the wild-card characters ? and *. You can enter up to 20 file names in this list. You can use the list, for instance, when you want to protect all the EXE files except the ones on which you are currently working (editing, compiling, and so on).

After you type or choose all the options you want for Disk Protect, choose **On**. This choice saves all the options you have chosen, activates disk protection, and takes you out of the Disk Protect dialog box. If you choose **Off**, the settings you have chosen are saved, and you exit the dialog box. However, Disk Protect is turned off. If you choose **Cancel**, you exit the dialog box, and all changes are discarded.

Handling Disk Protect Warning Messages

After you choose the files to protect and you enter **DISKMON** at the DOS prompt, Disk Monitor runs in the background, monitoring messages to the operating system to determine whether a protected file is about to be altered. If, for example, a protected file is about to be erased, a warning message appears. Figure 6.3 shows a warning message displayed when the protected file, TESTFILE.MON, was about to be erased.

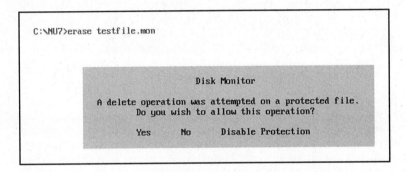

Fig. 6.3

A Disk Monitor warning message.

When such a warning message is displayed, you can choose **Yes** to allow the alteration to happen, **No** to tell Disk Monitor to protect the file, or **D**isable Protection to turn file protection off.

If you choose **Yes** or **D**isable Protection, the file is deleted. If you choose **No**, the file is not deleted, and the program you are running must then deal with the inability to perform its function. This inability may cause a warning or error message to appear. In the TESTFILE.MON case, when the erase was attempted with the DOS ERASE command and then not allowed, DOS responded with the message File not found.

Depending on the application you are running, you may have to respond to the warning message several times when the application writes to the file. If the process becomes too cumbersome, choose to discontinue protection.

Controlling Warning Messages for Graphics Mode

When you are running a graphics program such as Microsoft Windows, Disk Monitor cannot display the warning message on-screen. Instead, if the file is protected, the disk write (writing information to a protected file or erasing a protected file) is rejected. As a result, a warning or error message, such as Access denied or Write protect error, may appear in the graphics program.

If you are running a graphics application while using Disk Monitor, turning protection off while the graphics program is running is best. Then turn Disk Monitor back on when you exit the program. Because you might forget, an easy way to handle this situation is to write a batch program that turns protection off while the program is running, and then turns it back on when you exit the graphics program. Here is a sample batch program that runs the Windows program:

```
DISKMON \PROTECT-
WIN
DISKMON \PROTECT+
```

When you execute this batch file, disk protection is turned off, and the WIN (Windows) program is then run. When you exit Windows, disk protection is resumed. Disk Monitor command-line switches are discussed in the section "Using Disk Monitor from the DOS Prompt."

Adding a Disk Light

If you choose Disk Light from the Disk Monitor dialog box, the Disk Light dialog box appears (see fig. 6.4). From this box, you can turn the Disk Light feature on (**On**) or off (**Off**) or cancel any changes (**Cancel**).

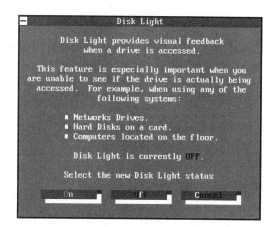

After you turn on the Disk Light feature, a blinking light in the upper-right corner of your monitor tells you when the hard disk is being accessed.

This light is helpful if you cannot easily see the disk light on your hard disk. The light also shows you when information is being written to a network drive. Being able to see when your disk is being accessed is important so that you can monitor this activity visually. If you notice a program accessing a disk when it should not be using the disk, you may want to test that program for possible virus infection.

Parking the Disk

The Disk **P**ark option in the Disk Monitor dialog box enables you to move the heads on your disk drive to a safe place; then you can move the computer without destroying data. On many new computers, the heads park automatically when you turn off the computer. If you do not know whether the heads park automatically, use Disk **P**ark before you move your computer.

When you select Disk **P**ark, the Disk Park dialog box appears (see fig. 6.5). Two beeps signal that the disk heads have been parked. Turn off the computer's power after you hear the two beeps. Or press Enter or choose **C**ancel to cancel the disk park and return to the Disk Monitor dialog box.

Using Disk Monitor from the DOS Prompt

After you run the Disk Monitor program and choose options, you can begin the program by entering **DISKMON** at the DOS prompt. Or you can set or change options by typing the options on the command line. You use the following syntax:

DISKMON [*switches*]

Here are the available switches for the Disk Monitor command:

Switch	Description
/LIGHT+ or /LIGHT-	Turns the Disk Light feature on (+) or off (-).
/PARK	Parks all drives.
/PROTECT+ or /PROTECT-	Turns the Disk Protect feature on (+) or off (-). When this feature is turned on, protection is set to your selections, which were stored in DISKMON.INI when you ran the command interactively.
	If you have not made previous selections (that is, you do not have a DISKMON.INI file), the system files are protected by default.
/SKIPHIGH	Tells the program that you do not want Disk Monitor loaded into high memory.
/STATUS	Displays a summary of the Disk Monitor status on-screen.
/UNINSTALL	Uninstalls Disk Monitor from memory if it was the last TSR (memory-resident program) loaded into memory.

The /LIGHT option controls the Disk Light feature; this option is the same as the Disk Light option in the Disk Monitor dialog box. You can use the /PARK option to control the Disk Park feature. Use the /PRO-TECT option to turn disk protection on or off. The /STATUS option allows you to display information about what portions of Disk Monitor are currently active. For example, if you enter **DISKMON /STATUS** when you have file protection and the Disk Light feature is activated, the program responds with the following messages:

```
Disk Light ON
Disk Protect ON, Files protected
```

The /SKIPHIGH option refers to the use of your computer's RAM (random-access memory). The initial 640K RAM in your computer is referred to as low memory. Memory above 640K is called high memory. When a program is stored in high memory (as DISKMON is by default, if space is available), you have more low memory to be used by your applications programs. If you are using a memory manager (or DOS 5.0 or later) that uses your high memory, use /SKIPHIGH to store the DISKMON program in low memory.

The /UNINSTALL option removes the DISKMON program from memory, deactivating disk protection. When you end DISKMON by using this option, you can reactivate it by issuing the DISKMON command again. If you attempt to run a large application program and you get a message that not enough memory is available, you might try uninstalling DISKMON (or other TSR programs) to free up enough memory so that the application program can run.

Using Disk Monitor on a Network

Disk Monitor can work on a network to prevent the modification of some files on your local or network drives. The command is not designed, however, to protect the system area of a network server. Usually, the server contains its own protection capabilities. The Disk Light option enables you to "see" the network disk as it is accessed. This feature often gives you a better feel for network usage. Disk Park does not park network heads.

Summary

Disk Monitor provides a "seeing eye" that watches your computer, making sure that important files do not get erased or altered without your permission. It is an invaluable feature in your arsenal against data loss. The Disk Light feature helps you have a better feel for disk access on local and network drives. Finally, Disk Park protects your disk when it is being moved.

Sometimes data protection is more than just protecting files against being erased or altered; it may involve protecting data in other ways. Turn to the next chapter to discover how Norton Utilities can protect your data from unauthorized use.

Using Diskreet

When only large mainframe computers stored computer information, computer systems personnel took great pains to protect the information from unauthorized use. All the data was housed in vaultlike rooms, and access to the computer was protected by one or more passwords.

With more than 100 million personal computers used today, most containing readily accessible information, data safety has plummeted. Corporations, organizations, governments, and individuals have some need to protect their data from unauthorized use. In many cases, anyone (such as the person cleaning up your room at night, a corporate spy, or another office worker) could turn on a computer and access information in any file—such as personnel, financial, medical, legal, corporate, or strategy papers—that should not fall into the wrong hands. The Norton Utilities solution to this problem is called Diskreet.

The Norton Diskreet utility enables you to protect files so that users cannot access the files without permission. Users must know a password before they can access files. The Diskreet command provides much more protection than the Disk Monitor command or file attributes. Files stored by Diskreet are encrypted so that they are unreadable, even by the Disk Editor program. You can protect files individually or by group with a pseudodisk called an *NDisk*.

An NDisk operates as a disk drive does, but Diskreet automatically encrypts files stored on this drive, and only users who know the password can access the files. If you try to access an NDisk, you are prompted to enter a password. If you do not know the password, you cannot type, read, or otherwise access the files on that "disk" successfully. After you supply the correct password and open an NDisk, you can access these files, which are decrypted as you access them. When you close the NDisk, the files become inaccessible again.

You can regulate access to an NDisk interactively or from a DOS prompt. You can regulate the automatic closing of an NDisk after it has been inactive for a certain period, or you can create a hot key that quickly closes an NDisk. In addition, you can audit access to an NDisk to determine whether someone has tried to access your information without permission.

You can choose between two versions of NDisk encrypting: fast encryption (a Norton proprietary method) and Government Standard DES (data encryption standard). The fast encryption option is effective but not quite as secure as the DES method. That is, the fast method can be more easily deciphered than the DES method because the fast method's algorithm for encoding is not as complex as the DES scheme. The DES method is slow but secure; you probably will want to use it only if the protected information is as top secret as the Manhattan Project.

When you store information in an NDisk, the data is secure. If you forget your password, even Norton cannot help you unscramble your files.

Installing Diskreet

The Diskreet program is a terminate-and-stay-resident (TSR) program—when the program loads, it stays in memory and monitors the computer as you run other programs. You can install the Diskreet program during installation (see Appendix C). You can install the program also by changing the Norton configuration (see Chapter 2), or you can install Diskreet manually. This section describes how to install Diskreet manually.

Before you use the Diskreet program, you must add the following line to your CONFIG.SYS file:

> DEVICE=*path*\DISKREET.SYS

The *path* is the name of the directory in which your Norton files are stored. If your Norton Utilities programs are stored in the directory named NORTON, you use this command:

> DEVICE=\NORTON\DISKREET.SYS

Here are the switches that you can use with DISKREET:

Switch	Description
/A20ON	If you experience problems on a network drive or lose characters during serial communication, use this switch. It causes communications to be handled differently and usually solves the problem.
/NOHMA	Tells the command not to use the high memory area. Use this switch when you are running Windows.
/Q	Tells the command to operate in *quiet mode*; that is, it disables the warning message that appears when you run Windows.
/SKIPHIGH	Tells the command not to load into an upper memory block. Use this switch when you are running Windows or when you are using a memory manager such as QEMM or 386MAX.

When you boot the computer, the Diskreet DEVICE command tells DOS to make the Diskreet driver available for use. The first time you boot with the Diskreet device driver installed, you see a screen similar to that in figure 7.1. This screen gives you information about the Diskreet program, including all the default settings. Diskreet creates a file named DISKREET.INI, which contains the settings for the program. When you boot again, you see only the copyright notice for Diskreet.

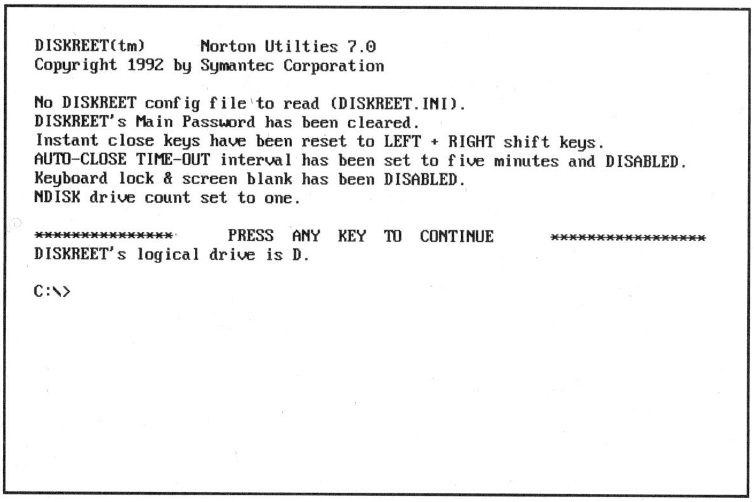

```
DISKREET(tm)        Norton Utilties 7.0
Copyright 1992 by Symantec Corporation

No DISKREET config file to read (DISKREET.INI).
DISKREET's Main Password has been cleared.
Instant close keys have been reset to LEFT + RIGHT shift keys.
AUTO-CLOSE TIME-OUT interval has been set to five minutes and DISABLED.
Keyboard lock & screen blank has been DISABLED.
NDISK drive count set to one.

****************    PRESS  ANY  KEY  TO  CONTINUE    ******************
DISKREET's logical drive is D.

C:\>
```

Fig. 7.1

The message that appears the first time you use Diskreet.

When you run Diskreet under Windows in standard or enhanced mode, a message appears, advising you that some Diskreet features (Auto-Open, Quick-Close, and Auto-Close Timeout) are disabled while you are in Windows. To prevent this message from displaying, place a /Q switch at the end of the DEVICE statement in your CONFIG.SYS file. For example, use this command:

    DEVICE=\NORTON\DISKREET.SYS /Q

The Diskreet driver takes up some of the RAM in your computer. If your computer has extended memory (over 640K), save some space for your program to use by placing the HIMEM.SYS driver (or PCSHADOW.SYS for COMPAQ computers) in your CONFIG.SYS file.

For example, to place the HIMEM.SYS driver (in the NORTON directory) in the CONFIG.SYS file, use the following command:

    DEVICE=\NORTON\HIMEM.SYS

Place this DEVICE command before the command DEVICE= \NORTON\DISKREET.SYS in your CONFIG.SYS file. If you are using an 80386-based computer, you can use an alternative memory manager such as QEMM or 386MAX in place of HIMEM.SYS.

Using Passwords

Information stored with Diskreet is only as safe as your password. Choose it with care. The more important your information, the more careful you should be about choosing and protecting your password. Diskreet requires passwords of six or more characters.

For a password, do *not* use your name, names of relatives, names of pets, license plate numbers, or any other kind of name or number associated with you or your company. When attempting to access your information, someone would try these combinations first.

The most effective passwords are random characters, such as ZTLFEWBDD, but these passwords are hard to remember. You could pick a strange word out of the dictionary, but a real hacker may even use some method of trying every word in the dictionary (spelled forward and backward) to get to your files. A compromise is to combine two easy-to-remember words that have no real meaning. Examples are LAUGH.BOOK, TREE/COMPUTER, and WHITE:RING. If you write down your password, place it in a protected area, such as a safe or a locked drawer.

In Diskreet, you can use three kinds of passwords. The *master* password protects the Diskreet settings and affects all NDisks. The *disk* password protects a specific NDisk or group of files. The *file* password protects an individual file.

Running Diskreet

To enter the Diskreet command, choose Diskreet from the Norton main screen or enter **DISKREET** at the DOS prompt. If you are using Diskreet for the first time or have not defined any NDisks, you see the dialog box shown in figure 7.2.

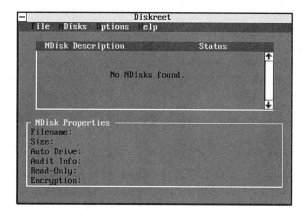

Fig. 7.2

The Diskreet dialog box.

From this dialog box, you can access the File, NDisks, **O**ptions, and **H**elp menus and then choose from a number of options located in these menus. The **H**elp option accesses the Norton Help screens; the other menus are described in the following sections.

Encrypting and Decrypting Files

If you choose the Encrypt option from the File menu, a dialog box similar to the one in figure 7.3 appears. From this dialog box, you can choose which file to encrypt. Notice that the current path listed just above the **D**irectories box is C:\NU. This tells you that the files in the Files list box are those contained in the C:\NU directory. This dialog box is similar to others in Norton Utilities; it is a "browse" dialog box, which means that you can look for the file or files you want to select for a particular task. In this case, the task is encrypting.

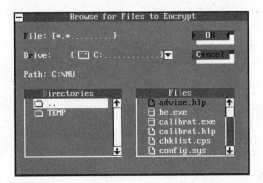

Fig. 7.3

The Browse for
Files to Encrypt
dialog box.

Specifying the Files To Encrypt

You can use the **Directories** list box to look for a directory. To browse
for files in a directory other than the current directory (C:\NU), select
the .. entry in the **Directories** box by pressing Alt+D. Press Enter
or double-click ... The **Directories** list box displays a list of the subdirectories of that parent directory. With this list box displayed, you
can then select a directory name with the arrow keys or the mouse
pointer. When you select a directory name, the files in that directory
appear in the Files list box.

T I P   To quickly locate a directory name in the **Directories** list box or to
find a file name in the Files list box, you can press the first character
of the directory or file name. The highlight in the list box jumps to
the first name (alphabetically) in the list beginning with the character you typed. Then you can scroll to find the specific directory or
file name.

To select a file in the Files list box, highlight the file name and press the
space bar, or just double-click the name with the mouse. When you
click or press the space bar, a check mark appears beside the highlighted name, which means that the file is selected. Select as many files
as you want to encrypt.

To choose files on a different drive, select a new drive name from the
Drive drop-down list. To see this list, highlight the list and press PgDn,
or point to the triangle to the right of the Drive field and click. A list of
available drives appears. Select the drive you want to browse.

T I P

To avoid selecting a drive and directory, enter the DISKREET command from the drive and directory that contain the files you want to encrypt or decrypt.

If you encrypt a single file or a group of files that can be easily described with the DOS wild-card characters ? and *, you can enter a file specification in the File field. For example, you can enter a single file name, such as MYFILE.TXT, or a file specification that includes a number of files, such as *.TXT.

After you define the files to encrypt, choose **OK** or press Enter to begin the encryption process. To exit the Browse for File to Encrypt dialog box without encrypting files, choose **C**ancel.

Specifying the File Name and Password

After you choose to encrypt the selected file or files, another dialog box appears (see fig. 7.4). This Encrypt a File dialog box enables you to specify the file in which the encrypted information is stored, and prompts you to enter the password for the encryption.

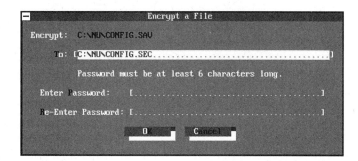

Fig. 7.4

The Encrypt a File dialog box.

If the **T**o file name is acceptable, enter the password. To change the name of the file that contains the encrypted information, enter the new file name in the **T**o Field.

Passwords must contain a minimum of 6 characters and a maximum of 40 characters. Each encrypted file can be protected with a different password, or you can enter the same password for each file. The encryption password must be entered twice. Type the password the first time in the Enter **P**assword field. To verify that the password is accurate, you must then reenter the password in the **R**e-Enter Password field.

> **CAUTION:** Remember the password. You cannot recover the encrypted information without it.

To proceed with the encryption, choose **OK** or press Enter. To exit the dialog box without encrypting the file, choose **Cancel**.

When the file has been encrypted, a message is displayed telling you that the file encryption was successful. After you press Enter, another message is displayed asking whether you want to permanently delete the original files (see fig. 7.5). If you choose **Delete**, the original file or files you encrypted are wiped from the disk (as with WipeInfo, discussed in Chapter 8). That is, after the file is deleted, it *cannot* be unerased. If you choose **Cancel** to cancel the message (not delete the file), the original files remain on disk. If you choose the **Disable This Message** option, this question no longer appears when you have encrypted a file.

Fig. 7.5

Diskreet asking whether you want to delete the original file permanently.

T I P If you allow a file to remain on disk after you encrypt it, you do not have protection from someone who might look at the contents of the file. The DOS DEL or ERASE command does not protect you, because the file can be unerased. The *only* way to get rid of the contents of the unencrypted file is to allow Diskreet to permanently delete it, or to delete it with the WipeInfo command (see Chapter 8).

Decrypting the File

After the file is encrypted, it looks like gibberish when you try to read it. To get the file back to normal, you must decrypt it. To decrypt a file, choose the **Decrypt** option from the Diskreet File menu. You see a file-selection dialog box like the one you use for choosing a file to encrypt (see fig. 7.6). The encrypted file may actually contain several encrypted files. After you choose the file to decrypt, you are asked for the password. If you enter the correct password, the file is decrypted. If you do not enter the correct password, the file is not decrypted. A message appears telling you that the password was incorrect, and the Diskreet main dialog box is displayed again.

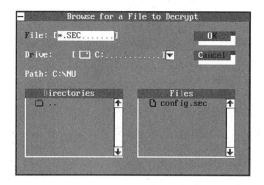

Fig. 7.6

Selecting a file to decrypt.

If a file with the same name as the file being decrypted already exists, a dialog box like the one in figure 7.7 appears. You can choose **O**verwrite, **S**kip, or **C**ancel. **O**verwrite overwrites the existing file with the one being decrypted. **S**kip causes Diskreet to skip decrypting the named file. **C**ancel terminates the decryption, and you return to the Diskreet menu.

Fig. 7.7

The dialog box for overwriting an existing file.

Creating a Diskreet NDisk

A Diskreet NDisk provides a method for automatically encrypting and decrypting all files that are written to or read from disk. When you first use Diskreet, the message No NDisks found appears. As noted earlier, an NDisk is a Norton encrypted disk; it is not a physical disk, but a portion of your hard disk set aside to behave as a separate disk. When you create an NDisk, you can use it as you would use any other disk (D:, E:, and so on). You can write and read files from this disk and use them in any program. When you close the NDisk (using Diskreet), however, all information on the disk is protected by encryption and cannot be read until you open the NDisk again with Diskreet and the correct password.

Before you can use an NDisk, you must create one. The following
sections lead you through the creation of an NDisk.

Specifying NDisk Options

To begin the process of creating an NDisk, open the **N**Disks menu in the
Diskreet dialog box. The first time you choose this option, you see a
menu like the one in figure 7.8. To create an NDisk, you must choose
the Create option from this menu. You then see the Create an NDisk
dialog box (see fig. 7.9).

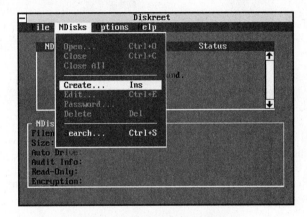

This dialog box contains options that enable you to specify how you
want the NDisk created. Here are the available options:

- **N**ame specifies the name of your NDisk. You can type a name up to eight characters in length. The name must obey standard file-naming conventions for DOS.

- **L**ocation indicates the disk that is to store the NDisk. To change the current disk, click the triangle or press PgDn and select the disk from the list of disk drives.

- **D**escription enables you to type a brief description of the NDisk. (The program requires a description for each NDisk you create.) This description (up to 30 characters) can be any words that fit into the field. Use a description that helps you remember the purpose of the NDisk.

- **S**ize sets the size of the NDisk. If you do not like the default size, choose **S**ize and specify a different disk size. The default size given depends on your disk's free space, but it is usually 5120K (the size of a 5M hard disk), if you have that much space available. Choose a size that reflects the amount of data you plan to store in the NDisk.

- **E**ncryption Method specifies which encryption method is used to store the information. The options in the list are Fast Proprietary Method and Government Standard (DES). As mentioned earlier, the fast method is fairly secure and fast. The second method is slower (meeting government standards) but more secure.

- Show **A**udit Info indicates whether you want audit information shown when an NDisk is opened. This information shows you how many successful and unsuccessful attempts have been made to open your disk. A check mark means that this option is chosen.

After you choose your settings, choose **O**K. If you choose **C**ancel, all the settings revert to their previous states, and the dialog box closes.

Setting the Password and Drive

After you specify the NDisk options in the Create an NDisk dialog box and choose **O**K, the Set Password dialog box shown in figure 7.10 appears. At the top of the box is the Assigned **D**rive Letter option. Next to this is the default drive letter (usually the next available drive letter) that will be assigned to this NDisk. In this case, it is drive D. To make the NDisk a different drive, select the drive from the drop-down list of available drives.

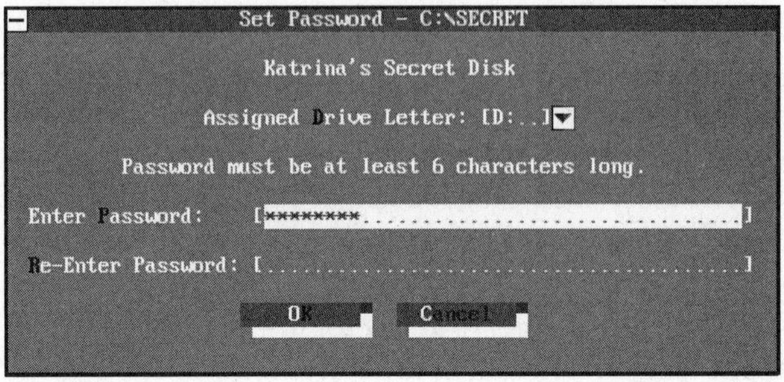

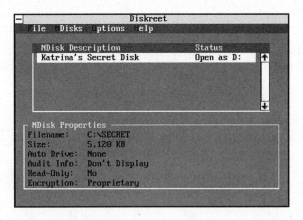

Fig. 7.10

The Set Password dialog box.

To set the password for this NDisk, choose the Enter **P**assword option. Then type a password containing at least six characters. Enter the same password in the **R**e-Enter Password field to verify the spelling. These passwords must match exactly (but uppercase and lowercase do not have to match because case is not checked). If the passwords do not match, you must reenter both.

When you have chosen a drive letter and set the password for the NDisk, choose **O**K to close this dialog box and save the information about the new NDisk. To cancel this dialog box without setting a password, choose **C**ancel.

The Diskreet dialog box is again displayed. If you created an NDisk, it now appears in the NDisk Description list box, as shown in figure 7.11. The next section discusses opening, closing, and managing NDisks.

Fig. 7.11

The current list of NDisks, displayed in the Diskreet dialog box.

Managing NDisks

After you create one or more NDisks, the names appear in the Diskreet NDisk Description list in the Diskreet dialog box. To open, close, or perform other management tasks on these NDisks, use the **NDisks** menu. Before you open the **NDisks** menu, highlight the particular NDisk you want to manage by using the up- and down-arrow keys, or just click the name. If you compare the resulting menu in figure 7.12 with the menu in figure 7.8, you notice that the NDisk options now are available.

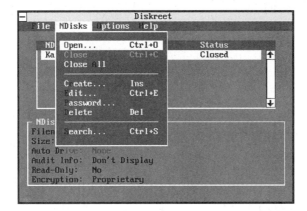

Fig. 7.12

The **N**Disks menu with active options.

> **NOTE** When an option is in parentheses or grayed (dimmed), you cannot currently choose that option. In figure 7.12, the **C**lose option is not available because no NDisks are currently open. To choose an item when the menu is not pulled down, use the shortcut keys. When the menu is pulled down, choose an item by pressing the hot key or clicking the item.

The following sections describe the options in the **NDisks** menu.

Opening and Closing an NDisk

The **O**pen option in the **NDisks** menu enables you to open an NDisk; you can open multiple NDisks simultaneously. First highlight the name of the NDisk to open from the Diskreet NDisk Description list (refer to fig. 7.11); then choose the **O**pen option. Or you can double-click an NDisk description from the Diskreet dialog box.

When you attempt to open an NDisk, you are prompted to enter the password for that NDisk. If you enter the password correctly, the NDisk is opened and becomes available. If you do not enter the correct password, the message Password Incorrect appears, and the NDisk does not open.

If you chose to display audit information (refer to fig. 7.9), the program displays the following information:

Audit Information	Meaning
Last opened	The date and time the NDisk was last opened
Last password change	The date and time the password was last changed
Total failed attempts	The number of failed attempts to open the NDisk
Total open attempts	The number of successful attempts to open the NDisk

This audit information can be valuable when you want to determine whether someone attempted to open this NDisk. If you notice a large number of failed attempts, for example, someone may be trying to guess your password.

To close an NDisk, highlight the currently opened NDisk in the Diskreet NDisk Description list and then choose the Close option from the NDisks menu. This closes the NDisk so that files cannot be written or read from it. The Close All option in the NDisks menu can be used to close all currently opened NDisks.

Editing an NDisk

The Edit option in the NDisks menu enables you to change information about the currently highlighted NDisk, such as what drive name will be used and when you are prompted to enter the password. Before you choose the Edit option, highlight the NDisk with the information that you want to edit. (Note that the NDisk must be closed for you to edit it. To close an NDisk, choose Close from the NDisks menu. To close multiple NDisks, choose Close All from the NDisks menu. If you attempt to open an NDisk, Diskreet displays a warning message; choose Close to close the selected NDisk.) Then choose Edit from the NDisks menu or press Ctrl+E. The Edit an NDisk dialog box is displayed (see fig. 7.13).

Fig. 7.13

The Edit an
NDisk dialog
box.

There are three drop-down lists in the Edit an NDisk dialog box: Auto Drive, **P**rompt, and Pro**m**pt At. The **Au**to Drive list contains possible drive names to be used for the NDisk.

The **P**rompt list contains the options Pop-Up, Automatic (the default setting), and Beep. The Pro**m**pt At list contains the options Boot and First Access (the default setting). These options enable you to choose when you are prompted for the password to use an NDisk—either when you boot your computer or when you first try to access the disk.

The **D**escription field enables you to change the brief description of the NDisk. In the **S**ize field, you can change the size currently allocated for the NDisk. You cannot make the size smaller than the current size of the files in that NDisk. If you anticipate storing more information in an NDisk, you might want to increase its size. The Show **A**udit Info check box allows you to specify that information about the disk's usage be displayed when you open the NDisk. (See the earlier section "Opening and Closing an NDisk" for more information on the audit information.) The **R**ead-Only check box allows you to set the file attribute of the NDisk as read-only. This means that the information in the NDisk can be read, but not written to or changed. You might want to check this option if the NDisk contains information that should not be altered.

Changing the NDisk Password and Encryption Method

The **P**assword option in the NDisks menu enables you to change the password for an NDisk. Before you choose this option, highlight an NDisk name in the NDisk Description list in the Diskreet dialog box.

Then choose **Password** from the **NDisks** menu. The Set Password dialog box appears, as shown in figure 7.14. This dialog box enables you to change the current password. You must first enter the current password in the Enter Old **Password** text box and then enter a new password in the Enter **New** Password text box. Verify the new password by entering the identical new password again in the **Re-**Enter New Password text box.

From this dialog box, you can also choose to change the encryption method with either the Secure or Quick option from the Re-Encryption Type list box.

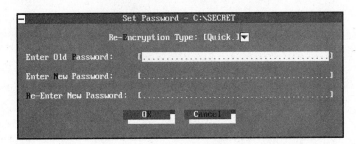

Fig. 7.14

The Set Password dialog box.

Deleting NDisks

To delete an NDisk, choose **Delete** from the **NDisks** menu. Diskreet displays a warning message, as shown in figure 7.15, and requires you to type the password for the selected NDisk before you can delete it. If you don't want to delete the NDisk, choose **C**ancel or press Esc. To delete the NDisk, type the password; then choose **D**elete (pressing Enter doesn't work). If the password you type is incorrect or if you fail to type a password, Diskreet just returns to the Diskreet dialog box without deleting the NDisk.

```
┌─┤ Delete an NDisk ├────────────────────────┐
│  If you delete C:\SECRET, all the data      │
│    on it will be irretrievably lost.        │
│                                             │
│  Are you sure you want to delete this NDisk?│
│ Password: [............................]    │
│        ┌ Delete ┐    ┌ Cancel ┐             │
└─────────────────────────────────────────────┘
```

Fig. 7.15

The Delete an NDisk dialog box.

Searching for NDisks

The **S**earch option in the **NDisks** menu enables you to search disks on your computer for an NDisk. This option can help if your NDisk is stored on a disk other than your default drive, or if you have NDisks on several disks or disk partitions. When you choose the **S**earch option, the dialog box shown in figure 7.16 appears. The Drives list on the left side of the dialog box contains a list of all the disks known to Diskreet. To select a disk to search, highlight that disk name and press the space bar; a check mark appears beside the disk name. Or double-click a disk name. Choose as many disks as you want from the Drives list.

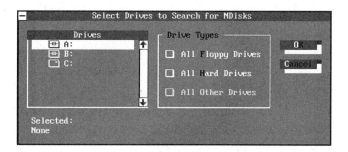

Fig. 7.16

Specifying drives to search for NDisks.

Three other selection options appear on the right side of the dialog box. Instead of selecting floppy disk drives manually from the Drives list, choose the All **F**loppy Drives option, which selects all floppy drives. Select all hard drives in the same way, by choosing All **H**ard Drives. The **A**ll Other Drives option is available only if you have other drives, such as network drives.

| If you just placed a floppy disk in a disk drive, Diskreet does not know that the disk is there until you choose the All **F**loppy Drives option. Notice that you can press Ctrl+S at any time in the Diskreet program to run the **S**earch option. | T I P |

After you choose the drives you want to search, choose **OK** to begin searching. The NDisks in the Diskreet Description list reflect those found on the drives you chose to search. To cancel this box without choosing drives to search, choose **C**ancel.

The **N**Disks menu enables you to manage how your NDisks are named and accessed. The next Diskreet menu, **O**ptions, enables you to set options for file and disk access.

Specifying Diskreet Options

The Diskreet **O**ptions menu enables you to choose a number of options that deal with how your NDisks operate. The options on this menu are described in the following sections (see fig. 7.17).

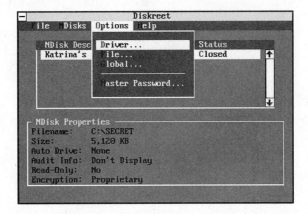

Fig. 7.17

The Diskreet **O**ptions menu.

Driver Options

When you choose the **D**river option in the **O**ptions menu, Diskreet displays the Driver Options dialog box (see fig. 7.18). This dialog box enables you to specify the number of drive letters to reserve for use with NDisks. You can choose from 1 to 5, according to the number of drives you want to have available. If, for example, your computer already uses up to disk D: and you choose three drive letters to reserve, the drives E:, F:, and G: are available for use as NDisks.

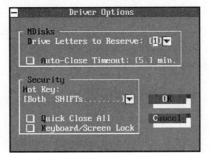

Fig. 7.18

The Driver Options dialog box.

When chosen, the Auto-Close Timeout option enables you to specify that an NDisk will automatically close after the NDisk has not been used for a certain amount of time. The default time is five minutes. This option enables you to protect yourself if you happen to leave your computer unexpectedly without closing your NDisk. When the system calculates that you have been gone the selected amount of time, the NDisk is automatically closed.

In the Security section of the dialog box, you can choose Hot Key for keystroke options that quickly close your NDisks. Choose from the following options:

Both SHIFTs

Both SHIFTs+CTRL

Left SHIFT+CTRL

Right SHIFT+CTRL

Both SHIFTs+ALT

Left SHIFT+ALT

Right SHIFT+ALT

CTRL+ALT

Other options in the Security section are Quick Close All and Keyboard/Screen Lock. When checked, the Quick Close All option causes all NDisks to close when you press the Security hot keys. If this box is not checked, the keystrokes do not close your NDisks. By default, the Quick Close All option is selected.

If the Keyboard/Screen Lock option is checked, your keyboard locks, and your screen clears (you are unable to access the keyboard or screen) after you press the Security hot key. To regain use of the computer, you must enter the main password. Because your screen is blank, you are not prompted to enter the password. You must enter it on the keyboard. Nothing appears on-screen until you correctly enter the password; then the screen again becomes visible. Your only other alternative is to reboot the computer.

When you have chosen and saved a Security hot key and you have one or more NDisks opened, you can quickly close the NDisks by pressing the hot keys. Several versions of the hot keys are available because some terminate-and-stay-resident (TSR) programs that you use may already use one of these hot key combinations. In that case, choose one of the combinations not used by any TSR program you are using.

Choose **OK** when you have chosen the options you want from the Driver Options dialog box. If you choose **C**ancel, any options you chose are canceled.

File Encryption Options

When you choose the **F**ile option from the Diskreet **O**ptions menu, the File Encryption Options dialog box appears (see fig. 7.19).

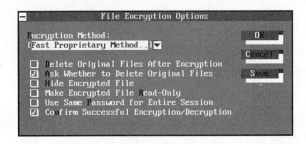

Fig. 7.19

The File Encryption Options dialog box.

From this dialog box, you can choose the following options:

■ **E**ncryption Method specifies the encryption method used to encrypt files: Fast Proprietary Method or Government Standard (DES). The fast method is fairly secure and fast. The second method is slower (meeting government standards) but more secure, as described earlier.

■ **D**elete Original Files After Encryption deletes the original files that you encrypted. Then only the encrypted files remain on your disk. This option is deselected by default. If you do not choose this option, your old file remains unprotected on disk.

■ With **A**sk Whether To Delete Original Files, you are asked whether you want to delete the original file each time a file is encrypted. This option is selected by default. If you choose this option, an overwrite warning message appears after each encryption (refer to fig. 7.7).

■ **H**ide Encrypted File sets the hidden file attribute on the encrypted file so that the file does not appear in a directory listing. This option is deselected by default.

■ Make Encrypted File **R**ead-Only sets the read-only file attribute on the encrypted file so that the file cannot be deleted or altered. This option is deselected by default. Making an encrypted file hidden or read-only refers to setting the file attribute of the encrypted file, as described in Chapter 9.

■ With Use Same **P**assword for Entire Session, you use just one
   password as long as you are in Diskreet and have not returned to
   the DOS prompt or the Norton main screen. That way, you do not
   have to enter a password each time to encrypt or decrypt a file.
   When this option is selected, you are prompted only once during
   an entire session for the password. By default, this option is
   deselected.

■ With Co**n**firm Successful Encryption/Decryption, a confirmation
   dialog box tells you whether an encryption or decryption has
   been successful. This option is selected by default.

After you choose settings on-screen, choose **S**ave to save this information to disk. If you choose **O**K or press Enter, these options are available only until you reboot the computer. To exit this dialog box, choose
OK or press Enter. To cancel all changes you made and exit the screen,
choose **C**ancel.

Global Options

When you choose the **G**lobal option from the **O**ptions menu, the Global
Options dialog box appears (see fig. 7.20). From this dialog box, you
can choose which method to use for clearing data (erasing files) when
Diskreet deletes the original files after encrypting a file. The options for
data clearing are None, Overwrite Once, and Government Wipe (DOD
Spec). Wiping techniques are described in Chapter 8.

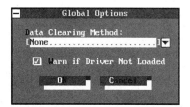

Fig. 7.20

The Global
Options dialog
box.

The **W**arn if Driver Not Loaded option enables you to decide whether
a warning box is displayed when you start Diskreet and the Diskreet
driver is not loaded. By default, this option is selected. If the drive is
not loaded, the following message appears:

```
The Diskreet Driver (DISKREET.SYS) has not been loaded. It
must be running for you to work with NDISKS.
```

If the Diskreet driver is not loaded on your computer, see the section "Installing Diskreet," earlier in this chapter.

After you choose options in the Global Options dialog box, choose **OK** to exit the dialog box. If you choose Cancel, any options you chose are canceled.

Master Password Option

When you choose the **Master Password** option from the **Options** menu, the Change Master Password dialog box appears. From this box, you can change the master Diskreet password. You must enter the current old password, if any, and then enter a new password twice to set the new password. To exit with the password reset, choose **OK**; or choose **Cancel** to exit and not reset the password.

Controlling Diskreet from the DOS Prompt

Many items that you can control through the Diskreet dialog boxes may also be controlled with the DISKREET command from the DOS prompt. You use this syntax:

DISKREET [*switches*]

The following switches are available with DISKREET:

Switch	Description
/CLOSE	Closes all NDisks
/D:*filespec*	Decrypts the specified file
/E:*filespec*	Encrypts the specified file
/T:*filespec*	Specifies the target file for encryption (use with the /E switch)
/HIDE[:*d*]	Hides the specified drive (NDisk)
/OFF	Disables use of the Diskreet driver
/ON	Enables the Diskreet driver
/P:*password*	Tells Diskreet which password to use for encryption or decryption of a file
/SHOW[:*d*]	Shows hidden drives (NDisks) being used to store files

You cannot use both /D and /E in the same command. The switches /CLOSE, /HIDE, /ON, /OFF, and /SHOW must be used alone, without any other options on the command line.

When encrypting a file from the DOS prompt, use this command:

DISKREET /E:*filespec* /T:*filespec* /P:*password*

The first *filespec* is the name of the file to be encrypted; the second *filespec* is the name of the target file for encryption.

When decrypting a file from the DOS prompt, use the following command:

DISKREET /D:*filespec* /P:*password*

For an example of using DISKREET to encrypt and decrypt files, see the upcoming section "Transferring Encrypted Files to Other Computers."

Using Diskreet on a Network

Diskreet NDisks are not designed to work as network drives. You can back up your NDisks, however, by copying them to a network drive. To read information from the network disk, you need to copy the information back onto your local computer's drive. With the DISKREET command, you can encrypt and decrypt individual files on a network drive. If you are on a Novell network, the NetWare command MAP attempts to locate any NDisks on your computer and prompts you for a password. To disable this prompt, enter the following commands at the DOS prompt or create a batch file to issue these commands:

```
C:\NORTON\DISKREET /OFF
MAP
C:\NORTON\DISKREET /ON
```

Transferring Encrypted Files to Other Computers

When a file or files are encrypted with Diskreet, the result is another file. This file, which contains encrypted information, cannot be read or used by your word processor or any other application program because the information contained in the file looks like gibberish. A user can access the information in the file only by decrypting the file with Diskreet. Because the file is protected by the Diskreet encryption, you can safely send this file to other people without worrying that the file will be intercepted and deciphered on its way. The following sections explain how to transfer the encrypted files.

 NOTE   If you transfer highly sensitive information, you may not want to telephone and tell the password to the recipient if the telephone might be tapped. Your encrypted file is only as protected as the password.

Transferring Encrypted Files by Disk

To transfer an encrypted file from one computer to another by disk, copy the file to a floppy disk, take that disk to another computer, read the file onto the new computer, and decrypt the file with Diskreet. Because the information on the disk is protected, you can be comfortable sending the information by courier or mail. If the disk is intercepted, the information cannot be read unless the person intercepting it knows your Diskreet password. Therefore, it is important for the password to be protected. For example, do not send the disk and the password together in the same package.

To transfer important information from one computer to another with Diskreet encryption, follow these steps:

1. Encrypt the file (or files) you want to send with a password known to the person who is receiving the disk. (Make sure that the password is transferred with a safe method.) For example, you can encrypt a file named MYFILE.ENC into a file named MYFILE.SEC with the following command at the DOS prompt:

    DISKREET /E:MYFILE.ENC /T:MYFILE.SEC /P:ITSIMPORTANT

2. Copy the encrypted file to a floppy disk. If your encrypted file is named MYFILE.ENC, you can copy that file to a disk in drive A with this DOS command:

    COPY MYFILE.SEC A:

3. Send the disk to the recipient.

4. When the disk arrives at the destination computer, the recipient copies the file onto the computer. The following command copies the file MYFILE.ENC from a floppy disk in drive A to drive C:

    COPY A:MYFILE.SEC C:

5. The recipient decrypts the file with Diskreet and the password provided for the file. The following command decrypts the file MYFILE.SEC with the DISKREET command at the DOS prompt:

DISKREET /D:MYFILE.SEC /P:ITSIMPORTANT

The decrypted file is named MYFILE.ENC—its original name—because DISKREET remembers the name of the original file. After the file is decrypted, it can be read and used by the application program for which it was intended.

Transferring Encrypted Files by Modem

Transferring encrypted files by modem is not really different from transferring nonencrypted files by modem; however, your information is protected from being read by others. Transferring files by modem enables you to send information quickly from your computer to any computer in the world with a modem and telephone hookup. If you are not familiar with the process, please refer to a book such as Que's *Using PROCOMM PLUS*.

Before you send a file by modem, encrypt the file with Diskreet. Even if the file is intercepted when you send it, the interceptor will not be able to read it unless that person knows the password. Be sure that you protect the password. Do not e-mail it to the recipient, for example. If a person can intercept your file, that person can also intercept your e-mail, and e-mail is not often protected by encryption. After the file has been transferred, the recipient can decrypt the file with Diskreet.

Transferring the information from your computer to the recipient's computer requires the same steps as those described in the preceding section, but instead you call the computer where you want to send the file and then send the file by modem, using your agreed-on transfer method. If you use PROCOMM PLUS, for example, you might transfer the file, using the ZMODEM transfer protocol.

Summary

The Norton Diskreet program allows you to protect important and confidential data from people who do not have authorized access (by way of a password). With Diskreet, you can encrypt and decrypt individual files. You can also create one or more pseudodisks, called NDisks, that can be used just like real disk drives—except that the information stored on an NDisk is protected by a password.

Another way to protect important information is to completely destroy it when it should no longer be on your disk. The WipeInfo command, described in the next chapter, can perform this task.

Destroying Files Permanently with WipeInfo

Because Norton Utilities and other programs offer the capability to bring back files after disks have been formatted, you may wonder how to get rid of files permanently. Amazingly, some people do not know or even think about this problem. A recent magazine story reported that a Fortune 100 company (a computer company, no less) auctioned off thousands of outdated PCs. Some were purchased by reporters who were able to unformat the hard disks and discover a great deal of important information.

How could this happen? The PC is particularly ornery about getting rid of information on disk permanently—it's harder than it seems. After you erase a file with the DOS ERASE or DELETE command, only one character in the disk directory changes. This character tells DOS that the file is deleted. The actual contents of the file are not changed, and most of the information about the file is still intact. When you format a disk, the system information and information in the root directory are erased, but most files' contents remain intact. For more information about how disks store files, see Chapter 3.

Even when a file is overwritten, parts of the disk may still contain file fragments. In fact, information that has appeared on your screen, which you have *never* saved to a file, may be written to your disk and could possibly be read by someone else. If you deal with very important data that must be protected from unauthorized use, you need to be aware of these potentially damaging situations. Here is how these problems arise.

Chapter 3 discussed how a file is saved on disk. If a file is less than a cluster in length, a portion of the cluster is not used for storing the file. This can be a cause for concern. Two kinds of information can be found in the remaining space assigned to a file but not actually used.

First, when DOS writes a file to be saved, it writes at least a sector of information. If the file saved is less than a sector long, DOS pads the remaining portion of the sector with whatever happens to be in RAM memory. This could be any of the following:

- A portion of a subdirectory
- Pieces of previously run programs
- Pieces of data used in previously run programs
- Other information in RAM

For example, suppose that you are a CIA agent. You write a memo to the President, send it by e-mail, and never save the e-mail for security reasons. Then you save another small file to disk. Information from the secret message may linger in RAM. When the small file is written to disk, DOS uses portions of RAM to pad out the remaining portion of the sector not used by the file. A critical portion of your secret message may have then been written to disk in that file!

Second, most disks store clusters more than one sector long. The preceding scenario just covers information padding out the rest of the last sector used to store a file. What if more sectors are left in the cluster? This unused cluster may contain information from a file that previously occupied that space. That leftover piece of a file could contain confidential information.

The following illustration shows what a disk may contain. The disk uses 2-sector clusters (1,024 bytes). Each sector is 512 bytes long. The first few bytes contain a file with the following memo:

```
Dave, let's meet for lunch at 11:30 this Friday — Al
```

This file is 54 bytes long. Therefore, the first sector of this file contains 512 minus 54 bytes (458 bytes) of unused space. The second sector of the cluster (512 bytes) is not needed to store any information from the file.

```
Bytes      Sector   Contents
1-64       1        Dave, let's meet for lunch at 11:30 this Friday — A1XXXXXXXXX
65-128              XXXXXXXXXXXXXXXXXXXXXXXXXXXXXXXXXXXXXXXXXXXXXXXXXXXXXXXXXXXXX
129-192             XXXXOOPS, SOME SECRET INFORMATIONXXXXXXXXXXXXXXXXXXXXXXXXXXXXX
193-256             XXXXXXXXXXXXXXXXXXXXXXXXXXXXXXXXXXXXXXXXMORE!!!XXXXXXXXXXXXXX
257-320             XXXXXTHIS SPACE PADDED BY DOS WHEN FILE WAS WRITTENXXXXXXXXXX
321-384             XXXXXXXXXXXXXXXXXXXXXXXXXXXXXXXXXXXXXXXXXXXXXXXXXXXXXXXXXXXXX
385-448             XXXXXXXXXXXXXXXXXXXXXXXXXXXXXXXXXXXXXXXXXXXXXXXXXXXXXXXXXXXXX
449-512             XXXXXXXXXXXXXXXXXXXXXXXXXXXXXXXXXXXXXXXXXXXXXXXXXXXXXXXXXXXXX
513-576    2        ...........................................................
577-640             ........THIS PORTION OF THE CLUSTER MAY CONTAIN LEFTOVERS....
641-704             ...........................................................
705-768             ........OOPS, HERE IS SALARY INFORMATION!!...................
769-832             ........FROM AN OLD REPORT...................................
833-896             ...........................................................
897-960             ...........................................................
961-1024            ...........................................................
```

The first sector (bytes 1–512) contains the file in bytes 1–54 and then padding from byte 55 through byte 512. Padded space in the first sector is shown in the graph as Xs. Bytes 513–1024 (the second sector in the cluster) contain whatever was left from the previous file. The second sector space is shown in the graph as dots. Notice that the first sector could contain in the padded area some information that happened to be in RAM at the time the file was saved. The second sector contains a piece of a file left from when that space stored a file that has now been deleted.

Of course, it is a problem that this secret information is on disk, but how could you read this "erased" information? You can read these areas with a disk editor such as Norton Disk Editor (see Chapter 17). A disk editor enables you to view the contents of a disk on a byte-by-byte basis (or even bit by bit). With a disk editor, you can read the information in the file slack space, as well as information in other areas of the disk.

Understanding WipeInfo

To give users a way to prevent important information from being seen by unauthorized eyes, Norton Utilities provides the WipeInfo command. This command *permanently* deletes files and disks by physically overwriting the contents of the disk, not just modifying the directory information. If you have information that should not fall into the wrong hands, WipeInfo should be an essential part of your information protection plan.

T I P If you demonstrate software, you should wipe program files instead of just deleting them. When you finish a demo, you might delete the files, but the files can easily be unerased and the program restored to the hard disk, which is, of course, illegal.

Before you use WipeInfo to delete important files permanently, you need a thorough understanding of this command and the way files are erased. WipeInfo overwrites the information on disk with several writes of random data. Unused areas of the disk are wiped clear so that they no longer contain residual files that were previously erased.

> **WARNING:** Be careful when you use the Wipeinfo command. Its results cannot be reversed.

WipeInfo includes a **G**overnment Wipe option that overwrites the information on a disk according to Department of Defense (DOD) specifications. These specifications call for a 1/0 pattern (a pattern of 1s and 0s) to be written to the disk three times, a random number to be written to the disk, and the last number written to the disk to be read back from the disk for verification (DOD 5220.22-M). The government adopted these specifications because a single erasure of magnetic information may not be enough. A faint magnetic "fingerprint" may remain on a disk after a single erasure.

 NOTE A Government Wipe of a file can take a few seconds or minutes (depending on the file size). A Government Wipe of a 1.44M disk can take two hours, and a wipe of a hard disk can last most of the day.

You can use WipeInfo interactively or as a command from the DOS prompt. The following sections describe how to use WipeInfo.

Using the WipeInfo Dialog Box

To use WipeInfo, choose WipeInfo from the Norton main screen or enter **WIPEINFO** at the DOS prompt. The WipeInfo dialog box appears, as shown in figure 8.1.

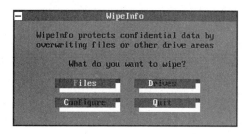

Fig. 8.1

The WipeInfo
dialog box.

The WipeInfo dialog box gives you four options. The **Q**uit option returns to the DOS prompt or the Norton main screen. The following sections describe the other options.

Specifying Files

If you choose **F**iles from the WipeInfo dialog box, Norton displays the Wipe Files dialog box (see fig. 8.2). In this dialog box, you can enter the names of the files to be wiped. To specify multiple files, use the * and ? wild-card characters.

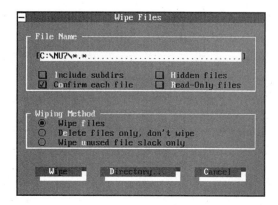

Fig. 8.2

The Wipe Files
dialog box.

The following options are available in the File Name section of the dialog box:

- To wipe files with matching file specifications in subdirectories, choose **I**nclude Subdirs.

- To have the program prompt you before it wipes each file, choose **C**onfirm Each File.

- To wipe hidden files or read-only files that match the file specification, choose **H**idden Files or **R**ead-Only Files.

In the Wiping Method section of the Wipe Files dialog box, you can specify whether you want to wipe the file or just delete it (as you would with DOS DELETE). The Wipe Unused File Slack Only option causes WipeInfo to wipe just those portions of the disk that are allocated to a file but unused. This process does not affect the file itself but wipes only the information in the slack space of the file. After you choose your options, choose the **W**ipe command button at the bottom of the dialog box to begin the wiping procedure; choose **C**ancel to cancel the wipe.

The **D**irectory option at the bottom of the dialog box enables you to change the current default directory. When you choose the option, a dialog box like the one in figure 8.3 appears. From the Change Directory dialog box, you can enter a new path, choose a new drive from a drop-down list box, or choose a new directory from the **S**ubdirectories list box. To display directories in the **S**ubdirectories list box, highlight the root directory symbol (\) and press Enter, or double-click the root directory. To choose a subdirectory, highlight the directory name in the **S**ubdirectories list and press Enter, or double-click. That directory name appears in the **P**ath field. To exit this dialog box and change to the specified directory, choose **O**K. Choose **C**ancel to exit without changing to another directory or drive.

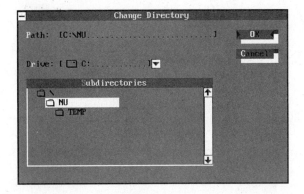

Fig. 8.3

The WipeInfo Change Directory dialog box.

Specifying Drives

The **D**rives option in the WipeInfo dialog box displays the Select Drives To Wipe dialog box (see fig. 8.4). From this dialog box, you can select which drives to wipe. You can also choose to wipe the entire disk (Wipe **E**ntire Drive) or just the unused portions of the disk (Wipe Un-used Areas Only). Wiping the unused portion of the disk gets rid of any erased files that someone could restore to see important information. After you choose the options in this menu, choose **O**K to begin wiping or **C**ancel to cancel the wipe.

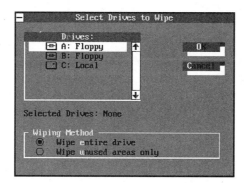

Fig. 8.4

The Select Drives
To Wipe dialog
box.

Configuring the Wipe Process

The **C**onfigure option in the WipeInfo dialog box displays the Wipe Configuration dialog box, enabling you to determine how information is wiped from the disk (see fig. 8.5). From this dialog box, choose the **F**ast Wipe (default) or **G**overnment Wipe option.

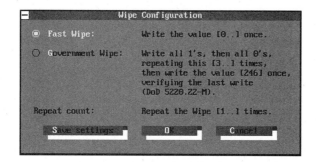

Fig. 8.5

The Wipe
Configuration
dialog box.

You can change several of the numbers in the options. Use the arrow keys, Tab, or mouse to move to those fields to change the numbers. The following list describes the changes you can make:

- For the **F**ast Wipe option, you can change the write value from 0 to another number (from 1 to 255).

- For the **G**overnment Wipe option, you can change the number of times the write is repeated (1s and 0s are written) from 3 to another number, such as 5. You can also change the final value written (the default is ASCII 246). This change enables you to provide an even more thorough wipe than the regular government standard.

- You can change the Repeat Count setting from 1 to another number.

After you choose these settings, choose **S**ave Settings and then choose **OK** to return to the WipeInfo dialog box.

Using WipeInfo from the DOS Prompt

The WipeInfo command overwrites information on disk so that the information cannot be recovered. This process includes wiping individual files or an entire disk. The syntax for the WipeInfo command is

WIPEINFO d:[/E] [/GOV*n*] [/R*n*] [/V*n*] [/BATCH]

or

WIPEINFO [*filespec*][/N][[/K][/S][/GOV*n*][/R*n*}[/V*n*][/BATCH]

The first version of the command is used to wipe information from disks. The second command is used to wipe files. Use only those switches listed for each version of the command. Here are descriptions of the switches available:

Switch	Description
/E	Causes the command to overwrite only information that is currently unused or is in "erased" files—files marked for erase by the DOS ERASE command but otherwise recoverable.
/K	Wipes out a file and any slack space allocated to it. (For more information on slack space, see Chapter 3.)
/N	Uses "no wipe" mode, which causes the WipeInfo command to behave like the ERASE command. The file is marked as erased but is not overwritten.
/S	Wipes out files that match the file specification in the current directory and all subdirectories.
/GOV*n*	Uses a government-standard overwriting procedure. The default for *n* (number of overwrites) is 3. The value written to disk is ASCII value 246.
/R*n*	Overwrites the disk *n* times. The default is 1.
/V*n*	Selects the value to be used to overwrite information on the disk. The *n* value can be from 0 to 255. Although the default is 0, the /GOV*n* switch overrides this default.
/BATCH	Executes the command without any prompts. This switch is helpful when the command is used in batch files. You can also use it from the DOS prompt, however. If you do use this switch, make sure that you know what you are doing, because the program begins wiping information without giving any chance to verify the correctness of the command.

> **CAUTION:** A few software products store copy-protection information in the slack space of a file. If you wipe out the slack space with the /K option, you may cause a program to lose its capability to run. Although this storage practice is not common, if you use software with protection schemes, you may want to check with the software manufacturer to see whether wiping the slack space affects the program's capability to run.

To wipe D: disk by using the government standard, enter the following command:

> WIPEINFO D:/GOV

WipeInfo is a convenient way to erase files throughout your hard disk. To "clean up" your hard disk, get rid of unnecessary files, and provide more space on the disk, you could use WipeInfo to erase all files (using the DOS style of erase) on your C: disk that match the specification TMP*.*. You would use the following command:

> WIPEINFO C:\TMP*.* /S /N

When you enter this command, you are prompted by a warning message (see fig. 8.6). To continue with the deletion, choose **Delete**. To cancel, press Enter or choose **Cancel**. If you choose to continue with the delete, WipeInfo identifies all the files that match the delete criteria and displays them in the Wiping Files dialog box (see fig. 8.7).

Fig. 8.6

The message box that appears when you delete files with WipeInfo.

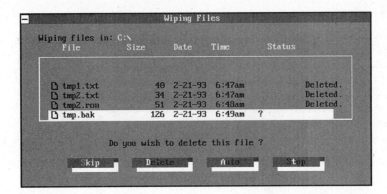

Fig. 8.7

The Wiping Files
dialog box.

The Wiping Files dialog box shows four files that have been listed thus far. As each file is highlighted on the list, you can choose **S**kip to skip that file (or **D**elete if you have chosen the delete mode rather than the wipe mode). Or you can choose the **A**uto option, which tells the program to continue deleting the rest of the files without prompting. Choose the S**t**op option to cancel any further deletions.

To skip the dialog boxes shown in figures 8.6 and 8.7 when entering the WipeInfo command at the DOS prompt, you place the /BATCH switch on the command line. For example, here is the same command used earlier, with the option to skip the warning and file list screens:

WIPEINFO C:\TMP*.* /S /N /BATCH

Be careful when you use the /BATCH switch because you do not get a second chance to stop the wipe. However, even if you go ahead and begin WipeInfo and suddenly have a change of heart or discover that you are wiping out the wrong disk, you can interrupt the process by pressing Ctrl+Break. If the operation has not proceeded too far, you may be able to recover some information on the disk. In fact, Norton designed WipeInfo so that it destroys the most unused part of the disk first; if you stop the procedure quickly, you have a good chance of being able to use some of the information on disk. Furthermore, if you use the /N switch, the files deleted are erased with the DOS erase procedure and are probably uneraseable with UnErase (see Chapter 10).

T   I   P   If you give a computer with a hard disk to another person and that computer contains information the recipient should not see, use WipeInfo. To wipe out only data files but leave programs intact on a computer, first erase all the confidential files and then use WipeInfo with the /E switch to wipe out all the erased files. The programs are left intact.

Summary

Norton Utilities offers you a number of ways to protect your information on disk. When protecting information means making sure that it does not get into the wrong hands, use WipeInfo to do an effective job of getting rid of information on disk. This command is more thorough than the DOS ERASE, DELETE, and FORMAT commands.

One final chapter in Part II covers ways to prevent files from being erased or changed. For information about setting file attributes, turn to Chapter 9.

Setting File Attributes

The last several chapters covered Norton programs that enable you to protect your data on disk in a number of ways. This chapter rounds out the protection schemes by covering two Norton Utilities commands that use file attributes to protect files: File Attributes and File Find. *File attributes* are pieces of information about a file that tell DOS how to manage the file. This chapter presents information about these attributes and shows how they can be used to protect your data.

The value of this method of protection is that it takes no overhead to protect the files. Unlike Diskreet and SmartCan, the File Attributes and File Find commands are built into DOS and do not require any memory-resident program to be active for files to be protected.

Understanding File Attributes

To protect your important files, prevent them from being erased or overwritten. Overwriting a file is different from erasing a file—and more destructive. When a file is overwritten, the information in the file is permanently replaced by the contents of the new file. Suppose that you have a valuable Lotus 1-2-3 worksheet named ABLE.WK3. Overwriting that file from 1-2-3 is possible (and sometimes easy). If you overwrite the file, you cannot recover the old file with the UnErase command because all or at least some of the information in the old file is gone. In particular, you want to protect certain files from erasure or change.

Examples are COMMAND.COM, AUTOEXEC.BAT, CONFIG.SYS, WIN.INI, SYSTEM.INI, and other configuration and system files for various application programs.

When one person gives a friend a floppy disk containing a program, a common problem can occur. The friend, who knows only enough about the COPY command to make himself dangerous, copies the program from the floppy disk to the hard disk with a command such as COPY A:*.* C:.

With this command, some files on the floppy disk may overwrite files on the hard disk, particularly COMMAND.COM. When you reboot the computer, the version of COMMAND.COM copied from the floppy disk may conflict with the other system files, so the computer may refuse to reboot. To recover from this problem, you can use Rescue Disk (see Chapter 14). Other important files, such as AUTOEXEC.BAT and CONFIG.SYS, may also have been overwritten on your hard disk's root directory. If you did not back up this information to your rescue disk or another disk, you may have to reconstruct these files.

Of course, it is ill-advised to copy a floppy disk onto the root directory of your hard disk without knowing much about the contents of the floppy. To protect against this kind of problem if it does occur, you can set attributes for important files in the root directory on the hard disk. Then if you copy a floppy disk that you do not know much about, you do not overwrite your original files.

Specifying File Attributes

When you create a file on disk, DOS stores the name of the file as well as other pieces of vital information. When you enter the DOS DIR command, you see some of this information—the size of the file, the date and time the file was created, and so on. DOS also stores four other pieces of information that you usually do not see. You can toggle on or off these four pieces of information, called *attributes* (see table 9.1).

Table 9.1 File Attributes

Attribute	Description
Archive	When the archive attribute is set (turned on), the file has not been backed up. When you create a file, DOS turns on the archive attribute. When you perform the backup procedure, the archive attribute is turned off.

Attribute	Description
Hidden	When the hidden attribute is set, the file does not appear in a directory when you perform the DIR command. On a bootable disk, the DOS files named IBMBIOS.COM and IBMDOS.COM usually are hidden files. When you perform a CHKDSK command, you may notice a report of hidden files.
Read-only	When the read-only attribute is set, the information in a file can be read or used by a program, but DOS prevents the file from being changed or erased.
System	System files are similar to hidden files. When the system attribute is set, DOS considers the file a system file and does not display it in a directory when you issue a DIR command.

With the commands File Attributes (FA) and File Find (FILEFIND or FF), you can control these attributes and protect important files from accidental change or erasure.

Protecting Files with File Attributes

The read-only attribute helps protect a file from accidental change. The hidden attribute helps hide files from normal view, preventing that file from being used or altered. The archive attribute can be reset to back up files a number of times, which gives you added protection. Specifically, here is how you can use the File Find and File Attributes commands to protect your files:

- *You can make all important files read-only.* When a file is read-only, you cannot change or erase that file. Be aware, however, that some files to which programs write should not be set to read-only. You should make at least the important files in the root directory read-only (including COMMAND.COM, AUTOEXEC.BAT, and CONFIG.SYS). You may have other critical files in your application programs, which should also be set to read-only. To change any of these files, turn off the read-only attribute temporarily.

- *You can hide valuable files.* You can prevent other people from accessing your secret information by hiding files. (This method is not foolproof. If other users know how to reset attributes, they can change the attribute back.) In fact, on most computers, two DOS files (IBMBIOS.COM and IBMDOS.COM) are hidden. Those files make up two-thirds of the information required to be on your disk in order for your computer to boot (the other third is supplied by COMMAND.COM). IBM and Microsoft chose to hide these files to help prevent their unauthorized use.

■ *For extra protection, you can turn off the archive attribute for some important files.* If you regularly back up your computer with incremental backups (backups of only those files that were changed since the last backup), those files are not backed up again. If you turn on the archive attribute for certain files, however, those files are included in the next backup, even if they were not changed since the last backup. You may want to take this step so that you have a duplicate copy of the backup in case one copy is damaged or lost.

 NOTE   The File Find command can do more than set attributes. A number of other features of the File Find command are not covered in this chapter. See Chapter 25 for more information about this command.

The next two sections discuss how to set file attributes with File Attributes and File Find. The File Attributes command is designed to be used as a DOS command-line utility. The File Find command enables you to set attributes interactively from a menu.

Setting Attributes from the DOS Prompt with the FA Command

The FA (File Attributes) command is similar to the DOS ATTRIB command. FA enables you to set file attributes from the DOS prompt. The syntax for this command is

FA [*filespec*][*attribute switches*][*other switches*]

or

FA [*filespec*] /DIR[+|−]

where *filespec* represents the specific files or directory to display or change, *attribute switches* represent the attributes you want to change, and *other switches* represent the other available switches you can use with file attributes. You can choose from the following attribute switches:

Switch	Description
/A	Sets the archive attribute
/DIR	Sets the hidden attribute for directories
/HID	Sets the hidden attribute for files
/R	Sets the read-only attribute
/SYS	Sets the system attribute

To use the FA command to set an attribute, follow the attribute switch with a plus (+) or minus (–). A plus sign turns on the attribute, and a minus sign turns off the attribute. To set the file COMMAND.COM to read-only, for example, you use this command:

    FA COMMAND.COM /R+

Additional switches are available for the FA command:

Switch	Description
/CLEAR	Clears (removes) all attributes. In other words, this command sets all attributes to the default condition, which is off (–).
/P	Pauses after each screen is displayed. This option is useful when you are displaying a list of files and attributes that is longer than the screen can display.
/S	Includes files in subdirectories. Use this option when you are setting attributes for files in the current directory and all subdirectories.
/T	Reports totals (number of files whose attributes have changed) only. Use this option when you are setting attributes but do not want a listing of the files that are changed. This option causes FA to report only how many files have been changed as a result of the command.
/U	Reports unusual files (with at least one attribute set).

To display a list of all files in the current directory with at least one attribute set, enter this command:

FA /U

The results of this command appear in figure 9.1. This listing is from a hard disk's root directory. Notice that several files are set to hidden, read-only, and system. These include key files for DOS (IO.SYS and MSDOS.SYS) and Norton Diskreet Ndisks (SECRET.@#!), as well as a copy of the file created by the Norton IMAGE command (IMAGE.IDX). Most of the other files are set to the Archive status, which means that those files have not yet been backed up.

```
C:\.
    io.sys              Archive Hidden Read-only System
    msdos.sys           Archive Hidden Read-only System
    command.com         Archive
    config1.npc         Archive
    config.old          Archive
    wina20.386          Archive
    descript.ion        Archive Hidden
    config.doc          Archive
    treeinfo.ncd        Archive
    treeinfo.dt         Archive
    treeinfo.idx        Archive
    secret.@#!                  Hidden Read-only System
    arrdesk.wbm         Archive
    autoexec.nd0        Archive
    config.nd0          Archive
    autoexec.ndw        Archive
    config.ndw          Archive
    smartcan.ini        Archive
    image.idx           Archive Hidden Read-only System
    image.doc           Archive        Read-only
Paused:  ENTER=Scroll line, SPACE=Scroll screen, ESC=Quit, Any other key=Resume
```

Fig. 9.1

A list of files and their attributes.

To clear (turn off) all attribute settings for all files in a directory, use the following command:

FA /CLEAR

To set all COM files to read-only, including those in subdirectories of the current directory, use the following command:

FA *.COM /R+ /S

The FA command is a quick and easy way to display or change attributes from the DOS prompt. You have to remember the command options, however. If you prefer to set attributes interactively, you can do so with the File Find command, as described in the next section.

Changing Attributes with File Find

Like the FA command, the File Find command contains options that enable you to examine and change file attributes. With File Find, you set these attributes interactively from a menu. This section describes how to use File Find to set file attributes. For more information on File Find, see Chapter 25 on finding files.

When you enter FILEFIND from the DOS prompt or the Norton main screen, the File Find dialog box appears (see fig. 9.2).

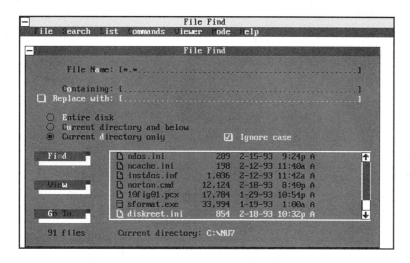

Fig. 9.2

The File Find
dialog box.

This screen contains several areas in which to enter information on setting file attributes. You enter in the File Name text box the files you want to affect. If, for example, you want to set attributes for all files named *.COM, enter the file specification ***.COM** in the File Name field.

When you set file attributes, you do not place any information in the Containing field or Replace With field. You use the radio buttons beneath Replace With to specify whether the files to be set are on the Entire Disk, the Current Directory and Below, or the Current Directory Only. The Ignore Case option is not relevant for setting file attributes.

To display the files that will be affected, select Find, which begins the search process. The Find button then changes to Stop. If you have a slow computer and a large hard disk, a search of the entire disk may take a long time. As files that match criteria are found, those files are listed in the file list box. To stop a search, choose Stop.

NOTE

The way that the program displays the files in the list box of the File Find dialog box is controlled by the **S**et List Display option, accessed from the **L**ist pull-down menu in the menu bar at the top of the screen. To display the format shown in figure 9.2, choose the **L**ist option from the menu bar and then choose the **S**et List Display option or press Ctrl+F to access the List Display dialog box. Then select Name, Size, **D**ate and Attributes.

The List Display dialog box is shown in figure 9.3. At the top of this dialog box are five List Format options. These options allow you to choose what information about the displayed files will be listed. The following options are available:

Name, Size, **D**ate and Attributes

Name and Date/**T**ime

Name and **S**ize

Name and **A**ttributes

Name

When you choose the Name and **A**ttributes option and then choose **O**K, the files in the list box will be displayed showing name and attributes. At the bottom of the List Display dialog box, you can also choose the order in which files will appear in the list box. Sort Criterion enables you to choose from the following options:

Unsorted

Name

Extension

Dat**e** & Time

Size

You can also choose whether the sorted files should be listed in Ascending or Descending order.

To specify attributes for a particular file, first highlight that file name in the list box by using the Tab key and the up- and down-arrow keys, or by clicking on the file name. Then open the Commands pull-down menu. From this menu, choose the Set Attributes option. The Change Attributes dialog box appears (see fig. 9.4). In this box, choose **F**or *filename* to set the attributes for the highlighted file in the file list (in this example, DISKREET.INI). To set the attributes for the entire list of files that match the search criteria, select For Entire File List.

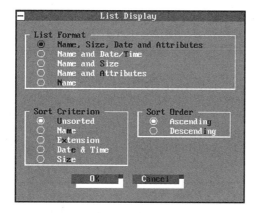

Fig. 9.3

The List Display dialog box.

Fig. 9.4

The Change Attributes dialog box.

The bottom half of the Change Attributes dialog box contains four options: **A**rchive, **R**ead Only, **H**idden, and **S**ystem. These options refer to the four attributes you can set for a file. A dark box next to the attribute name means that nothing is set, a white box means that the attribute is cleared, and a check indicates that the attribute is set. You can specify the attributes with any of the following methods:

■ Use the hot key to select the attribute (**A**rchive, **R**ead Only, **H**idden, and/or **S**ystem).

■ Use the arrow keys to highlight your choice; then press the space bar to lock in your choice.

■ If you are using a mouse, point to the attribute and click to set it.

Choose **OK** to save your changes; to cancel your changes, choose **Ca**n-cel. After you make all your selections and choose **OK**, another dialog box appears, informing you that the requested attributes are set.

If you chose to set attributes only for the single matching file and you choose the **S**et Attributes option again, the single file name listed in the Change Attributes dialog box will be the next file that matches the search criteria.

The File Find command contains a number of other options not described in this chapter. For more information about File Find, see Chapter 25.

Summary

If you set file attributes with the File Attributes (FA) or File Find command, you can protect your files from being accidentally erased or overwritten. Either method is a simple and easy way to protect files. Neither of these file-protection schemes requires any memory-resident program to be active to protect the files, because both schemes are built into DOS.

This chapter concludes Part II of this book. These chapters form the core of a protection plan for your data (along with a backup plan). If you use the information contained in Part II, you decrease the need for the recovery techniques described in the following chapters. However, Murphy's Law seems to reign, so no matter how hard you try, there may be a time when you must recover information that was accidentally or maliciously erased or lost. To learn how Norton Utilities has provided state-of-the-art recovery techniques, turn to Part III, "Basic Recovery Techniques." The first chapter of Part III explores strategies for using the UnErase command.

Basic Recovery Techniques

PART

III

OUTLINE

Unerasing Files and Directories

T he inevitable happens! You implemented procedures to protect your files, as described in Part II. Then you accidentally erased some important files. Or, for some reason, a file on your hard disk cannot be read. Who you gonna call? File Busters?

You may not need a professional file-recovery specialist. With the information in this chapter and Norton Utilities 7, the prospects are good that you can recover erased or damaged files from your disk by yourself.

Part II, "Protecting Your Files," covered preventive measures for protecting the information on your disk. At times, however, the best prevention does not work. For example, on a floppy disk that was not protected by SmartCan, you might use the DEL command accidentally, when you meant to use DIR. The consequences of these commands are quite different. The DIR command displays a list of files, and the DEL command deletes files.

The most common way to lose files is probably through accidental erasing. Accidental formatting is another common cause of information loss. Some information losses, however, are hard to control. You can lose files, for example, through excessive fragmentation on disk. Furthermore, the magnetic image on your disk can be damaged if the magnetic field weakens.

Part III shows you how to recover lost information and describes Norton UnErase (unerases files or directories), UnFormat (recovers disks that were formatted), Norton Disk Doctor (searches for and corrects file problems on disk), Disk Tools (fixes various disk problems), Rescue Disk (creates a rescue disk containing important recovery information and programs), and File Fix (fixes dBASE, 1-2-3, WordPerfect, Symphony, and compatible application program files). If these automatic techniques are not sufficient to recover your data, Part IV includes information on advanced techniques for data recovery, such as Manual UnErase techniques and Disk Editor. Before you learn how to use these Norton data-recovery commands, however, you may want to review the information in Chapter 3, "Understanding How Disks Work."

This chapter describes one of the most widely known Norton programs, the UnErase utility. This utility has likely saved computer users worldwide millions of dollars in time and energy that would have been used to recover files and directories manually.

Using UnErase

When a file is erased on your disk, only the information in the disk's directory is actually deleted (see Chapter 3). The contents of the file still remain on disk for a while—until that area of the disk is reused by another file. If the file space used by an erased file has not been used by a subsequent write to disk, you can usually recover the file with the UnErase command. Because an erased file can have its contents overwritten at any time, you must decide as soon as possible that a file must be unerased. You should have no problem unerasing a file immediately after the file has been erased. If you create one or more files after erasing a file, however, the original file may no longer be unerasable.

T I P   To protect an unerased file for a period of time, use the SmartCan utility described in Chapter 5. To prevent certain important files from being erased, use the Disk Monitor utility, covered in Chapter 6.

To use the UnErase utility, choose UnErase from the Commands list in the Norton main screen or enter **UNERASE** at the DOS prompt. When you begin UnErase, the program searches in the current directory for all files that can be unerased. If the program finds erased files, the file names (as far as UnErase can figure out, without the first character) are

displayed. If, for example, the file README.BAT has been erased, the
UnErase program reports that the file ?EADME.BAT can be recovered.
Figure 10.1 shows the UnErase menu and a list of erased files that are
candidates for unerasing.

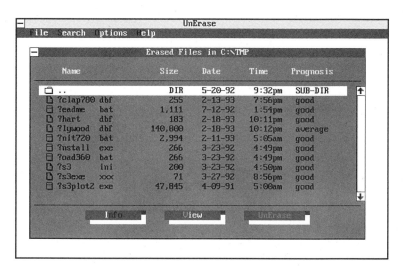

Fig. 10.1

Listing potential
files to unerase.

UnErase provides a prognosis of the likelihood that these files can be
unerased successfully. The possible prognoses are excellent, good,
average, and poor.

> To give UnErase a good chance of recovering files, particularly those
> that were in existence when you booted your computer, make sure
> that you place the IMAGE command in your AUTOEXEC.BAT file. For
> more information about the Image program, see Chapter 4.
>
> T I P

To choose which file to unerase, highlight the file name and choose
UnErase. If you choose to unerase the file ?EADME.BAT, for example,
you see the dialog box in figure 10.2, which asks you for the first letter
in the file's name.

To complete the process, press R to unerase the file README.BAT. You
return to the screen shown in figure 10.1, where you can choose other
files to unerase.

Fig. 10.2

Supplying the
first letter of an
erased file's
name.

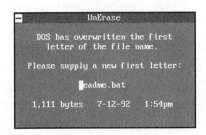

If a file cannot be unerased automatically, you see a message like the
one in figure 10.3. In this case, you can use the **S**earch For **L**ost Names
option (see the section "The UnErase Search Menu" later in this chapter), or you may need to use the Manual UnErase procedure discussed
in Chapter 16.

Fig. 10.3

A message telling
you that a file
cannot be
unerased.

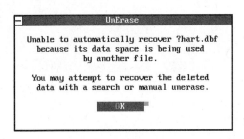

To locate files in other directories, you can go to another directory
from the current directory by using the following procedure. The first
entry listed in figure 10.1 is directory information. If you highlight the
parent directory listing (shown on-screen as . .) and press Enter or
double-click, you go to the preceding directory—in this example, the
root directory—where a list of all directories appears. Then you can
highlight another directory name, press Enter (or click), and go to another directory to look for more files to unerase. As you see in the next
section, you can use UnErase to recover directories also.

T I P   If a file or directory cannot be unerased or is unerased only partially,
you still may be able to recover portions of the file or directory by
using Disk Editor (see Chapter 17). Always try to use the automatic
UnErase techniques to erase files and directories before resorting to
the more complicated DISKEDIT command. Your chance of successfully unerasing a directory or file depends mostly on whether you
have created files that have overwritten the disk space used by the
directory or file.

The **Info** option in the Erased Files dialog box (refer to fig. 10.1) enables you to display information about the currently highlighted file. For example, figure 10.4 shows information about the file ?hart.dbf. This information includes the time and date the file was created or last changed, the file's size, and the file's attributes. For example, the file in figure 10.4 was created on February 13, 1993, at 7:56 p.m. Its size was 255 bytes, and it had the archive attribute set. (See Chapter 9 for information about file attributes.) The Information dialog box also gives you information about the likelihood that an unerase for this file will be successful. In this case, the prognosis for unerasing is poor. If you cannot unerase the file by using the automatic UnErase technique, the information about the starting cluster and the clusters needed can be helpful in manual unerasing (see Chapter 16).

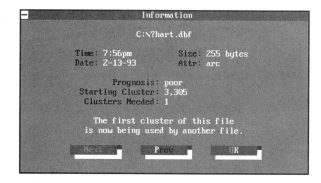

Fig. 10.4

The Information dialog box.

As you view an Information dialog box for an erased file, you can go to the dialog box for the next erased file in the list by choosing **Next**. Or you can go to the dialog box for the previous file in the list by choosing **Prev**. You exit the dialog box by choosing **OK**.

The **View** option in the Erased Files dialog box enables you to view the contents of the highlighted file (see fig. 10.5). If you are not sure what a file contains—for example, if you are not sure whether it is the specific file you want to unerase, or if you can't tell by its name what kind of file it is—you can use the viewer to examine the contents of the file to determine whether you want to unerase it. For example, you can tell by the contents of the current file being viewed that this is obviously an AUTOEXEC.BAT file.

If the file being viewed is a program file (such as an EXE file or a COM file), the contents may look like gibberish. If the file is a program application file, such as a 1-2-3 file or WordPerfect file, the file may look as though it contains a number of strange characters, as well as some phrases you can recognize. The purpose of the viewer is to help you find something in the file that can help you decide what kind of file it is and what the original file name was.

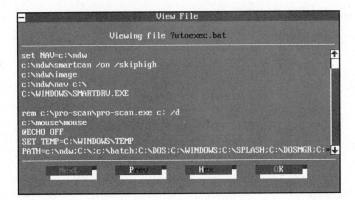

Fig. 10.5

Viewing an
erased file.

For some files, particularly program files, it may make sense to view them in hexadecimal format by choosing **H**ex in the View File dialog box. This format displays the contents of the file as hexadecimal numbers—numbers whose digits range from 0 to F. Although a display of hexadecimal numbers may not seem useful to the average person, certain patterns of these numbers can give clues that reveal the source of the file to a programmer. While you view the file, you go to the next or previous file in the erased file list by choosing **N**ext or **P**rev. Choose **O**K to exit the viewer and return to the erased file list.

Unerasing a Directory

Along with erased files, erased directories show in the UnErase list (if any exist), but instead of a number appearing in the Size column, the word DIR appears. Figure 10.6 contains information about an erased directory named TEMP. Its name in the list is ?EMP, and under the Size column, the directory is listed as DIR. To unerase this directory, highlight its name and choose the UnErase option.

If the directory can be unerased, you are prompted to enter the first letter of its name. After the directory is unerased, you can go to that directory by clicking its name to see whether the directory contains any files that can be unerased. Unerasing the directory does not automatically unerase files which were in that directory. You must specifically unerase files in the directory after you have unerased the directory itself.

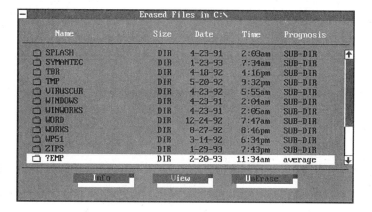

Name	Size	Date	Time	Prognosis
SPLASH	DIR	4-23-91	2:03am	SUB-DIR
SYMANTEC	DIR	1-23-93	7:34am	SUB-DIR
TBR	DIR	4-18-92	4:16pm	SUB-DIR
TMP	DIR	5-20-92	9:32pm	SUB-DIR
VIRUSCUR	DIR	4-23-92	5:55am	SUB-DIR
WINDOWS	DIR	4-23-91	2:04am	SUB-DIR
WINWORKS	DIR	4-23-91	2:05am	SUB-DIR
WORD	DIR	12-24-92	7:47am	SUB-DIR
WORKS	DIR	8-27-92	8:46pm	SUB-DIR
WP51	DIR	3-14-92	6:34pm	SUB-DIR
ZIPS	DIR	1-29-93	7:43pm	SUB-DIR
?EMP	DIR	2-20-93	11:34am	average

Erased Files in C:\

Info   View   UnErase

Fig. 10.6

Selecting a
directory to
unerase.

> After recovering a directory, you should run Norton Disk Doctor
> (NDD), as described in Chapter 12, to make sure that your disk does
> not contain any lost clusters or other logical problems.
>
> **T I P**

Using the UnErase Menus

As mentioned in previous sections, you can use the UnErase command
to erase files displayed in the Erased Files dialog box. Notice a menu
bar at the top of the UnErase screen. This menu bar gives you a number of other options to use when you unerase files. To display one of
the pull-down menus, press Alt plus the first letter of the menu name
(such as Alt+F for File), or just click the menu name.

The **Help** menu accesses the Norton Help system, which was described
in Chapter 1. The following sections cover the other menu selections.

The UnErase File Menu

The File menu at the top of the UnErase screen provides options for
listing, selecting, and naming files (see fig. 10.7). Notice the shortcut
keys beside some of the options. You can choose the corresponding
option from the UnErase screen without opening the File menu. To
choose the View Current Directory option, for example, press Alt+C.

You cannot choose options when they appear in parentheses or grayed (dimmed). In figure 10.7, the Rename option appears grayed because no file to be unerased has been chosen yet. If you highlight a file name for a restored (unerased) file, Rename becomes available and appears on the list either without parentheses or in the normal color for menu items.

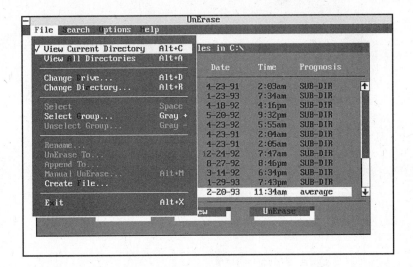

Fig. 10.7

The UnErase **F**ile menu.

The following sections describe the File menu options.

Specifying the Drive and Directory

The View **C**urrent Directory option in the File menu displays a list of all erased files in the current directory. This list includes the file name (with a question mark as the first character), date, time, and prognosis for recovery. Use this option when you want to find a file in the directory to unerase.

The View **A**ll Directories option displays a list of all erased files in all directories on the current disk. Erased files are listed by directory in the UnErase list. You can highlight and unerase files in this list. Use this option if you want to unerase files in a number of directories, or when you are not sure which directory contains the files you want to unerase.

Choose Change **D**rive to display a list of erased files on another drive. This option also displays a list of available drives, from which you can choose the drive to view. To display the erased files in another directory, choose Change Directory. A list of directories is displayed, from which you can choose the directory you want to view.

Selecting Files and Groups

To select an individual file to unerase, highlight the file name and choose the **S**elect option from the **F**ile menu. You can choose **S**elect only if a file name is highlighted in the UnErase list. The file name otherwise appears in parentheses or grayed, which means that you cannot choose the file then. Another way to select an individual file is to highlight the file name and press the space bar. After you select a file, triangles appear on both sides of the file name in the UnErase list of files.

Sometimes you may want to unerase a group of files simultaneously. For this purpose, choose Select **G**roup from the **F**ile menu. You are prompted to enter a file specification for the files to select. If you type ***.G***, for example, you select all files with extensions beginning with the letter G. Triangles appear on each side of each selected file name. You also can press the gray + key (on your numeric keypad) to invoke the Select **G**roup option. After you select the files to unerase, choose the UnErase option. You then are prompted to enter the first character of each file name in your selection list.

If the group you selected includes some files that you don't want to unerase, you can unselect the group by choosing the **U**nselect Group option from the **F**ile menu or by pressing the gray – key on your numeric keypad. You then are prompted to enter a file specification. If you type ***.GBK**, for example, all files now selected with the extension GBK are unselected, and the triangles at the sides of those names disappear.

Changing the Name of an Unerased File

If a file in the UnErase list is recovered, you can rename that file by highlighting its file name and choosing the Re**n**ame option. You are prompted to enter a new name for the file.

Specifying the Target Location for the Unerased File

The UnErase **T**o option on the **F**ile menu unerases and saves files to another disk drive. After you choose UnErase **T**o, you are prompted to choose the drive name where you want the file to be copied as the file is unerased. To activate the UnErase **T**o option, you must highlight a file name that can be unerased.

If you want to append additional, unerased information to a recovered or existing file, you can use the **A**ppend To option. First unerase a file and then choose **A**ppend To. The Manual UnErase dialog box appears.

In this dialog box, the file you just unerased is designated as the starting point for any other clusters you might want to add with the Manual UnErase features. See Chapter 16 for specific information about using Manual UnErase.

Advanced Unerasing

Two options are available for files that require special unerasing treatment. The **M**anual UnErase option in the **F**ile menu unerases a file that you cannot unerase automatically with the UnErase program. Usually, files with a poor prognosis cannot be recovered automatically (see Chapters 16 and 17 for advanced recovery techniques). Create **F**ile creates a new file by searching for erased clusters and building a new file from unerased material on disk. This process is similar to a Manual UnErase (see Chapter 16) except that it creates a new file instead of simply unerasing erased space.

The UnErase Search Menu

With the UnErase **S**earch menu, you can specify criteria to use in searching for erased files (see fig. 10.8). You can search for the kind of file (text, dBASE, 1-2-3, Symphony, and so on), for files containing a text string, or for file names that may not appear on the UnErase list, such as files in erased subdirectories. You can also specify searches within a range of clusters on the disk.

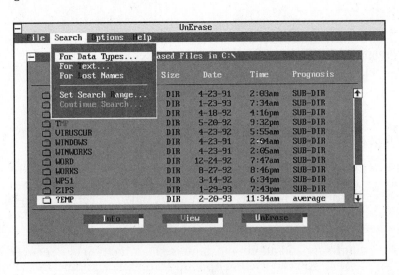

Fig. 10.8

The UnErase **S**earch menu.

The UnErase Search menu options are described in the following sections.

Searching for Specific Data Types

You use the For **D**ata Types option in the **S**earch menu to search the disk for normal ASCII text files, dBASE-type files, Lotus 1-2-3-type files, or Symphony-type files. After you choose the For **D**ata Types option, UnErase displays the Search for Data Types dialog box. In this dialog box, you specify which file types you want to find. Choose **N**ormal Text, **L**otus 1-2-3 and Symphony, **d**BASE, or Othe**r** Data. Then choose **O**K or Cancel. After you finish the search, the files listed in the UnErase list are the types you selected.

A text search can find erased files containing a certain *string* of characters. When you choose For **T**ext in the **S**earch menu, UnErase displays the Search for Text dialog box, where you can specify the text you want to find. If, for instance, you are looking for files that contain information about the 1992 budget, type **1992 Budget** as your text string and press Enter. Choose the **I**gnore Case check box option if you want to find this text in uppercase, lowercase, or any combination of uppercase and lowercase (the default). To match the case of the text that you typed in the dialog box, deselect the **I**gnore Case check box option.

After the program finishes the search, the files listed in the UnErase list are those that contain the text you specified.

Finding Lost Names

The For **L**ost Names option in the **S**earch menu searches for file names that usually don't appear in the UnErase list, such as erased files that have been part of an erased directory. If these lost file names are listed in the UnErase list, you can unerase them, as you can any other files. When you choose this option, UnErase immediately begins a search of the specified drives and directories and puts in the UnErase list any names that are found.

Specifying the Search Range

You can tell UnErase which clusters to search by choosing Set Search **R**ange from the **S**earch menu. You are asked to enter the beginning and ending cluster number. This procedure may save time if you have a large disk.

Continuing an Interrupted Search

If you stopped a search by pressing Esc—for example, when searching the entire disk for lost names—you can continue searching from the point where you stopped. Choose Continue Search from the Search menu to continue the search.

The UnErase Options Menu

The UnErase Options menu enables you to choose a sort order to use for the file names in the UnErase list. You may choose also to include nonerased (all) files in the list. Figure 10.9 shows the Options menu.

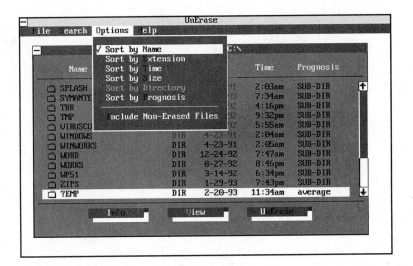

Fig. 10.9

The UnErase Options menu.

From the list of options, you may choose to list files in sorted order by file name (default), extension, time, size, or prognosis. You can use the Sort by Directory option only if you chose earlier the View All Directories option from the UnErase File menu. You may choose also to include nonerased files in the list. You may want to have these files listed for using the Rename or Append To option from the File menu.

Summary

This chapter described how to use Norton UnErase to recover files and directories that have been erased. Usually, if the file space on disk has not been overwritten, the UnErase command can automatically recover the erased file or directory. If, for some reason, you cannot unerase a file with this program, you need to move to Part IV, which covers advanced recovery techniques.

Unformatting Disks

I t is about the scariest disaster that can happen to your hard disk—it has been accidentally formatted! All your data is in danger of being lost; your programs, reports, databases, and spreadsheets are in a never-never land, the purgatory of bits and bytes. Like a paramedic, Norton Utilities can almost magically bring your files and programs back to life. If you took precautions to keep your disk healthy by using some of the measures outlined in Part II of this book, your hard disk has a good chance of being revived.

This chapter describes techniques for recovering a hard disk when the IMAGE (or MIRROR) file has been created (see Chapter 4), as well as techniques to use when the IMAGE or MIRROR files have not been created.

Recovering a Formatted Hard Disk

If you planned ahead and issued the Image command recently, you will have a much easier time recovering your data. However, even if you formatted your hard disk and do not have an IMAGE.DAT file, you may be able to recover the data.

> **CAUTION:** If your hard disk has just been formatted, proceed with care. Do not write new information to the hard disk before you attempt to perform a recovery.

To recover data from a formatted hard disk, follow these steps:

1. Boot the computer from a floppy disk, using the same version of DOS that was on the hard disk before it was formatted.

2. If your boot floppy disk does not contain the UnFormat command, place a disk containing that command in the floppy disk drive.

3. From the disk containing the UnFormat command (drive A, for example), enter the following command:

   UNFORMAT *d*:

   The *d*: parameter is the name of the disk to unformat. If you know that you used the Image command to create a recovery information file, use this command:

   UNFORMAT *d*: /IMAGE

   If you know that you used the MIRROR command (a command similar to Norton's Image command and available in DOS 5.0 and later versions) to create a recovery information file, enter this command:

   UNFORMAT *d*: /MIRROR

An explanation of the UnFormat procedure appears on-screen (see fig. 11.1). Choose **Q**uit if you want to cancel the procedure. If you choose **C**ontinue, you are prompted to select the drive to unformat (see fig. 11.2). Use the arrow keys or the mouse to select the drive and then choose **OK** to continue. If you don't want to unformat, choose **C**ancel.

You are then asked whether the disk to be unformatted used the program IMAGE.EXE or MIRROR.COM to save recovery information (see fig. 11.3). Choose **Y**es if you know that IMAGE.DAT or MIRROR.FIL was saved or if you are not sure. (If you choose **Y**es but the program does not find either of these files, the UnFormat process that occurs is the one described in the section "Unformatting without IMAGE or MIRROR Information" later in this chapter.) The next section describes the UnFormat process that occurs if IMAGE or MIRROR information is available.

If you know for sure that no IMAGE.DAT file is on the disk, choose **N**o. If you choose **N**o, see the section "Unformatting without Image or MIRROR Information" for instructions on completing the UnFormat process.

Fig. 11.1

The UnFormat
dialog box.

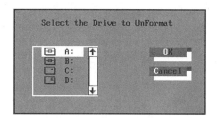

Fig. 11.2

Selecting the
drive to
unformat.

Fig. 11.3

The dialog box
where you
indicate whether
IMAGE or
MIRROR informa-
tion exists.

Recovering with IMAGE or MIRROR Information

At this point in the recovery procedure, Norton gives you another chance to cancel the UnFormat command (see fig. 11.4). If you answer **Yes** in this verification dialog box, the unformatting process begins.

The UnFormat program begins to look for the IMAGE.DAT and IMAGE.BAK (or MIRROR.FIL or MIRROR.BAK) information on the disk. A graphic may appear on-screen with the following message:

```
Searching for IMAGE info...
```

When the IMAGE information is found, a message appears like the one shown in figure 11.5. If two versions of the IMAGE or MIRROR information (one named IMAGE.BAK or MIRROR.BAK) are found, as in this example, a message tells you that two versions have been found. You may choose to use the most recent version (choose **R**ecent) or the previous version (choose **P**revious). If the most recent IMAGE.DAT (or MIRROR.FIL) information is not usable (perhaps you ran the Image program after the disk had been formatted), you may want to use the previous version—the IMAGE.BAK (or MIRROR.BAK) information. If you decide not to continue the UnFormat process, choose **C**ancel.

Fig. 11.4

The UnFormat verification box.

Fig. 11.5

The message displayed after UnFormat finds IMAGE.DAT.

After you select the IMAGE version you want, another message asks whether you are sure that you want to restore the recovery information (see fig. 11.6). Answer **Y**es to continue or **N**o to cancel. If you choose **Y**es, you are prompted to choose between a full or partial restoration. Choosing **P**artial restores only parts of the system area, including the boot record and the file allocation table. Usually, you choose **F**ull (see fig. 11.7).

CAUTION: Use the **P**artial restore option only when you use the UnFormat command to restore a damaged portion of your disk, such as the boot record. This is an uncommon option to use, and it is made available primarily for persons with a great deal of experience with the disk structure.

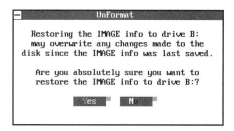

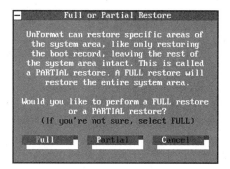

Fig. 11.6

Choosing to restore the recovery information.

Fig. 11.7

Selecting full or partial recovery.

Finally, the restoration begins. The drive may "churn" as the information is recovered. The recovery process generally takes only a few minutes. When the recovery is finished, a message tells you that the drive has been restored successfully to its previous state (see fig. 11.8).

After the recovery finishes, you still may have some problems with a few files—those that were changed since you issued the last Image command. If so, UnFormat suggests that you run Norton Disk Doctor (NDD) to clear up any additional problems. These problems may include sectors that remain unallocated to files. The NDD command often can sort out these problems and recover the remaining files. To run Norton Disk Doctor, enter this command at the DOS prompt:

NDD *d:* /QUICK

Fig. 11.8

The message
indicating a
successful
recovery.

Here *d*: is the drive name of the disk just restored. If the recovery was
performed on the disk from which your computer boots, reboot your
computer after running NDD. See Chapter 12 for more information on
Norton Disk Doctor.

> **T I P**   The best way to learn how to use UnFormat is on a practice disk—
> when all you have to lose is some time. Place several files on a for-
> matted disk. You may even want to include a few subdirectories.
> Now reformat the disk, using the Save Image Info option from the
> Safe Format dialog box (see Chapter 4). After you format the test
> disk, run the UnFormat program and see how it can restore the disk.
> This procedure gives you some experience and confidence for the
> time when you really may need to restore your disk.

You can run the UnFormat command from a network to unformat a disk
on your local computer, but UnFormat will not unformat a network
drive.

Unformatting without IMAGE or MIRROR Information

If you didn't prepare the disk to be unformatted—that is, you did not
use Norton's Image command, the DOS MIRROR command, or Norton's
Safe Format command—Norton Utilities may be able to help, but the
recovery requires more work.

 The UnFormat command often can help you recover files from a hard disk that has been formatted. You cannot, however, use UnFormat to restore a floppy disk that has been reformatted using a regular DOS format. When a hard disk is reformatted, only the system area is overwritten, not the entire disk. When a floppy disk is formatted with DOS FORMAT, the entire disk is overwritten.

Begin the UnFormat program, as described earlier in this chapter. If any chance exists that IMAGE.DAT or MIRROR.FIL is on disk, allow the UnFormat command to search for it. If you cannot find IMAGE.DAT or MIRROR.FIL, you must attempt to recover your data without it.

The UnFormat command attempts to recover as many files as possible. First the program must search the disk, looking for directory and file names. This search may take some time.

UnFormat usually can recover all directories and all files in those directories except for the files in the root directory. Some versions of DOS (COMPAQ 3.1 and AT&T 2.11) overwrite information thoroughly with a format, and recovery is not possible.

When the UnFormat command finishes what it can do, your disk should contain directories named DIR0000, DIR0001, DIR0002, and so on. The original names of the directories are lost, but files are grouped in the new directories as they were in the original directories. All Lotus 1-2-3 files are in one directory, for example, and all WordPerfect files are in another directory. If you have many kinds of files in one directory, the recovery process can be more difficult because it may not be easy to identify the original file name.

NOTE Only upper-level directory names are lost. If you have a subdirectory, its name will be recovered.

You can retrieve the original names of the directories in one of two ways. If you are using a version of DOS earlier than 3.0, you need to make new directories, copy the files from each recovered directory into each new directory, and then delete the old directories and files.

If you are working with DOS 3.0 or a later version, you can use a second, much easier method. This technique uses the Norton Change Directory (NCD) command (see Chapter 23). Use the NCD command to change the name of the directories.

To decide what to name your directories, look at the files contained in the directory. If, for instance, you see that the 1-2-3-type files are in a directory, you can easily conclude that this directory should be LOTUS.

After you decide what the names of the directories should be (for example, DIR0000 is WP51, DIR0001 is LOTUS, and so on), you can change the directory names.

After you rename the upper-level directories on your disk, run Norton Disk Doctor (NDD) to clear up problems with the recovered files (see Chapter 12 for more about NDD). These problems usually are unallocated sectors—portions of the disk that have not been assigned properly to a file or free space. Use the following command to run the NDD program:

    NDD C:/QUICK

The /QUICK switch tells NDD to test the system area of the disk only—not the entire disk. (The system area is where the unallocated sectors' information is located.)

If your disk is supposed to be bootable but is not, use Norton Disk Doctor to make the disk bootable. See the section "Making a Disk Bootable" in Chapter 13.

The UnFormat command is not perfect, but it restores all the information that was not erased during the formatting process. One of the major problems is that all the files in the root directory, such as the AUTOEXEC.BAT and CONFIG.SYS files, are lost. You must reconstruct these files. If you do not have backup copies of the files, you must rebuild them in a text editor.

Using UnFormat To Recover from a Virus Attack

The UnFormat command can also help you recover from some versions of destruction brought about by a computer virus. If your disk has become unusable because of a virus attack, use the UnFormat command to attempt recovery, just as if the disk had been formatted. If you have a recent copy of IMAGE.DAT or MIRROR.FIL on your disk, your chances for recovery are good.

Summary

Norton Utilities has turned a frightening experience into a simple procedure. Working together, the Image and UnFormat commands can help you protect your disks against accidental formatting. Even if you have not used Image or DOS MIRROR to help protect your disk, Norton is often still able to recover most or all information from your formatted disk. This chapter described the techniques used for recovering disks in both situations.

The next chapter shows a different sort of recovery technique, one that can help correct problems with the way files are stored on disk, and can help detect and correct other problems with your disk before it becomes too late. Turn to Chapter 12 to learn about Norton Disk Doctor.

Diagnosing and Treating Disks with Disk Doctor

I nformation stored on disk is dependent on the reliability of the physical disk to hold magnetic signals; these signals contain the 0s and 1s that make up the bits used to store the file. Information storage also relies on DOS's system area to keep track of where all the bits and pieces of all the files on disk are stored.

Maintaining the integrity of the data on disk is a Herculean task. How millions (sometimes billions) of pieces of information can be reliably stored on a disk is a real mystery to most people.

Unfortunately, problems sometimes occur. A small flaw may be on the disk where the magnetic coating is not thick enough. Information stored in this location is OK for a while, but eventually the disk loses some of its magnetic image. Files may also be broken into so many pieces on disk (called fragmentation) that the file allocation table (FAT) somehow loses information about what cluster belongs to what file.

The FAT may think that the same cluster is being used by two files at the same time. Unstable software that does not properly close files or that manipulates file information outside the standard DOS guidelines can sometimes cause this situation.

When these kinds of problems begin to happen, they can often be easily solved if they are caught in time. Fortunately, Norton Disk Doctor can help locate and correct such problems.

Using detailed knowledge about the structure of the boot record, the file allocation table, and the system area, Norton Disk Doctor can often figure out where problems exist on a disk and what can be done to eliminate those problems. Whenever any problem related to reading or writing files to disk occurs (for example, you get a DOS message that indicates Unable to read disk in drive A), you can use Disk Doctor to diagnose the problem and usually restore the disk to health.

Diagnosing and Doctoring Disks

You can begin Norton Disk Doctor (NDD) from the Norton main screen or by entering **NDD** at the DOS prompt. (For details on using the Norton main screen, see Chapter 1, "Norton Utilities Basics.") To begin from the main screen, use the up- and down-arrow keys to highlight Disk Doctor in the Commands list and press Enter, or point to Disk Doctor and click twice. The Norton Disk Doctor menu appears (see fig. 12.1).

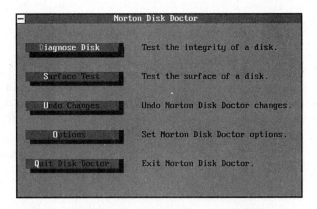

Fig. 12.1

The Norton Disk Doctor menu.

The menu contains the following choices:

Option	Description
Diagnose Disk	Examines your disk to check the integrity of the information stored on it
Surface Test	Tests the surface of the disk for existing or potential read/write problems
Undo Changes	Undoes any changes made by NDD and returns your disk to its original state
Options	Sets certain options for the program
Quit Disk Doctor	Ends the NDD program

If you enter the NDD command with no switches, the command operates in interactive mode; you choose the options you want from the menu. Or you can use this command syntax from the DOS prompt:

NDD [*d*:][*d*:][*switches*]

The *d*: designations are disk drive names; you can specify more than one drive. (Norton does not mention any limit.)

The following switches may be used with NDD:

Switch	Description
/COMPLETE or /C	Tests for bad cylinders on the disk and tests the partition table, boot record, root directory, and lost clusters.
/QUICK or /Q	Omits the test for bad cylinders but tests the partition table, boot record, root directory, and lost clusters.
/R:*file*	Instructs NDD to write to the designated *file* a report about the results of NDD's testing. Use with /QUICK or /COMPLETE.
/RA:*file*	Instructs NDD to write a report about the results of NDD's testing and append the report to a designated *file* (instead of making a new file). Use with /QUICK or /COMPLETE.
/REBUILD	Tells NDD to try to rebuild the entire disk.
/X:*d*	Excludes drive *d* from examination.
/UNDELETE	Tells NDD to undelete a DOS partition detected in an earlier run but not undeleted at that time. When you run NDD and find an old DOS partition, for example, NDD asks whether you want to undelete the partition. If you answer no, the /UNDELETE switch enables you to try to undelete the partition later.

Details about the first four NDD options in the Norton Disk Doctor menu are covered in the next few sections.

Performing a Quick Disk Test

Disk Doctor is designed to perform a quick disk test or a series of more extensive tests. For example, to run a quick test on drive C from the DOS prompt, enter **NDD C: /Q**. This command causes Disk Doctor to examine your disk's system area for flaws in the disk's directory and file structure and to examine the disk for lost clusters. For more information on how disks are organized and how they manage data, see Chapter 3.

Using the **C**onfiguration option in the Norton main screen (see Chapter 2), you can place the quick Disk Doctor command in your AUTOEXEC.BAT file so that your disk is examined each time your computer is booted. The process usually takes less than a minute. If you do not choose to place this command in your AUTOEXEC.BAT file, you may want to perform this quick test only occasionally, or the more extensive tests discussed in the following section.

Diagnosing a Disk

The Disk Doctor **D**iagnose Disk option performs various tests on your disk to check whether you can access the stored information properly. Use **D**iagnose Disk occasionally as preventive maintenance on your hard disk. If your disk access becomes erratic—for example, you experience trouble trying to read a file or your computer no longer boots properly—use this option to diagnose the problem. **D**iagnose Disk performs more than 100 tests to analyze your disk.

NOTE   If you have never used NDD on your hard disk, you may want to perform a full test so that you can find and resolve any problems or potential problems. Afterward, using the quick test (/Q) may be enough to find most file problems. Under normal disk operation, use the NDD diagnosis about once a month.

Problems on a disk usually result from corrupted information being placed on the disk or from bad spots on the disk that cause information to be unreadable. Loss of the magnetic signal (image), for instance, can cause a bad spot. NDD tries to read information from all parts of the disk. If part of the disk cannot be read and no file is using the bad part, the problem is simple to fix. NDD marks that area as bad, and DOS then knows not to use the area.

If the bad spot is located where a file is stored, however, NDD must try to read as much of the file as possible and move the file to a safe location on disk. Then NDD marks the bad area so that it is not used again.

 NOTE Often when NDD finds a problem on disk, a prompt asks whether you want the problem to be fixed or ignored. Unless you have a specific reason not to fix a problem, let NDD try to correct it.

After you choose the **Di**agnose Disk option from the NDD menu, you see a list of possible disk drives to test (see fig. 12.2). Specify the disk drive to test by highlighting the disk drive of your choice and pressing the space bar, or by clicking with the mouse pointer. A check mark appears next to your choice. You can then choose any other disk drive to test. After you make your selections, press Enter or choose **D**iagnose to begin the test procedures. Choose **C**ancel if you don't want to diagnose the disk drives.

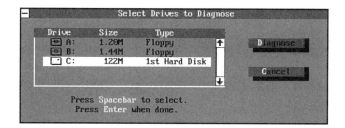

Fig. 12.2

Specifying the drives to diagnose.

Figure 12.3 shows the first test screen during a test of the hard disk. Notice the six-part test list, titled `Diagnosing drive C:`, at the top of the screen. This list contains only five parts if you are diagnosing a floppy disk, because the partition table test is not performed. As each part of the test progresses, the corresponding description for that test area is highlighted on-screen, and a blinking dot appears before the description name. When a test for an area is complete, a check mark appears next to the test description.

Information about the progress of the current test being performed appears at the bottom of the screen. In figure 12.3, a test of the file allocation tables is in progress. You can stop the test at any time by pressing Esc.

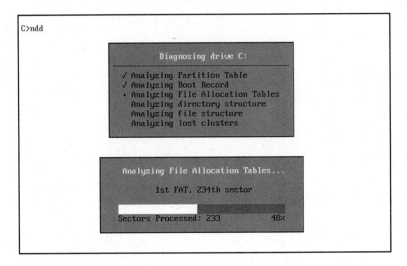

```
C>ndd
```

```
              Diagnosing drive C:

        √ Analyzing Partition Table
        √ Analyzing Boot Record
        • Analyzing File Allocation Tables
          Analyzing directory structure
          Analyzing file structure
          Analyzing lost clusters
```

```
        Analyzing File Allocation Tables...

           1st FAT, 234th sector

        Sectors Processed: 233        48%
```

Fig. 12.3

The NDD test in progress.

Norton Disk Doctor first tests to see whether bad information is located in the system area or data area of the disk. If your hard disk is partitioned into several disks (C and D, for example), the NDD partition table checks to see whether the allocation of space is properly accounted for on the drive being tested.

The tests of the boot record, file allocation table (FAT), and directory structure examine the integrity of the system information on disk. NDD determines whether the system information can be read from disk and whether the system information makes sense. In the system area of the disk, NDD reads the information and compares what has been read from disk to what should be on the disk; the process is like looking at a manuscript to see whether all the parts—the title, contents, body, and index—are there. If NDD finds that something is missing, wrong, or out of place, the program usually knows how to fix the problem. While NDD is going through the list of diagnostic tests, it may detect a problem on the disk. See the section "Dealing with a Bad Diagnosis" later in this chapter.

When testing the file allocation table, NDD analyzes the FAT to see whether available space on disk is accounted for as space being used by a file, as sectors marked as bad spots on the disk, or as free space. Space on a disk may be unaccounted for when a file is not properly saved to disk. This unaccounted space appears in the FAT as a *lost cluster*, a place on disk reserved for use by a file but never used. Lost clusters can occur when you turn off the computer or reboot it, or when the power fails while a file is open. A series of lost clusters related to one file is called a *chain*.

The file structure test examines how your files are stored on disk to make sure that the file allocation is OK. The lost clusters test looks for information about files not stored properly—a problem sometimes caused by programs that are abruptly stopped, as in a power outage.

The surface test checks for physical defects on your disk. When the list of diagnostic tests is completed, the Surface Test dialog box automatically appears (see fig. 12.4). From this dialog box, you can choose several options that determine how the test for physical defects is performed. Specify the options you want for the test (the following sections describe the options). Then press Enter or choose the **B**egin Test option to begin the test. To end the operation without testing, choose **C**ancel. To exit the test while in progress, press Esc and then select **C**ancel. To resume after pressing Esc, select **R**esume.

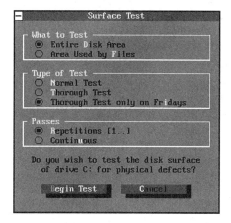

Fig. 12.4

The Surface Test dialog box.

Choosing Which Test To Run

The testing options in the What to Test section of the Surface Test dialog box tell Disk Doctor to look at the surface of the entire disk (Entire **D**isk Test) or to test only the portions of the disk occupied by files (Area Used by **F**iles). The Areas Used by **F**iles option is faster, but Entire **D**isk Test is more thorough.

Specifying the Type of Test

You can choose from three types of tests in the Type of Test section of the Surface Test dialog box. **N**ormal Test performs a quick scan of the disk. **T**horough Test tests the disk more thoroughly than the **N**ormal Test but takes twice the time. Thorough Test Only on **F**ridays combines elements of the two other tests and takes a little longer than the **N**ormal Test. The default test is Thorough Test Only on **F**ridays.

Selecting the Number of Passes

The Passes options specify how often to repeat the test or to perform the test until you press Esc. Usually, one repetition (the default) is sufficient. If intermittent problems exist, however, you may want to run the test for a number of repetitions or continuously (testing continues indefinitely until you press Esc) to try to locate the problem. To specify the number of repetitions, choose **R**epetitions and indicate a number in the field (from 1 to 999). To run the test continuously, choose Contin**u**ous. To begin the tests, choose **B**egin Test; to cancel NDD, choose **C**ancel.

Figure 12.5 shows the screen that is displayed while a surface test is in progress. The Time section tells you the estimated amount of time that it takes to perform the test and the current amount of elapsed time. The Sector section tells you what sector is currently being tested and how many clusters are on the disk.

You can see a blinking box on the disk map that occupies one block of the map. As the box progresses, it shows you which block is being tested. The Legend section tells you what the boxes on the disk map mean. For example, if the disk has a bad block, a B appears on the disk map in the location of the bad block. At the bottom of the Legend section is an indication of the size of a block. For this disk, a block is 232 sectors.

The progress graph at the bottom left shows you how much of the test has been completed. This graph also has an indicator, such as Pass 1 of 1, that tells you the number of times the test will be performed. The test in progress in figure 12.5 will be performed only once. If you had requested 10 tests, the indicator would read Pass 1 of 10, then Pass 2 of 10, and so on; it would continue until 10 different surface tests had registered.

After the test is finished, you are given the chance to print a report. See the section "Creating a Disk Doctor Report" later in this chapter. If Disk Doctor finds a problem during the surface test and you have indicated that you want NDD to prompt you before making repairs, the program gives you an opportunity to correct the problem. See the next section for more information.

Dealing with a Bad Diagnosis

While diagnosing a disk or running a surface test, NDD tells you when and if any problems are found. Usually, a report of an error on the disk includes a description of the error and a recommendation. This section illustrates some of the disk errors you may encounter while running Disk Doctor.

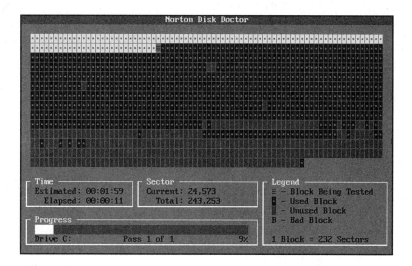

Fig. 12.5

The progress screen for the surface test.

Figure 12.6 shows an error involving the file allocation table that occurred during a diagnosis of drive B. This report tells you that the FAT copies are not the same. If you remember from Chapter 3, a physical error occurs when a physical problem with the disk exists, such as a bad spot on the disk caused by age, liquids, or some other physical damage. This physical problem is in contrast to a logical problem, which means that the disk may be physically OK but the information stored is bad. Note the error message in figure 12.6, the description of what caused the error, and the recommendation for action.

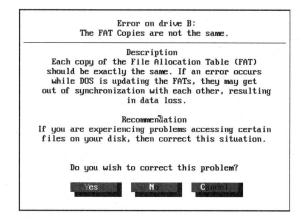

Fig. 12.6

An error message reporting a problem with the FAT.

If you encounter a physical error on the disk, first end NDD by pressing Esc or choosing Cancel, and return to the DOS prompt. Then attempt to copy all the files from the floppy disk containing the error to another disk. DO NOT WRITE ANY INFORMATION TO THE BAD DISK; writing information may make the situation worse. If you can copy all the files from the disk, you should trash or reformat the bad disk.

If you cannot copy all the files from the bad disk, run NDD again on the disk and have the program attempt to correct the problem with the FAT. If NDD is successful in correcting the disk, immediately copy all files from the disk and then trash the disk or reformat it. Do not continue to use the disk as is—even if NDD was successful in fixing it. The evidence of this problem means that the disk may be susceptible to the same problem in the future.

If NDD cannot solve the problem and you cannot copy files from the disk, turn to Part IV, "Advanced Recovery Techniques."

When NDD finds an error on a disk and you choose to allow the program to attempt a fix, NDD first gives you the option of creating an Undo file (see fig. 12.7).

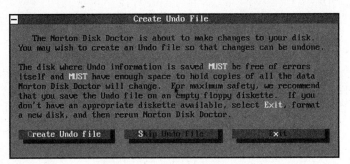

Fig. 12.7

The NDD
Create Undo File
dialog box.

An *Undo file* is a file that contains information about changes that NDD has made to a disk. When you create an Undo file, it allows you to return a disk to its original state in case something goes wrong during the time NDD is attempting to fix the disk. The Undo file must be written to a different disk from the one currently being checked. Thus, when you choose the option **C**reate Undo File, you are prompted to choose the drive where you want to save the Undo information (see fig. 12.8). If you choose **S**kip Undo File, no undo information is stored. If you choose Exit, the NDD diagnosis ends.

When a severe problem occurs, like the error shown in figure 12.6, and you choose **Y**es to correct the problem, NDD may present a solution (see fig. 12.9). The message in figure 12.9 indicates that NDD cannot fix the problem and that you should run Disk Tools to correct the problem. The Disk Tools program is described in Chapter 13.

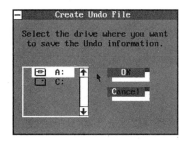

Fig. 12.8

The prompt for the drive where the Undo file will be stored.

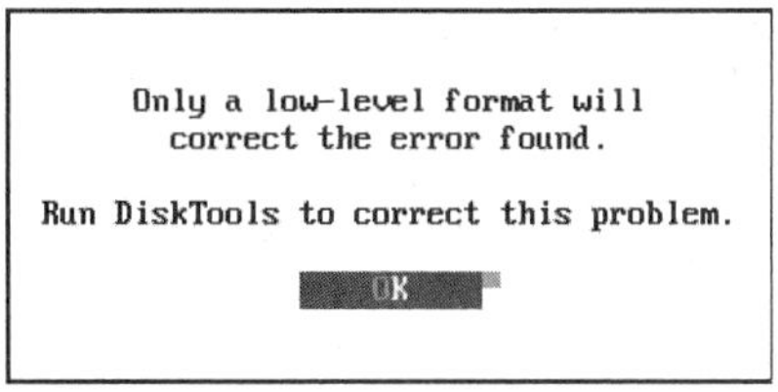

Fig. 12.9

An NDD message telling you to perform a low-level format on the defective disk.

Another solution to a FAT problem that may be reported is shown in figure 12.10. In this case, NDD recommends that the Calibrate program be run on the disk. Calibrate is discussed in Chapter 20.

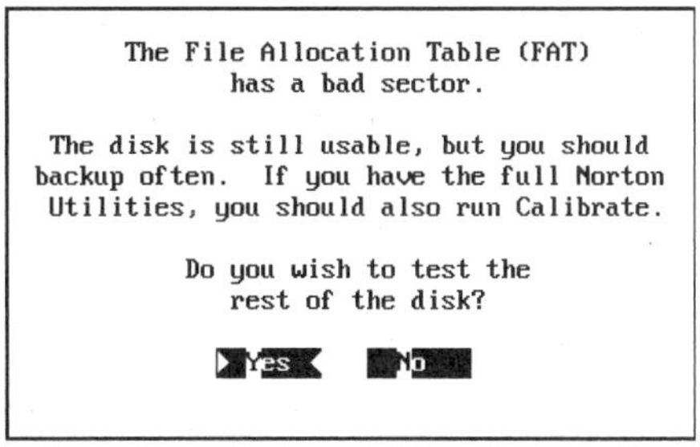

Fig. 12.10

NDD recommending that you run the Calibrate program on a defective disk.

Figure 12.11 shows an error message reported by NDD as it attempts to read the root directory. If you recall, the root directory of a disk is the area where top-level file names and directory names are stored. If the root directory cannot be read, you cannot read or access any of the files on the disk. Figure 12.11 shows that NDD can attempt to correct this problem. As in figure 12.6, you can allow NDD to attempt to correct the problem by choosing **Yes** (again, you are given the opportunity to create an Undo file). If you choose **No**, no attempt is made to correct the error, and diagnosing continues. If you choose **C**ancel, the NDD program ends without correcting this problem.

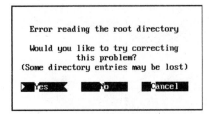

Fig. 12.11

Disk Doctor reporting an error when reading the root directory.

If the error is so severe that NDD cannot correct the problem, a message similar to the one in figure 12.12 appears. In this case, you are not even given the opportunity to tell NDD to fix the problem. You will probably not be able to read anything from a disk as severely damaged as the one that caused this error. You do not need to give up, however. You can try the Revive a Defective Diskette option in Disk Tools, as described in Chapter 13; or you can use the techniques for recovering files described in Part IV, "Advanced Recovery Techniques."

Fig. 12.12

A Disk Doctor message telling you that the disk can't be repaired.

```
The root directory on drive A:
      CAN'T be repaired.

Unable to continue testing the drive.

            OK
```

The problems previously discussed were all related to a disk diagnosis. Disk Doctor may also encounter errors when running a surface test. During the surface test, Disk Doctor reads and writes information to every sector on the disk, testing the disk's memory. This process is somewhat comparable to what happens during a format, except that the information on the disk is not destroyed. If the surface test locates an area on disk where information cannot be reliably read and written, a report like the one in figure 12.13 is generated.

In this case, cluster 137 is found to contain a bad sector. You can choose to move the data in this cluster to a safe location. Moving the data means that you can no longer use the cluster; however, the data in the file will be moved to a good cluster. Notice the message that says

        This cluster is in use by UNKNOWN.

This message means that the bad cluster is being used to store the file. It does not necessarily mean that the file is damaged. The bad sector may be in slack space. Still, you want to allow NDD to move this cluster to a safe location; then check to see whether the file is OK. If this cluster does not contain data used in a file, NDD marks, rather than moves, the cluster. Moving the data in the cluster (using **Move**) places the file information in a new cluster that is good, enabling you to try to save the file information. Marking the cluster as bad prevents new information from being written to that cluster. If you choose the **Skip** option, the cluster is not affected. If you choose **Auto**, this sector and all subsequent bad sectors found in this test are marked or moved. Choose **Cancel** to end the test.

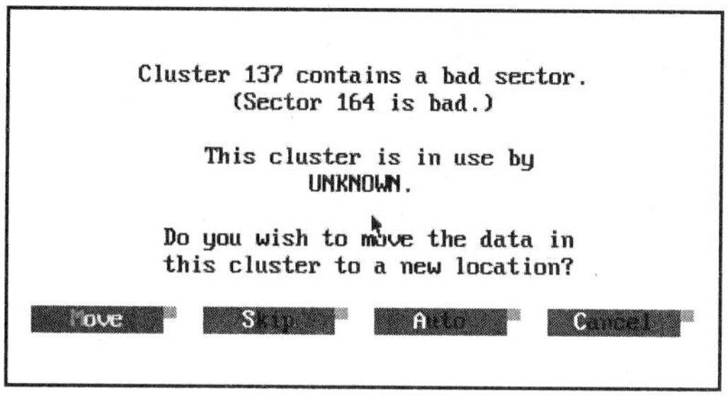

```
┌────────────────────────────────────────────────┐
│                                                │
│        Cluster 137 contains a bad sector.       │
│            (Sector 164 is bad.)                 │
│                                                │
│          This cluster is in use by              │
│                 UNKNOWN.                        │
│                                                │
│        Do you wish to move the data in          │
│        this cluster to a new location?          │
│                                                │
│    ▐ Move ▌    ▐ Skip ▌   ▐ Auto ▌   ▐ Cancel ▌ │
└────────────────────────────────────────────────┘
```

Fig. 12.13

A message telling you that a bad sector has been found.

T I P

Always check any file for which NDD finds a problem. First let NDD attempt to fix the file; then use the file to verify that it is OK. For example, if the file is a word processing file, examine it in your word processor; if the file is a spreadsheet file, look at it with your spreadsheet program.

After you have used Disk Doctor to correct problems on the disk, you are given an opportunity to create a report that summarizes information about the disk and tells what fixes were performed. The next section describes how to create and interpret a report.

Creating a Disk Doctor Report

When the disk analysis is complete, a brief summary appears on-screen (see fig. 12.14). The test results tell you that no problems were found during most of the tests, but a problem was fixed as a result of the boot record test.

You may want to produce a report about the disk test, particularly if disk problems are found. To produce a report, press Enter or choose **Report**. To end without producing a report, choose **Done**. Figure 12.15 is a sample report. Keep these reports as a record of your disk problems.

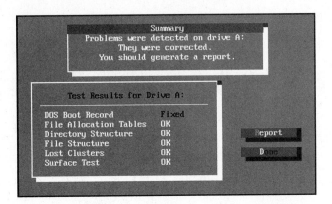

Fig. 12.14

A brief NDD
report following
a disk diagnosis.

The report's header provides the date and time of the analysis. The Disk Totals section tells about the disk's storage capacity. The Total Disk Space is the number of bytes of information the disk can hold. The User Files entry describes the file on the disk. Bad sectors are places on disk that have been found (usually by the format procedure) to be unsuitable for storing information. If you subtract from the total the number of bytes taken up by the user files and bad sectors, you get the number of bytes available on the disk.

The Logical Disk Information section of the report describes the logical parameters used to store information on the disk. The Media Descriptor gives a code for what kind of disk is used. Note the possible codes:

Code	Description
F0	1.4M 3 1/2-inch disk
F8	Hard disk
F9	1.2M 5 1/4-inch disk or 720K 3 1/2-inch disk
FD	360K 5 1/4-inch disk
FE	160K 5 1/4-inch disk
FF	320K 5 1/4-inch disk

In the example in figure 12.15, the analyzed disk is a 360K 5 1/4-inch disk. The media descriptor of FD is a hexadecimal number code.

The Physical Disk Information section includes information about how the data is physically on disk. The Drive Number tells you which drive the disk is in when analyzed. Drive number 0 refers to drive A, drive number 1 refers to drive B, and so on. In figure 12.15, the disk is analyzed in drive A (drive number 0).

```
                    Norton Disk Doctor
                    Norton Utilities 7.0
                   April  21, 1993 5:07pm

               **************************
               *  Report for Drive A:  *
               **************************

                        DISK TOTALS
          --------------------------------------------
           362,496 bytes Total Disk Space
           349,184 bytes in 22 User Files
             2,048 bytes in Bad Sectors
            11,264 bytes Available on the Disk


                  LOGICAL DISK INFORMATION
          --------------------------------------------
                Media Descriptor:  FD
                 Large Partition:  No
                        FAT Type:  12-bit
                   Total Sectors:  720
                  Total Clusters:  354
                Bytes Per Sector:  512
              Sectors Per Cluster:  2
               Bytes Per Cluster:  1,024
                  Number of FATs:  2
             First Sector of FAT:  1
       Number of Sectors Per FAT:  2
        First Sector of Root Dir:  5
    Number of Sectors in Root Dir:  7
     Maximum Root Dir File Entries:  112
        First Sector of Data Area:  12


                 PHYSICAL DISK INFORMATION
          --------------------------------------------
                    Drive Number:  0
                           Heads:  2
                       Cylinders:  40
               Sectors Per Track:  9
                   Starting Head:  0
               Starting Cylinder:  0
                 Starting Sector:  1
                     Ending Head:  1
                 Ending Cylinder:  39
                   Ending Sector:  9


                  SYSTEM AREA STATUS
          --------------------------------------------
             Invalid signature in Boot Record
                   Status: Corrected
```

Fig. 12.15

A report generated by Norton Disk Doctor.

```
                   FILE STRUCTURE STATUS
      -----------------------------------------------
         No errors in the file structure


                   SURFACE TEST STATUS
      -----------------------------------------------
                     Test Settings
                 ------------------------
                    Test:  Disk Test
               Test Type:  Daily
          Repair Setting:  Prompt before Repairing
         Passes Requested:  1
         Passes Completed:  1
            Elapsed Time:  1 minute, 34 seconds


      Error reading sector 629 in cluster 310
        Cluster 310 was used by \wamprpts.cai
           Contents relocated to cluster 344
      Status: Corrected and marked as unusable

      Error reading sector 683 in cluster 337
           Cluster in use by \nu70305.pcx
           Status: NOT Corrected. Skipped.
```

Fig. 12.15

Continued

The System Area Status section reports any problems found in the system area or the file structure. This section provides information on what problems exist and how (and whether) they are fixed. Figure 12.15 shows that the boot record was invalid but has been corrected.

Problems reported in the File Structure Status section are fixes related to cleaning up files that are cross-linked or that contain lost chains. Both conditions refer to a misallocation of clusters to a file.

The material provided in the Surface Test Status section of the report shows any problems found on the disk during the scan. Figure 12.15 shows that error reading sectors were in clusters 629 and 683. The first cluster contained information about a file; the cluster was corrected and marked as unusable. The second cluster was not corrected; the **S**kip option was chosen.

If a bad cluster is found but no information exists in that area, the cluster is marked as bad, and no file information is damaged. If the cluster contains information, as in this example, NDD tries to move as much good information as possible to a good cluster and reports that the files are moved but that they may not be fully recovered or usable.

If you discover by reading the report that NDD moved some of your files, examine those files to see whether they contain any damaged areas. You can examine word processing files in your word processor. If NDD moved program files (EXE or COM files, for example), recopy them from the original source to the disk to guarantee that the contents of the file are OK.

Performing a Surface Test Only

Instead of performing the entire suite of NDD tests, you can choose to perform only the surface test. You may want to skip the earlier tests, for instance, if you have already performed them and simply want to repeat the surface test. From the Norton Disk Doctor menu (refer to fig. 12.1), you can choose the **S**urface Test option. When you choose **S**urface Test, the Surface Test dialog box appears (refer to fig. 12.4). Choose the options you want and then begin the test. The test runs exactly as described earlier, and errors that are detected during the test are handled in the same way as previously described.

Undoing Changes

You may want to reverse any changes made after running the NDD program on your disk. For example, you can no longer use a moved file, and you want to try some other way, such as using Disk Editor, to recover the file. As NDD makes changes to your disk, the program stores the information about those changes in a file called NDDUNDO.DAT. If you choose the Undo Changes option from the NDD menu, the disk is restored to its original condition.

Setting Disk Doctor Options

If you choose Options from the NDD menu, you see the Norton Disk Doctor Options dialog box (see fig. 12.16). Using this dialog box, you can specify settings for the surface test and create a custom error message.

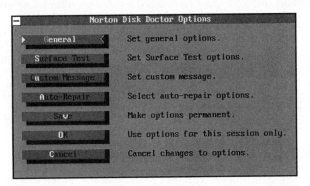

The Norton Disk Doctor Options dialog box contains several options:

■ The General option displays the General Options dialog box (see fig. 12.17). This dialog box offers radio button options for handling surface tests (Prompt Before Surface Test, Never Perform Surface Test, and Always Perform Surface Test). Five check box options for skipping tests are also provided (Skip Partition Tests, Skip CMOS Tests, Skip Compression Tests, Skip Host Drive Test, and Only 1 Hard Disk). You usually need these skip options if your computer is not 100-percent compatible with IBM PCs. In this dialog box, you may also include a list of Drives to Exclude.

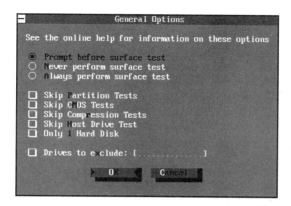

Fig. 12.17

The General
Options
dialog box.

■ The **S**urface Test option displays the Surface Test dialog box (refer to fig. 12.4). You can use the options in this dialog box to change the default settings for the surface test, and then save this information to disk. When NDD is used again interactively or as a command from the DOS prompt, your new defaults are used.

■ The **Cu**stom Message option allows you to customize the message that appears on-screen when NDD encounters an error in the system area test. The Set Custom Message dialog box is shown in figure 12.18. Suppose that you have placed the NDD command on several computers in your company, but you do not want inexperienced users to make corrections on their disks without the company computer-support team knowing about the problem. In this case, you can create a custom message. With the Set Custom Message dialog box displayed, type a message such as the one shown in the box in figure 12.18. Select the **P**rompt with Custom Message option to cause that message to be displayed when an error is found. Choose O**K** to exit the box. Then, if NDD finds a system area problem, this message appears on-screen.

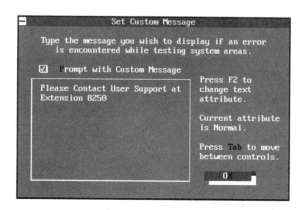

Fig. 12.18

Creating an NDD
custom error
message.

■ The **A**uto-Repair option enables you to choose how NDD will respond to problems (see fig. 12.19). Each of the options describes
a kind of problem that NDD might encounter, and each problem
description contains three radio button options: Prompt, Auto,
and Never. If you choose the Prompt option (the default for all
repair options), NDD will prompt you with a question before repairing a problem. If you choose Auto, NDD will attempt to repair
the problem but will not prompt you before doing so. (The repair
will be noted in the NDD report.) If you choose the Never option,
the problem will not be repaired but will be noted in the report.
Two other radio button options in this dialog box are Save Lost
Clusters as Files (the default) and Delete **L**ost Clusters. These two
options are activated when you select the Auto option for one or
more of the items to be repaired by NDD.

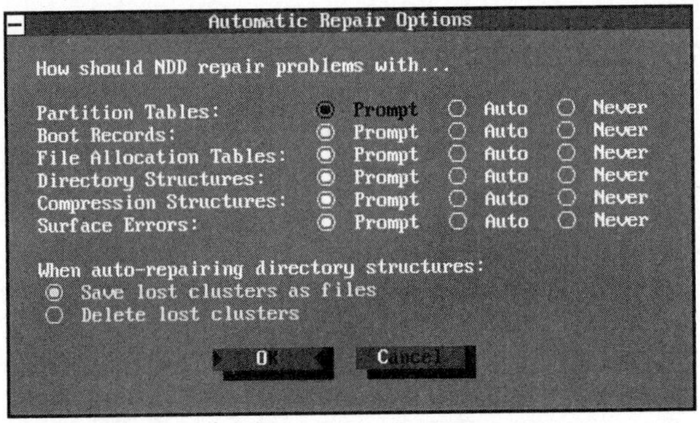

Fig. 12.19

The Automatic
Repair Options
dialog box.

After you make selections from the Surface Test, Set Custom Message,
and Automatic Repair Options dialog boxes, choose Save from the
Norton Disk Doctor Options dialog box to save this information permanently to disk. The new settings take effect immediately. To use the
new settings for the current session only, choose **O**K or press Enter.
If you don't want to save your changes, choose **C**ancel.

Summary

This chapter covered the Norton Disk Doctor utility. If your disk has problems, such as not enabling you to read files from a disk that used to work, try Disk Doctor to cure what ails the disk. It performs a battery of more than 100 tests on your disk, creates a report showing the current condition of your disk, and attempts to correct problems relating to file allocation or disk storage.

Sometimes Disk Doctor is unable to revive a disk. Often the NDD program recommends that you use the utilities in the Disk Tools program. Now turn to the next chapter to find out how to use Disk Tools.

Using Disk Tools

The Disk Tools utility in Norton Utilities 7 contains several recovery programs that don't seem to fit in any of the other major utilities. Actually, several of the Disk Tools functions were in Norton Disk Doctor in earlier versions of Norton Utilities. The Disk Tools program in Version 6 also included Rescue Disk options, which are now offered as a separate command (described in Chapter 14).

This chapter explores the four disk tools (procedures) included with Norton Utilities 7:

- *Make a Disk Bootable.* This procedure enables you to turn any disk (hard disk or floppy disk) into a bootable disk—even if the disk has not been formatted with the /S (System) option. The disk must have sufficient room on it to hold the DOS files.

- *Recover from DOS's Recover.* The inappropriate use of the DOS RECOVER command can cause you to lose all the files on a disk. This procedure helps you recover your files after such a disaster.

- *Revive a Defective Diskette.* The system area of a floppy disk may become unreadable or be damaged in some other way. This procedure revives a disk and restores it to usability.

- *Mark a Cluster.* At times, the FORMAT command misses marking a cluster that is bad. If you discover that a cluster on a disk is having problems, you can use this procedure to mark the cluster so that it is no longer used to store files.

Running Disk Tools

To begin Disk Tools, choose the Disk Tools option from the Norton main screen or enter **DISKTOOL** at the DOS prompt. The Disk Tools dialog box appears (see fig. 13.1). The options in this dialog box are described in the following sections.

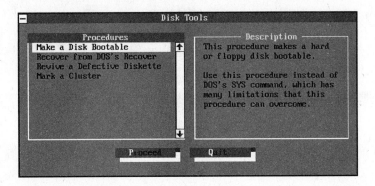

Making a Disk Bootable

Sometimes you may want to give an unbootable disk booting capabilities. This feature may be of particular importance for a hard disk. A disk can lose its booting capability if the magnetic signal on the boot record becomes weak or if the low-level format loses alignment with the read/write head. In addition, software programs may accidentally overwrite important system information required for booting. The Make a Disk Bootable option can place a fresh copy of the system information on the disk, making the disk bootable again.

Sometimes a disk may not have been set up properly as a bootable disk. If the disk was originally formatted as a nonbootable disk, DOS cannot make the disk bootable. Although DOS has a SYS command that should copy the system files to a nonbootable disk, the command works only if you told the format procedure to leave room on the disk to receive the system files. Otherwise, DOS writes data to the area of the disk reserved for the system information so that the SYS command cannot work for that disk. Disk Tools, however, can move files around, copy system information to the disk, and make the disk bootable.

Using Disk Tools to make a disk bootable can save you a great deal of time. Without Disk Tools, you must copy all files off the disk, reformat the disk with the /S switch, and copy files back to the disk. This process can take several minutes to a few hours; the Disk Tools procedure takes only a few minutes.

When you choose the Make a Disk Bootable option from the Disk Tools dialog box, you are prompted by the program to select the disk drive that contains the disk to make bootable (see fig. 13.2). Make sure that the correct disk is in the drive; then select the drive and either choose **OK** or press Enter.

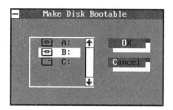

Fig. 13.2

The Make
Disk Bootable
dialog box.

The program first makes sure that you have enough free space on the disk to make the disk bootable. To make a disk bootable, the program must copy three files to the disk: COMMAND.COM and two hidden files. In PC DOS, two system files that contain part of DOS are stored on the disk as hidden files and do not appear when you use the DIR command. If the disk does not have enough room to accept the files, you see a message telling you that not enough room is available. To make this disk bootable, erase some files from the disk and try the procedure again.

During the procedure, you see messages that the files COMMAND.COM, IBMBIOS.COM, and IBMDOS.COM are being copied to the disk. These files are the DOS system files. When they have been successfully copied, the disk becomes a bootable disk, and you can use it to boot your computer. Figure 13.3 shows one of the messages that appears while the disk is being made bootable.

```
Preparing drive B: for the system files

        This may take a moment...
```

Fig. 13.3

Disk Tools
indicating that it
is preparing the
disk to receive
the system files.

> **T I P**
>
> If you have a hard disk that no longer boots from drive C, you can often recover from this problem by booting the computer with the rescue disk (see Chapter 14) or your original DOS disk. Then run the Make A Disk Bootable option on the hard disk. However, first check the hard disk by running Disk Doctor on the disk (see Chapter 12).

T   I   P   If you are using a one-disk computer (a desktop or laptop) that boots from a floppy disk, often you must first boot the computer with your DOS disk and then place your program disk (for example, a word processor) in the disk drive and begin that program. Making your application disk a bootable disk may be simpler. Then you can boot from the disk and begin your application program without having to change disks. The drawback of this procedure is that placing DOS on the disk (making it bootable) can take up about 100K of the disk's space.

Recovering from DOS's RECOVER Command

Many people see the poorly named DOS RECOVER command and assume that it can recover lost files or turn bad files into good files. You actually use the DOS RECOVER command to recover files with a defective sector. This DOS command is primitive, though, compared with what you can do in Norton Utilities.

The DOS manual states that the RECOVER command "recovers a disk with a bad sector." The recovery process used by DOS, however, eliminates all subdirectories on your disk and renames all your files with obscure names. Trying to find the contents of each file can take hours, and for some files, the task may be nearly impossible. If you use Norton Utilities, you should never have a reason to use the DOS RECOVER command.

If you have used the RECOVER command by accident or because you thought the command recovered damaged files, you can use Norton Disk Doctor to place files back into their proper directories—as long as you have not written other files to the disk. You must rename files in the root directory and subdirectories.

The next few paragraphs illustrate how the DOS RECOVER command affects your disk and how you can revive it with Disk Tools. Suppose that you have a disk containing a root directory and three subdirectories.

The files in the root directory:

COMMAND	COM	47845	01-08-92	6:00p
AUTOEXEC	BAT	641	12-11-92	11:04p
IMAGE	DAT	12800	12-22-92	11:03a
WP		<DIR>	12-22-92	11:00a
123		<DIR>	12-22-92	11:00a
DB3		<DIR>	12-22-92	11:00a

The files in the WP directory:

LETTER	WP	5799	11-08-93	3:09p
REPORT	WP	7012	11-08-93	3:09p

The files in the 123 directory:

SALES	WK1	6185	11-30-93	10:19p
BUDGET	WK1	7623	11-30-93	10:20p

The files in the DB3 directory:

SALES	DBF	37376	03-24-93	9:56p
CUSTOM	DBF	5158	02-23-93	8:14p

After the DOS RECOVER command has been run on this disk, the contents look like this:

FILE0001 REC	1024	12-22-93	11:04a
FILE0002 REC	512	12-22-93	11:04a
FILE0003 REC	512	12-22-93	11:04a
FILE0004 REC	512	12-22-93	11:04a
FILE0005 REC	37376	12-22-93	11:04a
FILE0006 REC	33792	12-22-93	11:04a
FILE0007 REC	37888	12-22-93	11:04a
FILE0008 REC	48128	12-22-93	11:04a
FILE0009 REC	5632	12-22-93	11:04a
FILE0010 REC	6656	12-22-93	11:04a
FILE0011 REC	7680	12-22-93	11:04a
FILE0012 REC	6144	12-22-93	11:04a
FILE0013 REC	7168	12-22-93	11:04a
FILE0014 REC	12800	12-22-93	11:04a
FILE0015 REC	512	12-22-93	11:04a

Notice that all the directories are gone, and all file names have been changed to FILE00*??*.REC. If you have only 15 files, as illustrated here, you might be able to determine quickly what these files were and rename them appropriately. However, with more files, the task becomes quite formidable. Fortunately, Disk Tools' Recover from DOS's Recover option can help.

T I P   If you are recovering a floppy disk, make a copy of that disk with the DUPDISK command in case something goes wrong during the recovery (see Chapter 26). Then you still have the original disk that can be used for another attempt at recovering the files.

If you choose the Recover from DOS's Recover option from the Disk Tools dialog box, you see the message shown in figure 13.4. If you choose **OK** when this message is displayed, you are asked to select the drive name of the disk you want to recover (see fig. 13.5).

A warning message then reminds you that you should use this procedure *only* if you have run DOS's RECOVER command or your root directory is destroyed (see fig. 13.6). To proceed with the recovery, choose **Yes**; to cancel the recovery, choose **No**. If you choose to proceed, a final message is displayed before the actual recovery begins (see fig. 13.7).

Fig. 13.4

A message displayed when you choose the Recover from DOS's Recover option.

> Recover from DOS's RECOVER
>
> After running DOS's RECOVER command, all previous directories on the disk are lost. This procedure can also be used AFTER running RECOVER to UNDO what RECOVER did and do it the right way.
>
> [OK]   [Cancel]

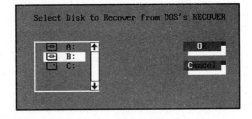

Fig. 13.5

Specifying what disk to recover.

> Select Disk to Recover from DOS's RECOVER
>
> A:
> B:
> C:
>
> [0]
> [Cancel]

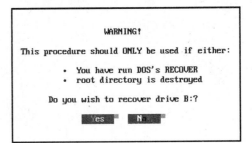

Fig. 13.6

A warning message.

> WARNING!
>
> This procedure should ONLY be used if either:
>
> • You have run DOS's RECOVER
> • root directory is destroyed
>
> Do you wish to recover drive B:?
>
> [Yes]   [No]

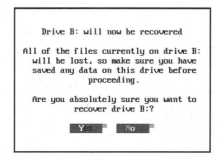

Drive B: will now be recovered

All of the files currently on drive B:
will be lost, so make sure you have
saved any data on this drive before
proceeding.

Are you absolutely sure you want to
recover drive B:?

Yes   No

Fig. 13.7

Last warning
message before
recovering the
specified disk.

Answer **No** to cancel the recovery procedure. If you answer **Yes** to have
the program proceed, a screen appears showing you the progress of
the recovery (see fig. 13.8).

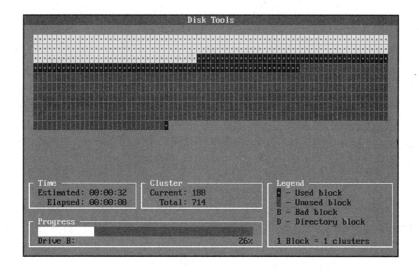

Fig. 13.8

A progress
screen for disk
recovery.

When the recovery is complete, you see a final message (see fig. 13.9).
You are told that Disk Tools has recovered the directories and named
them DIR0000, DIR0001, and so on. Most files in the root directory are
named FILE0000.*???*, FILE0001.*???*, and so on. Any files in directories
other than the root directory are recovered with their full names intact.

After the recovery is finished, the files in the root directory are the
following:

```
DIR0000      <DIR>         12-22-92  11:00a
DIR0001      <DIR>         12-22-92  11:00a
DIR0002      <DIR>         12-22-92  11:00a
FILE0003               1024 12-22-92  11:10a
```

```
FILE0004  COM      33792  12-22-92   11:10a
FILE0005  COM      37888  12-22-92   11:10a
FILE0006  COM      48128  12-22-92   11:10a
IMAGE     DAT      12800  12-22-92   11:10a
```

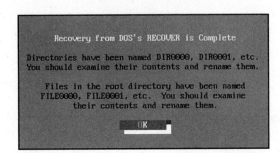

> Recovery from DOS's RECOVER is Complete
>
> Directories have been named DIR0000, DIR0001, etc.
> You should examine their contents and rename them.
>
> Files in the root directory have been named
> FILE0000, FILE0001, etc. You should examine
> their contents and rename them.
>
> [OK]

Fig. 13.9

The message telling you that the recovery is complete.

Notice that Norton recognized the file IMAGE.DAT and recovered its name in the root directory. The other files are called FILE000?.COM. You must examine the files to determine their contents. One way to examine them is to use Norton Disk Editor (see Chapter 17). In this case, FILE0003 is the AUTOEXEC.BAT file. You can use the RENAME command to rename that file:

RENAME FILE0003 AUTOEXEC.BAT

The file named FILE0006.COM is COMMAND.COM. The other two files do not match any files in the original directory. They are the hidden files IBMBIOS.COM and IBMDOS.COM, which make up the DOS system. After you recover IBMBIOS.COM and IBMDOS.COM, use the FA command to set their attributes to read-only, system, and hidden (see Chapter 9).

Although the directory names have been lost, the files in the directories are intact. For example, a directory listing of DIR0000 reveals the following files:

```
LETTER       WP       5799       11-08-93    3:09p
REPORT       WP       7012       11-08-93    3:09p
```

You can recognize these files as being from the original WP directory. To rename the directories, use the Norton Change Directory (NCD) command (see Chapter 23). After you have renamed files and directories, the disk is back to its original state.

Reviving a Defective Disk

The next option in the Disk Tools dialog box is the Revive a Defective Diskette option. This option mainly puts fresh format information on the disk. The procedure can be helpful if a disk has become difficult or impossible to read, which may happen if you use a floppy disk often. Sometimes the disk begins to wear out, the software program over-writes the system area, the disk becomes scratched, or other problems cause the disk to lose some information. If you have accessed the FAT so often that its information has begun to wear thin, the Revive a Defective Diskette option can place a new copy on disk for you.

When you choose Revive a Defective Diskette, you are first asked to specify the drive where the disk to be revived is located (see fig. 13.10).

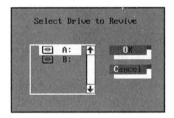

Fig. 13.10

Selecting the disk that you want to revive.

During a normal format procedure, a disk is checked for bad spots. If found, these spots are marked and not used to store information. A disk, however, can develop bad places after the original format has taken place. At times, the magnetic signal that stores information on disk may become weak and unreadable.

Furthermore, on some parts of a hard disk, the magnetic coating may be thin in spots and wear out over an extended period of use. If this problem occurs, you can use Disk Tools to mark bad spots and move data to safe areas on the disk.

These bad areas in the magnetic media can limit access to data in a particular file or can sometimes make a disk completely unreadable. Such problems often show up as read errors when you try to access information on a disk. You may get the following message while trying to read a disk that you know was readable earlier:

        Abort, Retry, Ignore, Fail?

The Disk Tools program can try to recover information from this kind of disk. Disk Tools may perform a type of reformatting of certain areas of the disk. This formatting does not destroy information as normal formatting does. Instead, it re-creates certain vital parts of the disk to make the disk readable again. Disk Tools performs various tests on the disk to see whether the program can recover questionable information and rework defective areas to make the disk usable again.

A dialog box reports the progress of the procedure (see fig. 13.11). When the process is finished, you see a message that the floppy disk has been revived (see fig. 13.12). Diagnose the disk with Disk Doctor to check that the system information is not lost.

Fig. 13.11

A progress report from Revive a Defective Diskette.

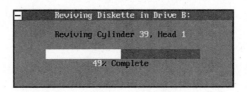

Fig. 13.12

The final message from Revive a Defective Diskette, telling you to run NDD on the revived disk.

If you have problems with a disk and have revived or recovered it with Disk Tools, copy the information from the original floppy disk to another disk. If the first disk is one that you use frequently and it may be wearing out, copy the information to a new floppy disk and use that one.

If you cannot revive a disk with Disk Tools, the prognosis of recovery is bad. The NDD program may be able to fix bad information in the FAT and recover lost clusters. Your last possible choice is to use Disk Editor to attempt to recover portions of the disk (see Chapter 17).

T   I   P   If you have problems with a hard disk, make sure that you keep backups. In fact, always keep backup copies of all important files even before you have problems with a hard disk.

Marking a Cluster

The Mark a Cluster option in the Disk Tools dialog box enables you to mark any cluster on a disk as bad or good. You may want to mark a cluster as bad—meaning that you can no longer use the cluster to store file information—if you discover that the cluster has intermittent problems. By running NDD or other programs, you may find specific clusters that are bad (the cluster number is reported to you on-screen or in a report). You may run NDD, for example, to generate a list of bad clusters; then you can use Disk Tools to mark the clusters as bad. (Of course, you can allow NDD to automatically mark the bad clusters.) You can also mark a cluster as bad if you want to hide and protect information; the information in that cluster is not overwritten as long as the cluster remains bad. When you choose this option from Disk Tools, an information message appears (see fig. 13.13). This message explains that when a cluster is marked as good, DOS can use it to store file information. If a cluster is marked as bad, DOS does not use it.

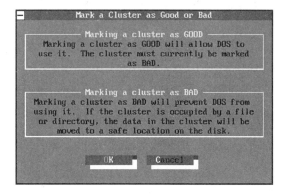

Fig. 13.13

The information message from Mark a Cluster.

To cancel the Mark a Cluster procedure, choose **C**ancel. If you choose **O**K, you are prompted to choose the drive on which to mark a cluster (see fig. 13.14).

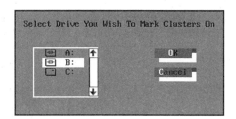

Fig. 13.14

Mark a Cluster prompting you to choose what drive to use.

If you mark a cluster being used by a file as bad, the information in that cluster is copied to a safe location on disk so that the information in the file remains intact. Marking a cluster as good means that the cluster is available to store file information. You can also use Mark a Cluster to bring back clusters you have marked as bad. You mark a cluster as bad to protect new information from being written to that bad spot.

After you tell which disk drive you plan to use (such as drive A, B, or C), you are prompted to type the number of the cluster that you want to mark and whether you want to mark the cluster as bad or good (see fig. 13.15). The Mark Cluster dialog box tells you the range of clusters you can mark. Type a cluster number in the Cluster number field; then choose the Good or Bad radio button, according to your intention.

Fig. 13.15

The Mark Cluster dialog box where you mark clusters as bad or good.

You can mark as many clusters as you want. After you enter your choices, choose **OK** to mark the cluster or choose **C**ancel to end the program and return to the Disk Tools dialog box.

Using the DISKTOOL Command from the DOS Prompt

When you enter **DISKTOOL** at the DOS prompt without any command-line options or you choose Disk Tools from the Norton main screen, the program runs interactively, as described in the previous sections. You can also run the program from the DOS prompt by using command-line options and bypassing the Disk Tools dialog box.

Here are four versions of this command's syntax:

DISKTOOL [/MAKEBOOT] [/SKIPHIGH]

DISKTOOL [/DOSRECOVER] [/SKIPHIGH]

DISKTOOL [/REVIVE] [/SKIPHIGH]

DISKTOOL [/MARKCLUSTER] [/SKIPHIGH]

The following switches are available for use with DISKTOOL:

Switch	Description
/DOSRECOVER	Skips the Disk Tools dialog box and goes to the Recover from DOS's Recover option.
/MAKEBOOT	Skips the Disk Tools dialog box and goes to the Make a Disk Bootable option.
/REVIVE	Skips the Disk Tools dialog box and goes to the Revive a Defective Diskette option.
/MARKCLUSTER	Marks a cluster.
/SKIPHIGH	Tells the program that you do not want Disk Tools loaded into high memory. Use this option if you are using a memory manager that is already using DOS high memory.

The Disk Tools program is primarily designed for interactive use. However, you can select which tool to use and tell the program not to use DOS high memory by including one or more switches on the command line. When you begin the program from the DOS prompt and use /DOSRECOVER, /MAKEBOOT, /REVIVE, or /MARKCLUSTER, the opening Disk Tools dialog box is bypassed, and the dialog box associated with the chosen tool is displayed exactly as if you had arrived there by way of the Procedure list box in the Disk Tools dialog box.

 NOTE Previous versions of the Disk Tools command included Rescue Disk options. To create or use a rescue disk in Version 7, use the RESCUE command (see Chapter 14).

Summary

This chapter described four important Disk Tools procedures that can help you revive or restore a disk, make a disk bootable, and manually mark clusters as good or bad. Disk Tools is a valuable part of your rescue arsenal and should be on your rescue disk. To learn how to make and use a rescue disk, turn to the next chapter.

Creating and Using a Rescue Disk

When your hard disk is having access problems or has been accidentally formatted, you cannot use the hard disk to help you correct the problem. That is the purpose of the rescue disk—a disk that contains information about your hard disk, plus important programs that can help you recover, revive, or unformat the hard disk. If you have not yet made a rescue disk for your computer, do so now! This chapter shows you how to create and use a rescue disk.

Understanding How the Rescue Disk Works

Your disk contains a number of pieces of information that could take much time and effort to re-create if they happen to be lost or corrupted (perhaps by a virus). They include your setup information (CMOS), information about how your hard disk boots (the DOS boot program), and information about how your hard disk is partitioned (for example, into disks C and D). Norton Utilities provides a way to keep a separate copy of this information on a disk called a *rescue disk*.

As noted, a rescue disk contains information about your disk, including information about your partition tables, boot records, and setup values (CMOS data). When you create a rescue disk, this information is written to a disk (usually a floppy disk) and stored in three files: PARTINFO.DAT, BOOTINFO.DAT, and CMOSINFO.DAT.

The *partition information* tells how your hard disk was set up originally, when you used the FDISK command to inform DOS how the hard disk was to be used (one drive, two drives, the size of the drives, and so on). The *boot information* tells how your disk is formatted (under which version of DOS) and includes other system information.

The *CMOS setup information* stored in RAM is kept active by a battery. The PC AT was the first computer to use this kind of setup. Many new computers no longer store information in CMOS. If you must run the setup program to configure your computer, your computer has CMOS. If your battery dies, your computer loses its CMOS settings.

You can create a rescue disk by choosing the Rescue Disk command from the Norton main menu or by entering **RESCUE** at the DOS prompt. With either method, you see the Rescue Disk dialog box shown in figure 14.1.

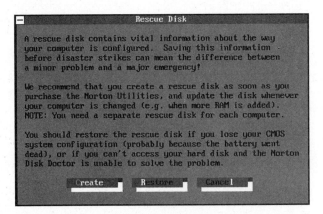

NOTE You may have created a rescue disk when you installed Norton Utilities. If you did, you do not have to do that again. If you have not created a rescue disk, it is important to do so now!

You must create a rescue disk for each computer. The information on a rescue disk for one computer may not work on another computer.

Specifying the Contents of the Rescue Disk

After you choose **C**reate from the Rescue Disk dialog box, the Create Rescue Disk dialog box appears (see fig. 14.2). This dialog box enables you to specify where to create the disk and what files will be included. At the top of the dialog box is the **S**ave Rescue Information To field. Here you specify the disk drive where you want the information saved. Usually, this will be drive A. You can specify another drive, however, by selecting a drive name from the drop-down list box. Choose the drive that contains the floppy disk to be used as your rescue disk; then specify the disk size in the Rescue **D**iskette Type field. Usually, the disk size in this field is the appropriate size, but sometimes you may need to change it. If, for example, you have a high-density (1.44M) 3 1/2-inch drive but your floppy disk is a double-density (720K) 3 1/2-inch disk, you should change this setting from 1.2M to 720K.

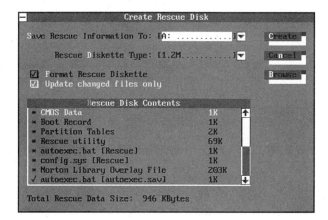

Fig. 14.2

The Create Rescue Disk dialog box.

The **F**ormat Rescue Diskette option allows you to decide whether the diskette that will be used will be formatted before the rescue information is stored on it. This option is selected by default. Usually, it is preferable to format the rescue disk so that it will contain the current DOS system information. That way, you can boot your computer from the rescue disk, if needed.

The **U**pdate Changed Files Only option is available only if the **F**ormat Rescue Diskette option is deselected. Choose this option if you have made changes to your computer (such as added more RAM) and you want to update your current rescue disk without starting over from scratch. When you choose this option, only updated information is copied to the rescue disk.

The **R**escue Disk Contents list box contains the information that will be saved to the rescue disk. Usually, you will want to use this list as is, neither adding nor deleting from the list. On occasion, though, you may want to add or delete information from this list. The information that has an asterisk (*) on the left is always saved; you cannot deselect those items. Items that have a check mark next to their names can be deselected. Normally, these are the items that you can select or deselect to save to the rescue disk:

> AUTOEXEC.BAT (the startup batch file)
> CONFIG.SYS (the startup configuration file)
> Norton Disk Doctor
> Norton Safe Format
> UnErase
> UnFormat
> FDISK (a disk-partitioning program)
> Norton Diagnostics

This list box may include other startup programs, such as your mouse and DISKREET programs or drivers, which appear in your AUTOEXEC.BAT or CONFIG.SYS file.

To select or deselect information in the list, highlight the item (such as Norton Safe Format) and press the space bar to select or deselect the item.

If you want to locate other files on the drive to add to the **R**escue Disk Contents list, choose the **B**rowse option. The Browse For Files To Add dialog box appears, as shown in figure 14.3. In this box, you can choose additional files to add to the rescue disk.

To select a group of files, type a file specification in the **F**ile text box (for example, type ***.EXE**). This causes all files that meet the specification to be selected in the **Fi**les list box at the lower right of the dialog box. To select or deselect individual files, highlight the file name in the **Fi**les list box and press the space bar. (A check mark appears to the left of selected file names.)

To change drives, specify the drive you want in the **D**rive drop-down list box. To change directories, use the **D**irectories list box. To list additional directories, highlight the parent directory (. .) and press Enter, or click the parent directory. If you are several directories deep, you may have to choose .. more than once before arriving at the root directory. The **D**irectories list box then displays a list of all directories at the root level. To locate a directory, use the up- and down-arrow keys, use the scroll bar to move the highlight, or begin entering the name of the directory. The highlight will move to the directory name that matches the letters you type. Then press Enter. After you have highlighted the directory you want, press Enter or double-click the directory. This causes the **F**iles list box to display the file names in the selected directory.

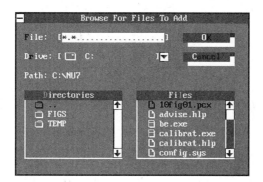

Fig. 14.3

The Browse For Files To Add dialog box.

After you have selected files to add to the rescue disk, choose **O**K. If you want to cancel the Browse For Files To Add dialog box, choose **C**ancel. Be careful not to choose more files than can fit on the rescue disk.

Once the **R**escue Disk Contents list contains all the files you want included on the rescue disk, you can begin to create the rescue disk by choosing **C**reate in the Create Rescue Disk dialog box. To cancel the creation of a rescue disk, choose Ca**n**cel.

Creating the Rescue Disk

When you choose **C**reate in the Create Rescue Disk dialog box to begin the creation process, a warning message appears, telling you that information currently on this disk will be lost (see fig. 14.4). Choose **O**K to proceed or choose **C**ancel to stop the process.

If you proceed and you chose to format the disk that will be the rescue disk, the format begins. You then see a progress dialog box, as shown in figure 14.5. Notice in this dialog box that the disk being formatted will contain system files (see the System Mode entry at the upper right of the dialog box). This means that the rescue disk will be bootable.

Fig. 14.4

A Rescue Disk
Warning box,
indicating that
files on the
disk will be
destroyed.

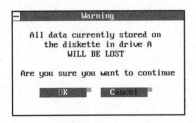

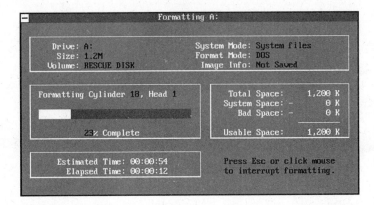

Fig. 14.5

Formatting the
rescue disk.

After the disk is formatted, the Rescue Disk program begins to copy
information to the rescue disk. Another progress dialog box appears
(see fig. 14.6). This dialog box tells you how much (a percentage) of the
rescue information has been copied to the rescue disk.

When all the information has been successfully copied to the rescue
disk, a final message tells you that all the rescue information was saved
(see fig. 14.7).

T I P Store your rescue disk in a safe place. It should be accessible in case
you need it for restoring information to your computer.

Restoring from the Rescue Disk

If your computer develops problems that prevent you from booting
from its hard disk, the Rescue Disk program can help solve the problem. Here is the procedure for using Rescue Disk:

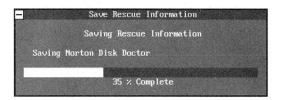

Fig 14.6

A Rescue Disk progress dialog box.

Fig. 14.7

The message that appears when the rescue disk is complete.

1. Place the rescue disk in the boot drive of your computer (usually drive A) and turn on the computer.

2. After the computer boots, enter **RESCUE** at the DOS prompt. The Restore Rescue Information dialog box appears (see fig. 14.8).

3. In this dialog box, you can choose the items you want to restore (**C**MOS Information, **B**oot Records, and **P**artition Tables). A selected option has a check mark in its box. Choose **C**MOS Information if your computer has lost information about disk drive sizes and types. This loss may occur if your computer's CMOS battery has run down or been replaced. Choose **B**oot Records if your hard disk will not boot. Choose **P**artition Tables if your computer has lost information about your hard disk partitions. If your rescue disk information is in a drive or path other than the one shown in the Restore Information **F**rom field, you can choose New Path, which displays a dialog box enabling you to choose another drive or path.

4. After making your selections, choose the **R**estore option. The information will be restored to your disk. If you change your mind, choose Cance**l**.

5. End the Rescue Disk program by pressing Esc and reboot your computer.

If you continue to have problems, reboot with the rescue disk and run Norton Disk Doctor on your hard disk to see whether it can detect problems with your disk (see Chapter 12). You also might try the Make a Disk Bootable option in the Disk Tools utility (discussed in Chapter 13) if your computer will not boot from its hard disk.

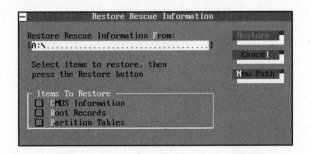

Fig. 14.8

Using the rescue disk to restore information to your disk.

Summary

The rescue disk is an important tool in the medicine bag for your computer. It contains a number of utility programs, plus information about your computer that can help you restore, revive, or unformat your hard disk. This chapter explained how to create and use a rescue disk. If you have not created one for each of your computers, do so now. Then store the disk in a safe but accessible place so that it will be there when you need it.

Now turn to Chapter 15 on restoring files with File Fix, the final chapter in Part III of this book.

Restoring Files with File Fix

The File Fix program recovers corrupted database, spreadsheet, and word processing files. These files can become corrupted when the power is turned off abruptly, when a program accesses a file incorrectly, or when the information stored on disk is damaged because of a bad spot on the disk. Specifically, File Fix is designed to fix the following types of files:

Database files	dBASE (II, III Plus, and IV)
	Clipper
Spreadsheet files	Lotus 1-2-3 (through Version 3.1)
	Symphony (Versions 1.0 and 1.1)
	Quattro Pro (Version 3.0)
	Excel (Versions 2.0 through 4.0)
Word processing files	WordPerfect (Version 5.1)

You can use File Fix also to fix files that are created by other programs but are compatible with one of these file formats. For example, some database programs create DBF (dBASE-type) files. Sometimes these "compatible" files are not quite compatible and may cause problems when you use them. File Fix often can take these marginally compatible files and turn them into fully compatible files.

Furthermore, if you have erased all records in a dBASE database, File Fix sometimes can recover those records. File Fix uses knowledge about how these files are created to try to recover the file information. Even if all information in the file cannot be recovered, File Fix may be capable of recovering some information.

Starting the File Fix Program

Begin File Fix by choosing the File Fix option from the Norton main
menu or entering **FILEFIX** at the DOS prompt. Figure 15.1 shows the
File Fix dialog box. From this dialog box, you can choose to fix files for
Lotus 1-2-3, Symphony (spreadsheet files only), Quattro Pro (spreadsheet), Excel (spreadsheet), dBASE and Clipper (and similar formats),
and WordPerfect.

Fig. 15.1

The File Fix
dialog box.

To fix a file, highlight the file type in the File Formats list box and
choose **P**roceed. To cancel or end the procedure, choose **Q**uit. If you
choose **Q**uit, you return to the Norton main screen or to DOS, depending on where you began the program. After you choose **P**roceed, you
see the Choose File To Repair dialog box (see fig. 15.2).

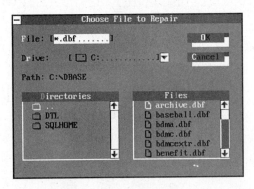

Fig. 15.2

Selecting a file to
fix.

This dialog box is similar to others in Norton Utilities in that you can
use it to browse for the file (or files) you want to select for a particular
task. If you want to choose files on a different drive, you can select
a new drive name from the **D**rive drop-down list box. You use the
Directories list box to look for a directory. If, for example, you want to
browse for files in a directory other than the current directory, you can

select the parent directory (. .) entry in the **Directories** list and then press Enter, or just double-click the entry. If you are several directories deep, you will have to do this several times before getting to the root directory. Once you are in the root directory, the **Directories** list displays all directories off the root directory on the current drive. With this list displayed, you can then select a directory name by using the arrow keys or mouse. When you select a directory name, the files in that directory appear in the **Files** list box.

> **T I P**
>
> Another way to quickly locate a directory name in the **Directories** list box or a file name in the **Files** list box is to move to the list box and type the first character of the directory or file name you want. The highlight in the list box jumps to the first name (alphabetically) in the list beginning with the character you typed. Then you can scroll to find the specific directory or file name.

To select a file in the **Files** list box, use the up- and down-arrow keys to highlight the file name. To begin the repair process, press Enter, choose **OK**, or double-click the file name.

> **T I P**
>
> To avoid having to select a drive and directory, enter **FILEFIX** from the drive and directory that contain the files you want to fix.

After you specify the file type and the file you want to fix, the File Fix procedure varies, depending on the type of file you are fixing. The following sections describe the procedures for repairing database, spreadsheet, and WordPerfect word processing files.

Fixing Database Files

File Fix can often fix damaged database files that are compatible with the dBASE and Clipper standard database formats. These programs include dBASE II, dBASE III Plus, dBASE IV, FoxBASE, Clipper, Wampum, Kwikstat, and any other programs that create standard DBF format files.

If you specified the dBASE & Clipper file type in the File Fix dialog box, after you specify the file to be repaired, File Fix displays the first Repair dBASE File dialog box. This dialog box gives you several options for fixing the file (see fig. 15.3).

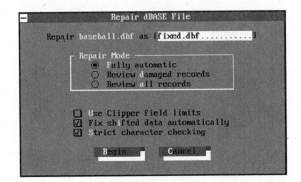

Fig. 15.3

Selecting dBASE
file fix options.

At the top of the dialog box, you see that the selected DBF file will be repaired as a file named FIXED.DBF. If you want to change the name of the repaired file, enter a new name in the Repair As field.

Before you choose a repair mode, notice the options at the bottom of the dialog box. To select or deselect an option (a check mark in the box means that the option is selected), press Alt plus the highlighted letter in the option name, or just click the option's check box.

You should choose the first option, **U**se Clipper Field Limits, if your DBF file was created by Clipper. The other two options, Fix Shifted Data Automatically and **S**trict Character Checking, are selected by default. Sometimes when dBASE files are damaged, the information in the database is shifted and not aligned properly in the fields. In that case, choose Fix Shifted Data Automatically. If this option does not work, you must correct the shifting manually. The **S**trict Character Checking option means that only characters which are usually allowed in records should be allowed. A few programs, such as the SBT Accounting series, enable special graphics characters in the record. If you use such a program, deselect the **S**trict Character Checking option.

In the Repair Mode section of the dialog box, you indicate the method with which you want to try to repair the file. If this attempt is your first pass at fixing the file, choose **F**ully Automatic. If that method does not work, choose Review **D**amaged Records, which enables you to look at only those records that are corrupted. If the database is extremely corrupted, choose Review **A**ll Records.

After you set all the options for the repair process, choose **B**egin. When you begin the fix, File Fix lets you choose whether you want to review the fields in the database file (see fig. 15.4). It is a good idea to review the fields to see whether all the field names and specifications are OK, as far as you know. To review the fields, choose **R**eview Fields. If you don't want to review the fields, choose S**k**ip Review to continue with the repair process.

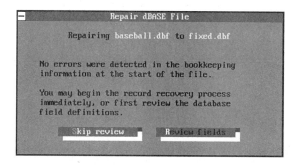

Fig. 15.4

File Fix asking
whether you
want to review
the fields.

If you choose fully automatic mode, Norton proceeds with the repair
without further prompts. If you choose to review the dBASE file, you
see the dialog box shown in figure 15.5. This dialog box lists the structure of the database as far as File Fix can determine. If this data has
been corrupted, you can revise this information by choosing **R**evise.
Otherwise, choose **A**ccept. If you choose **R**evise, another dialog box is
displayed, enabling you to correct information about the file's database
structure (see fig. 15.6). You can choose to import a database structure
from another file, edit the structure, or cancel this repair. Choose **Im**-
port if you have another dBASE file with the same structure (same field
names, types, and widths) as that of the database file you are repairing.
File Fix can graft the good database structure onto the damaged file. If
you are not able to import a structure, choose **E**dit.

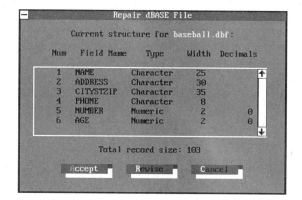

Fig. 15.5

The structure of
the file that is
being fixed.

When you choose **E**dit, you see a dialog box similar to that shown in
figure 15.7. The purpose of this dialog box is to allow you to locate the
first of the data fields in the damaged database. The box in the middle
of the dialog box shows the data in the database. You want the first
record in the database to begin at the top line on the left side of the

box. When you press the right- or left-arrow key, the information in the box moves to the right or left. Move the information in this box until the information in the first record begins at the top line on the left side of the box, or change the file position at the bottom of the dialog box. Choose **OK** to continue with the repair or choose **Cancel** to cancel it.

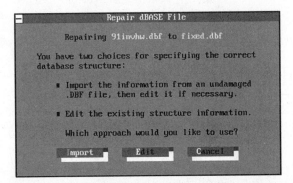

Specifying the file's database structure.

Adjusting the starting point for data in the database file being repaired.

When you choose **OK** after adjusting the starting point, another dialog box appears (see fig. 15.8). The purpose of this dialog box is to enable you to line up the database fields. Figure 15.8 shows fields that are lined up correctly, with each field making a column of data. If the fields in the box are not lined up in columns, change the record size. Then choose **OK** to continue with the repair or choose **Cancel** to cancel it.

When you choose **OK** after lining up the fields, the dialog box shown in figure 15.9 is displayed. In this dialog box, you can adjust the width of each database field. The name of each field is listed at the left side of the dialog box, and the data in that field is shown in the File Data area.

If the data matches the field widths, the data in the File Data area should fit correctly into the field widths. If the data does not fit, you can adjust the width of one or more fields. Highlight the field name and press the right- or left-arrow key to make the field wider or narrower. The data in the record is adjusted to fit the new field width. You can adjust as many fields as you want to make the data fit correctly.

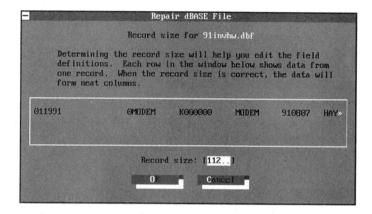

Fig. 15.8

Lining up fields in the database being repaired.

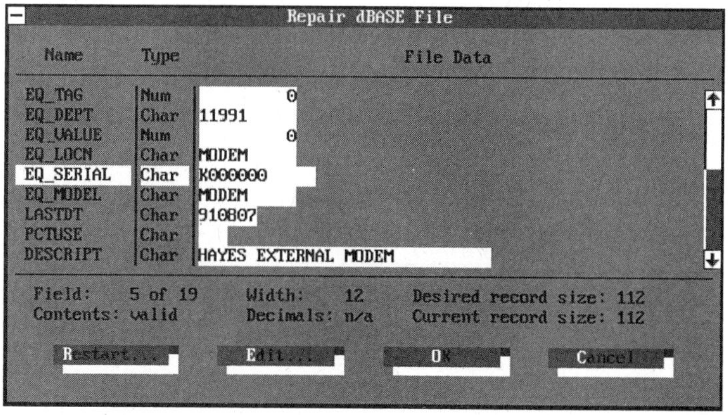

Fig. 15.9

Adjusting the field widths in the database being repaired.

You can edit other information about a highlighted field by choosing Edit at the bottom of this dialog box. When you choose Edit, the dialog box shown in figure 15.10 is displayed. In this dialog box, you can change the name of the field and its type, width, and decimals. Choose OK to exit the dialog box. The changes you made are then applied to the highlighted field.

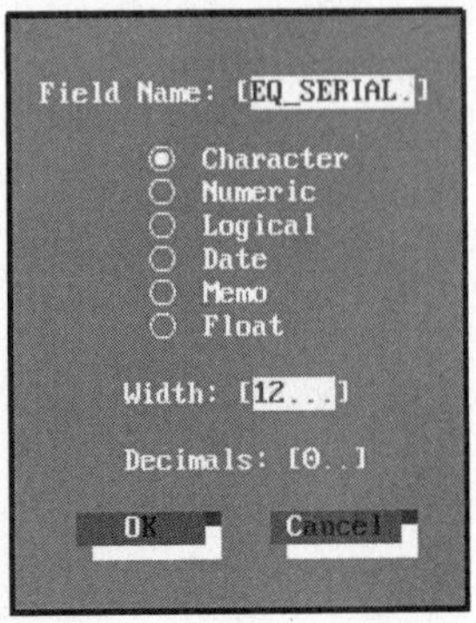

Fig. 15.10

Editing the structure of a field.

When you have adjusted the widths of fields and made any other edits to the field specifications, you choose **OK** in the Repair dBASE dialog box shown in figure 15.9 to continue with the repair process. If you choose **Restart**, you return to the database file as it was before any of the adjustments were made, and you can begin making new adjustments. You could choose this option if you royally messed up the adjustments and want to begin again. Choose **Cancel** to exit this dialog box without applying any of the changes you have made. After you have made the necessary adjustments, the current structure is displayed again, as shown in figure 15.5.

After you accept the database structure, you see the dialog box shown in figure 15.11, displaying the contents of a record. If the record looks OK, choose **Accept**, and the next record is displayed. If the data does not line up in the fields, you can shift the data by choosing **Shift**. When you choose this option, you can then use the right- and left-arrow keys to move the information in the record until the information lines up with the fields. If you want to reject a record, choose **Reject**. If you reject a record, it is not written to the fixed file. If you want to return to fully automatic mode for the rest of the records, choose **Mode** and then choose **Fully Automatic**. Choose **Cancel** to cancel the fix.

After a file is fixed, File Fix tells you how much of the file is accepted and how much is rejected (see fig. 15.12). If a large number of bytes are rejected, it may mean that some of the file was lost. Always examine carefully the file in the program for which the file is intended before making a decision to recover the information fully. In this case, use dBASE to browse through the fixed file to determine whether all the records have been properly fixed.

At this point, you must decide what to do with the fixed file. If you choose **No Report**, File Fix ends. If you choose **Printer** or **File**, a report summarizing the repair is generated and sent to a file (you specify the name) or to the printer. The report summarizes all the options you chose in fixing the file and contains information on how many records were unchanged and how many were fixed. A sample report is shown in figure 15.13.

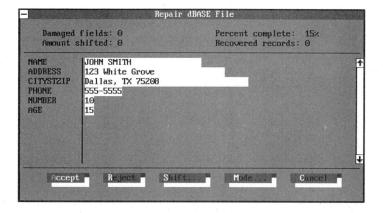

Fig. 15.11

Viewing a dBASE record in File Fix.

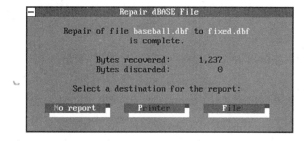

Fig. 15.12

The results of a file fix.

Fixing Spreadsheet Files

File Fix can fix several types of spreadsheet files, including Lotus 1-2-3, Symphony, Microsoft Excel, and Quattro Pro files. After you specify the file format—Lotus 1-2-3, Symphony spreadsheet files, Excel, or Quattro Pro—in the File Fix dialog box (refer to fig. 15.1), you specify the file to fix in the Choose File To Repair dialog box (refer to fig. 15.2).

When you specify the file you want to fix (in this case, a 1-2-3 file), File Fix displays the Repair Lotus 1-2-3 File dialog box (see fig. 15.14). At the top of the box is a message that the selected WK1 file will be repaired as the file named FIXED.WK1. If you want to change the name of the repaired file, enter a new name in the Repair As field. Then choose one of two repair modes. The default setting is Attempt Recovery of All Data (which includes formulas, macros, and so on). Usually, you choose to recover all data. If this option does not work, however, use the alternative option, Recover Cell Data Only.

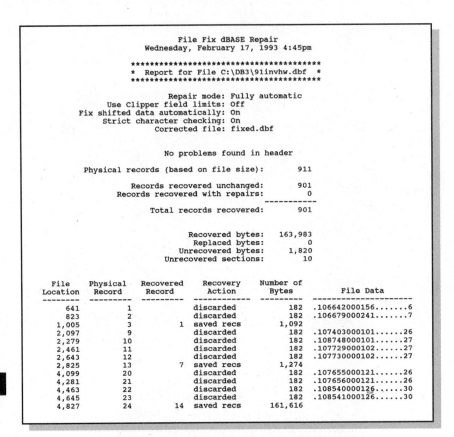

```
                    File Fix dBASE Repair
              Wednesday, February 17, 1993 4:45pm

              *******************************************
              *   Report for File C:\DB3\91invhw.dbf   *
              *******************************************
                        Repair mode: Fully automatic
               Use Clipper field limits: Off
         Fix shifted data automatically: On
                Strict character checking: On
                         Corrected file: fixed.dbf


                      No problems found in header

         Physical records (based on file size):      911

                Records recovered unchanged:          901
           Records recovered with repairs:              0
                                                 -----------
                     Total records recovered:         901


                            Recovered bytes:   163,983
                             Replaced bytes:         0
                          Unrecovered bytes:     1,820
                       Unrecovered sections:        10


     File      Physical   Recovered    Recovery    Number of
   Location     Record     Record       Action       Bytes        File Data
   --------    --------   ---------   -----------   ---------   --------------------
        641        1                  discarded        182     .106642000156.......6
        823        2                  discarded        182     .106679000241.......7
      1,005        3          1       saved recs     1,092
      2,097        9                  discarded        182     .107403000101......26
      2,279       10                  discarded        182     .108748000101......27
      2,461       11                  discarded        182     .107729000102......27
      2,643       12                  discarded        182     .107730000102......27
      2,825       13          7       saved recs     1,274
      4,099       20                  discarded        182     .107655000121......26
      4,281       21                  discarded        182     .107656000121......26
      4,463       22                  discarded        182     .108540000126......30
      4,645       23                  discarded        182     .108541000126......30
      4,827       24         14       saved recs   161,616
```

Fig. 15.13

A File Fix report for a dBASE file.

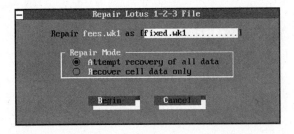

Fig. 15.14

The Repair Lotus 1-2-3 File dialog box.

To begin the recovery process, choose **B**egin. To stop the process, choose **C**ancel. While the recovery is in progress, File Fix displays a summary dialog box (similar to the one in fig. 15.12) that indicates how much of the file is recovered. For other spreadsheet types, the process is similar to the 1-2-3 method described here.

Fixing WordPerfect Files

File Fix can fix WordPerfect word processing files that have been damaged. For example, you may have unerased a WordPerfect file, but all of the file was not able to be unerased. WordPerfect may not be able to recognize or import the damaged file. File Fix may be able to fix the rest of the file so that you can then use it in WordPerfect. The procedures and options are similar to those used in the dBASE file fix described earlier. After you select the WordPerfect format from the File Fix dialog box, you choose the file to fix from a dialog box like the one in figure 15.2. Then the Repair WordPerfect File dialog box appears, offering two Repair Mode options (see fig. 15.15).

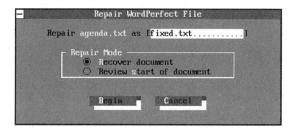

Fig. 15.15

WordPerfect
Repair Mode
options.

At the top of the box, you see that the file selected will be repaired as the file named FIXED.*ext* (for this example, the extension is TXT). If you want to change the name of the repaired file, enter a new name in the Repair As field.

From this dialog box, you can choose to recover the document (**Re**cover Document, which is the default setting) or review the start of the document (Review **S**tart of Document). If the document is damaged, you may need to tell File Fix where the document starts. If you choose Review **S**tart of Document, you see the dialog box shown in figure 15.16.

Usually, WordPerfect documents begin with a series of codes that tell WordPerfect what printer is being used, what fonts are being used, and so on. The document shown in figure 15.16 is not damaged. Therefore, you can see what the beginning of the document should look like. Notice that the first three letters in the document are .WPC, indicating to WordPerfect that the document is indeed a WordPerfect file. If you are repairing a WordPerfect file, it would be a good idea to look first at a similar nondamaged file to see what the start of the file should look like.

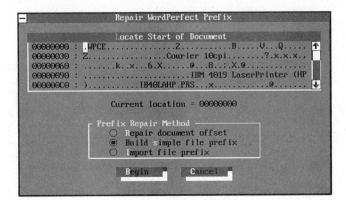

Fig. 15.16

Reviewing the
start of a
WordPerfect
document.

Options in the Repair WordPerfect Prefix dialog box include **R**epair
Document Offset, Build **S**imple File Prefix, and **I**mport File Prefix. A
WordPerfect prefix is information in the file that tells WordPerfect the
version of the file, the printer used, and other settings for the file. If you
choose the **R**epair Document Offset option, File Fix creates a minimal
prefix for the file. The Build **S**imple File Prefix option tells File Fix to
construct from the current prefix a new file prefix that is not damaged.
This version of a prefix repair should retain more information than the
Repair Document Offset option. The **I**mport File Prefix option enables
you to graft a good file prefix from another WordPerfect file. For example, if you have another WordPerfect file that you know is OK, your
best option may be to copy its file prefix onto the damaged file. When
you choose this option, a dialog box similar to that shown in figure 15.2
appears. You can choose the name of the file from which to copy the
file prefix.

Once you have repaired the file prefix, FileFix proceeds to write the
fixed document into the file name chosen for the fixed file. You should
examine the fixed document in WordPerfect to verify that it has been
recovered. If it is still damaged, you might run File Fix again and choose
a different method of repairing the prefix to the file.

Summary

The chapters in Part III covered the core of Norton Utilities' automatic
file-recovery options, beginning with the easiest and quickest way to
unerase a file—using the UnErase command. This command should
always be your first choice when trying to unerase a file. If your disk
has other problems, such as not enabling you to read files from a disk

that used to work, try Norton Disk Doctor to cure what ails the disk. To recover a defective disk or make a disk bootable, use Disk Tools. To recover database, spreadsheet, or WordPerfect files, use the File Fix command, as described in this Chapter.

If you need to do some real "surgery" on your disk to recover a file or to correct information on your disk, proceed to Part IV, "Advanced Recovery Techniques."

Advanced Recovery Techniques

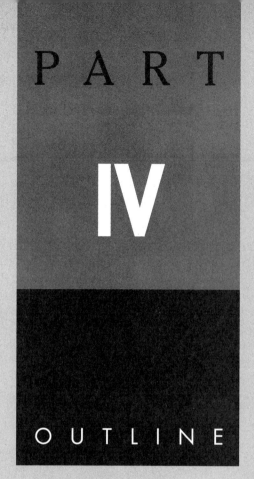

Recovering Files with Manual UnErase

T he chapters in Part III described the automatic Norton Utilities
file-recovery programs, which you should always use first when
attempting to recover data. For difficult problems that the automatic
methods cannot correct, Norton provides the Manual UnErase option,
discussed in this chapter. Disk Editor, described in the next chapter, is
designed for more delicate data fixes. Because Disk Editor can change
information directly on the disk, you can use it to re-create missing
sections of the data or system area.

This chapter and the next one require more knowledge of computers
than the rest of the book requires. To understand the descriptions and
instructions in these chapters, you need to know how clusters and sectors work to store files on disk. Some knowledge of the structure of
system files is also helpful. For more information on clusters, see Chapter 3, "Understanding How Disks Work," or refer to *Que's Guide to Data
Recovery*.

Unerasing Files Manually

When you cannot unerase a file automatically with UnErase, you can try to assemble the file manually with the **M**anual UnErase or Create **F**ile procedure. Start UnErase by entering **UNERASE** at the DOS prompt or choosing UnErase from the Norton main screen. The UnErase screen appears, displaying a list of erased files in the Erased Files dialog box. To use the **M**anual UnErase procedure on one of the files, highlight the file name and then choose **F**ile to access the UnErase **F**ile menu (see fig. 16.1).

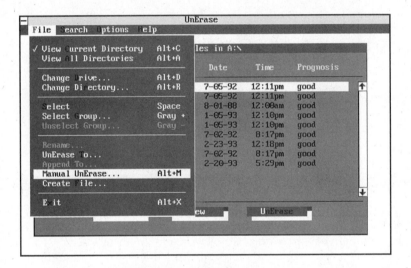

Fig. 16.1

The UnErase **F**ile menu.

Choose the **M**anual UnErase option from the **F**ile menu. The program then prompts you to enter the first character of the name of the erased file, as shown in figure 16.2.

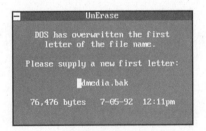

Fig. 16.2

Entering the first character of the erased file's name.

When you type the missing character, the program displays the corrected file name in the Manual UnErase dialog box, along with information about the file's attributes, the first cluster in the file, the file size, and other information (see fig. 16.3). The process of manually unerasing files is somewhat like solving a mystery—you must find all the clusters that make up the file (if possible) and place those clusters in order. If you know how many clusters are needed to make up the file, you know when you have completed the task of finding all the clusters in a file.

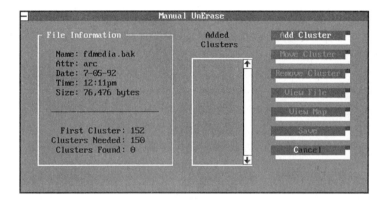

Fig. 16.3

The Manual UnErase dialog box.

The options on the right side of the Manual UnErase dialog box help you piece together the file to unerase. The Added Clusters list box shows which clusters have been located and added to the recovered file to make up the unerased file.

 If you cannot recover the file with **M**anual UnErase, you still may be able to recover all or parts of the file with Norton Disk Editor. See Chapter 17 for more information on that program.

The following sections describe the processes involved in assembling the clusters of the file, viewing the file, correcting the file, and completing the manual unerase procedure. To cancel this procedure without saving, choose the **C**ancel option or press Esc. UnErase displays the following message in a dialog box:

```
Do you wish to abandon the work in progress?
```

To return to unerasing the file, choose **N**o or press Enter. To stop the unerase process, choose **Y**es; the program returns to the Erased Files dialog box.

Adding Clusters

To begin the process of restoring a file, choose the **A**dd Cluster option from the Manual UnErase dialog box. The Add Clusters dialog box appears (see fig. 16.4). Choose **A**ll Clusters first to try to restore the erased file. When you use this option, the program finds all clusters that probably belong to the file and displays them in the Added Clusters list box in the Manual UnErase dialog box. If you need to choose other clusters and add them to the file individually, refer to the next section.

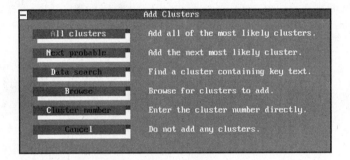

Fig. 16.4

The Add Clusters dialog box.

Finding Missing Clusters

Generally, the **A**ll Clusters option in the Add Clusters dialog box can assemble the entire file. If viewing the unerased file reveals that some parts of the file are still missing after you use this option, you must use a different technique to locate the missing information. The following sections describe three techniques for finding missing clusters.

Adding the Next Probable Cluster

The **N**ext Probable option in the Add Clusters dialog box adds to the file the cluster that the program determines is the next probable cluster belonging to the file. After you add such a cluster, choose the View **F**ile option in the Manual UnErase dialog box to look at the file's contents. If the cluster you added belongs to the file but is in the wrong order, you can change the order of the clusters as described in the section "Moving and Deleting Clusters" later in this chapter.

Searching for Data in the File

Use the **D**ata Search option if **N**ext Probable cannot locate the next cluster. First view the file and determine what is missing from it. If you are unerasing a report with seven sections, for example, and you find sections labeled I through VI, you may want to search for the text *VII* to find the next cluster. In other words, you must be familiar with the text of the file you are unerasing in order to use the **D**ata Search option effectively.

When you choose **D**ata Search, the Data Search dialog box appears (see fig. 16.5). You can enter the search text in ASCII or hexadecimal code (hex), but ASCII is generally easier. When you enter search text in ASCII, the text also appears in hex. Type the text in the appropriate text box (**A**SCII or **H**ex) for the format you want to use. If you want the search to be case-sensitive, deselect the **I**gnore Case option. If you want to begin the search at a particular sector location on disk, choose the **S**earch at Specified Sector Offset option. This option is helpful if you suspect that the data for which you are searching is toward the end of the disk; you can speed up the search by starting the search at some sector later in the disk instead of starting the search at sector 0 (which is the default).

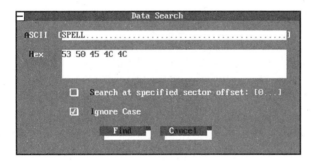

Fig. 16.5

Entering search text in the Data Search dialog box.

After you enter your search text, choose **F**ind. A search for the text begins. If the search text is found, a few lines of the cluster appear in the View File dialog box. You can then choose any of the following options:

Option	Description
Add Cluster	Adds this cluster to the list
Find Next	Continues search for next matching text
Hex	Displays the find in hexadecimal format (if currently in text mode)

continues

Option	Description
Text	Displays the find in text mode (if currently in hexadecimal mode)
Done	Stops the search

In the View File dialog box, the **H**ex option is provided if you have searched in text mode. If you have searched for hexadecimal characters, the dialog box provides the **T**ext option. When you choose the **H**ex option, the program redisplays the text file in hexadecimal characters with text characters in the right side of the dialog box. If the file is displayed in hexadecimal characters and you choose **T**ext, the program switches the view to text characters.

Continue the search until you find the right cluster to add.

Searching for a Numbered Cluster

The **C**luster Number option in the Add Clusters dialog box allows you to add one or more clusters to the list of clusters in the file. When you choose this option, you see a dialog box similar to the one shown in figure 16.6. In this dialog box, you can specify **S**tarting and **E**nding Cluster numbers for adding clusters in the file being unerased. In some cases, you may know the number of the cluster or clusters you want to add to the file. Perhaps you intentionally placed clusters in particular locations on the disk to hide them for a special reason (for more on clusters, see Chapter 13 on Disk Tools). Or you may have located a cluster by using a technique other than UnErase. Specify the clusters to add here, and then choose **O**K to add those cluster numbers to the Added Clusters list box in the Manual UnErase dialog box, or choose **C**ancel to exit this dialog box without adding any clusters.

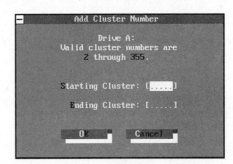

Fig. 16.6

The Add Cluster Number dialog box.

Viewing the File

From the Manual UnErase dialog box, you can view the unerased file as you assemble it from clusters, or you can view a map of the file. Viewing the file enables you to verify that all clusters have been found and are in correct order. For database, text, or word processing files, this verification is fairly easy if you are familiar with the information in the file. For files whose information is stored in cryptic codes, such as some spreadsheet files or program files, determining whether the file is intact may be more difficult.

Choose View File from the Manual UnErase dialog box to see the file in progress. Figure 16.7 shows the file SPELL.TXT being viewed. You can use the up- and down-arrow keys or the mouse and scroll bar to scroll through the entire file to determine whether it is complete.

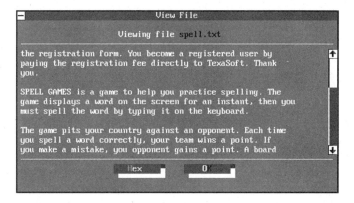

Fig. 16.7

Viewing a file in the Manual UnErase viewer.

At the bottom of the viewer, you can choose the **H**ex option to cause the viewer to switch to hexadecimal format mode. For some files, you may know of markers in the file that are documented in hexadecimal format; looking for these codes in hexadecimal format may be easier than looking for them in ASCII. Figure 16.8 shows the same file in hex mode.

Notice in the hex viewer that the ASCII version of the text appears at the far right of the dialog box, with the equivalent hex codes at the left of the dialog box. To switch back to text mode, choose the **T**ext button. To end the viewer, choose **OK**.

You may want to know the location of the file in relation to the rest of the disk—for example, whether the file is in one location or fragmented. If the file is fragmented, finding the pieces may be more difficult. Knowing that the file is fragmented, however, may give you some clues as to where to look on the disk for file fragments. Choose View **M**ap from the

Manual UnErase dialog box to see a map of your hard disk, showing where found clusters are located relative to one another (see fig. 16.9). The F in the upper portion of the map locates the portion of the current file being unerased. For large or fragmented files, the F marker may appear at more than one location on the map.

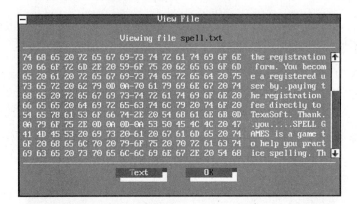

Fig. 16.8

Viewing a file in hexadecimal mode.

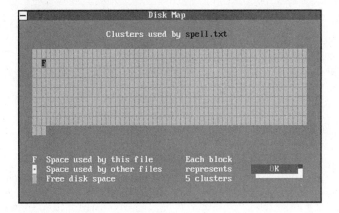

Fig. 16.9

A map of clusters known to be used by the file being unerased.

Moving and Deleting Clusters

Whether you add clusters automatically or individually as you recover clusters of a file, you may find that some of the clusters are out of order in the Added Clusters list box. To move a cluster to another location in the cluster list, use the arrow keys or the mouse to highlight the cluster you want to move. Press the space bar or choose Move Cluster to select the cluster. Triangles will appear to the left and right of the selected cluster. Use the up- and down-arrow keys to move the cluster to a new location in the list. Press the space bar again or choose End Move to anchor the cluster.

If you determine that a cluster does not belong to the file you are trying to unerase, use the arrow keys (or mouse) and the space bar to select that cluster. Then press Del or choose **R**emove Cluster to delete it from the Added Clusters list box.

Saving the Restored File

When you have found all the clusters and placed them in the correct order, choose **S**ave from the Manual UnErase dialog box to save the file to disk and end the manual unerase procedure. The program returns to the Erased Files dialog box and displays the word RECOVERED next to the file. If all the file's clusters were not recovered, a dialog box appears with the following message:

You have selected **less** data than the erased file originally held.

If you have specified too many clusters in the Added Clusters list box, the following message appears:

You have selected **more** data than the erased file originally held.

Choose **S**ave Anyway if you want to save the file with the information that you restored. Choose **R**esume to return to the Manual UnErase dialog box and continue the unerase process.

On occasion, you may want to create a new file rather than unerase an existing file. For this process, refer to the next section.

Creating a New File from Clusters

The Create File option in the UnErase File menu is similar to the **M**anual UnErase option. The difference is that you create an entirely new file rather than restore the pieces of an unerased file. You can use this option to create a new file from file particles that are on disk but may not necessarily be part of an unerased file as detected by the UnErase procedure. This situation may occur, for example, with a file that has been erased for a period of time so that its initial directory information has been overwritten by another file.

To create a new file, you must start with a new name. When you choose the Create **F**ile option from the UnErase **F**ile menu, you are prompted to enter the name of the new file, as shown in figure 16.10.

Entering a name
for the file to
create.

When you enter the new file name, the Manual UnErase dialog box is
displayed (refer to fig. 16.3). At this point, you can use the search procedures already described to locate clusters to form a file. After you
have added all the clusters you want to use in the new file, choose
the **S**ave option. The file is stored to disk under the name you have
indicated.

Summary

The **M**anual UnErase and Create **F**ile procedures enable you to search
the clusters of your disk for file fragments and then piece them together to re-create an erased file or to recover portions of files. This
chapter described how to locate all the clusters known to belong to a
file and how to use search techniques to search for clusters that belong
to the file but could not be found automatically by the UnErase program. The chapter also showed you how to view a file to determine
whether all its pieces have been found. When you have found as much
of a file as possible, you can then save the file back to disk.

The **M**anual UnErase command enables you to view your disk one cluster at a time. To learn how you can obtain an even more detailed look
at your disk, turn to the next chapter, which discusses Norton Disk
Editor.

Using Disk Editor

U nErase and Norton Disk Doctor (NDD) are powerful programs, but sometimes even these programs cannot solve your problem. If you first tried UnErase (including Manual UnErase) and NDD to recover some information from a disk but still have important data to recover, your next step is Norton Disk Editor.

Disk Editor is a set of routines that enables you to explore the information on the disk, down to the level of examining each individual byte. With Disk Editor, you can display and directly edit information on a disk, including system areas. You can search for lost data, try to fix problems in programs, and recover some or all portions of erased files.

 NOTE Data recovery at this level is beyond the scope of this book. This chapter provides an overview of just the essentials of the Disk Editor program. For details on the program, consult the *Norton Utilities 7 User's Guide*.

To use Disk Editor, you need more knowledge about the way the disk works and the way the information is stored than you need for the NDD and UnErase commands. The Disk Editor program is not as easy to use or as automated as UnErase and NDD. To learn to use the Disk Editor program effectively, you may need a significant amount of time. If you try to recover some information that takes only an hour to re-create, using Disk Editor to get the data back may not be worth the trouble— you may just want to retype the information.

> **WARNING:** Unless you are very knowledgeable about the structure of a disk, using Disk Editor for all but simple fixes can cause data to become unusable and unrecoverable. To benefit from this discussion of Disk Editor, you should know disk storage terms, such as *cluster*, *sector*, *partition table*, and *FAT*. The Disk Editor program enables you to recover disk information as well as destroy it. The program is powerful enough that you could destroy your entire disk. For more information, see Chapter 3, "Understanding How Disks Work," or *Que's Guide to Data Recovery.*

Running Disk Editor

To begin Disk Editor, choose the Disk Editor option from the Norton main menu or enter **DISKEDIT** at the DOS prompt. Note the syntax of this command:

DISKEDIT [*d:*][*path*][*filespec*][*switches*]

The following switches are available:

Switch	Description
/M	Selects maintenance mode, which means that Norton Utilities bypasses the DOS logical organization. If a disk is badly damaged, you may need to use this mode. If Norton does not begin to analyze a disk when you run the command, try the /M switch to see whether that helps. You cannot work with files or unerase files in maintenance mode.
/X:*d*	Excludes certain drives from absolute sector processing. Use this switch if you have nonexistent drives allocated. The letter *d* represents the list of drives to exclude. For example, DEF excludes drives D, E, and F from absolute sector processing.
/W	Enables the write mode for Disk Editor (turns off read-only mode). You can also turn write mode off with the Configuration option in the **Tools** pull-down menu.

When Disk Editor begins, you will likely see the screen shown in figure 17.1, indicating that you are in read-only mode. This screen tells you that you can safely explore your disk without worrying about changing important information.

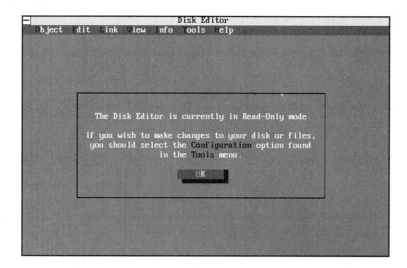

In read-only mode, you can use the editor to examine your disk, but you cannot write anything to your disk. Later in this chapter, the procedure to change the mode is discussed. When you first begin to use Disk Editor, it is a good idea to keep it in read-only mode to protect yourself against accidental writes to the disk.

When you choose **OK** in the message screen or press Enter, the Disk Editor main screen appears (see fig. 17.2).

This screen displays the files found on the disk, listing file specification, size, date, time, the cluster where the file begins, and attributes now set. The Disk Editor menu bar is at the top of the screen. To open the pull-down menus, press Alt plus the highlighted letter of the menu item, point to the menu name and click, or press the shortcut key combination shown on the menu for that item. Generally, you use the options on this menu to find something on disk that you want to change, you make the change, and you write the change back to disk.

Suppose that you have a directory which cannot be erased with the DOS or Norton Remove Directory command. This situation can occur if a file or subdirectory has been corrupted and does not erase properly. DOS does not erase the directory because the operating system thinks the directory still contains information. To erase this directory manually, you must locate the directory name in the Disk Editor main screen and replace the first character of the name with the hexadecimal number E5, which is the symbol DOS uses to denote an erased file. The easiest way to replace the first character is to display the directory in hex mode (choose the As **H**ex option in the **V**iew menu); then change the first character of the subdirectory name to E5.

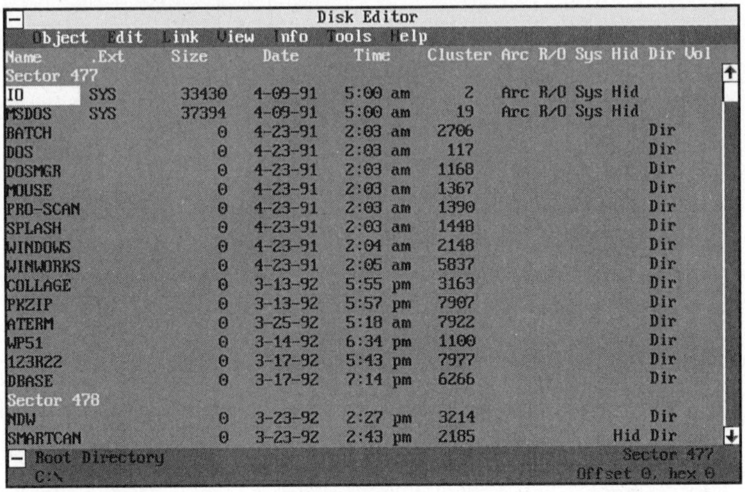

Fig. 17.2

The Disk Editor main screen.

With Disk Editor, you can locate the directory name, change the first character, and then write the change back to disk. (In this example, you also run the CHKDSK /F command or NDD to clean up any lost clusters caused by the change.)

Using the Object Menu

Generally, before you do any editing on the disk, you choose which object to edit. You choose the object with the **O**bject menu (see fig. 17.3). The objects that you can choose include the drive, directory, file, cluster, sector, physical sector, partition table, boot record, and copies of the file allocation table (FAT).

The **C**lipboard option enables you to store (in the clipboard) a block of information from the disk and later place that block elsewhere on disk. With the **M**emory Dump option, you can view, search, and copy information from RAM. RAM may contain information not on disk if an application crashes before your information has been written to disk.

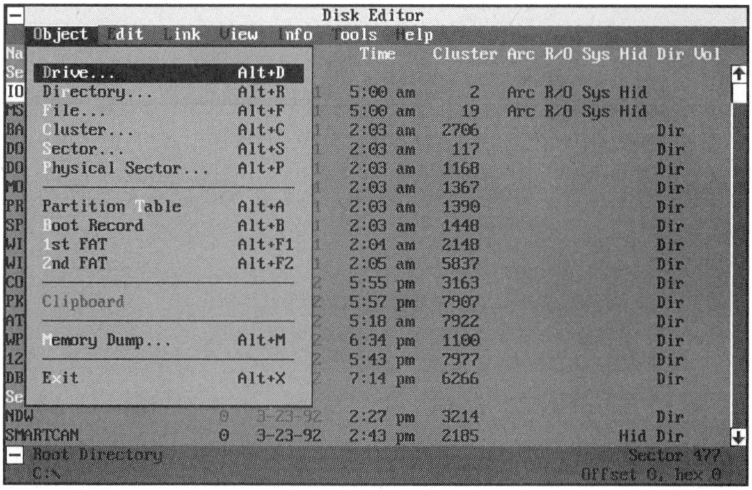

Fig. 17.3

The Disk Editor
Object menu.

WARNING: Use Memory Dump with care. This option may
cause some computers to lock up, and then require a boot, which
causes you to lose information in RAM (in this case, the information you currently have in the clipboard). This problem is particularly true of PS/2 computers.

Using the Edit Menu

The Edit menu enables you to edit information on disk (see fig. 17.4).
The Undo option in the menu enables you to undo the last items you
edited. Undo remembers 512 bytes of information and undoes items
in the reverse order of how you edited them. Undo, however, undoes
items only within a sector boundary. If you have moved to another
sector, Undo undoes items just in the current sector. If parentheses
appear around this command or it appears grayed, you have nothing
to undo.

The Mark, Copy, Paste Over, and Fill options enable you to manipulate
information on the disk. You use Mark to capture data from the disk
and place the data in the clipboard so that it can be copied elsewhere.

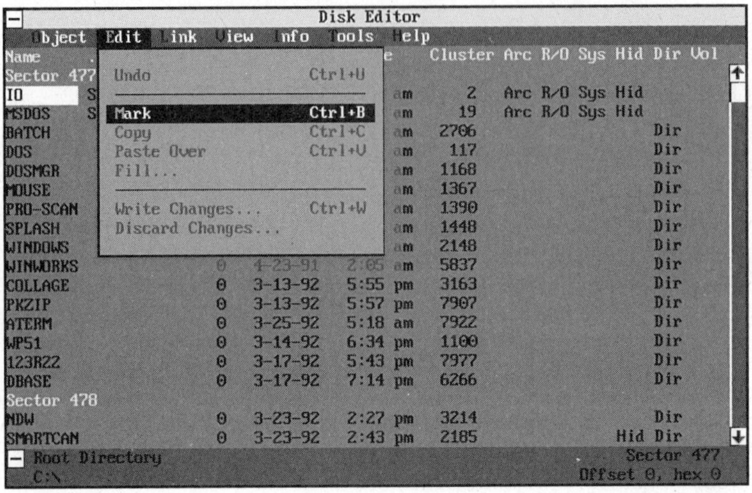

Fig. 17.4

The Disk Editor
Edit menu.

While viewing a portion of the disk in Disk Editor (viewing is usually easiest in hex mode), you can copy information by placing the cursor at the beginning of the block you want to copy. Choose **M**ark from the **E**dit menu and move the cursor to the end of the block. If you use a mouse, set the mouse pointer at the beginning of the block, press the mouse button, and drag the mouse pointer to the end of the block. To place the information in the clipboard, select **C**opy from the **E**dit menu.

The clipboard can hold up to 4,096 bytes (characters) of information. The information remains in the clipboard until replaced with other information. To copy the information from the clipboard to somewhere else on the disk, go to that location, place the cursor where you want the information to begin, and choose **P**aste Over from the **E**dit menu.

NOTE The paste-over procedure overwrites information now in that location; no insert mode is available.

Use the **F**ill option to fill a block of space with a single character. Mark a block, as described in the copy procedure. After you choose **F**ill from the **E**dit menu, you are prompted to select the character with which to fill the block. You can choose an ASCII character from a list box, and that character fills the entire marked region. This method erases sensitive information from disks.

After you change a disk by copying or filling, these changes are not actually written to the disk until you choose the **W**rite Changes option from the **E**dit menu. To choose not to make these changes, use **D**isregard Changes.

Using the Link Menu

Each file on disk is related to a directory and a FAT entry. When you edit the contents of the file, you may need to reference information in the directory or file allocation table (FAT). How can you locate on disk the directory related to the file, or how can you locate in the FAT table the information associated with the file? The answer is the Link menu.

The Link menu enables you to travel back and forth to areas related to a particular file (see fig. 17.5). If you choose the **D**irectory option from the Link menu (while you examine a file), Disk Editor takes you to the place on disk that contains the directory entry related to that file, and places you in the appropriate directory viewer. Similarly, choosing the Cluster Chain (FAT) option takes you to the place in the FAT related to that file. If you choose the File option, you are returned to the actual contents of the file.

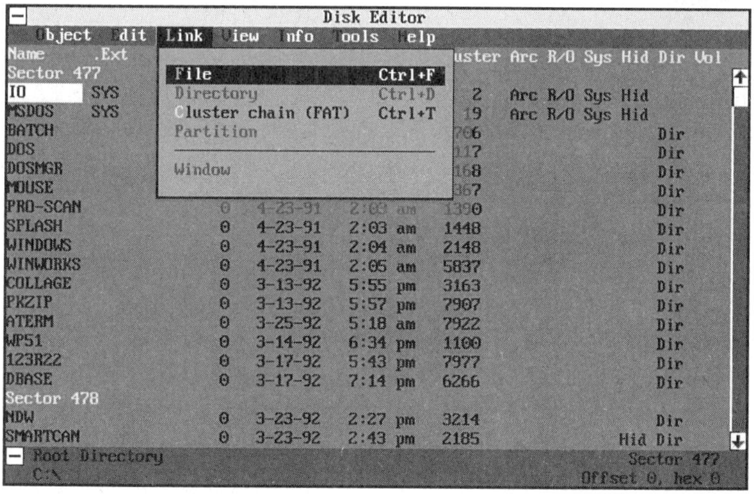

Fig. 17.5

The Disk Editor Link menu.

If you edit a partition rather than a file, the Link menu enables you to link to the partition table or boot record. In each case, the allowable links are noted by Link menu options not surrounded by parentheses or grayed.

The **W**indow option in the Link menu enables you to look at the FAT table in one half of the screen as you examine the contents of a file in the other half. To use this option, you must first be viewing a copy of the FAT. To view the 1st or 2nd FAT, choose the appropriate FAT option from the **O**bject menu. To split the screen, press Shift+F5 (or choose **S**plit Window from the View menu). To link the screens, choose the **W**indow option from the **L**ink menu. You then see a screen similar to the one in figure 17.6.

Using the View Menu

The **V**iew menu enables you to choose various options when viewing information on disk (see fig. 17.7). The As **H**ex and As **T**ext options enable you to see the information on-screen as hexadecimal code and ASCII text, respectively. Text files usually are viewed in text mode. Programs or coded files may be viewed in hex format. The other modes enable you to see data appropriate to what you are viewing. If you look at the FAT, for example, you usually choose the As FAT option.

The window options in the **V**iew menu enable you to split the screen and view two items simultaneously. You can split the screen with **S**plit Window (Shift+F5), switch from window to window with **S**witch Windows (Shift+F8), and adjust the size of the window with **G**row Window (Shift+F6) or Sh**r**ink Window (Shift+F7).

Using the Info Menu

The **I**nfo menu enables you to display information about the object or drive you are viewing, or to look at a map of the object (a graphic display that shows the object in relation to all the clusters on disk).

The Info menu is shown in figure 17.8. To look at a map of the IMAGE.DAT file created by the Norton Image program, select the File option from the Object menu and then select the file IMAGE.DAT from the list of files. Choose the Map of Object option from the Info menu, and a dialog box similar to the one in figure 17.9 appears. Notice the Fs on the map. These Fs show where within the disk space the selected object is stored.

The FF at the upper right of the map shows the location of this file on the disk.

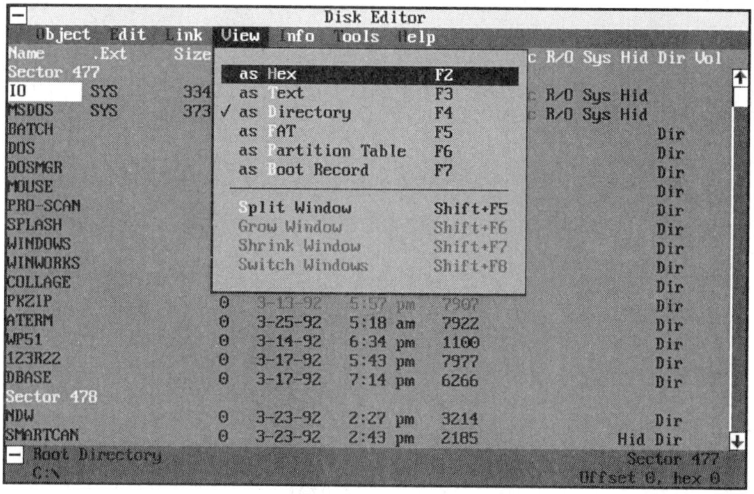

Fig. 17.7

The Disk Editor
View menu.

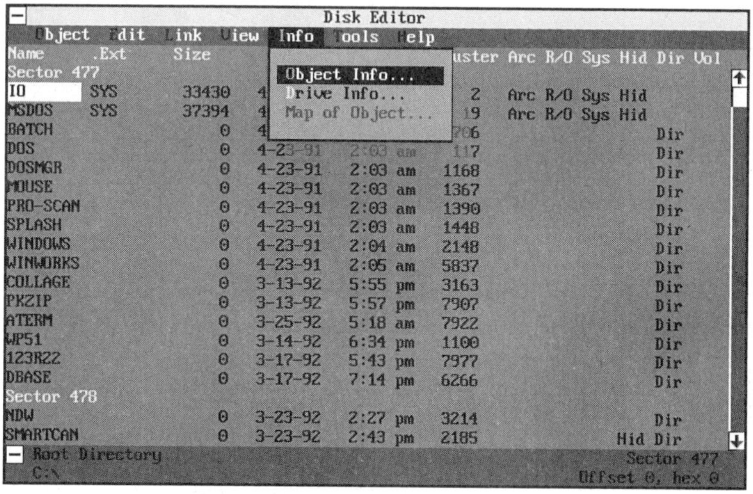

Fig. 17.8

The Disk Editor
Info menu.

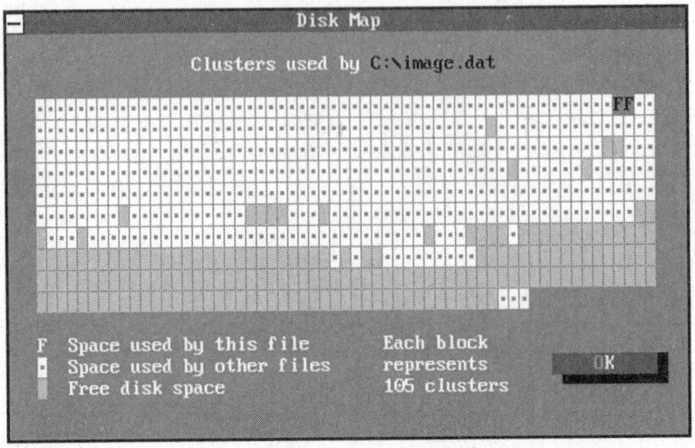

Fig. 17.9

The Disk Editor
Disk Map.

Using the Tools Menu

The Tools menu, shown in figure 17.10, gives you several tools for exploring the contents of a disk.

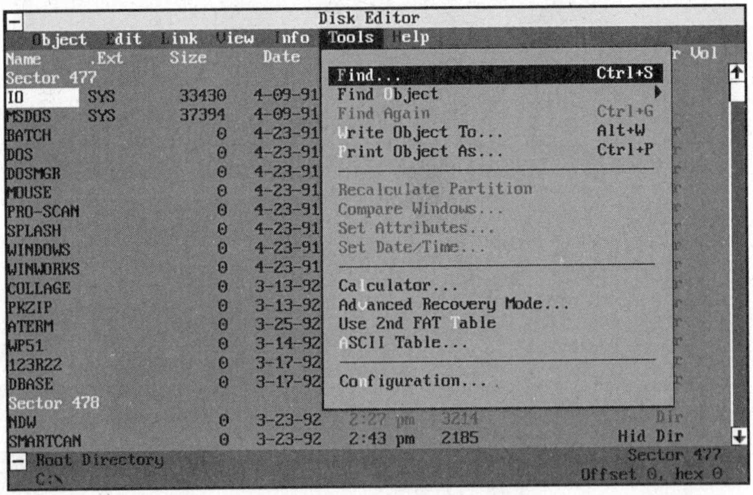

Fig. 17.10

The Disk Editor
Tools menu.

Here are the options in the Tools menu:

Option	Description
Find	Searches for a string of text on a disk. Find can be helpful if you are looking for information on disk but do not know which file (or erased space) contains the information.

Option	Description
Find **O**bject	Allows you to specify a search for a partition or boot record, a FAT, or a subdirectory.
Find A**g**ain	Repeats the last **F**ind command.
Write Object To	Writes the object you are currently editing to disk. You are asked to specify a file name, starting cluster number, or sector number. With this option, you can find pieces of an erased file and write out the information to disk. The **W**rite Object To option is a way to recover information that you cannot recover with UnErase or Disk Tools.
Print Object As	Prints the object you are currently editing to the printer. You can choose to print the information in hexadecimal, directory, FAT, boot sector, or partition table format.
Recalculate Partition	Calculates two items (available when you are in partition table view): the relative sector number from the starting sector coordinates, and the number of sectors from the starting and ending sector coordinates.
Compare Windows	Compares two windows and places the cursor at the first point where the information in the two windows disagrees.
Set **A**ttributes	Changes the attributes for a group of files (available when a directory object is displayed and when one or more entries are highlighted).
Set **D**ate/Time	Changes the date and time for a group of files (available when a directory object is displayed and when one or more entries are highlighted).
Calculator	Enables you to perform arithmetic with binary, hexadecimal, or decimal numbers.
Ad**v**anced Recovery Mode	Allows you to specify and test settings for the hard disk, including physical characteristics and partition settings.
Use 2nd FAT **T**able	Uses the second FAT table information rather than the first table. Use this option when the information in the first FAT table is corrupted.
ASCII Table	Displays the ASCII character set and gives the decimal and hexadecimal value for each character.
Configuration	Sets several options for using Disk Editor.

If you choose the Configuration option from the Tools menu, the program displays the Configuration dialog box (see fig. 17.11) in which you can set additional options for using Disk Editor.

Fig. 17.11

The Disk Editor Configuration dialog box.

The following Configuration options are available in Disk Editor:

Option	Description
Read Only	Prevents you from writing changed information to disk. You can change the default setting of read-only to enable users to write changed information to disk.
Quick Move	Speeds up response time by omitting the rewriting of file names in the status bar of the Disk Editor main screen.
Auto View	Tells Disk Editor to choose the most appropriate view to be used.
Quick **L**inks	Links from one object to a related object when you press Enter or click the mouse.
Exit Prompt	Tells Disk Editor to display a warning prompt when you press Esc to exit the program.
S**h**ow All Characters	Shows all characters as stored in the object. (This is a character filter that tells the program how to display text.)
View WordStar Files	Specifies that the text being viewed is stored in WordStar format. Thus, the characters shown are converted from WordStar codes to readable characters.

Option	Description
Save	Saves configuration selections to the file NU.INI.
OK	Uses the current settings for the current session only; these settings are not saved to disk as default settings.
Cancel	Exits the Configuration dialog box without making any changes.

Summary

Norton Disk Editor enables you to make real changes on the disk drive—viewing and changing information directly on the disk for files and disk system areas. With Disk Editor, you can change information on the disk that cannot otherwise be changed.

Disk Editor is both a powerful and a dangerous tool. The best way to learn to use it is by practicing on a floppy disk—particularly one that has been formatted with the System Files option in Safe Format or with the /S option in the DOS FORMAT command. With this practice disk, you can explore all of Disk Editor's options and become comfortable with using them before you edit a "live" disk. This chapter concludes Part IV on advanced recovery techniques. Part V deals with Norton commands that can help you fine-tune your computer to make it run more efficiently. Turn now to Chapter 18 to learn about the System Info command.

Making Your Computer Work More Efficiently

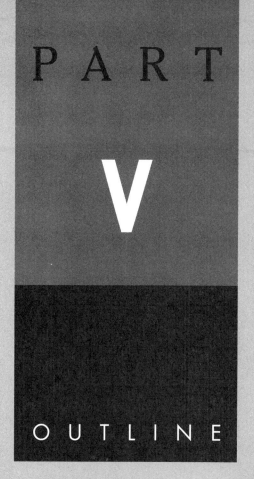

P A R T

V

O U T L I N E

Using System Info

Norton Utilities provides you with ways to safeguard the data in your computer and to use your computer more efficiently. The gold in Fort Knox is safe but not very accessible. The data in your computer should be both safe and efficient to use.

Part V of this book, "Making Your Computer Work More Efficiently," helps you understand your computer's capabilities better and shows you how to fine-tune your computer to run faster and more efficiently. This first chapter in Part V discusses the System Info (SYSINFO) utility. System Info is like a stethoscope, giving you information about what is going on inside your computer.

This information is valuable in several ways. Some programs, for example, cannot run on computers with older ROM BIOS chips (which contain basic system programming). With System Info, you can determine quickly the date of the current ROM BIOS chip on your computer. If you are going to upgrade or replace hardware, such as a modem card, you should know what kind of bus you have. Because the DOS CHKDSK command does not report any memory over 640K, System Info is valuable in finding out how much memory your computer has and what kinds of memory you have (that is, main, extended, and expanded memory). These pieces of information and much more are revealed through the System Info program.

You can use all the utilities discussed in Part V to make hard disk access faster and more efficient and to compare your computer's speed and efficiency with those of other computers. These utilities—System Info, Speed Disk, Calibrate, and Norton Cache—not only make your programs run faster, but also reduce wear and tear on your hard disk (and may prolong its life).

Understanding System Info

The old saying "Know thyself" often is quoted to emphasize the fact that before you can do much with your life, you must know your capabilities and limitations. A new saying should be "Know thy computer." If you are to get the most out of your computer, you should know it well. True to form, Norton Utilities provides you with a way to know your computer well: the System Info utility. System Info enables you to look into the heart of your computer and to discover how powerful (or weak) it is, compared with other computers. System Info also shows you what is contained in your computer's memory and what key devices (such as disk drives) are available for its use.

With the Norton System Info (SYSINFO) command, you can compare your computer with other computers in terms of processing and disk speeds. The System Info test compares the performance of your computer with that of the following computers:

- A standard IBM PC XT using the Intel 8088 microprocessor and running at 4.77 MHz

- An IBM PC AT using the Intel 80286 microprocessor and running at 8 MHz

- A COMPAQ 486 computer using the Intel 80486 microprocessor and running at 33 MHz

The System Info command also gives you fast access to vital information about a computer. If you help other people with their computers (as a user-support technician, for example), the System Info command can help you discover information about a computer that you have never used before. You may be interested in the existence of a math coprocessor, the type of video display being used, the existence of parallel and serial ports, the amount of memory available and used, and other items described by the System Info command.

When you run the System Info command from the Norton main screen or from the DOS prompt with no switches, the program presents about 20 different dialog boxes (depending on your computer's configuration). These dialog boxes and their contents are described in the following sections.

Starting System Info

You can begin the System Info program by choosing it from the Norton main screen or by entering **SYSINFO** at the DOS prompt. You use the following syntax at the DOS prompt:

SYSINFO [*d*:] [*switches*]

The *d*: option is the letter of the hard disk drive that you want to test. The available *switches* for the System Info command are the following:

Switch	Description
/AUTO:*n*	Tells the command to operate in automatic mode. In this mode, the system information is shown dialog box by dialog box, with a pause of *n* seconds between dialog boxes. If you do not specify *n* in the switch, the pause between dialog boxes is five seconds.
/DEMO	Causes System Info to operate in demo mode and to scroll continuously through four dialog boxes: System Summary, CPU Benchmark, Disk Speed Benchmark, and Overall Performance. You can use this switch to see how the performance of your computer measures up to that of other well-known computers.
/DI	Produces only the Drive Information summary dialog box.
/N	Skips the live-memory probe. In some computers, the live-memory probe forces you to reboot after the System Info test. Use the /N switch to get around this problem. This switch is necessary if your computer is not a 100-percent-compatible IBM clone. If the System Info command causes your computer to freeze, use the /N switch to avert this problem in the future.
/REP:*file1*	Causes a report to be printed to the file specified by *file1*.
/SPEC:*file2*	Causes the report to use settings stored in the file named *file2*.
/SOUND	Beeps between CPU tests.
/SUMMARY	Displays information about a specific drive.
/TSR	Shows all TSR (terminate-and-stay-resident) programs in memory.

Viewing the System Summary Dialog Box

A System Info test on drive C of a 386SX/10 computer with a 122M hard disk was used to create these dialog boxes. The first dialog box that appears when you issue the System Info command is the System Summary dialog box (see fig. 18.1).

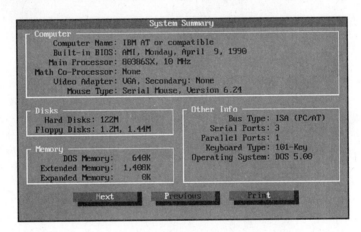

The System Summary dialog box for a 386SX/10.

Notice the three options at the bottom of the dialog box: **Next**, **Previous**, and **Print**. To scroll through the dialog boxes, you can use the mouse or arrow keys to choose **Next** or **Previous**. Choose Print to print a summary of the information to the printer.

To exit the current dialog box and return to DOS or the Norton main screen, press Esc or double-click the control box in the upper-left corner of the System Information main screen.

NOTE A menu bar appears at the top of the System Information main screen. You can use this menu bar to display any of the dialog boxes that are available in System Info. For information on how to use this menu, see "Using the Menu Bar and Printing Reports" later in this chapter.

Computer Processor Information

The System Summary dialog box displays information about the computer being tested in four areas: Computer, Disks, Memory, and Other Info. The first item in the Computer section is the Computer Name. In this case, the program gives the name as an IBM AT or compatible. The computer being tested (a 386SX/10) is an AT-compatible computer because it uses the ISA bus type (discussed in the following section).

The Built-in BIOS information tells you the date of the BIOS (basic input/output system). The BIOS contains an essential set of software—sometimes called *firmware*—in ROM (read-only memory) that you can access when you turn on your computer. This BIOS software tells the computer how to initiate a system boot. In this case, the BIOS is an AMI type, with a date of Monday, April 9, 1990. This date can be important because some newer software programs will not run with older versions of the BIOS.

A surprising number of versions of BIOS exist. IBM has used more than 20 versions in its computers, ranging from the original PC to the current PS/2 and PS/1 lines. Other third-party companies manufacture "clone" BIOSs—one reason why so many IBM-compatible computers have been sold.

If you need to call your computer manufacturer's support line, you may want to supply the date of the BIOS you are using. Like software, older BIOSs may contain bugs, and the date will tell the support representative whether the problem you are having could be related to a buggy BIOS. Providing the date and type of BIOS that you are using is helpful when you are calling for support on software or a peripheral device (for example, a disk drive, audio card, network card, or backup tape system). For example, to install a 1.44M disk drive in an older PC, you must upgrade the BIOS to a version that supports that kind of drive.

 **NOTE** The BIOS is contained in a small ROM chip in your system board. If you are comfortable working inside the computer box, you can update your ROM BIOS chip fairly easily by pulling off the old chip and replacing it with a newer chip. (Be certain that you replace the chip with one that is compatible with your computer.) If you decide to upgrade the chip yourself, purchase the chip from a dealer who is familiar with your brand of computer, or buy the chip from your computer's manufacturer.

The Main Processor reported for this computer is an 80386SX, 10 MHz. Several Intel microprocessors, however, can be reported. Some of the most common microprocessors are listed in table 18.1.

NOTE Some processors come in more than one variety. One version of the 80386 microprocessor, for example, is the 80386SX (which was used to capture the figures in this chapter). This chip has all the characteristics of the normal 80386 chip except that it has a 16-bit external data bus structure instead of the 32-bit structure used by the 80386 chip. Machines built around the SX chips are less expensive.

Table 18.1 Intel Microprocessor Chips and Math Coprocessors

Chip Name	Computer	Math Coprocessor	Common Speeds	Internal/External Processor Bits
8086	PC	8087	4.77, 8, 10 MHz	16/16
8088	PC	8087	4.77, 8, 10 MHz	16/8
80286	IBM AT class	80287	6, 8, 10, 12 MHz	16/16
80386SL	Wide variety	80387	16, 20, 25 MHz	32/16
80386SX	Wide variety	80387SX	16, 20 MHz	32/16
80386DX	Wide variety	80387	16, 20, 25, 33 MHz	32/32
80486	Wide variety	Built-in	20, 25 MHz	32/32
80486SX	Wide variety	80486 Overdrive	16, 20, 25, 33 MHz	32/32
80486DX	Wide variety	Built-in	25, 33, 50 MHz	32/32
80486DX2	Wide variety	Built-in	50, 66 MHz	32/32
Pentium (80586)	Wide variety	Built-in		

Another factor in the functionality of the microprocessor is its speed. Table 18.1 shows common speeds (in megahertz) for the processors listed. Speed alone, however, does not determine the power of a processor. A 25 MHz 80486, for example, is more powerful than a 25 MHz 80386 because the 80486 chip can do more in the same amount of time. Therefore, you should not use clock speed alone as a measure of system power.

Other factors influence the power of a computer, so two computers, each using a 50 MHz 80486DX, may have different actual processing speeds. See "Viewing the Overall Performance Index Dialog Box" later in this chapter for more information on how to compare the processing power of two computers.

The DX2 version of the 80486 uses a process called *clock doubling* to achieve higher speed. Thus, the 80486DX2 running at 50 MHz actually is a 25 MHz chip with its speed doubled. The Overdrive-SX chip is an up-grade of the 486SX chip that doubles the chip's speed. A 486SX running at 16 MHz with Overdrive, for example, runs at 32 MHz.

Some processors come in low-power versions. The 80C88 and 80C286 processors, for example, use less power than the 8088 and 80286 use. These chips often are used in laptop computers because of the power limitation of batteries.

The math coprocessor is a "sister" microcomputer processor that gives the computer the capability to perform mathematical calculations faster. For many number-intensive tasks, a math coprocessor can cut processing time dramatically. A sophisticated statistical analysis such as a multiple regression, for example, may take 30 seconds to perform on a computer with an 80286 processor. Add an 80287 coprocessor, and the same calculation may take only 1 to 3 seconds.

Beginning with some versions of the 80486 chip, the math coprocessor was built into the main processor chip. The Overdrive-SX chip is an upgrade of the 486SX chip that doubles the chip's speed. A 486SX running at 16 MHz with Overdrive, for example, runs at 32MHz.

The Video Adapter entry in the System Summary dialog box shows what kind of computer monitor is attached to your computer and whether a secondary monitor is available. (For detailed information about various video adapters, see "Viewing the Video Summary Dialog Box" later in this chapter.) For this report, the adapter is listed as a VGA (Video Graphics Array) adapter. No secondary adapter is listed.

Also reported in the Computer section is the Mouse Type (if any) that you are using. Common mouse types are Microsoft, Microsoft-compatible, and PS/2. If available, a version number is reported also. For this computer, the mouse type reported is a Serial Mouse, Version 6.24.

Disk Drives, Memory, and Other Information

The Disks section tells you the size of your hard disk(s) and floppy disk(s). For this computer, the disks reported are a 122M hard disk and two floppy disks: a 1.2M 5 1/4-inch disk and a 1.44M 3 1/2-inch disk. (For more information about disks, see "Viewing the Disk Characteristics Dialog Box" later in this chapter.)

The Memory section tells you how much DOS memory you have and how much (if any) extended or expanded memory you have. (The various kinds of memory are discussed in "Viewing the Memory Summary Dialog Box" later in this chapter.)

The Other Info section contains information about other characteristics of your computer. The Bus Type entry refers to one of the following buses:

Bus	Description
ISA	Standard bus for IBM PCs and compatibles and for AT-type computers
MCA	Microchannel bus; used in most IBM PS/2s
EISA	Extended Industry Standard Architecture bus (similar in capability to the newer MCA bus but still compatible with the older ISA bus)

The *bus* is the internal pathway along which electronic signals are sent from one part of the computer to another part. For example, the bus carries information from the microprocessor to the memory chips and back.

The type of bus that your computer uses determines the type of expansion cards you can install. The ISA bus accepts only standard PC/AT-type expansion cards. The MCA bus accepts only MCA cards. The EISA bus accepts EISA or ISA cards. As indicated in figure 18.1, this computer contains an ISA (PC/AT) bus.

The Serial Ports entry in the Other Info section shows how many serial ports are available to the computer. These ports generally are used for communications—for example, hooking up a modem. Some mice also connect to serial ports.

A serial port sends a stream of data, bit after bit, over two wires (like a telephone wire) to the connected device in a process called *asynchronous communication*. Serial cables can extend hundreds of feet from the computer to the connecting device. The computer described in figure 18.1 contains three serial ports.

The Parallel Ports entry shows how many parallel ports are available to the computer. You usually use parallel ports to communicate with a printer, although some other devices (such as backup tape drives) can connect to a parallel port. Parallel ports send eight parallel data bits through eight wires—one bit per wire—simultaneously. This process is called *synchronous communication*. Usually, parallel communications are limited to cables no more than 15 feet long. The computer described in figure 18.1 has one parallel port.

> Information can be sent through a parallel port connection faster than through a serial port connection. Data travels through a serial connection the way cars travel on a one-lane highway: in single file. A parallel connection is like an eight-lane highway with eight cars (pieces of information) running side by side. Thus, a parallel connection can send much more information in the same amount of time than a serial connection can. Some printers can connect to the computer through either a serial port or a parallel port. If you have this option and if your printer is less than 15 feet away from the computer, choose the parallel-port hookup.
>
> **T I P**

The Keyboard Type entry shows the type of keyboard you are using. The computer described in figure 18.1 has a 101-key keyboard, which currently is the standard. For earlier computers, such as the PC, the standard was an 84-key keyboard. The main difference between the keyboards is that the old 84-key PC keyboard does not contain the function keys F11 and F12 or a separate cursor-movement keypad.

The Operating System entry shows what version of DOS you are using. The computer described in figure 18.1 is using DOS 5. DOS versions currently range from 1 to 6.

Viewing the Video Summary Dialog Box

If you press Enter or choose Next in the System Summary dialog box, the Video Summary dialog box appears (see fig. 18.2).

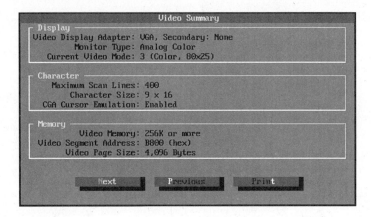

Fig. 18.2

The Video Summary dialog box.

The Video Summary dialog box displays information about the type of monitor you are using. The Display section provides information about your computer's display adapter and monitor. The Character section displays information about the resolution of characters on-screen. Finally, the Memory section shows how much memory is available to your video adapter. The following sections describe the items in each of these three areas of the dialog box.

Video Display Features

The Display section in the Video Summary dialog box tells you which type of display adapter is attached to the computer, the monitor type, and the current video mode. The computer that produced the dialog box shown in figure 18.2 uses a VGA video display adapter.

The Secondary entry shows the type of alternative video adapter that is attached to the computer (if any). The computer described in figure 18.2 has no secondary adapter.

Table 18.2 summarizes several kinds of video adapters. The Resolution column lists the number of dots, or *pixels*, that appear on-screen. The more pixels, the greater the clarity of the screen image.

Table 18.2 Common Video Adapters for IBM-Compatible Computers	
Adapter Type	**Resolution**
Monochrome (text only)	720 x 350
Color Graphics Monitor (CGA)	320 x 200 color mode 640 x 200 single-color mode

Adapter Type	Resolution
Enhanced Graphics (EGA)	640 x 350
Multicolor Graphics (MCGA)	640 x 350, 64 shades of gray or 16 colors
Video Graphics (VGA)	640 x 480, 256 colors
Super VGA	800 x 600 and 1,024 x 768

The Monochrome Display Adapter (MDA) is a single-color adapter that was used mostly for early PCs. This adapter displays text only; no graphics are supported. The resolution of the monochrome adapter is 720 pixels by 350 pixels, and characters are created in a 7-by-9 pixel matrix.

The Color Graphics Adapter (CGA) supports up to four colors simultaneously and has a resolution of 320 by 200 pixels. When only one color is displayed, the adapter has a resolution of 640 by 200 pixels. This adapter supports single-color composite and RBG (red-blue-green) monitors. Its text resolution is inferior to that of the monochrome adapter.

The Enhanced Graphics Adapter (EGA) supports up to 16 colors simultaneously and has a resolution of 640 by 350 pixels. EGA was a transition standard between the CGA and VGA adapters. Although EGA and VGA adapters cost about the same amount of money, the VGA monitor is preferable because it preserves the aspect ratio of graphics. *Aspect ratio* means that certain graphics, such as pie charts, retain their correct aspect (round) instead of being distorted (egg-shaped).

The Multicolor Graphics Array (MCGA) adapter supports up to 64 gray-scale shades in CGA mode and supports up to 16 colors in EGA mode with a resolution of 640 x 350 pixels.

The Video Graphics Array (VGA) adapter, introduced in 1987, supports up to 256 colors simultaneously with a resolution of 640 by 480 pixels. The VGA standard has been pushed to higher levels of resolution (800 x 600 and 1,024 x 768) in Super VGA adapters. VGA became the standard for displays in the late 1980s and continues to be the most common type of display in the early 1990s. The VGA display can also display information for programs that use the older MDA, CGA, and EGA monitor modes.

Video Character and Memory Features

The Character section in the Video Summary dialog box tells you the number of scan lines on-screen, the number of pixels used to create a character (the computer described in this chapter has 400 scan lines, and the character size is 9 x 16 pixels), and the CGA cursor emulation. The more scan lines, the better the clarity of graphics. The more pixels used to display a character, the better the clarity of text. If CGA Cursor Emulation is enabled, EGA or VGA monitors can respond to cursor-sizing calls in the same manner as CGA monitors. (Cursor sizing is discussed in Chapter 22.)

The Memory section contains information about how much memory is allocated to your display and how that memory is used. The Video Segment Address entry tells you where the video memory begins. This information may be important if you are writing a computer program to take advantage of the features of a particular video adapter or if you have a program that requires a particular level of video features. The Video Page Size entry shows how many bytes of information are required to hold one screen's worth of information in the current video mode.

Viewing the Hardware Interrupts Dialog Box

Pressing Enter or choosing Next in the Video Summary dialog box brings you to the Hardware Interrupts dialog box (see fig. 18.3).

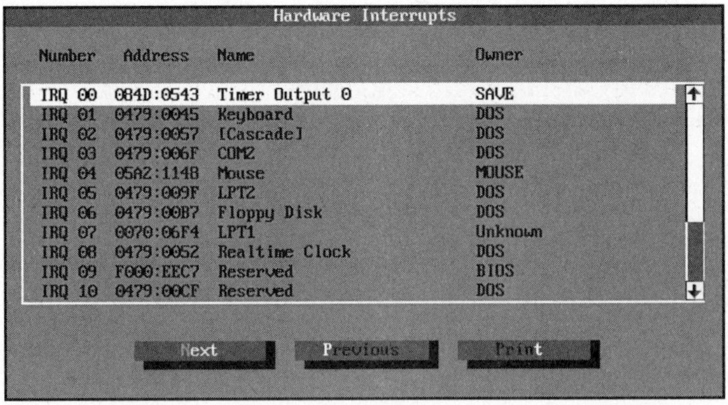

Number	Address	Name	Owner
IRQ 00	084D:0543	Timer Output 0	SAVE
IRQ 01	0479:0045	Keyboard	DOS
IRQ 02	0479:0057	[Cascade]	DOS
IRQ 03	0479:006F	COM2	DOS
IRQ 04	05A2:1148	Mouse	MOUSE
IRQ 05	0479:009F	LPT2	DOS
IRQ 06	0479:00B7	Floppy Disk	DOS
IRQ 07	0070:06F4	LPT1	Unknown
IRQ 08	0479:0052	Realtime Clock	DOS
IRQ 09	F000:EEC7	Reserved	BIOS
IRQ 10	0479:00CF	Reserved	DOS

Next   Previous   Print

Fig. 18.3

The Hardware Interrupts dialog box.

A *hardware interrupt* is a way for hardware devices to request service from the computer. Notice that the devices listed in the Name column of the Hardware Interrupts dialog box include the keyboard, communication ports, and disks. When one of these devices wants to convey information to the computer or to request service from DOS, the device sends an interrupt signal to the computer. Each device is assigned a unique interrupt signal so that the computer knows which device is requesting service. The interrupt names are designated as IRQ numbers. The IRQ number for the keyboard, for example, is 01.

Occasionally, when you add a new device to the computer, you are asked to set its interrupt (IRQ number) to one that currently is not being used. Check the Number, Name, and Owner columns of the Hardware Interrupts dialog box to find out which interrupts are available. If the Name associated with the interrupt is Reserved, the interrupt is not associated with a device now and is therefore available for use. To see interrupts other than the ones listed, use the arrow keys to scroll the list, or click the down arrow on the scroll bar.

Viewing the Software Interrupts Dialog Box

Pressing Enter or choosing Next in the Hardware Interrupts dialog box displays the Software Interrupts dialog box (see fig. 18.4).

```
                        Software Interrupts
   #   Interrupt Name              Address   Owner

  00   Divide by Zero              0116:108A  DOS System Area  ▲
  01   Single Step                 0070:06F4  Unknown
  02   Nonmaskable                 0479:0016  DOS
  03   Breakpoint                  0070:06F4  Unknown
  04   Overflow                    0070:06F4  Unknown
  05   Print Screen                084D:042C  SAVE
  06   Invalid Opcode              F000:EB52  BIOS
  07   Reserved                    F000:EAA6  BIOS
  08   IRQ0 - System Timer         084D:0543  SAVE
  09   IRQ1 - Keyboard             0479:0045  DOS
  0A   IRQ2 - Reserved             0479:0057  DOS             ▼

         Next          Previous          Print
```

Fig. 18.4

The Software Interrupts dialog box.

Software interrupts are similar to hardware interrupts except that a software program is requesting service. The interrupts listed in this dialog box may be useful if you are writing software programs that must take advantage of these interrupts. If, for example, you were writing a software program that needed to communicate with the keyboard, you know that the interrupt associated with the keyboard is IRQ1. To see interrupts other than the ones listed, use the arrow keys to scroll the list, or click the down arrow on the scroll bar.

Viewing the Network Information Dialog Box

If your computer is part of a network, pressing Enter or choosing Next in the Software Interrupts dialog box brings you to the Network Information dialog box. Only information for Novell NetWare networks is supported.

The information displayed about the network user includes the user ID, log-in date, and log-in time. Information displayed about the network includes the default server name, vendor, software, revision date, and copyright. You can find this information useful for software support because different software programs require certain versions of NetWare in order to run properly. If your computer is not part of a network, the CMOS Values dialog box appears (described in the following section).

Viewing the CMOS Values Dialog Box

Pressing Enter or choosing Next in the Network Information dialog box (or in the Software Interrupts dialog box, if your computer is not part of a network) brings you to the CMOS Values dialog box, which contains information about the way your computer is configured (see fig. 18.5).

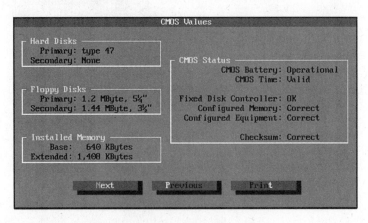

Fig. 18.5

The CMOS Values dialog box.

CMOS (complementary metal-oxide semiconductor) is a chip that stores important setup information about your computer, such as the hard disk type, how many floppy disk drives it has, and how much memory it has. If System Info determines that any of these entries are incorrect, the incorrect values will appear in red or boldfaced.

An important piece of information in this dialog box is the CMOS Battery entry. If your computer begins to operate erratically (if, for example, you are losing time and date information and having problems finding your disks), check this dialog box to see whether the battery is listed as operational. If the battery is not listed as operational, the computer may have lost information about its configuration. (See Chapter 14 for information on Rescue Disk.)

Computers that retain setup information in CMOS have a battery that causes the chip to remember the setup information when the computer is turned off. If the battery loses its charge, the computer loses its setup information. Most CMOS batteries are attached to a battery holder on the inside back panel of the computer. To change batteries, simply unplug the old battery and plug in a new one. (Make sure that the replacement battery is the correct type.) After you replace the battery, you have to run the setup program for your computer or use Rescue Disk (see Chapter 14) to restore your CMOS values.

T I P

The Hard Disks section in the CMOS Values dialog box reports the drive types for your hard disks. For the computer described in this chapter, the hard drive is type 47. Some PCs, however, don't need this information, and the field may contain None even if you have a hard disk.

The Floppy Disks section reports the sizes of your floppy disk drives. The Installed Memory section reports the CMOS values for base and extended memory. The CMOS Status section reports on your computer's current CMOS values. If any of these fields contains Error, you may need to run your computer's setup program and/or replace your battery.

Viewing the Disk Summary Dialog Box

Pressing Enter or choosing **Next** in the CMOS Values dialog box takes you to the Disk Summary dialog box (see fig. 18.6).

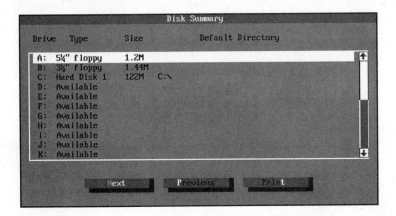

The Disk Summary dialog box tells you how many disk drives the computer can use and which drives are available. In figure 18.6, drives A, B, and C are being used. Drives A and B are floppy disk drives, and drive C is a hard disk. The hard disk is currently using the root directory (C:\). The other drives, listed as available, are currently not being used.

Viewing the Disk Characteristics Dialog Box

Pressing Enter or choosing **Next** in the Disk Summary dialog box brings you to the Disk Characteristics dialog box, which provides information about the current disk (see fig. 18.7).

A list of available disks appears in the box at the upper-right corner of the dialog box. You can change to another disk to see information about that disk. Use the up- and down-arrow keys to highlight a disk name in this list, or click a disk name (A:, for example) in the list. This way, you change the information in the dialog box to reflect information about the selected disk drive.

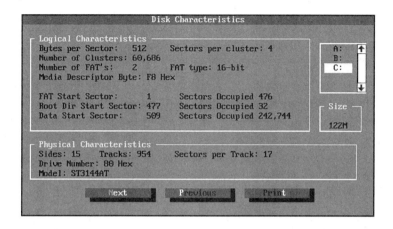

Fig. 18.7

The Disk Characteristics dialog box.

The Logical Characteristics section contains information about how magnetic information is stored on the disk. The number of bytes per sector is usually 512—that is, when a track on a disk is broken into sectors, each sector holds 512 bytes of information.

DOS reads a certain minimum amount of information from a disk at a time. That amount is called a *cluster.* Usually, the number of sectors per cluster is two for floppy disks and four or more for hard disks. The size of the cluster often determines how much wasted space (*slack space*) is on disk. The computer described in this chapter has four sectors per cluster, meaning that the smallest amount of space that a single file will occupy is 2,048 bytes (4 × 512). All files will take up space that is a multiple of 2,048. Space not used by the file, but in the cluster used to store the file, is slack space.

NOTE The difference in cluster size accounts for the difference in space required to store a file on the hard disk compared with a floppy disk. For the computer described in this chapter, a 500-byte file would take up 2,048 bytes on the hard disk. If you copy the file to a floppy disk that uses two sectors per cluster, however, the file takes up only 1,024 bytes. The Norton File Size (FS) command can help you determine whether a group of files from a hard disk will fit on a floppy disk. For more information about the FS command, see Chapter 26.

The number of FATs (file allocation tables) almost always is 2 except in the case of RAM disks (memory disks), which may have only one copy of the FAT. On a disk with more than 20,740 sectors (such as the disk used by the computer described in this chapter, which has $60,686 \times 4$ sectors), DOS uses a 16-bit FAT. If the disk has 20,740 or fewer sectors, DOS creates a 12-bit FAT.

The Media Descriptor Byte entry tells you what kind or size of disk has been formatted. Table 18.3 interprets the Media Descriptor Byte codes displayed in the Disk Characteristics dialog box. Thus, the disk shown here is a hard disk (code F8 Hex). *Hex* refers to the fact that this number (F8) is in hexadecimal format.

Table 18.3 Media Descriptor Byte Codes	
Reported Code	**Disk Represented**
F0	1.44M 3 1/2-inch floppy disk
F8	Hard disk
F9	1.2M 5 1/4-inch floppy disk or 720K 3 1/2-inch floppy disk
FD	360K 5 1/4-inch floppy disk
FE	160K 5 1/4-inch floppy disk
FF	320K 5 1/4-inch floppy disk

The remaining technical information listed in the Disk Characteristics dialog box is useful if you are editing or rebuilding the system area of a disk with a program such as Norton Disk Editor (see Chapter 17). The FAT Start Sector entry tells you which sector on disk is the starting point for the file allocation table. In this case, the FAT begins in sector 1. The Sectors Occupied entry (in this case, 476) tells you how long the FAT is. The dialog box also lists information about the starting location and length of the root directory area and about the data area on disk.

The Physical Characteristics section describes the inner workings of the disk. In this case, the hard disk has 15 sides (8 platters). Actually, the disk has 16 sides, but one side of one platter is used as a map that guides the actuator to the correct tracks on the other platters. Therefore, the disk has 15 sides that actually hold information. This box also reports the number of sectors per track, the drive number, and the model number of the disk drive (if available).

 NOTE Some hard disk drives use one side of a disk for an actuator guide; some do not. If your hard disk shows an even number of sides, it probably does not use an actuator disk map.

Viewing the Partition Tables Dialog Box

Pressing Enter or choosing **Next** in the Disk Characteristics dialog box displays the Partition Tables dialog box, which provides information about the partitions in your hard disk (see fig. 18.8).

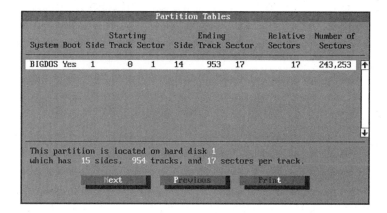

Fig. 18.8

The Partition Tables dialog box.

In this case, only one hard disk exists. If you use the FDISK command to partition your hard disk into more than one drive (for example, drives C and D), each drive shows up as a partition. You can use this information to determine the number and size of partitions in the hard disk(s) and to find out where the sectors start and end.

Viewing the Memory Summary Dialog Box

Pressing Enter or choosing **Next** in the Partition Tables dialog box brings you to the Memory Summary dialog box, which reports how your computer uses memory (see fig. 18.9).

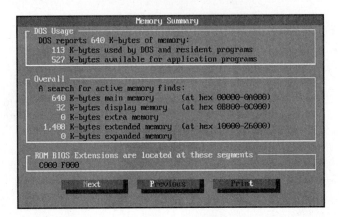

Fig. 18.9

The Memory
Summary dialog
box.

The Norton System Info command looks at the computer's RAM (random-access memory) in two ways. The first section of the dialog box is DOS Usage. In figure 18.9, DOS reports 640K of available RAM, which is divided into two parts: 113K is being used by DOS and resident programs, and 527K is available for use by other applications.

The reason for this 113K/527K split of the 640K of main memory is that when you boot your computer, the computer reads DOS information on the boot disk and moves some of that information into RAM so that the information is available when needed. DOS information, therefore, takes up some of your RAM. If you have loaded any RAM-resident programs (pop-up, terminate-and-stay-resident, and so on), those programs also are loaded into a portion of RAM when you boot your computer. If memory-resident programs occupy too much of your RAM, you may have a hard time running large programs such as Microsoft Windows or Aldus PageMaker.

The Overall section in the Memory Summary dialog box provides an overall report on the computer's memory locations. The report includes the following kinds of memory:

Memory	Description
Main memory	About the same as the total memory reported by the DOS method.
Display memory	RAM located in the display adapter card and used by the monitor.
Extra memory	Any read/write memory between 640K and 1M.
Extended memory	Memory beyond 1M (available only in 286-class and newer computers). To use this memory, you must have an XMS memory manager, such as MS-DOS's HIMEM.SYS.

Memory	Description
Expanded memory	Add-on memory available to certain programs that subscribe to a special way of using memory developed by Lotus, Microsoft, Intel, and AST. Many programs, such as Lotus 1-2-3, use this memory to work with large amounts of data (spreadsheets, databases, and so on) at one time.

The ROM BIOS extended memory, if present, is located in add-in boards (such as video display boards) or hard disks but is not a part of normal RAM. (The location of any ROM BIOS extensions is reported in the ROM BIOS Extensions section in the Memory Summary dialog box.) Allocation of memory is important in running such programs as Lotus 1-2-3 and in networking. Some programs, such as QEMM, enable you to reallocate memory among the memory areas for the purpose of providing enough memory for certain tasks.

Viewing the Extended (XMS) and Expanded (EMS) Memory Dialog Boxes

Pressing Enter or choosing Next in the Memory Summary dialog box takes you to the Extended Memory dialog box (see fig. 18.10).

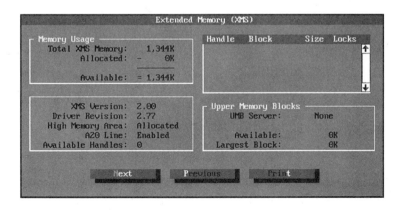

Fig. 18.10

The Extended Memory (XMS) dialog box.

If you are using an extended memory manager, information about the manager's allocation of memory appears in this dialog box. The most commonly used memory manager is Microsoft's HIMEM.SYS, which may be preloaded on your computer, particularly if the computer came preloaded with Windows. An extended memory manager enables you to allocate a block of memory for use by a program.

In the Extended Memory dialog box, the amount of allocated memory appears in the Memory Usage section. The box to the right of that section lists information about the XMS memory handle. Unlike DOS memory that is allocated to a specific address, extended memory's location is indicated by a *handle* (a pointer) to a memory block where the extended memory resides. Memory may be locked when you are running under a multitasking environment such as Windows or DesqView.

The Upper Memory Blocks section reports on your system's use of upper memory blocks (UMBs). UMBs are "holes" in memory between 640K and 1M; a memory manager can fill these holes with memory. Usually, memory between 640K and 1M is used only in 386-class and later computers and is managed by programs such as QEMM/386. DOS 5 and 6 also use UMBs.

If your system has expanded memory (EMS), that memory will be reported in a dialog box similar to the one shown in figure 18.10. EMS memory is not allocated like DOS memory (by size); EMS memory is specified by pages. Thus, the EMS address is a pointer to an EMS block of memory that consists of one or more pages. The standard LIM page size is 16K. (LIM stands for Lotus, Intel, and Microsoft—the companies that set the standards for EMS memory.)

The Expanded Memory (EMS) dialog box shows information about each EMS block that currently is allocated. This dialog box also reports the number of pages controlled by a handle and the size of each block (in bytes).

Viewing the DOS Memory Blocks Dialog Box

Pressing Enter or choosing Next in the Extended Memory or Expanded Memory dialog box brings you to the DOS Memory Blocks dialog box (see fig. 18.11).

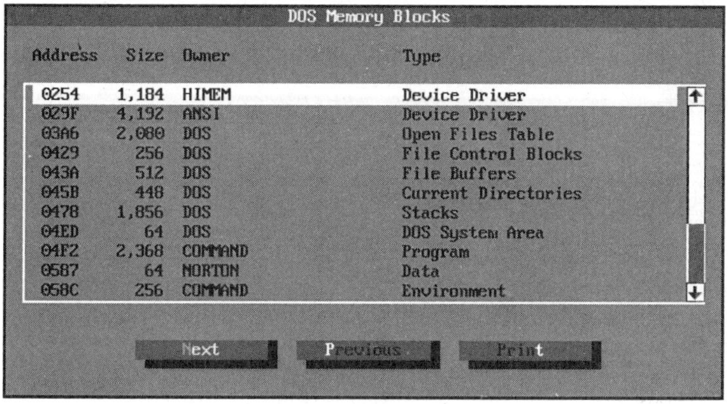

```
                          DOS Memory Blocks
    Address   Size  Owner            Type

    0254     1,184  HIMEM            Device Driver
    029F     4,192  ANSI             Device Driver
    03A6     2,080  DOS              Open Files Table
    0429       256  DOS              File Control Blocks
    043A       512  DOS              File Buffers
    045B       448  DOS              Current Directories
    0478     1,856  DOS              Stacks
    04ED        64  DOS              DOS System Area
    04F2     2,368  COMMAND          Program
    0587        64  NORTON           Data
    058C       256  COMMAND          Environment

         Next          Previous          Print
```

Fig. 18.11

The DOS
Memory Blocks
dialog box.

This dialog box lists the memory locations for various components of the DOS system. (You can scroll through this list by pressing the arrow keys or clicking the scroll bar.) In figure 18.11, the COMMAND program (COMMAND.COM) is stored in memory beginning at memory address 04F2 and is 2,368 bytes long. The information in this list can be helpful if you are diagnosing system problems related to DOS operation. If your system is infected with a virus program, for example, that virus may appear in this list. If you know what this list should look like (if you have a hard copy of the report on file), the presence of an unknown program or the change in size of a program (such as COMMAND.COM) may indicate the presence of a virus.

Examining the DOS memory blocks can help you find out how your memory is being allocated. You might be particularly interested in "free" memory. This memory—a gap in the allocation of DOS memory—usually cannot be used. Free memory sometimes is caused by the execution of a TSR (terminate-and-stay-resident program) and its subsequent removal. Free memory may reduce the amount of memory available for running programs.

Viewing the TSR Programs Dialog Box

Pressing Enter or choosing **Next** in the DOS Memory Blocks dialog box brings you to the TSR Programs dialog box (see fig. 18.12).

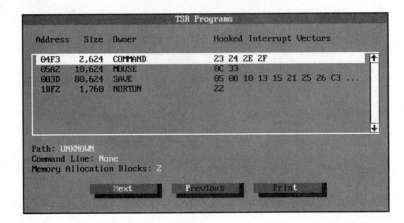

Fig. 18.12

The TSR Programs dialog box.

TSR (terminate-and-stay-resident) programs—also called *memory-resident programs*—are programs that, when begun, stay in the computer's RAM while other programs are running. By staying in memory, these programs are using some of the RAM, making the memory unusable by other programs. Therefore, you need to be aware of how much space TSR programs are using. The TSR Programs dialog box lists the TSR programs and their sizes, owners, and hooked interrupt vectors (the interrupt vector used by the software program to communicate with DOS).

In the dialog box shown in figure 18.12, the COMMAND program (COMMAND.COM)—a portion of the operating system (DOS)—is in memory. The MOUSE program tells DOS how to use a mouse, and the SAVE program is a program used to capture this screen image. Because each of these programs takes up memory and because large programs will not run if not enough memory is available, you may be interested in knowing precisely how much of your memory each program is using.

You may be interested also in the order of these memory-resident programs because some programs can be uninstalled only if they are the last program loaded into memory. This dialog box shows you which programs are in memory as well as the order of the programs.

If you use the Norton Disk Monitor program (a TSR program), for example, and then want to uninstall the program, you can enter the following command:

DISKMON /UNINSTALL

This command takes the program out of memory only if it is the last TSR program in the list. Therefore, you need to uninstall these programs in reverse order. (See Chapter 6 for more information on Disk Monitor.) Two other Norton TSR programs that have an /UNINSTALL switch are Norton Cache and SmartCan.

You can uninstall most TSR programs (check each program's documentation). If you load a TSR program as a result of a command in your AUTOEXEC.BAT or CONFIG.SYS files, you also can remove that program from the batch file and then reboot.

Viewing the Device Drivers Dialog Box

Pressing Enter or choosing Next in the TSR Programs dialog box brings you to the Device Drivers dialog box (see fig. 18.13).

```
                        Device Drivers
     Address    Name      Description

    0116:0048  NUL       NUL Device                        ↑
    02A0:0000  CON       Console Keyboard/Screen
    0255:0000  XMSXXXX0  Extended Memory Manager (XMS)
    0072:0003  CON       Console Keyboard/Screen
    0073:0005  AUX       First Serial Port
    0074:0007  PRN       First Parallel Printer
    0075:0009  CLOCK$    System Clock Interface
    0076:000B  A: - C:   DOS Supported Drives
    0077:000B  COM1      First Serial Port
    0078:000D  LPT1      First Parallel Printer
    0079:000F  LPT2      Second Parallel Printer           ↓

        Next          Previous          Print
```

Fig. 18.13

The Device Drivers dialog box.

A *device driver* is a program that tells DOS how to interact with a specific hardware device, such as a disk drive, printer, plotter, or mouse. These programs are stored in memory and are accessed by DOS when DOS needs to "talk" to a specific device. Like the information on DOS memory blocks and TSRs discussed in the preceding sections, device driver information can be helpful if you are diagnosing memory problems related to DOS operation.

Viewing the CPU Speed Dialog Box

Pressing Enter or choosing Next in the Device Drivers dialog box brings you to the CPU Speed dialog box, which compares the speed of the current computer with the speeds of three other popular computers (see fig. 18.14).

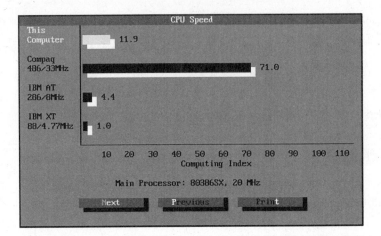

Fig. 18.14

The CPU Speed
dialog box.

In this dialog box, the original IBM/XT, running at 4.77 MHz, is used as
the base (1.0). A fast machine, the COMPAQ 486/33, is used as an example of a powerful computer. This computer is running about 11.9
times faster than an XT computer.

Keep in mind that this test may be somewhat misleading because the
processing speed of a computer has much to do with the data you are
processing. One computer may be better at processing numbers, for
example, whereas another is more adept at processing text fields. But
this dialog box and the following two dialog boxes are good bench-
marks to use when you compare computer power.

Be aware that two computers using identical Intel processors at the
same clock speed (for example, two 486/50 computers) could generate
different reports in the CPU Speed, Disk Speed, and Overall Performance Index Speed dialog boxes. Speed capabilities depend on the
architecture of the machine as well as the primary speed of the microprocessor. All cars with V-8 engines, for example, do not have the same
acceleration because the engine is only part of the drive train; the
transmission, differential, and other components also are factored
into the power of the car.

When you shop for a computer, you may want to take a copy of System
Info with you and run the utility on several computers to determine
their relative speed. In fact, some computer stores will have System
Info or a similar program available so that you can make this kind of
comparison.

Viewing the Disk Speed Dialog Box

Pressing Enter or choosing Next in the CPU Speed dialog box brings you to the Disk Speed dialog box, which compares the speed of your hard disk with the speed of three other popular computers' hard disks (see fig. 18.15).

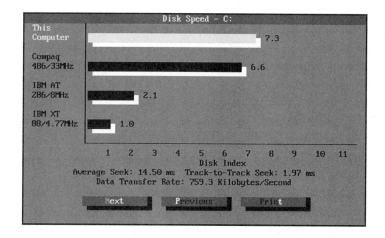

Fig. 18.15

The Disk Speed dialog box.

The hard disk of an IBM/XT computer is used as the base (1.0). The hard disk being compared can access information about 7.3 times as fast as the hard disk in the XT computer. Be aware, however, that hard disk access is affected by how much information is on the disk and whether the files on the disk are fragmented. Cache programs such as Norton Cache (see Chapter 21) and Calibrate (see Chapter 20) also can affect the efficiency of data access on your hard disk.

When you shop for a computer, the speed of the disk drive is an important consideration, particularly if you will be using programs that tend to read and write large amounts of information frequently from the disk (these programs include desktop publishers such as PageMaker). Some computer manufacturers advertise "power" machines with fast CPUs (such as 486/50s) but don't mention the fact that the hard drive is *slow*. If you use such a machine, you are likely to be disappointed in its overall power. That fact is a good reason to use this Disk Speed feature to compare hard drives before you buy.

Viewing the Overall Performance Index Dialog Box

Pressing Enter or choosing Next in the Disk Speed dialog box displays the Overall Performance Index dialog box. This index is a weighted combination of disk and CPU indexes that compares your computer's overall performance with that of three other popular computers (see fig. 18.16).

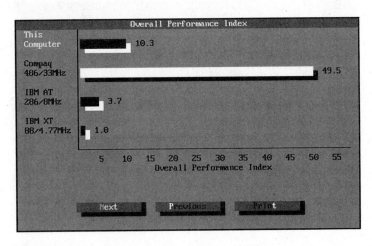

Fig. 18.16

The Overall Performance Index dialog box.

You should look at these indexes in the same way that you look at the miles-per-gallon figures reported for automobiles. The numbers are for comparison only; your actual "mileage" may vary. Like the CPU Speed and Disk Speed dialog boxes, however, this dialog box can be an extremely helpful tool when you compare one machine with another.

Viewing the Network Drive Benchmark Dialog Box

If you are connected to a network, you can view an additional dialog box. When you press Enter or choose Next in the Overall Performance Index dialog box, a dialog box that lists network drives appears, displaying the following prompt:

```
Select Network Drive
```

Use the up- and down-arrow keys to point to a drive name and then press Enter, or double-click the drive name.

To perform a benchmark test on a network drive, you must have read-and-write privileges for that drive. If you do not have those privileges, a warning message appears, telling you that the benchmark test cannot be run. If you have read-and-write privileges, however, you see a dialog box similar to the one shown in figure 18.17.

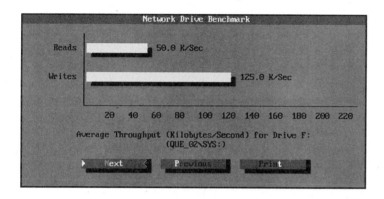

Fig. 18.17

The Network Drive Benchmark dialog box.

This dialog box graphically shows the average access times for this network drive. You may want to compare this dialog box with the Disk Speed dialog box (refer to fig. 18.15). Usually, network drives have slower access times than the access time of your computer's hard disk.

Viewing the CONFIG.SYS and AUTOEXEC.BAT Files

The next two dialog boxes in the System Info report describe your CONFIG.SYS and AUTOEXEC.BAT files (see figs. 18.18 and 18.19). You may want to look at the CONFIG.SYS file dialog box to see which device drivers you have installed; you can check the AUTOEXEC.BAT dialog box to see which TSR programs you begin at boot time.

Three other files may be displayed in the same way as the CONFIG.SYS and AUTOEXEC.BAT files. These three files—NDOS.INI, WIN.INI, and SYSTEM.INI—are displayed only if the programs that they support are loaded on your computer. The WIN.INI file, for example, will not exist on your computer unless you have a copy of Windows on your disk. The NDOS.INI file contains settings for the NDOS command processor. This file is explained in Chapter 28. The WIN.INI and SYSTEM.INI files contain settings for the Microsoft Windows program.

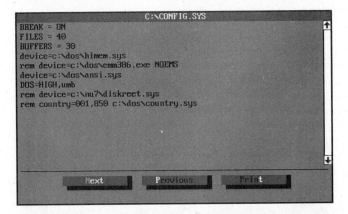

Fig. 18.18

The
CONFIG.SYS
dialog box.

Fig. 18.19

The
AUTOEXEC.BAT
dialog box.

After you scroll through all the dialog boxes, System Info cycles back to
the original System Summary dialog box. To end the System Info program at this point (or from any of the report dialog boxes), press Esc,
choose Exit from the File menu, or double-click the control box.

If you want to review one or more of the System Info dialog boxes but
do not want to scroll through many other dialog boxes to get to it, use
the pull-down menu options to display any of the report dialog boxes,
as described in the following section.

Using the Menu Bar and Printing Reports

You can view any of the dialog boxes described in this chapter by
choosing the appropriate option from the menu bar at the top of the

System Information screen. The menus are **F**ile, **S**ystem, **D**isks, **M**emory, **B**enchmarks, and **H**elp. You can use the File menu to view and print reports.

To open these pull-down menus, press Alt (or F10) and the first letter of the menu name, or point to a menu and click. After you extend the menus, you can use the right- and left-arrow keys to move from menu to menu, and the up- and down-arrow keys to choose options in the menus.

Using the File Menu

From the **F**ile menu, you can choose one of the following options:

> View **C**ONFIG.SYS
>
> View **A**UTOEXEC.BAT
>
> View **N**DOS.INI
>
> View **W**IN.INI
>
> View **S**YSTEM.INI
>
> Print **R**eport
>
> **E**xit

Each report dialog box contains a Print option to print a brief report about that item, but not an option to print the entire System Info report. The **F**ile menu has a Print **R**eport option that enables you to print such a report. When you choose Print **R**eport, the Report dialog box appears (see fig. 18.20).

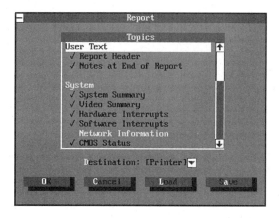

Fig. 18.20

The Report dialog box.

Notice that this dialog box contains a Topics list box. The items in the Topics list box correspond to the dialog boxes that were discussed earlier in this chapter. Each item is an independent part of the report. Therefore, you can select specific items that will be in your report. (You might want your report to contain the System Summary report, for example, but not interrupt information.) When an item is selected, a check mark appears to the left of the item name.

The first two items in the list, under the User Text heading, enable you to include your own information in the title (header) of the report and to add notes at the end of the report.

Following are the report items displayed in the Report dialog box:

- User Text
  Report Header
  Notes at End of Report

- System
  System Summary
  Video Summary
  Hardware Interrupts
  Software Interrupts
  Network Information
  CMOS Status

- Disk
  Disk Summary
  Disk Characteristics
  Partition Tables

- Memory
  Memory Usage Summary
  EMS Usage Summary
  XMS Usage Summary
  DOS Memory Block Allocation
  Installed TSR Programs
  Device Driver List

- Benchmark
  CPU Speed
  Hard Disk Speed
  Performance Index
  Network Performance

- System Files
  CONFIG.SYS File
  AUTOEXEC.BAT File
  NDOS.INI File
  WIN.INI File
  SYSTEM.INI File

Some of the items in the list may appear in parentheses or may appear grayed, indicating that the item is not available for the report. The Network Information item, for example, will not be available if your computer is not part of a network.

When the report is created, only items selected in the Report dialog box will be included. By default, all available items are selected. A report on all items will be about 15 pages long. If you want to shorten this report, deselect the Hardware and Software Interrupts items.

The command buttons at the bottom of the Report dialog box are **OK**, **C**ancel, **L**oad, and **S**ave. If you choose **OK**, the report uses all the selected report items. Choosing **C**ancel closes the Report dialog box and returns you to the dialog box in which you were working when you chose Print **R**eport from the **F**ile menu.

The **L**oad and **S**ave buttons enable you to save the current selections in the Topics list box to a report-options file and then later load them back to produce a similar report. For example, you could create and save several different reports: a short report, a medium-sized report, and a comprehensive report.

To save a group of topics, first select the items in the Topics list box and then choose **S**ave. You are prompted to enter the name of the file, as shown in figure 18.21. The report-options file is stored with an SIR extension.

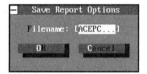

Fig. 18.21

Saving a Report Topics selection.

Later, when you choose the Print **R**eport option again, you can choose the **L**oad option in the Report dialog box. A list of previously saved report-options files appears (see fig. 18.22).

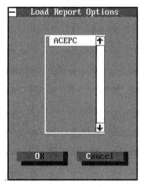

Fig. 18.22

Selecting a file from the Load Report Options dialog box.

Select the name of the report-options file you want to use. All the selections in the Topics list box will revert to the settings that were in effect when the report-options file was saved.

Below the Topics list box is a drop-down list box titled **Destination** (refer to fig. 18.20). In this box, you can choose to output the report to the printer or a file. The default setting is Printer. To change this setting, press PgDn to display the drop-down list and then choose either Printer or File. If you choose the File option, you are prompted to enter a file name for the report (see fig. 18.23). The default name is SIREPORT.TXT. You can use this name or enter your own file name.

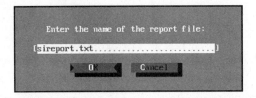

If you chose the Report Header option in the Report dialog box, you then are prompted to enter a single line of information to appear in the title of the report (see fig. 18.24).

If you chose the Notes at End of Report option in the Report dialog box, a User Notes dialog box appears (see fig. 18.25).

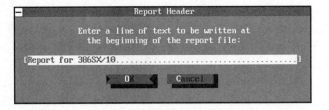

The Notes at End of Report message can be up to 10 lines long. You may want the message to include information such as the serial number of the computer, warranty information, the physical location of the computer, and so on.

After you enter the Report Header and User Notes information, the report prints to your printer or is stored in a file, according to the destination you selected. A portion of the report, consisting of the System Summary and Video Summary options, is shown in figure 18.26.

```
                      System Information
                        System Report
                  Friday, March  5, 1993 5:11am
                     Report for 386SX/10

                ***********************
                *   System Summary    *
                ***********************

           --------------- Computer ---------------
           Computer Name: IBM AT or compatible
           Built-in BIOS: AMI, Monday, April  9, 1990
          Main Processor: 80386SX, 10 MHz
       Math Co-Processor: None
           Video Adapter: VGA, Secondary: None
              Mouse Type: Serial Mouse, Version 6.24

           --------------- Disks ---------------
           Hard Disks: 122M
        Floppy Disks: 1.2M, 1.44M

           --------------- Memory ---------------
              DOS Memory:    640K
         Extended Memory:  1,408K
         Expanded Memory:      0K

           --------------- Other Info ---------------
                Bus Type: ISA (PC/AT)
            Serial Ports: 3
          Parallel Ports: 1
           Keyboard Type: 101-Key
        Operating System: DOS 5.00



                ***********************
                *   Video Summary     *
                ***********************

           --------------- Display ---------------
     Video Display Adapter: VGA, Secondary: None
            Monitor Type: Analog Color
       Current Video Mode: 3 (Color, 80x25)

           --------------- Character ---------------
       Maximum Scan Lines: 400
           Character Size: 9 x 16
      CGA Cursor Emulation: Enabled

           --------------- Memory ---------------
             Video Memory: 256K or more
     Video Segment Address: B800 (hex)
```

Fig. 18.26

A portion of the printed System Info report.

For purposes of comparison, upkeep, diagnostics, and support, you may want to run this type of report on each computer you use and then file the information for future use. These reports may be valuable if you ever need to rebuild a hard disk or recover from a virus attack.

Using Other Menu Options

The rest of the System Info menu options enable you to view individual report items. If you do not want to print an entire report, you can display one report dialog box and then print that information.

From the **S**ystem menu, you can choose one of the following dialog boxes to view:

> **S**ystem Summary
>
> **V**ideo Summary
>
> **H**ardware Interrupts
>
> Software **I**nterrupts
>
> **N**etwork Information (if available)
>
> **C**MOS Status (if available)

From the **D**isks menu, you can choose one of the following dialog boxes to view:

> **D**isk Summary
>
> Disk **C**haracteristics
>
> **P**artition Tables

From the **M**emory menu, you can choose one of these dialog boxes to view:

> Memory **U**sage Summary
>
> **E**xpanded Memory (EMS)
>
> E**x**tended Memory (XMS)
>
> Memory **B**lock List
>
> **T**SR Programs
>
> **D**evice Drivers

From the **B**enchmarks menu, you can choose one of the following dialog boxes to view:

CPU Speed

Hard Disk Speed

Overall Performance Index

Network Performance Speed (if available)

The **H**elp menu enables you to access Norton's Help system (discussed in Chapter 1). When you are viewing a particular dialog box, you can press F1 for interactive Help information or choose the **H**elp option to display information about the dialog box.

Exiting System Info

To exit the System Info program, press Esc, choose E**x**it from the **F**ile menu, or double-click the control box in the upper-left corner of the System Information screen.

Summary

This chapter covered the use of the Norton System Info utility. System Info produces a variety of reports about what components are used in your computer, how fast your computer operates, and what operating system and support software your computer uses. The Print **R**eport option in this program enables you to print a detailed report about your computer. This report can be a helpful tool in diagnosing or correcting problems related to your computer's performance.

Chapters 19 through 21 discuss other Norton Utilities that can help you make your computer run more efficiently.

Making Your Disk Run Faster with Speed Disk

After a great deal of use, your files on disk can become fragmented. Fragmentation occurs when the disk does not have enough space for storing the file in one contiguous area, so DOS stores part of a file in one cluster, part in the next available cluster (which may not be near the first cluster), and so on.

Because fragmentation causes DOS to look here and there to find a file, access to the hard disk can slow considerably. Excessive fragmentation can even cause DOS to lose information on some files, although data loss from fragmentation usually isn't a major problem.

Because slower data access caused by fragmentation is a common problem, Norton Utilities offers a solution—the Speed Disk utility. Speed Disk safely reorganizes the files on your disk without erasing or losing any data. If your disk drive grinds when it reads and saves a file, or if the drive seems to operate slowly, you may be able to regain speed with Speed Disk. Speed Disk optimizes a disk by rearranging the disk's files so that each file is stored in contiguous clusters. Instead of taking up to 30 seconds on a fragmented disk, for example, DOS can save a word processing file to an optimized disk in only 5 seconds.

Trimming the time needed to save files is not the Speed Disk command's only contribution. A number of programs, such as Aldus PageMaker and Ventura Publisher, access your disk many times as you use them. With a slow hard disk, the use of these programs can resemble a crawl. So when you use Speed Disk periodically, you can have some real productivity advantages.

Because your disk undergoes drastic reorganization, take the following precautions before executing the Speed Disk program:

- Run Disk Doctor to make sure that no current problems with your hard disk exist (see Chapter 12).

- Make sure that no memory-resident programs are running. (Use the System Info command, covered in Chapter 18, to check this out.) Some programs may access particular places on disk that the disk reorganization will move.

T I P   If you have a complicated AUTOEXEC.BAT file that loads several programs into memory, you may want to boot from a floppy disk that contains only DOS and Speed Disk. This way, you ensure that no memory-resident programs are being used.

- Although SPEEDISK generally is safe, keep a backup of your hard disk before you do anything that significantly alters the disk.

- Get rid of unneeded files, such as backup (BAK) files. The more full your disk is, the greater the likelihood of disk fragmentation.

T I P   To eliminate unneeded files, use the WipeInfo command in "non-wiping" or DOS ERASE mode across directories (use the /N switch). For example, to erase all BAK files on disk, use this command:

WIPEINFO C:*.BAK /N/S

The /N switch tells the command to erase files just as DOS ERASE does. The /S command tells the command to search for all files (in all subdirectories) that match the *.BAK specification. Because your initial search is in the root directory, this command erases all *.BAK files on disk.

NOTE If your computer is attached to a network, you can use Speed Disk to optimize local disks on your own computer, but you cannot use Speed Disk to optimize a network drive. The program does not include network drives on the list of drives to optimize.

Starting Speed Disk

Although you can make a number of choices when you use Speed Disk, the easiest way to use the program is to allow it to make a recommendation about how to optimize your disk, and then follow that recommendation. The following sections tell you how to use Speed Disk, how to follow its recommendations, and how to choose options to optimize your disk.

To begin the Speed Disk program, you can choose it from the Norton main screen or enter **SPEEDISK** at the DOS prompt. When you begin Speed Disk, the program reads information from system memory. You then see the Speed Disk screen, displaying information like that in figure 19.1. The drives that appear on-screen may be different, depending on the drives you have available on your computer.

From the dialog box that is displayed, you can choose which disk to optimize. Highlight the drive name of the disk you want to optimize and choose **OK**, or point to the drive with the mouse and double-click.

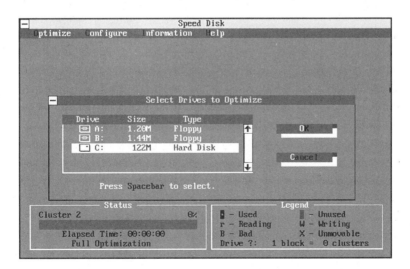

Fig. 19.1

The Select Drives to Optimize dialog box.

After you choose the drive to optimize, Speed Disk analyzes the information on the drive and produces a Recommendation dialog box (see fig. 19.2). This box contains a recommended course of action. In this example, the program recommends unfragmenting files only. To accept this recommendation, choose the **U**nfragment Files Only option and then choose **O**ptimize. To choose another optimization method, select the radio button for that method. The meanings of these methods are described in table 19.1. To cancel the optimization, choose **C**ancel.

Fig. 19.2

The Speed Disk
Recommendation
dialog box.

Table 19.1 Speed Disk Optimization Methods

Method	Action
Full Optimization	Optimizes your disk by unfragmenting all files but does not reorder your directories. Reorders files if you specified which files should go first. When finished, no holes in the directory structure exist.
Full with **D**irectories First	Moves directories to the front of the disk space, making their access faster; does everything the full optimization method does. Offers the best overall performance gain.
Full with File **R**eorder	Reorders files by directory; does everything the full optimization method does. Files associated with directories that are placed first are also placed first in the file list. This method takes the most time to run.

Method	Action
Unfragment Files Only	Attempts to unfragment as many files as possible without removing all the holes in the directory, as the full optimization method does. This sort is fast, and Norton recommends that you run it about twice a week.
Unfragment Free **S**pace	Moves data forward on the disk to fill in any free space; does not unfragment any files. May not provide significant speed for old files, but provides space for new files to be stored as unfragmented files.

After you specify the optimization method, the optimization begins immediately. During this process, do not turn off your computer. If you need to stop the program, press Esc; then choose **C**ancel or **R**esume at the prompt.

During the optimization process, Speed Disk displays a map of the computer's disk space (see fig. 19.3). The legend in the lower-right corner of the screen explains what each symbol on the map means. During the process, you can watch the movement of used clusters to the top of the map and the movement of unused clusters to the bottom. For full optimization, all unused clusters are positioned at the bottom of the map.

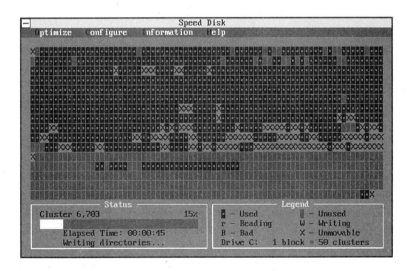

Fig. 19.3

Speed Disk in action.

T I P   If you have never optimized your disk, it is likely that full optimiza-
           tion will be recommended the first time you use Speed Disk. This
           method is the most thorough and takes the longest time—maybe an
           hour, depending on your hard disk size. After you have fully opti-
           mized your disk, you may want to use the recommended approach
           on a weekly basis. Subsequent recommended optimization methods
           may be one of the faster approaches, which takes only a few
           minutes.

T I P   If by some slight chance you lose power during an optimization,
           run Disk Doctor on your disk to check for and correct any disk
           problems as soon as you are able to bring your computer back up
           (see Chapter 12).

Using the Speed Disk Menus

In addition to choosing an optimization method from the Recommendation dialog box, you can make this choice and others from the Speed
Disk pull-down menus. To display a pull-down menu, press Alt plus the
highlighted character in the menu name, or just click the menu name.
The pull-down menus enable you to specify Speed Disk options manually. The menu choices are Optimize, Configure, and Information. The
following sections describe the options available on each menu. The
Help option displays the Norton Help menu as described in Chapter 1.

Selecting Optimization Options

The Speed Disk Optimize menu, shown in figure 19.4, contains a number of options that you can use to control the optimization process.
Although the Begin Optimization option is first in the menu, you should
set all options in the other menus to your choice before you choose
Begin Optimization. (Notice that you can press Alt+B to begin optimization, even if you are not in this menu.)

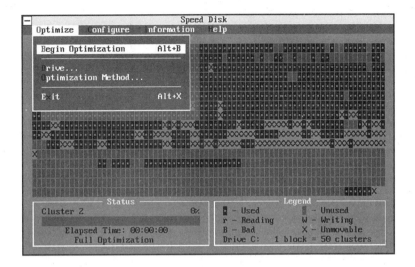

Fig. 19.4

The Speed Disk **O**ptimize menu.

You use the **D**rive option in the **O**ptimize menu to specify which drive to optimize.

The **O**ptimization Method option opens the Select Optimization Method dialog box from which you can choose the methods to use (see fig. 19.5). Use the up- and down-arrow keys to highlight the radio button of the method you want, and press the space bar to choose the option. You can also point to the button and click the mouse. Press Enter or choose **OK** to lock in the option; press Esc or choose **C**ancel to cancel this menu.

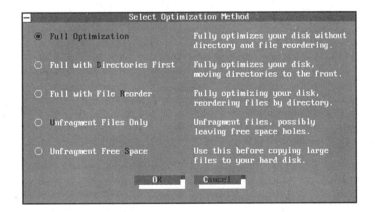

Fig. 19.5

The Select Optimization Method dialog box.

To leave the Speed Disk program, choose E**x**it.

Configuring the Speed Disk Program

The Configure menu enables you to choose options concerning how files and directories are ordered in the optimization process (see fig. 19.6). The following sections describe these options.

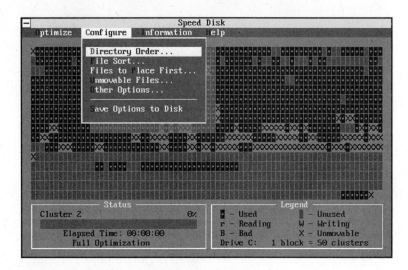

Changing Directory Order

The Directory Order option accesses the Select Directory Order dialog box, which enables you to specify the order in which directories are placed on the disk (see fig. 19.7). The directories at the beginning of the disk have the fastest access time. By default, the order that Speed Disk uses is the order you specified in your PATH statement, which usually is found in your AUTOEXEC.BAT file.

The Directory List box displays all directories on the disk. The Directory Order list box contains the list of directories to be reordered on your disk during optimization. To specify a customized directory order, you can move the files already in the Directory Order list to new locations in the list, add new directories to the list, or delete directories from the list.

 NOTE   Changing the directory order in Speed Disk in no way affects the order of directories in your PATH statement or AUTOEXEC.BAT file.

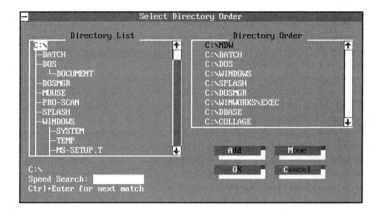

Fig. 19.7

The Select Directory Order dialog box.

To move a directory name in the Directory Order list, follow these steps:

1. Highlight the directory name in the Directory Order list. Choose **M**ove, press the space bar, or double-click the directory name.

2. Press the up- or down-arrow key to move the directory name to its new place in the list; or highlight the directory name, press and hold down the left mouse button, and drag the directory to the new location. As you move the directory up or down in the list, the other listed directory names move to accommodate the selected directory. To anchor the directory name in the list, press Enter (or double-click again).

3. Repeat steps 1 and 2 until you have all the directories in the order you want.

To add a new name to the Directory Order list, you must copy the directory's name from the Directory List box. Follow these steps:

1. If the highlight is not in the Directory List box, press the Tab key to move it there.

2. In the Directory List box, use the up- and down-arrow keys to highlight the directory you want. Choose **A**dd to add the selected directory to the list in the Directory Order box.

   Alternatively, you can double-click the directory name in the Directory List box to add it to the Directory Order list.

3. Repeat step 2 to add all the directories you want to the Directory Order list.

> **T   I   P**   When choosing a directory name in the Directory List box, you can use the Speed Search field in the Select Directory Order dialog box to locate a directory name quickly. With the highlight in the Directory List box, type the first letter of the directory you want to highlight (for example, type **K** to search for the KWIKSTAT directory). If the highlighted directory is not the one you want, you can type the next letter of the name (**W**, for example). Continue typing letters of the name until the directory you want is highlighted. Usually, typing one or two letters is sufficient.

If you often change the files in a directory, you may not want this directory in the Directory Order box. To delete a directory from the Directory Order box, follow these steps:

1. Make sure that the highlight is in the Directory Order box. If necessary, press Tab to move the highlight.

2. Highlight the directory name you want to delete.

3. Choose **D**elete.

4. To delete additional directories, repeat this procedure.

NOTE   These steps do not delete the directory from the disk.

NOTE   You cannot delete directories when the highlight is in the Directory List box on the left. The **D**elete option is available only when the highlight is in the Directory Order box; **D**elete becomes **A**dd when the highlight is in the Directory List box.

After you finish your changes, choose **OK**. Choose **C**ancel if you decide not to change the directory order.

Specifying File Order

The Speed Disk **C**onfigure menu offers two options for specifying the order of files on the disk during reorganization. The File Sort option controls a general sorting of files into ascending or descending order by name, extension, date and time of last revision, or size. The Files To **P**lace First option moves selected files so that they precede all other files on the disk.

Because sorting files reorganizes file names, you can find the files quickly in a directory of names. When you create a file, DOS locates an empty spot in the disk directory and places the name and information about that file in the directory. Usually, files in the directory are listed in the order in which they were created. Sorting enables you to place these files in the order you want. This feature can help you find certain files faster and determine easily which file is smallest or largest, which files were created last or first, and so on.

With the File Sort option in the Configure menu, you can specify the way that files are sorted within directories. In the File Sort dialog box, you can set Sort Criterion and Sort Order (see fig. 19.8). The options from which you can choose are Unsorted, Name, Extension, Date and Time, and Size. You can also choose to make the sort Ascending or Descending.

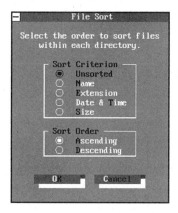

The File Sort dialog box.

Because files placed at the beginning of the disk are accessed faster than those placed later on the disk, you may want to place your most commonly used files at the beginning of the disk. Usually, this includes program files—files with the EXE or COM extension. For this process, use the Files To Place First option on the Speed Disk Configure menu. Choose this option to access the Files To Place First dialog box, where you can place the file specifications for those files that you want to place at the beginning of the disk during optimization (see fig. 19.9).

To add a new file to the end of the list, use the up- and down-arrow keys to move the highlight to a blank line and then enter a new file specification. You can use the wild-card characters ? and * in your file specification. To insert a new file in the list, move the cursor to a file specification and choose the Insert option. Insert adds a blank line above the highlighted file specification so that you can enter a new file specification.

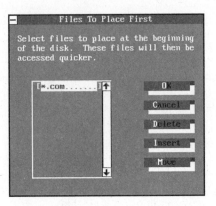

Fig. 19.9

The Files To Place
First dialog box.

To move a file specification, highlight the file specification and choose
the **M**ove option. Then move the file specification up or down by using
the arrow keys or dragging it with the mouse.

To delete a file from the list, highlight the file specification and choose
Delete. Choose **OK** to exit this dialog box and save the changes you
have made. Choose **C**ancel to exit the box without saving any of the
changes you have made.

Specifying Unmovable Files

Unmovable files are not physically moved on disk during an optimization. Speed Disk analyzes your disk and marks all hidden files and files
related to copy-protection schemes as unmovable. However, because
the nature of protection schemes that may be created in the future
cannot be predicted, Norton has allowed you to manually designate
files to remain unmovable. If you have other files not recognized by
Norton as needing to remain unmovable, you can choose **U**nmovable
Files in the **C**onfigure menu and then specify the file names manually
in the Unmovable Files dialog box (see fig. 19.10). Files used in copy-
protection schemes are becoming more rare, but if you have a
copy-protected program, you may want to specify any files used in the
protection scheme as unmovable. If you have copy-protection files that
have been moved, you may no longer be able to run the program associated with the copy-protection scheme. In that unlikely case, you may
have to contact the program's owner for a disk that will put the protection back into place, or reload the program from its original disks.

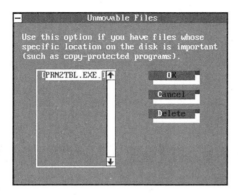

Fig. 19.10

The Unmovable
Files dialog box.

To add a new file to the list of unmovable files, press the down arrow to
go to a blank line, and enter the new name. To delete a file from the list,
highlight the file name and choose **D**elete. Choose **O**K to exit this dialog
box and save the changes you have made. Choose **C**ancel to exit the
dialog box without saving any of the changes you have made.

Selecting Other Options

If you choose **O**ther Options from the Speed Disk **C**onfigure menu,
Speed Disk displays the Other Options dialog box, containing three
check boxes (see fig. 19.11). The **R**ead-After-Write option causes Speed
Disk to verify that information moved to different locations on the disk
during optimization matches the original information. You can also
choose the Clear **U**nused Space option. This option blanks out unused
file space on disk so that old file information cannot be recovered from
the disk. To protect your old data from discovery by others, use Clear
Unused Space. The **B**eep When Done option causes a beep to sound
when optimization is complete.

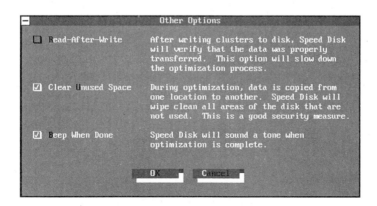

Fig. 19.11

The Other
Options dialog
box.

Saving Configuration Settings to Disk

After you make selections for the various Configure menu options, you can save the selections to disk by choosing Save Options to Disk from the Configure menu. Then when you begin Speed Disk again, these options are in effect. If you don't choose Save Options to Disk, the configuration changes you made for this optimization session apply only to the current session. Speed Disk returns to the default settings (or the last set of saved settings) for the next optimization session.

Obtaining Additional Information about the Disk

The Information menu enables you to look at a number of pieces of information that relate to the way your disk is optimized. The Information menu is shown in figure 19.12.

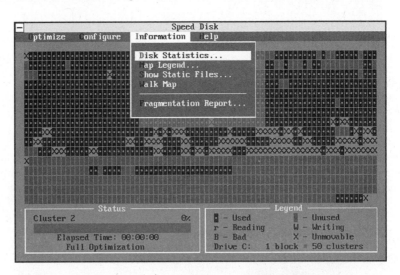

Fig. 19.12

The Speed Disk Information menu.

The Disk Statistics option gives you information about the disk to be optimized (see fig. 19.13). The most important information in the Disk Statistics dialog box is the Percentage of Unfragmented Files field. If this number is 95 percent or more, you have little fragmentation. If the number is about 90 percent, you probably should perform an optimization. If the number is under 90 percent, you need a full optimization.

```
            Disk Statistics for Drive C:

    Disk Size:                            122M
    Percentage of Disk Used:              67%
    Percentage of Unfragmented Files:     96%
    Number of Directories on Drive:       88
    Number of Files on Drive:             2,648

    Clusters Allocated to Movable Files:    40,656
    Clusters Allocated to Unmovable Files:  +  2,597
    Clusters Allocated to Directories:      +    106
    Clusters Marked as Bad:                 +      0
    Unused (Free) Clusters:                 + 17,327

    Total Clusters on Drive:              60,686

                    OK
```

Fig. 19.13

The Disk Statistics dialog box.

The **M**ap Legend option gives you a key for the symbols used on the disk map that is in view during the optimization (see fig. 19.14). This legend provides a more detailed explanation of the symbols than the explanation that appears in the legend on the disk map.

```
─                        Speed Disk
 Optimize   Configure   Information   Help

                    Disk Map Legend
      ▓  – Disk space used by files
      ░  – Disk space optimized already
      ·  – optimized pass one (compressed volumes)
         – Unused disk space
      X  – Disk space used by files that will not be moved
      B  – Bad disk space (untouched by Speed Disk)
      r  – Disk space that is being read
      W  – Disk space that is being written
      V  – Disk space that is being verified
      C  – Unused disk space that is being cleared

                      OK

 Cluster                                     r – Reading      W – Writing
                                             B – Bad          X – Unmovable
    Elapsed Time: 00:00:00                   Drive C:  1 block = 50 clusters
    Full Optimization
```

Fig. 19.14

The Disk Map Legend dialog box.

The **S**how Static Files option gives you a list of files that the program has determined should not be moved (see fig. 19.15).

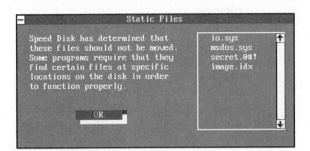

Fig. 19.15

The Static Files
dialog box.

The **W**alk Map option displays the disk map and enables you to use the
arrow keys to highlight blocks on the map. When you highlight a block,
a cluster range is displayed. If you want to know where a bad block is
located on disk, use the **W**alk Map option to determine the location of
the bad cluster. You may want to examine this cluster by using Disk
Editor (see Chapter 17).

With the **F**ragmentation Report option, you can examine the amount of
fragmentation of individual files (see fig. 19.16). In this figure, the left
side of the dialog box is a directory tree; the files for the directory highlighted in the directory tree appear on the right side of the dialog box.
If the file listing shows files with dots in front of their names, those files
are fragmented. The percent of fragmentation is listed in the % column.
Files that have 100 percent listed are completely unfragmented. Any file
with 90 percent or less is considered highly fragmented. The lower this
number, the more fragmented the file is.

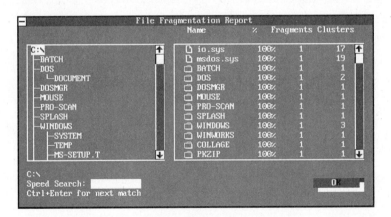

Fig. 19.16

The File Fragmen-
tation Report
dialog box.

Using Speed Disk Switches

The Speed Disk command reorganizes your disk so that fragmented files can be unfragmented. Files may be packed and rearranged to help your disk run at top speed. When entering this command at the DOS prompt, use this syntax:

SPEEDISK [*d:*] [*switches*]

You can use the following switches with the Speed Disk command:

Switch	Description
/B	Reboots after the command finishes.
/F	Performs a full optimization of the disk.
/FD	Performs a full optimization with directories first.
/FF	Performs a full optimization with a file reorder.
/Q	Unfragments free space and fills unused gaps (quick compression).
/SD[–]	Sorts files by date. If you include the minus parameter, the sort is from the most recent date to the oldest date.
/SE[–]	Sorts files by extension. If you include the minus parameter, the sort is in descending alphabetical order.
/SN[–]	Sorts by file name. If you include the minus parameter, the sort is in descending alphabetical order.
/SS[–]	Sorts by file size. If you include the minus parameter, the sort is from largest to smallest.
/U	Unfragments as many files as possible without moving parts of the directory structure. Some damaged files may not be capable of unfragmenting.
/V	Uses verify-after-write data verification. That is, whenever information is written to the disk, it is read from the disk to verify that it was correctly written.

For example, to optimize your hard disk C: with a full optimization and then reboot the computer after the optimization, use the following command:

SPEEDISK C: /F/B

NOTE You run Speed Disk in interactive mode by entering **SPEEDISK** with no switches. In interactive mode, you can choose the options from the Speed Disk menus. You can also choose which files not to move and which files to place first on the disk (nearest track 0).

Summary

In this chapter, you learned how to use the Speed Disk program to optimize your disks so that you can access files quickly. When the disk begins to fill, files can become fragmented, and your hard disk access time can slow considerably. If you use Speed Disk regularly, you can prevent file fragmentation and enhance your computer's productivity.

The Calibrate program can help some disks improve their access speeds. Turn to the next chapter for a discussion of Calibrate.

Using Calibrate

T he Calibrate program optimizes the speed and reliability of reading and writing information to and from your hard disk. In order for Calibrate to know how to optimize your hard disk, the program runs a series of tests to determine some of the disk's logical and physical characteristics. Calibrate is designed specifically for use on your hard disk. It is not intended to work on floppy disks, network disks, RAM disks, assigned disks (DOS ASSIGN command), or substitute disks (DOS SUBST command).

You use Calibrate for two reasons. First, you use it to check the interleave factor to see whether the disk is working efficiently. You need to test the disk only once. Second, if your hard disk gives intermittent errors when reading and writing files, you must run Calibrate to evaluate and solve the problem. Norton recommends that you run Calibrate every three months to test your hard disk for problems.

Understanding Calibrate

Calibrate can improve the speed at which data is read from your hard disk by adjusting the disk's interleave factor. The interleave factor has to do with the way DOS reads and writes information from your hard disk. Because the hard disk is spinning at a rapid speed, the read/write head cannot always get information off the disk in one long stream.

Often information is read and written from the disk in spurts of 512K (a sector). In reading information from the disk, the head may read one 512K sector on the disk, skip the next sector while the first sector of information is being sent to the computer, read the next sector, skip the next, read the next, and so on.

The number of sectors skipped between reads is called the *interleave factor*. In this example, the interleave factor is 2 (sometimes called 2:1). Each hard disk has an optimum interleave factor that makes reading information from the hard disk as fast as possible. Some hard disks, however, may have been formatted at a less-than-optimum interleave factor. If this is true for your hard disk, the Calibrate program can adjust the disk to make it work faster.

Calibrate adjusts the interleave factor by performing a low-level format. This kind of format does not destroy the data on your disk. It simply adjusts how the information is stored on disk and tests the reliability of information storage on the disk. A low-level format, unlike the normal high-level format (FORMAT command) of a hard disk, actually reads and writes information to every area of the disk to verify its capability to store magnetic information. A high-level format does not do this kind of thorough testing of the disk.

Calibrate cannot perform a low-level format on some hard disks, however, and cannot adjust the interleave factor on these disks. When you run the Calibrate program, it informs you if you have a hard disk that the program cannot adjust. Some of the disk types on which Calibrate cannot adjust the interleave factor include the following:

Drives with SCSI controllers or IDE-type controllers

Drives that are not 100-percent IBM compatible

Drives with controllers that perform a sector translation

Drives with on-board disk caching

Iomega Bernoulli Box drives

Novell file servers

Any hard disk with a sector size other than 512K

Even if you have one of these disk types, however, Calibrate can still perform some valuable tests for you. It can test each byte of your hard disk for reliability and move any data that is in danger to a reliable portion of the disk.

NOTE Before you run Calibrate the first time, back up your hard disk. Although Calibrate is safe and reliable, you may run into problems on drives that are not 100-percent IBM compatible. After you run Calibrate on your computer and verify that your disks are compatible, you no longer need to back up each time you use the program.

Before you run Calibrate, you should also remove all TSR programs from memory and have only essential device drivers (in your CONFIG.SYS file) in use when you issue the Calibrate command. Many times, the easiest way to do this is to boot with your original DOS floppy disk in drive A.

Calibrating Your Hard Disk

You can run Calibrate by choosing it from the Norton main screen or by entering **CALIBRAT** at the DOS prompt. If you run Calibrate without any switches, you see an opening dialog box like the one in figure 20.1. The first Calibrate dialog box gives you a brief description of what Calibrate does. To continue with the calibration, choose Continue; choose Quit to stop the calibration process.

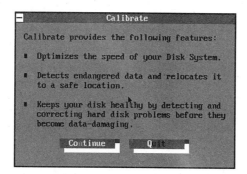

Fig. 20.1

The Calibrate opening dialog box.

If you choose Continue and have more than one hard disk, Calibrate prompts you to choose which hard disk to analyze. If you have only one hard disk, you are not prompted; you go directly to the next dialog box. An additional message may appear, warning you to make sure that you have a backup copy of your hard disk before performing the Calibrate low-level format and tests. Again, choose Continue or Quit.

The next dialog box that you see, shown in figure 20.2, lists the preliminary tests that Calibrate can perform on your hard disk. (On certain types of drives, such as RLL drives and MFM drives, this dialog box may list the Seek tests also.) These compatibility tests tell Calibrate what it needs to know about the logical and physical characteristics of your disk. Choose the Continue option from this dialog box to go to the next dialog box, or choose Cancel to stop the procedure.

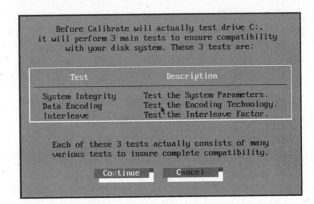

Fig. 20.2

The Calibrate compatibility tests.

System Integrity Tests

When you continue to the System Integrity Tests dialog box, the System Integrity tests begin (see fig. 20.3). While each test is in progress, a dot appears to the left of the test name. The Test Status progress bar lets you know how much of the test has been performed. When Calibrate finishes the test, a check mark appears beside the name. Choose the Stop option if you want to cancel a test in progress.

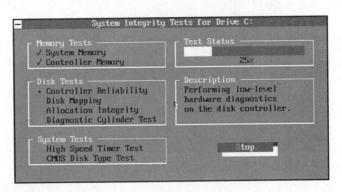

Fig. 20.3

The Calibrate System Integrity Tests dialog box.

As you continue with the calibration tests, you see the Seek Tests dialog box. The Seek tests examine how fast the read/write head on your hard disk can seek out information on the disk. While the tests are in progress, the movement of the head is animated on-screen, moving back and forth on the picture of the drive in the middle of the screen. The Value column gives you the time required to perform each of the tests (in milliseconds).

Seek performs the following four tests:

Test	Description
BIOS Seek Overhead	Tests the time spent getting ready to read information from the disk.
Track-to-Track	Tests how much time the head takes to move to the next track on disk.
Full Stroke	Measures how long the head takes to move from one track to another track on the other side of the disk.
Average Seek	Determines how long, on the average, the head takes to find and read information from the disk. The Average Seek is the number you most often see quoted in advertisements for hard disks. A fast disk has an average seek time of less than 20 ms. A slow hard disk has an average seek time from 60 ms to 80 ms. If you are using disk-intensive application programs on your computer, the average seek time can be a major factor in how efficiently your computer works.

When you run Calibrate from the DOS prompt, you can cause the program to skip the Seek tests if you use the /NOSEEK switch in the command.

Data Encoding Tests

The Data Encoding tests analyze the physical characteristics of the hard disk. The Calibrate program uses this information to do further testing. A technician who is examining a hard disk for problems may also need this information.

Interleave Test

If calibration is possible, Calibrate tests your hard disk by using a number of possible interleaves. This test takes several minutes, after which Calibrate indicates the current and the optimal settings (see fig. 20.4). If Calibrate indicates an optimal setting that varies from the current setting, the program also indicates an expected improvement in performance that you can gain by switching to the optimal setting. If you prefer, you can keep the current setting instead of using the optimal setting. Your disk works optimally at the interleave that is lowest on the graph. This interleave number is labeled Optimal on the graph. Your current interleave is also marked.

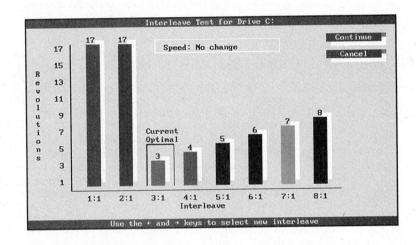

Fig. 20.4

A dialog box displaying the results of the Interleave test.

In figure 20.4, the box around the 3:1 bar indicates that the optimal interleave is 3:1, as determined during pattern testing. In this case, the current setting is the optimal setting. Note the message Speed:No change at the top of the dialog box. If Calibrate had found that adjusting the interleave to a new setting would help, this message would be something like Speed:Increase by 16%. This means that if the interleave is changed to the optimal setting, you increase the access speed to your hard disk by the stated amount (16%). If you do not want to reset your interleave to the setting indicated by the box, you can use the right- and left-arrow keys to move the box to another setting. Choose Continue to continue with the program or choose Cancel to end Calibrate.

If the Calibrate program is unable to perform the interleave tests, a dialog box like the one shown in figure 20.5 appears. This dialog box indicates that your hard disk controller contains an advanced translating controller (common on newer machines), and the Calibrate program cannot adjust it. (Depending on the equipment you are calibrating, you may get a different version of this dialog box.) If you have a cache program installed, such as NCACHE2, you can temporarily remove it from AUTOEXEC.BAT or CONFIG.SYS and try running Calibrate again.

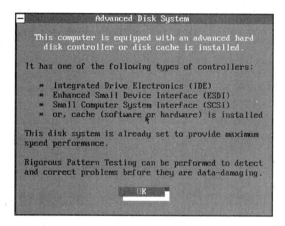

Pattern Testing

After interleave testing is complete, the Pattern Testing dialog box appears (see fig. 20.6). You use Calibrate pattern testing to test your hard disk for defects. You can choose the thoroughness of this test in the Pattern Testing dialog box. The options run from No Pattern Testing to Rigorous Pattern Testing. The higher the level of testing, the more time is required. The No Pattern Testing option may take 5 to 10 minutes, and the Rigorous Pattern Testing option may last overnight, depending on the size of your hard disk.

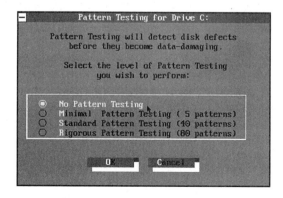

You use pattern testing to test the disk for its read/write capabilities. A pattern of magnetic signals, such as 101010101, is written to the disk and then read back. Pattern testing uses the alternating 1 and 0 pattern, which is the most difficult pattern to read. If you did not receive a warning that Calibrate could not perform a low-level format, then pattern testing also performs a low-level format as it tests the disk.

Use the No Pattern Testing option if you indicate a new interleave factor in the Interleave test. This option is the quickest way to update your interleave factor. Use one of the other pattern-testing options if you have had some problems with your disk, such as the loss of information or files becoming unreadable.

When pattern testing begins, you see a disk map (similar to the Speed Disk map discussed in Chapter 19) that shows the progress of the test. You can safely interrupt the test by pressing Esc. If you stop the pattern testing/low-level format in the middle of its run, Calibrate takes up where it left off when you begin it again (see fig. 20.7).

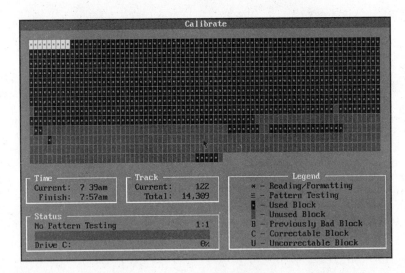

Fig. 20.7

The Calibrate program showing pattern testing in progress.

T I P Because pattern testing can take some time, Norton has a built-in, screen-blanking routine that enables you to blank your screen so that the image does not burn into the screen. During pattern testing, press the space bar to blank the screen. While the screen is blank, a floating message appears occasionally to tell you that the testing is still in progress. Press the space bar again to bring back the image.

Calibrate Report

After all the Calibrate tests are complete, you see a Test Summary message box like the one shown in figure 20.8. Choosing **OK** in this message box displays a report dialog box like the one in figure 20.9. This report summarizes the findings of all the Calibrate tests. Use the up- and down-arrow keys to view parts of the report not shown. It is a good idea to choose the **P**rint option in the report dialog box so that you can keep a folder of reports about your hard disk. Such reports may become important if a technician needs to diagnose problems with your disk in the future. Alternatively, you can choose the **S**ave As option to save the report to a file. Choosing **D**one returns you to the beginning of the Calibrate program, which displays an option dialog box that enables you to choose which disk to test. If you do not want to do further testing, press Esc to return to DOS or the Norton main screen.

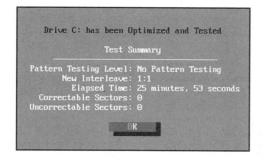

Fig. 20.8

The Test Summary message box.

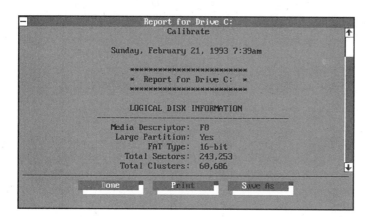

Fig. 20.9

The Calibrate Report dialog box.

Using the Calibrate Switches

You can use a number of switches when you run the CALIBRAT command from the DOS prompt. You use the following syntax:

CALIBRAT [*d:*] [*switches*]

Here are the available switches:

Switch	Description
/BATCH	Does not prompt for any input from the user; returns to DOS when finished. This switch automates the entire test procedure. If you use this option, you may also want to choose one of the /R options to create a report of the test findings.
/BLANK	Blanks the screen while performing the tests.
/NOCOPY	Does not make a duplicate copy of the track being tested. You might run this option to discover bad tracks before deciding to let Calibrate fix them.
/NOFORMAT	Performs pattern testing only and skips the low-level format. Use this option if you know Calibrate cannot perform a low-level format (or Interleave test) because you have an advanced controller. You can discover if you have such a controller by running the program interactively as described earlier in this chapter. If you get a message that the interleave testing cannot be done (refer to fig. 20.5), use this option from then on when you run the program from the DOS prompt. You should also use this option on any other computers you might have of the same brand and model.
/NOSEEK	Skips the Seek tests. Use this option when you do not want Calibrate to test the head-positioning mechanism of the disk. Usually, you need to use Calibrate once without this switch to test the seek-testing mechanism. Thereafter, use this switch.
/PATTERN:*n*	Tells Calibrate which testing level (*n*) to use during a pattern test. The parameter *n* can be 0, 5, 40, or 80. The higher the number, the more thorough the test, but the longer Calibrate takes to test the disk.
/R:*file*	Generates a report and writes it to the file name specified. You must also use the /BATCH switch when you use this option.

Switch	Description
/RA:*file*	Generates a report like that generated by /R:*file*, but appends information to the *file* instead of making a new file.
/X:*drives*	Excludes named drives from the test. For example, /X:DE excludes disks D and E from testing.

Summary

The Norton Calibrate program optimizes the speed and reliability of your hard disk. This chapter showed you how to run the Calibrate command interactively or from the DOS prompt. Calibrate is particularly useful for an older hard disk that may not have been set to its maximum interleave value. With Calibrate, you can set your hard disk to run at its optimum speed, and check the hard disk for flaws with the pattern testing option.

Now turn to Chapter 21 to learn how to use your computer's memory to make access to your disk faster and more efficient.

Using Norton Cache

The flow of information from the disk into a computer program often creates an information bottleneck. Although you can access information in the computer's RAM almost instantaneously, getting information from a disk can be very slow by comparison. If you are using disk-intensive programs, slow disk access can bring your program speed down to a crawl.

A solution to slow disk access is for the computer to read more information from the disk than is needed and to place the extra information into RAM—anticipating that the next piece of information requested by the program will be in RAM and therefore accessed faster. The computer stores this information in a disk buffer, or *cache*.

This chapter provides a brief description of the Norton Cache (NCACHE2) program. This program does more than just create an information buffer. By using two features—IntelliWrites and SmartReads—NCACHE2 tries to guess which data you will read or write from the disk next in order to place in the cache the information you are most likely to need. NCACHE2 predicts future disk access by analyzing the pattern of past disk access. This program can improve the speed at which your hard disk operates and can even help prolong the life of the hard disk.

 NOTE Advanced disk caching is beyond the scope of this book. For information on this subject, consult your *Norton Utilities 7 User's Guide*.

Understanding Disk Caching

Figure 21.1 shows how the information is read from the computer disk and stored in a buffer, called a *cache*, until the program requests the information. If your computer has 1M of memory, for example, and your software programs can access only 640K of that memory at one time, you have extra memory that you can use as a disk cache. The more extra memory you can use as a cache, the more potential speed you can experience in disk access.

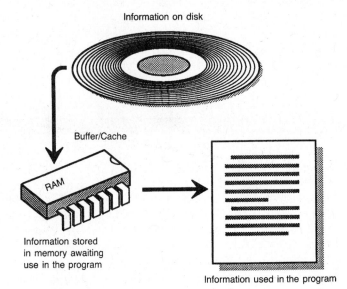

Information on disk

Buffer/Cache

RAM

Information stored
in memory awaiting
use in the program

Information used in the program

Fig. 21.1

How caching
works.

Extra memory is any memory beyond what your programs normally need. This memory may be regular DOS memory, which goes up to 640K. If all your programs in memory (including DOS) use only 320K, you have extra memory that you can use as a cache. Other kinds of extra memory are extended and expanded memory. *Extended memory* is memory above 1M. *Expanded memory* is add-on memory that can be accessed by certain programs that subscribe to the *LIM standard*—a special way to use memory developed by Lotus, Intel, and Microsoft.

A disk cache can provide speed and extend battery life in laptop computers (because the laptop doesn't need to use the motor to access the hard disk as often); the disk cache can also give your programs an enormous boost in speed. Reading information from a floppy disk can take around 200 ms, whereas reading the same information from a hard disk may take from 18 ms to 80 ms. Getting information from RAM takes less than 1 ms.

Installing Norton Cache (NCACHE2)

You can use the Norton Cache program in one of two ways. You can include the program command as a line in your AUTOEXEC.BAT file, or you can include the program as a device driver in your CONFIG.SYS file. If you requested that NCACHE2 be installed when you ran the Norton Install program, NCACHE2 was installed as a device driver in the CONFIG.SYS file. The benefit of installing NCACHE2 in the AUTOEXEC.BAT file is that if you install it as the last terminate-and-stay-resident (TSR) program, you can uninstall it from memory if you need to use the memory to run a large program. The advantage of placing NCACHE2 in CONFIG.SYS is that the command will have compatibility with more computers.

To run NCACHE2, your computer must use DOS 3.0 or a later version, with 640K or more of conventional (RAM) memory and at least 384K of extended or expanded memory. NCACHE2 is also compatible with DR DOS 5.0 from Digital Research, and NCACHE2 supports more storage devices than many other cache programs, including removable drives, external drives, and CD-ROMs.

Using NCACHE2 Options

You can use the Configuration menu in the Norton main screen or the NUCONFIG command to install NCACHE2 in your AUTOEXEC.BAT or CONFIG.SYS file automatically (see Chapter 2 for details). To place the NCACHE2 program in AUTOEXEC.BAT manually, use the following syntax:

> \path\NCACHE2 [switches]

The path refers to the directory name where the NCACHE2 file is stored. To place the program in CONFIG.SYS, use this syntax:

> DEVICE=\path\NCACHE2 [switches]

Many optional switches are explained later in this chapter.

Either of these commands causes the disk cache to be in effect when you boot your computer. (Do not use both commands; use one or the other.) As with the AUTOEXEC.BAT file, you can enter the NCACHE2 command from the DOS prompt at any time to begin or end the NCACHE2 program, using the switches described later.

NOTE Usually, NCACHE2 loads automatically into high memory. You should not use a memory manager (such as QEMM) to load NCACHE2 high. If you are using DOS 5.0 (or later) and EMM386, load NCACHE2 from your AUTOEXEC.BAT file in order to load into high memory.

You can use NCACHE2 with most default conditions on many computers. You should have to refer to the switches only if you are having problems getting your cache to work correctly. Some ways in which you can use NCACHE2 are described in the following sections. The commands listed are what you place in your AUTOEXEC.BAT file, although you can achieve the same effect by typing **DEVICE=** in front of the command and placing it in your CONFIG.SYS file.

Specifying the Cache Size

The Norton Cache program enables you to specify how much random-access memory (RAM) in your computer is to be used as a buffer when the computer is reading information from disk. The larger the cache, the faster your disk access tends to be.

The following command, for example, is used on a Dell 486P/50 computer (80486):

\NU7\NCACHE2 /INSTALL

Because programs used on this computer never use more than 640K, NCACHE2 is set to use 2968K of the memory as a cache. The NCACHE2 program is in the NU7 directory.

The /INSTALL switch causes the NCACHE2 program to be installed using a default cache size that is equal to all available expanded memory plus all available extended memory. If you do not have any extended or expanded memory, the /INSTALL option causes 128K of memory to be allocated to the cache. After you enter this command, you see a screen like the one shown in figure 21.2. Notice that 2968K is assigned as cache memory.

Fig. 21.2

Installing
NCACHE2 with
defaults.

```
Conventional memory:       0K cache    37K management   513K free
High DOS memory:           0K cache     0K management     0K free
Expanded (EMS) memory:     0K cache     0K management     0K free
Extended (XMS) memory:  2968K cache     0K management    40K free

     Total cache size is 2968.0K - Currently using 0.0K   (0.0%)

           The following drives are being cached: C:
```

You can use the /DOS, /EXT, and /EXP options to allocate some other amount of conventional (/DOS), extended (/EXT), or expanded (/EXP) memory for cache. Suppose that you want to create a small cache of 20K conventional memory. You use the following command:

       \NORTON\NCACHE2 /DOS=20

The examples in this section illustrate typical ways of using the NCACHE2 program. If you use one of these versions of the command, replace /DOS =20 with the amount of extra DOS memory you are willing to use as a cache. The most common command options you may want to use are the /+S and /+I options. The /+S option enables SmartReads; /+I enables IntelliWrites. These options can provide additional speed for some applications such as word processing and spreadsheet programs, but the options may not provide additional speed for database programs. You may have to experiment with these options to determine which combination gives you the best disk access for the type of application programs you run.

Another option that you may use is /USEHIGH=ON. If you are using an advanced memory manager such as QEMM or 386MAX on your computer, this option enables NCACHE2 to use less of your initial 640K DOS memory and may provide more memory for use in your application programs. If you need further options to make the program fast enough for your needs, refer to the additional parameters described in the following section.

Choosing Command Switches

As described earlier, you place the Norton Cache program in your AUTOEXEC.BAT file by using the following syntax:

       path\NCACHE2 [*switch*]

The *path* refers to the directory name where the NCACHE2 file is stored. To place the Norton Cache program in your CONFIG.SYS file, you can use this syntax:

       DEVICE=*path*\NCACHE2 [*switches*]

Many switches are available to specify how the NCACHE2 program creates and uses a disk buffer. The first group of switches contains the drive switches. They are used to control and fine-tune the cache for each drive. Notice that some of these switches are preceded by a plus (+) or minus (–), which tells the program to activate or deactivate the option. To use one of these drive switches for a particular drive, precede the switch with the drive designation. For example, to deactivate caching for drive D, use the switch D:/–A. Here are the drive switches that may be used with NCACHE2:

Drive Switch	Description
/+|–A	Activates or deactivates caching. Use this switch if you need to deactivate caching in order to run a program in which you do not want caching to be used.
/+|–C	Enables or disables caching of additional information. No new information is cached when this switch is disabled.
/+|–I	Enables or disables IntelliWrites. When on, this switch accelerates disk writes and returns control to the application before the write is finished.
/+|–P	Enables or disables write protection for drives.
/+|–S	Enables or disables SmartReads.
/+|–W	Enables or disables write-through caching. When write-through caching is disabled, writes are written directly to the disk, bypassing the cache.

Another group of switches contains the install switches. You use these switches when you are installing the NCACHE2 program. Here are the install switches that are available:

Install Switch	Description
/BLOCK=*n*	Sets the size of the cache blocks. The *n* is a number in kilobytes. Use large blocks if you are accessing large files and your disk is unfragmented. Use smaller blocks if you access small files or if your disk is fragmented.
/DOS=*n* or /DOS=–*n*	Specifies how much DOS (conventional) memory is to be used by the cache. Use this switch only when you do not have expanded or extended memory. A negative value tells the command to leave that much memory free for other programs to use.
/EXP=*n* or /EXP=–*n*	Specifies how much expanded memory (in kilobytes) is to be used by the cache. A negative value tells the command to leave that much memory free for other programs to use. /EXP=750, for example, tells the command to use 750K of expanded memory for the disk cache. Any expanded memory used must be compatible with LIM 4.0.

Install Switch	Description
/EXT=*n* or /EXT=-*n*	Specifies how much extended memory (in kilobytes) is to be used by the cache. A negative value tells the command to leave that much free memory for use by other programs. /EXT=256, for example, tells the command to use 256K of extended memory for the cache.
/G=*n*	Limits the caching of group sector reads for the specified drive(s).
/INI=*filespec*	Indicates where to look for the file that contains installation options. If, for example, your installation options are in your NORTON directory in a file named NCACHE.INI, you use the parameter /INI=\NORTON\NCACHE.INI.
/INSTALL	Installs Norton Cache with all default values, including the use of all available expanded and extended memory for the cache. This switch is often the easiest and quickest way to execute the command.
/OPTIMIZE=[S|E|M]	Optimizes for speed, efficiency, or memory.

The S (Speed) option sets the following parameters:

> /BLOCK=8K
> /DELAY=1.0
> /READ=8K
> /WRITE=*x* (*x* is the largest track, in kilobytes, of all tracks being cached)

The E (Efficiency) option sets the following parameters:

> /BLOCK=*s* (*s* is the smallest block size for the current cache size, usually 512K to 1M)
> /DELAY=1.0
> /READ=8K
> /WRITE=8K

The M (Memory) option sets the following parameters:

> /BLOCK=8K
> /DELAY=0.0
> /READ=0 (disables the read-ahead feature)
> /WRITE=0 (disables IntelliWrites)

continues

Install Switch	Description
/R=D*n*	Specifies how many sectors ahead should be read. A specification of /R=0 or /R=D0 disables read-aheads. /R=*n* causes read-aheads always, and /R=D*n* causes read-aheads only when the file being read is not a random file. For *n*, you can specify a number of sectors from 0 to 15.
/READ=*n*	Sets the maximum size (in kilobytes) for read-aheads. For *n*, use a whole number from 8 to 64.
/USEHMA=ON|OFF	Uses the XMS high memory area to reduce the use of DOS RAM (if set to ON). This option is available only if you have an extended memory manager.
/USEHIGH=ON|OFF	Minimizes the use of conventional (low) DOS memory if high memory is available (if set to ON). The default setting is OFF.
/WRITE=*n*	Sets maximum size (in kilobytes) for the IntelliWrites buffer. For *n*, use a whole number from 8 to 64.

A third group of switches contains the reconfigure switches. You use them to change something about the program after it has been installed. Here are the reconfigure switches:

Reconfigure Switch	Description
/DELAY=*ss.hh*	Delays writes to the disk in seconds or hundredths of a second (00.01 is one hundredth of a second). The default is 00.00. Slight writing delays can improve the speed of write-intensive programs.
/DISKRESET=ON|OFF	Specifies that all data be written to disk when an application makes a disk reset request.
/DUMP	Writes all information currently in the cache to disk.
/Help or /?	Displays a list of the command-line switches to the screen.
/MULTI ON|OFF	Specifies whether the multitasking feature of IntelliWrites should be enabled (ON) or disabled (OFF).
/QUIET	Specifies quiet mode. Only errors are reported.

Reconfigure Switch	Description
/QUICK=ON|OFF	Displays the DOS prompt even when information is being written to disk (ON), or waits until all writes to the disk have finished before displaying the DOS prompt (OFF).
/REPORT=ON|OFF	Displays status and performance information (ON) or does not display such information (OFF). An example of this report appears in figure 21.3.
/RESET	Resets the cache by writing all pending disk writes, flushing all data from all drives.
/SAVE	Saves current cache settings in the file specified by the /INI switch (or NCACHE.INI).
/STATUS=ON|OFF	Displays a condensed version of the cache report. If the OFF switch is used, the report is not displayed at install time.
/UNINSTALL	Removes the NCACHE2 (TSR) program from memory and discontinues caching. You can uninstall only if the program was loaded from the AUTOEXEC.BAT file (not from the CONFIG.SYS file).

```
   Conventional memory:        0K cache    37K management    513K free
   High DOS memory:            0K cache     0K management      0K free
   Expanded (EMS) memory:      0K cache     0K management      0K free
   Extended (XMS) memory:   2968K cache     0K management     40K free

      Total cache size is 2968.0K - Currently using 159.0K    (5.3%)

DOS = 0K             BLOCK = 8192   USEHIGH  = ON     DELAY = 1.00
EXP = 0K, 0K         READ  = 8K     USEHMA   = ON     QUICK = ON
EXT = 2968K, 1480K   WRITE = 8K     OPTIMIZE = SPEED  MULTI = OFF

      A  C  I  W  P     R     G     Cache Hits / Disk Reads
A:    -  +  -  +  -    DB   128          0 / 0           (0.0%)
B:    -  +  -  +  -    DB   128          0 / 0           (0.0%)
C:    +  +  +  +  -    DB   128        105 / 328        (32.0%)
```

Fig. 21.3

An NCACHE2 status and performance report.

 NOTE If your computer is using the Microsoft SmartDrive cache, you must remove it from your AUTOEXEC.BAT file or CONFIG.SYS file before using the NCACHE2 program.

When you install NCACHE2, you must specify a cache size. If you do not specify a size, the default conditions are /EXT=4096, 2048K.

To install the cache using default conditions, enter the following command:

NCACHE2 /INSTALL

To install this program using all but 64K of extended memory and using read-ahead of 32K only for disk C, enter the following command:

NCACHE2 /EXT=–64 /READ=32K /–A C:/+A

Note that /–A deactivates caching for all drives, and then C:/+A activates caching for drive C. Thus, only disk C is cached.

Using Batch Files To Simplify NCACHE2 Options

Because NCACHE2 contains so many options, you may want to create a few batch files to issue versions of the command that you use most often. To make the uninstall procedure easier, you can place the following line in a batch file called UNI.BAT:

NCACHE2 /UNINSTALL

Suppose that you want to deactivate NCACHE2 during the use of a program. You can place the following command in a batch file called DEACTIVE.BAT:

NCACHE2 /–A

Then, to reactivate the command, you can have a batch file called ACTIVE.BAT containing this command:

NCACHE2 /+A

If you use a complicated NCACHE2 command from the DOS prompt, you can place the following command line in a file called CACHE.BAT:

NCACHE2 /USEHIGH=ON /EXT=920 /+S /+I

Then you just enter **CACHE** to begin the NCACHE2 program. Assigning these batch file names to such tasks makes working with long commands that have difficult-to-remember options much easier.

Summary

This chapter explored the Norton Utilities NCACHE2 command. The NCACHE2 program helps make your disk access more efficient and speeds up disk access as well as the operation of many programs. You can run NCACHE2 on computers that use MS-DOS or PC DOS 3.0 (or later) or that use DR DOS 5.0 (or later).

The next chapter begins a tour of the Norton Utilities programs for managing computer resources.

PART

VI

OUTLINE

Managing Your Computer's Resources

Using Norton Control Center

S o far, this book has concentrated on issues of safety and maintenance. Part VI introduces various Norton Utilities commands that
make using your computer easier and more fun.

The Norton commands covered in Part VI include Norton Control
Center (NCC), Norton Change Directory (NCD), Batch Enhancer (BE),
commands for finding files, Norton command-line utilities, and Norton
Diagnostics. These commands enable you to navigate around your
computer faster and with fewer keystrokes than you can with DOS
commands. You can use the NCC command to modify some of your
computer's environment settings (such as colors, cursor size, and keyboard rate) and to create better batch files, search files by name or by
contents, duplicate disks, manage a file's date and time, and perform a
series of diagnostic tests on your computer. This chapter shows you
how to use Norton Control Center.

With Norton Control Center (NCC), you can change several settings on
your computer, including the size of your cursor, your monitor's colors, the number of lines displayed, and the date and time. The Time
Mark (TM) command that you may have used in Norton Utilities 4.5
is now part of the NCC command for Versions 5, 6, and 7.

You can use Norton Control Center interactively or from the DOS
prompt. This chapter first describes interactive mode and then the
options available from the DOS prompt.

Using Norton Control Center in Interactive Mode

If you run the NCC command at the DOS prompt or from the main Norton menu with no quick switches, you enter interactive mode, and the Norton Control Center screen appears (see fig. 22.1).

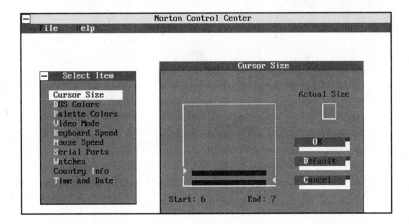

Fig. 22.1

The Norton Control Center screen.

Notice the list of options in the Select Item menu on the left side of the screen. These options represent the settings that you can change in Norton Control Center. When you enter the NCC command from the DOS prompt or from the Norton main menu, the first option, **C**ursor Size, is highlighted. When you highlight a Select Item option, a dialog box appears on the right side of the screen, displaying information on the highlighted option. (You can use the right- and left-arrow keys, Tab key, or mouse to move to the right or left side of the screen.)

After you choose your settings, open the **F**ile menu at the top of the screen. The **F**ile menu has three options:

Option	Description
Save Settings (F2)	Saves your settings to a file. From the DOS prompt, you must enter the NCC command with the /SETALL switch to save the settings so that you can activate the settings at any time. (See the command-line options described later in this chapter.)
Load Settings (F3)	Loads the previously set NCC options that were saved in a file.
E**x**it (Alt+X)	Exits the NCC program.

The following sections discuss the settings you can change with Norton Control Center in interactive mode.

Setting the Cursor Size

When you first enter Norton Control Center, the Cursor Size option is highlighted in the Select Item menu, and the Cursor Size dialog box appears on the right side of the screen (refer to fig. 22.1). Notice the two lines at the bottom of this dialog box and the fields labeled Start and End. In interactive video mode, the cursor consists of lines 6 and 7. (In higher-resolution modes, you may have as many as 14 cursor lines.) This combination of lines 6 and 7 creates a cursor that looks like a small underline—the normal setting for most computers.

If you are using a computer on which the cursor is hard to find—for example, a laptop with a hard-to-read display—you may want to create a larger cursor. You can use lines 0 to 7 for the cursor. If you want the cursor to be larger, press the up-arrow key to add more lines.

Figure 22.2 shows settings that display the cursor as a square rather than an underline. (The new version flashes in the upper-right corner of the dialog box.)

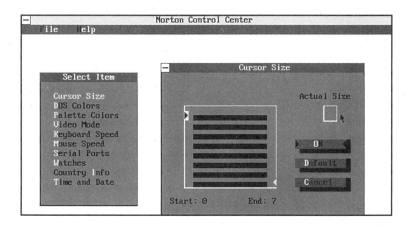

Fig. 22.2

Changing the cursor size.

After you size your cursor, choose **OK** to return to the Norton Control Center screen or press Esc to end the NCC command.

Setting Monitor Colors

The **D**OS Colors option in the Select Item menu enables you to choose color settings for your monitor. The settings that you can choose, however, depend on the kind of monitor you have. Some computers support only a few colors, whereas others support hundreds. If you tire of the black-and-white display that you normally see in DOS, you can use **D**OS Colors to specify colors that better fit your mood or decor.

When you choose **D**OS Colors, the DOS Colors dialog box appears (see fig. 22.3).

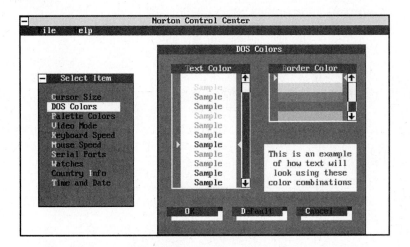

Fig. 22.3

The DOS Colors
dialog box.

The DOS Colors dialog box enables you to change the settings in two boxes: **T**ext Color (including the background color) and **B**order Color. You can use the arrow keys to move between these boxes.

To choose a color combination in the **T**ext Color box, scroll through the list of options. Arrows on the right and left sides of this box point to the currently selected color combination. When you choose an option, a sample of that color combination appears in the lower-right corner of the DOS Colors dialog box. The Text Color options include white on black, yellow on black, white on blue, and red on blue. You can also choose a Border color from the box in the upper right of the DOS Colors dialog box in the same way you choose a Text color.

After you choose color options, choose **O**K at the bottom of the box to return to the Select Item menu. If you want to revert to the default colors, choose **D**efault. To revert to the colors that you were using when you entered Norton Control Center and to return to the Select Item menu, choose **C**ancel.

Setting Palette Colors

The Select Item menu in Norton Control Center includes the **P**alette Colors option (available for EGA and VGA monitors only). When you choose the **D**OS Colors option, you can use only 16 colors at one time, even if your monitor can display more colors. You use the **P**alette Colors option to specify those 16 colors and how they are used (for the text, background, and so on).

If your monitor supports more than 16 colors, **P**alette Colors enables you to select alternative colors to be used as the 16 **D**OS Colors. (You can change the normal DOS blue to a lighter blue, for instance.) Some computers support as many as 256 colors, any of which you can use as a **D**OS Color.

When you choose the **P**alette Colors option, the Palette Colors dialog box appears (see fig. 22.4).

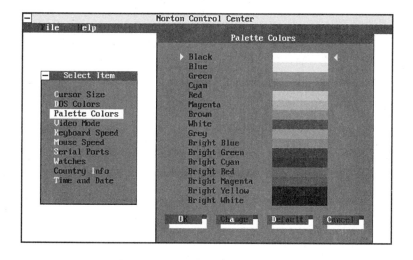

Fig. 22.4

The Palette Colors dialog box.

This dialog box displays a list of 16 colors, including black. (Although you cannot see the actual colors in this black-and-white figure, you can see the names of the colors on the left side of the Palette Colors dialog box.) When you first access this dialog box, the colors displayed are the 16 standard DOS colors. You can change any of these colors to any other supported color. You can change the color named Green, for example, to purple. The color will still be named Green on-screen, but whenever a program uses a color named Green, that color will actually be displayed as purple.

To choose an alternative color for one of these original DOS colors, highlight the original DOS color that you want to change and then choose the Change button. Another color menu appears. Scroll through this list to find a new color, select the color you want, and then press Enter to choose that color as the replacement for the original DOS color. You return to the Palette Colors dialog box. If, for example, you chose blue-green to replace DOS's original blue, DOS displays blue-green where the program usually displays blue.

After you select the colors you want to use, choose **OK** in the Palette Colors dialog box. If you want all the colors to revert to the normal DOS colors, choose **D**efault. If you want to cancel this option and revert to the colors that were in effect when you entered Norton Control Center, choose **C**ancel.

Setting the Video Mode

Although the typical DOS monitor displays 25 lines per screen, some monitors—EGA and VGA in particular—can display more. To change the display mode, choose **V**ideo Mode from the Select Item menu. The Video Mode dialog box appears (see fig. 22.5).

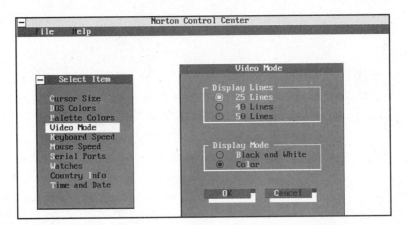

Fig. 22.5

The Video Mode
dialog box.

The options in this dialog box are **25** Lines, **40** Lines, **50** Lines, **B**lack and White, and **C**olor. After you choose the settings you want to use, choose **OK**. To revert to the preceding video mode, choose **C**ancel.

Setting the Keyboard Speed

You can use the NCC command to change the speed of the IBM PC keyboard. If you are a fast typist, for example, you may want to make the keyboard more responsive. To change the PC keyboard, choose **Keyboard Speed** from the Select Item menu. The Keyboard Speed dialog box appears (see fig. 22.6).

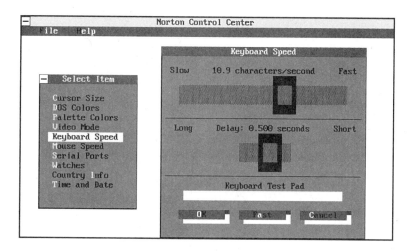

Fig. 22.6

The Keyboard Speed dialog box.

 NOTE The **Keyboard Speed** option is not available for some early versions of the PC (original PC and XTs, for example). If your computer does not support a change in keyboard speeds, Norton displays a message telling you that this option does not work on your computer.

The Keyboard Speed dialog box contains two areas in which you can set keyboard options. Use the top area to set the keyboard rate; use the bottom area to set the delay. *Keyboard rate* is how quickly a character repeats when you hold down that key. *Delay* is the time that elapses before the character begins to repeat.

The normal keyboard rate is 10.9 characters per second (cps). You can change this speed to a minimum of 2 cps or a maximum of 30 cps. The normal delay rate is 0.5 second. You can change this delay to a minimum of 0.25 second or a maximum of 1 second.

To change either setting, use the arrow keys or the mouse to move the box along the appropriate bar. To choose the fastest settings for keyboard rate and delay, choose the **Fast** button at the bottom of the Keyboard Speed dialog box.

You can experiment with these settings by typing in the Keyboard Test Pad box at the bottom of the dialog box. Press and hold down the A key, for example, and notice how much delay occurs before the letter starts repeating and how quickly the letter repeats.

When you are satisfied with your settings, choose **OK** to return to the Select Item menu. Choose **C**ancel to revert to the previous speed settings.

Setting the Mouse Speed

If you use a mouse, you may want to adjust the device's *sensitivity*—the way in which the movement of the mouse corresponds to the movement of the mouse pointer on-screen. *Slow sensitivity* means that you must move the mouse more to see movement on-screen. *Fast sensitivity* means that a small movement of the mouse on your mouse pad translates to a large movement on-screen.

When you choose the **M**ouse Speed option from the Select Item menu, the Mouse Speed dialog box appears (see fig. 22.7).

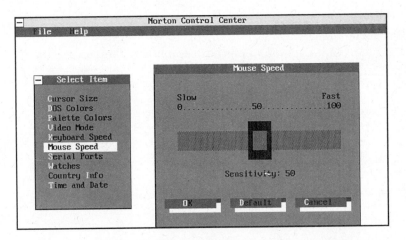

Fig. 22.7

The Mouse Speed dialog box.

The default sensitivity setting is 50; you can use any setting from 0 to 100. Change the sensitivity by using the arrow keys or the mouse to move the box along the bar in the middle of the dialog box.

After you select the mouse sensitivity that you want, choose **OK**. If you want to revert to the normal sensitivity (50), choose **Default**. If you want to cancel this option and revert to the sensitivity setting you were using when you entered Norton Control Center, choose **Cancel**.

 Setting the mouse sensitivity to 0 may cause the mouse pointer movement to stop completely.

Choosing Serial Port Settings

In Norton Control Center, you can choose the settings for your serial ports—a required task if you have a printer, a plotter, or another device that requires a serial port. A modem, for example, may require settings of 2400 baud, no parity, 8 data bits, and 1 stop bit. If you must choose settings for communication with a peripheral device (such as a printer) or another computer, these settings usually are specified in the peripheral device's manual.

When you choose **S**erial Ports from the Select Item menu, the Serial Ports dialog box appears (see fig. 22.8).

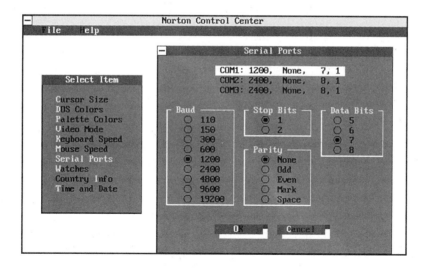

The following options determine how communications take place through as many as four COM (serial) ports:

Setting	Defines
Baud	Speed of communication. Common baud settings are 110, 150, 300, 600, 1200, 2400, 4800, 9600, and 19200. The higher the baud setting, the faster the communication.
Stop Bits	Number of stop-bit signals sent with each pulse of information. This option is usually 1 or 2.
Parity	Type of error-checking protocol to be used: None, Odd, Even, Mark, or Space. The most common setting is None.
Data Bits	Number of bits of information included in each communication pulse. This option is 5, 6, 7, or 8.

After you make your choices, choose **OK** to lock in all selections, or choose **Cancel** to revert to the preceding settings.

Setting Stopwatches

Norton Utilities provides four stopwatches that enable you to time certain events. You can use the **W**atches option to observe and reset these watches. You can use **W**atches also to reset the watches before you time something—for example, to compare the time that two different accounting packages take to generate an end-of-month report.

When you choose **W**atches from the Select Item menu, the Watches dialog box appears (see fig. 22.9).

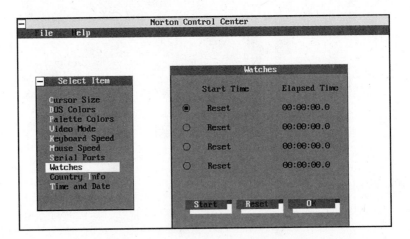

Fig. 22.9

The Watches
dialog box.

To use a watch, choose one of the four radio buttons, and then reset or start that watch by choosing **S**tart or **R**eset at the bottom of the dialog box. When you finish using the watch, choose **OK** to return to the Select Item menu.

Usually, you will use the watches by issuing the NCC command from the DOS prompt. For more information, see the section "Using Norton Control Center from the DOS Prompt" later in this chapter.

NOTE When you use the NCC command with the /START or /STOP switch, the elapsed times appear on-screen. If the result of a /START or /STOP operation scrolls off-screen, you can view the time by choosing Norton Control Center's **W**atches option.

Setting Country Info

Because many countries use PCs, you occasionally may have to change the formatting of certain items so that those items match another country's standard. In the United States, for example, dates are usually written in month-day-year format; Europeans, however, write dates in day-month-year format. Other formats that vary from country to country are time, currency (£ rather than $), lists (separated by semicolons rather than commas), and numbers (1.000 rather than 1,000). The Country **I**nfo option in the Select Item menu enables you to set these items for your computer. If, for instance, you are preparing a report to be sent to Europe, you can change the date format so that Europeans can understand the report.

For the Country **I**nfo option to work, you must have the COUNTRY.SYS driver in your CONFIG.SYS file. If the COUNTRY.SYS driver is not in CONFIG.SYS, a screen appears when you choose that option. This screen displays the current settings, which you cannot change (see fig. 22.10). If the driver is in the CONFIG.SYS file, however, you can change the settings in the Country Info dialog box.

If the driver is in CONFIG.SYS, a list box in the bottom-left corner of this dialog box lists several country options, including U.S.A., Arabic Speaking, and Australia. If you choose a country from this list, the Country Info information changes to match that country's normal usage. After you choose a country, choose **OK** to lock in the formats, or choose **C**ancel to revert to the preceding settings.

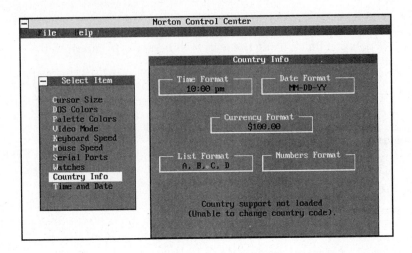

Fig. 22.10

The Country Info dialog box.

If you want to be able to change your country settings, place a line like this one in your CONFIG.SYS file:

COUNTRY=001,850 C:\DOS\COUNTRY.SYS

The 001 specifies the United States, and 850 is a selection for a character set. The other common character set used in the United States is 437. (See your DOS manual for more information on country settings.)

You must also enter a command similar to this one from the DOS prompt (or in AUTOEXEC.BAT):

NLSFUNC \DOS\COUNTRY.SYS

This command assumes that you stored the COUNTRY.SYS driver in a directory named DOS.

After you include the proper COUNTRY.SYS driver in your CONFIG.SYS file, reboot, and enter the NLSFUNC command, you can change your country settings in Norton Control Center.

Setting the Time and Date

If your clock battery has failed, the date and time settings for your computer will not be correct. On some computers, particularly the AT, you must use the diagnostics disk to reset the date and time so that the computer remembers the settings. Norton Control Center's Time and Date option, however, enables you to set these parameters without booting with the diagnostics disk.

NOTE You can use the Time and Date option to set the date and time for several DOS computers, but some computers may not respond to your setting if they use a nonstandard clock. You should experiment to see whether this Norton Control Center option works for your computer.

When you choose Time and Date from the Select Item menu, the Time and Date dialog box appears (see fig. 22.11).

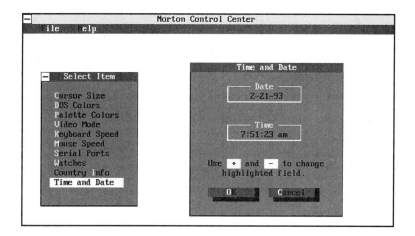

Fig. 22.11

The Time and Date dialog box.

To set the time or date, use the arrow keys to highlight the number and then press the plus (+) key or minus (–) key to increase or decrease the number. (Or you can enter the numbers.) Choose **OK** to lock in the changes, or choose **Cancel** to return the time and date to their previous settings.

Saving Norton Control Center Settings to Disk

To save the changes you made with Norton Control Center, choose **S**ave Settings from the **F**ile menu. When you are prompted for a file name, type the name and then press Enter. The settings you changed in Norton Control Center are saved to that file.

After you save the information to a file, you can use command-line switches to reset Norton Control Center to the settings you saved. Suppose that you chose certain colors, along with other settings that you want to use all the time, and then saved this information in a file named SETTINGS.NCC. You can place the NCC command in your AUTOEXEC.BAT file with the /SETALL switch, using the following command:

NCC \NORTON\SETTINGS.NCC /SETALL

This command reactivates all the settings (color choices, cursor size, and so on) that you saved in Norton Control Center. In this case, the SETTINGS.NCC file is in the NORTON directory, so the path name is necessary. Otherwise, the file is activated from the root (\) directory. If you do not want to include the command in your AUTOEXEC.BAT file, you can enter the same NCC command at the DOS prompt.

Using Norton Control Center from the DOS Prompt

Several settings that you can choose interactively in Norton Command Center can be set also from the DOS prompt with Norton Control Center command-line options. Here is the syntax:

NCC [*filespec*] [*switches*]

The *filespec* variable refers to a file that contains system-information specifications. Before you use this version of the command, you must create this file by using Norton Control Center to choose the settings you want and then save the information to a file.

The following switches are available for use with *filespec*:

Switch	Description
/CURSOR	Reads the information in the file named by *filespec* but sets only the cursor size
/DOSCOLOR	Reads the information in the file named by *filespec* but sets only the previously chosen DOS colors for foreground, background, and border
/PALETTE	Reads the information in the file named by *filespec* but sets only the palette colors
/SET	Reads the information in the file named by *filespec* and sets all the parameters

If you have not created a settings file by running the NCC command in interactive mode, you can set a few options with these quick switches:

Switch	Description
/25	Places the monitor in 25-line mode (same as /CO80)
/35	Places the monitor in 35-line mode (supported only by EGA monitors)
/40	Places the monitor in 40-line mode (supported only by VGA monitors)
/43	Places the monitor in 43-line mode (supported only by EGA monitors)
/50	Places the monitor in 50-line mode (supported only by VGA monitors)
/BW80	Places the monitor in black-and-white mode with 25 lines and 80 columns
/CO80	Places the monitor in color mode with 25 lines and 80 columns
/FAST	Sets the keyboard rate to its fastest possible value

You can use the NCC command to set stopwatches also. Here are the available switches:

Switch	Description
/C:*comment*	Displays the text string *comment* after you execute the command. This switch is useful for documenting which timer is being reported. If the *comment* contains any blanks, you must enclose the entire *comment* in quotation marks.
/L	Displays the time and date on the left side of the monitor.
/N	Suppresses display of the current time and date.
/START:*n*	Starts stopwatch number *n* (1 to 4).
/STOP:*n*	Stops stopwatch number *n* (1 to 4).

NOTE To access Norton Control Center interactively, enter the NCC command without using any file specification. The Norton Control Center menu appears, enabling you to choose interactively the same options that you can set with switches in command-line mode.

You can combine switches to change multiple settings. For example, to set your VGA computer so that 50 lines are displayed on-screen and the keyboard rate is the fastest value, use this command:

NCC /50/FAST

Summary

Norton Control Center gives you the capability of customizing your computer. If you have a laptop computer, for example, and want a large cursor, you can create that larger cursor in Norton Control Center. In this chapter, you learned how to change the colors that appear on your monitor, select the number of lines displayed, adjust keyboard and mouse speed, set up options for your serial ports, set up country formats, and use stopwatches to time various events.

Another Norton Utilities program that you can use to manage your computer resources is Norton Change Directory. The next chapter shows you how to use this utility to manage your disk directories.

Using Norton Change Directory

DOS provides commands to make, remove, and change directories. The Norton Change Directory (NCD) command, however, gives you even greater control over directory management. In the preceding chapter, you learned how to use Norton Control Center (NCC) to manage your computer's hardware settings. Similarly, you use Norton Change Directory to manage your files and directories. With NCD, you can efficiently manage your directories on disk and navigate easily between directories.

Norton Change Directory is actually two commands in one. If used in command-line mode (from the DOS prompt), Norton Change Directory replaces the DOS commands MD, CD, and RD, which are used to make, change, and remove directories, respectively. If used in interactive mode, Norton Change Directory acts as a directory-management tool. This chapter discusses Norton Change Directory in both modes.

Using Norton Change Directory in Interactive Mode

If you enter the NCD command without parameters, you activate the command's interactive mode, and a graphic representation of your directory structure appears on-screen (see fig. 23.1). The disk in figure 23.1 has four levels of directories. Directory ONE-A has a subdirectory called TWO-A, which has a subdirectory called THREE-A, which in turn has a subdirectory called FOUR-A. Directory ONE-B has only a single subdirectory, named TWO-B. Directory ONE-C has no subdirectories.

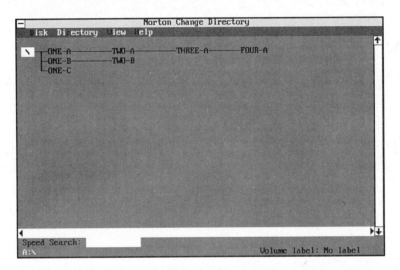

Fig. 23.1

Norton Change Directory in interactive mode, displaying a graphic representation of your directory tree.

To go to any directory on disk, use the arrow keys to move the highlight to the directory you want, and press Enter. You then exit the Norton Change Directory command and return to the DOS prompt—in the directory you chose.

You can do much more than just change directories on this screen. The menu bar at the top contains the menus **D**isk, Di**r**ectory, **V**iew, and **H**elp. To open any menu on the menu bar, press Alt plus the highlighted letter of the menu name or just click the menu name. These pull-down menus contain a number of options that allow you to manage the directory tree and to use the NCD program, such as choosing what drive tree is currently being viewed.

Using the NCD Disk Menu

The NCD **D**isk menu, shown in figure 23.2, contains several options. **C**hange Disk selects the disk for which you want to display a directory tree. **R**escan Disk updates Norton Change Directory's TREEINFO.NCD file, which contains the names of all directories. If you add or remove a directory without using the NCD command, you must select this option to ensure that the directory tree on-screen is accurate.

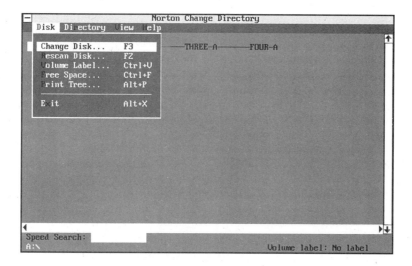

Fig. 23.2

The NCD
Disk menu.

With the **V**olume Label option, you can change the volume label on the disk or add a volume label if one is not present. (This function replaces the VL command in Norton Utilities 4.5.) **F**ree Space displays disk size, amount of space used, and amount of free space. With **P**rint Tree, you can print a copy of the directory tree. (This option is especially useful if your directory tree is too large to fit on-screen.) To exit Norton Change Directory, choose E**x**it.

Note that each option has a shortcut key or key combination. You can access the **C**hange Disk option, for example, by pressing the shortcut key F3 even if the **D**isk menu is not open. Alternatively, you can access **C**hange Disk by opening the menu (pressing Alt+D) and then choosing the option (pressing C) from that menu.

Using the NCD Directory Menu

The NCD Directory menu, shown in figure 23.3, offers options dealing
with the manipulation of directories on disk. In this menu, you can
choose to list the files in a directory; rename, make, or delete a directory; display the size of a directory; copy a directory from one part of
the tree to another part (or to another drive); remove a directory and
all its files; and move a directory to a different location on the tree. In
addition, you can choose configuration options for the NCD command
that allow you to permit or disable the copying, removing, and moving
of directories. The following paragraphs describe these options in more
detail.

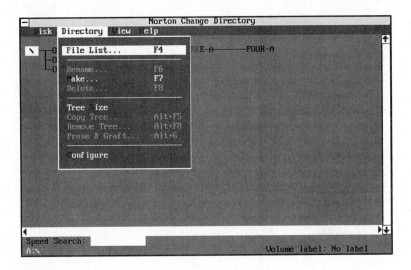

Fig. 23.3

The NCD
Directory menu.

With **F**ile List, you can display a list of files in the currently selected
directory (see fig. 23.4). You can sort the names in a certain order by
choosing options from the Sort Order list. You use **R**e-sort to revert to
the original listing.

The **R**ename option enables you to rename the highlighted directory.
This feature is particularly useful because you cannot rename a directory by using DOS commands.

You use **M**ake to create a new directory. Highlight the directory to
which you want to add a subdirectory, choose **M**ake, enter a name
for the new directory, and press Enter. **D**elete removes a directory.
Just highlight the directory (which must not contain any files or
subdirectories) and choose **D**elete.

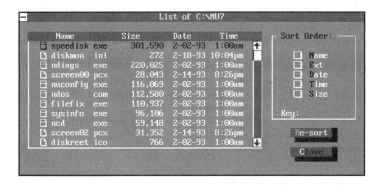

Fig. 23.4

Displaying files
with **F**ile List
from the NCD
Di**r**ectory menu.

The Tree **S**ize option displays the total size of all files in the currently
selected directory, as well as the total allocated disk space for the files.
With Cop**y** Tree, you can copy the selected directory and all its subdirectories to a new location on the tree or to another drive. Select the
directory to be copied, choose Cop**y** Tree, type the name of the directory or drive to which you want to copy the selected directory, and
press Enter. You are asked whether you want to delete the original
directories and files after the copy is complete.

Remove **T**ree deletes a directory and all its subdirectories. Select the
directory, choose Remove **T**ree, and verify at the prompt that you want
to remove the directory.

The **P**rune & Graft option enables you to rearrange directories in the
directory tree. Choose **P**rune & Graft and select the directory you want
to *prune* (to cut from the tree). Then indicate where to *graft* the directory into the existing directory tree. A dialog box prompts you to confirm the graft.

With the **C**onfigure option, you can enable or disable the Copy Tree,
Remove **T**ree, and **P**rune & Graft options (see fig. 23.5).

 Because the Copy **T**ree, Remove **T**ree, and **P**rune & Graft
options are potentially dangerous, these options are turned
off by default. To enable these options, you must choose
Configure from the Di**r**ectory menu.

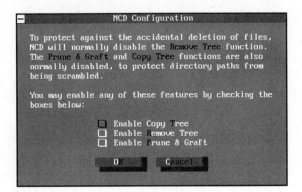

Using the NCD View Menu

Large directories may not fit on the Norton Change Directory screen.
The NCD View menu enables you to display as many lines on-screen as
your monitor type supports. (EGA screens can display up to 40 lines,
and VGA screens can display up to 50 lines.) The View menu contains
the following options:

> **25** lines
>
> **28** lines
>
> **43** lines
>
> **50** lines

The options shown in the View menu vary according to what kind of
monitor you have. For MDA and CGA monitors, the only option is **25**
lines. For EGA monitors, your choices are **25**, **35**, and **43** lines. For a
VGA monitor, the options are **25**, **40**, and **50** lines.

A check mark appears to the left of the current selection (usually
25 lines).

Using Norton Change Directory from the DOS Prompt

Norton Change Directory gives you more control over directory names
than do the normal DOS commands. The Norton Change Directory command is particularly well suited for interactive use, but you can also
use the command from the DOS prompt.

The syntax for the NCD command can be any of the following:

NCD [*dirname*] [*switches*]

NCD [*d:*][*pathname*] [/R] [/N]

NCD [*d:*] /V[:*label*]

NCD [*d:*] /L[:*output*] [/G|/NG|/T] [/P] [/A]

NCD MD [*dirname*]

NCD RD [*dirname*]

NCD SIZE [*dirname*]

NCD COPY *source destination* [/DELETE]

NCD GRAFT *source destination* [/DELETE]

NCD RMTREE *dirname* [/BATCH]

The *dirname* parameter is the name of the directory you want to change to, make, remove, or display the size of. The *source* and *destination* parameters tell the command the original location of the directory to be copied or grafted (*source*) and the target location (*destination*) for the directory.

Changing to Another Directory

To use Norton Change Directory to change directories, enter **NCD**, followed by a space, and then the name of the directory to which you want to change. (You do not need to type the names of all the directories in the path, as you do when using the DOS CD command.) For example, to change to the directory \ONE-A\TWO-A\THREE-A\FOUR-A, enter the following command:

NCD FOUR-A

Actually, you need to enter only enough characters of the target directory's name to make the command unique to that directory. You can, therefore, enter the command in this way:

NCD FOUR

If no other directories begin with the letter F, you can even enter the command like this:

NCD F

If you do have more than one directory that begins with the letter F, the NCD command switches to the first directory beginning with that letter. If you enter the command again (press F3 and then Enter), Norton Change Directory switches to the next directory beginning with F. As you name your directories, you may want to choose unique names to make the Norton Change Directory command faster to use. The more complicated your directory structure, the easier changing directories becomes if you use the Norton Change Directory command instead of the DOS CD command.

Understanding NCD Switches

The NCD command-line switches allow you to bypass the menus while still performing powerful directory operations. Notice from the command syntax descriptions shown earlier that some switches cannot be used together. For example, the designation [/G|/NG|/T] means that you can select only one of these switches at a time (the | means "or").

Here are the switches you can use with NCD:

Switch	Description
/A	Displays the directory tree for all drives except floppy disk drives.
/BATCH	Skips all prompts and exits to DOS after finishing.
/DELETE	Deletes copied files from their original directory.
/G	Displays the directory tree graphically.
/L:*output*	Prints the directory tree to the specified *output* file.
/N	Does not write to the file TREEINFO.NCD. If you use Norton Change Directory on a write-protected disk, you must use this switch.
/NG	Displays the tree in nongraphic characters (best if you use a printer that does not support graphic characters).
/P	Pauses after each screen of information is displayed.
/R	Updates the file TREEINFO.NCD, which contains information about your directory tree structure.
/T	Totals the number and sizes of all files.
/V:*label*	Places a volume label on the disk.

Note some other command-line options that may be used with NCD:

Option	Description
MD *path*	Makes a new directory specified in *path*
RD *path*	Removes a directory specified in *path*
SIZE *directory*	Displays the size of a branch on the tree
COPY	Copies a directory to a new location
GRAFT	Deletes files from the old location
RMTREE	Removes a directory and all associated files

 NOTE To use the COPY, GRAFT, and RMTREE options, you first must enable them in the NCD Configuration dialog box, which you access with the Directory Configure option.

Using a Nongraphic Version of the Tree Structure

To record a nongraphic version of the tree structure on all your hard drives to a file named MYDIRS, for example, enter the following command:

```
NCD /L:MYDIRS /A /NG
```

Changing the Volume Label

The /V:*label* switch enables you to change the volume label on the disk. To change the volume label on the disk in drive A to MYDISK, enter the following command:

```
NCD A: /V:MYDISK
```

Creating and Removing Directories

The MD and RD versions of the Norton Change Directory command are similar in function to the DOS MD and RD commands. You use these DOS commands to make a new directory or to remove an empty directory, respectively.

You can use the Norton Change Directory command rather than the DOS MD and RD commands to make and remove directories. To create a directory, such as \FIRST\SECOND, enter the following command:

NCD MD \FIRST\SECOND

 NOTE In this example, FIRST must already exist; otherwise, you get the error message Invalid path or path no longer exists.

To delete that directory, enter this command:

NCD RD \FIRST\SECOND

This deletes only the SECOND directory. It does not delete the FIRST directory.

You may be tempted to pass up the Norton Change Directory command and use MD and RD instead, but a good reason exists for using Norton Change Directory. The first time you run the NCD command, Norton analyzes and stores your entire directory structure in a file (TREEINFO.NCD) for quick access. If you use the DOS versions of RD and MD, the Norton file is not updated. If you use the Norton Change Directory versions, the Norton file is updated, and changing directories continues to be quick and easy.

If you accidentally use RD or MD, you can update the Norton file TREEINFO.NCD by using the /R switch with the NCD command. To update the NCD tree file, use this command:

NCD /R

Checking the Size of a Directory

The NCD SIZE command displays the amount of space taken up by the files in the directory. This information can be useful to you if you are planning to copy the directory to another drive; you would want to be sure that the target drive had enough space (see also the discussion of the File Size command in Chapter 26). To find out how much space your \WP51\DOCS directory takes, for example, enter the following command:

NCD SIZE \WP51\DOCS

This command reports two numbers, such as the following:

```
Total size of files : 5,656,832 Bytes
Total allocated space : 6,184,960 Bytes
```

The difference between the allocated space and the total size of the files is *slack space*—wasted space not taken up by actual file data, but unavailable for use. Slack space is discussed in Chapter 3, "Understanding How Disks Work," and in the discussion of the File Size (FS) command in Chapter 26.

Copying Directories and Their Files

Using the NCD COPY command, you can copy an entire directory and all its files to a new location. For example, to copy the directory MYDIR to its new location as a subdirectory of YOURDIR, enter the following command:

NCD COPY \MYDIR \YOURDIR

To copy the directory and then delete the old version of MYDIR and its files, enter this command:

NCD COPY \MYDIR \YOURDIR /DELETE

 NOTE The NCD COPY command is disabled by default and must be enabled in the NCD Configuration dialog box. You choose Configure from the NCD Directory menu to access this dialog box.

Moving Directories and Their Files

The NCD GRAFT command is similar in function to the NCD COPY command. NCD GRAFT doesn't copy, however, but actually moves the source directory, all its subdirectories, and all the files contained in these directories to the destination location. Suppose that you want to move the directory named MYLETS to the WP51 directory, resulting in the subdirectory \WP51\MYLETS. Use this command:

NCD GRAFT \MYLETS \WP51

You may need to add the /NET switch if you use this command on a network. Usually, you do not need this switch.

 NOTE The NCD GRAFT command is disabled by default and must be enabled in the NCD Configuration dialog box. You choose Configure from the NCD Directory menu to access this dialog box.

Removing a Directory and Its Files

The Norton Change Directory RMTREE command removes a directory and all its files from the directory tree. The command prompts you for confirmation before actually deleting the information. If you use the /BATCH switch, the prompt for confirmation does not appear. To remove the directory TMP from the tree, erasing all files in that directory, use the following command:

NCD RMTREE \TMP

NCD responds with this message:

```
You are about to remove ALL FILES in the directory
tree starting at C:\TMP.
Are you sure (Y/N)?
Enter Y to continue with the remove or enter N to
cancel.
```

 NOTE This potentially dangerous command is disabled by default and must be enabled in the NCD Configuration dialog box. To access this dialog box, choose **C**onfigure from the NCD Directory menu.

Summary

Although similar in some ways to such DOS commands as MD, CD, and RD, the Norton Change Directory command is more powerful, easier to use in its graphic mode, and capable of performing more tasks on your directories than are similar DOS commands. After you begin using the Norton Change Directory command, either from the DOS prompt or interactively, you are certain to find the command far superior to its DOS counterparts for managing directories.

In the next chapter, you learn how to use Norton Batch Enhancer to create better batch files.

Creating and Using Batch Files

N orton Batch Enhancer (BE) enables you to create more powerful and elaborate batch commands than you can create with DOS's batch language.

Batch files usually consist of several DOS commands listed one after another. These files are named with the BAT extension, such as AUTOEXEC.BAT. When a batch file is executed, DOS acts on the commands in the file one at a time, beginning with the first command in the file and continuing to the last command in the file. The DOS batch language, however, lacks a few useful batch file features. You may, for example, want to prompt for input in a batch file and then branch according to the user's response. In addition, you may want to set colors, draw windows or boxes, and print text from a batch file. The Batch Enhancer command enables you to perform these tasks.

You use one of the following versions of this command:

> BE *command* [/DEBUG]
>
> BE *filespec*

NOTE When you enter the *command* version, BE acts on the command; when you enter the *filespec* version, BE acts on the commands in the file.

These commands may be used with BE:

ASK	GOTO	SA
BEEP	JUMP	SHIFTSTATE
BOX	MONTHDAY	TRIGGER
CLS	PRINTCHAR	WEEKDAY
DELAY	REBOOT	WINDOW
EXIT	ROWCOL	

You can use the BE command at the DOS prompt, but the command is generally used in batch files. That is, you can place a BE command in a DOS batch file and use it just as you would from the DOS prompt. The following command, for example, produces a standard system beep:

BE BEEP

You may want to include this command at the end of a batch file so that your computer will signal you when the operation is finished.

Each BE command has its own parameters, which are described in the following sections.

NOTE Some of the BE commands are also implemented in NDOS, which is described in Chapter 28. These commands include the following:

ASK	MONTHDAY	SHIFTSTATE
BEEP	PRINTCHAR	TRIGGER
BOX	REBOOT	WEEKDAY
CLS	ROWCOL	WINDOW
DELAY	SA	

Using Script Files

A *script file* is similar to a batch file, but a script file executes commands through the Norton BE program instead of DOS. A script file can contain and will act on any of the Norton BE commands; however, DOS commands that are contained in the BE script will be ignored when the script is run. The advantage of writing a script file instead of a normal DOS batch file is that a script file runs faster and enables you to use features that are not available in DOS. Thus, BE commands can be used in DOS batch files, but DOS batch commands cannot be used in BE script files. The BE script command has the following syntax:

BE *scriptname* [[GOTO] *label*]

 When naming script files, avoid using the BAT extension so that you prevent confusion between script files and batch files.

Suppose that you create a script file named SETCOLOR which contains the following command:

SA BRIGHT WHITE ON BLUE

 You do not have to include BE in front of a command when the BE command is used in a script file. That is, you can use the command BEEP rather than BE BEEP. (See the section "Using the SA Command" later in this chapter.)

To run this script, issue the following command at the DOS prompt:

BE SETCOLOR

A script can contain several labels; you can have the command execute at a particular label by entering that label name in the command line. For example, all the lines that begin with a colon in the following SETCOLOR script file are labels:

```
:BLUE
SA BRIGHT WHITE ON BLUE
EXIT
:GREEN
SA BRIGHT WHITE ON GREEN
EXIT
:RED
SA BRIGHT WHITE ON RED
```

When you enter **BE SETCOLOR GREEN**, the program begins at the label :GREEN, executes the SA command, and then executes the EXIT command. (See the section "Using the EXIT Command" later in this chapter.)

NOTE The BE commands that can be used only in script files and not in regular DOS batch files include EXIT, GOTO, and JUMP.

Using the ASK Command

The ASK command enables you to capture a user's response and then act on that response. You can use the ASK command to create menus. If you use ASK in your AUTOEXEC.BAT file, you can control the way in which your computer boots. Sometimes you may want to load memory-resident programs, such as SideKick, at boot time. At other times, you may want to boot without loading those programs.

The ASK command has the following syntax:

BE ASK *prompt* [*keys*] [DEFAULT=*key*] [TIMEOUT=*n*] [ADJUST=*n*] [*color*] [/DEBUG]

The *prompt* is a text string that you want to display on-screen. (You must enclose the string in quotation marks.) The cursor is placed after the prompt to anticipate a single-character user response.

A simple example of the BE ASK command follows. Suppose that you want your AUTOEXEC.BAT file to give you the option of booting with no memory-resident programs. You want the computer to ask the following question:

```
Skip memory-resident programs (Y/N)?
```

If you press Y, you want to skip loading memory-resident programs. If you press N, you want the computer to go ahead and load those programs. Use the following ASK command:

BE ASK "Skip memory-resident programs (Y/N)?" YN

Notice that the expected responses are listed as the keys Y and N. The next two lines use the DOS IF ERRORLEVEL command to tell the computer what to do when the user makes one of the choices:

```
IF ERRORLEVEL 2 GOTO DOMEMORY
IF ERRORLEVEL 1 GOTO SKIP
```

If you press N, an errorlevel code 2 is generated, and these commands send the flow of the batch file to a label named DOMEMORY. If you press Y, an errorlevel code 1 is generated, and the flow of the batch file is sent to a label named SKIP. If you press any other key, the computer beeps, and the ASK command waits for you to press Y or N.

Here is how the complete batch file may look with the ASK command:

```
ECHO OFF
CLS
BE ASK "Skip memory resident programs(Y/N)?" YN
IF ERRORLEVEL 2 GOTO DOMEMORY
IF ERRORLEVEL 1 GOTO SKIP
:DOMEMORY
REM place commands for memory-resident programs here
:SKIP
REM place the rest of the AUTOEXEC.BAT command here
```

The REM lines are remarks about where to place the commands that load memory-resident programs and where to place other AUTOEXEC.BAT commands.

With the ASK command's DEFAULT=*key* parameter, you can specify what Enter means. DEFAULT=Y, for example, means that pressing Enter is the same as choosing **Yes**.

With the TIMEOUT=*n* parameter, you can specify how long the ASK command waits for an answer before taking the default answer (*n* denotes the number of seconds to wait).

If one menu will not hold all the options you want to use, you may have to use a multipart menu. You may have a two-layer menu, for example, with 10 options in the first layer. When BE returns an errorlevel code in the second layer, you can adjust the errorlevel by 10 by including the option ADJUST=10 so that the level matches your IF. . .GOTO statements. If you do not adjust the errorlevel, the errorlevels in the second menu are 1, 2, 3, and so on. With the adjustment, the errorlevels become 11, 12, 13, and so on. This adjustment enables you to tell the difference between option 1, menu 1 (errorlevel=1) and option 1, menu 2 (errorlevel=11).

ADJUST=*n* enables you to make the errorlevel numbers higher so that they do not conflict with numbers you have already used. If, for example, your first menu has four options, the menu could have an errorlevel value of 1 to 4. In a subsequent menu, you can include an ADJUST=4 command so that the menu begins with the errorlevel value 5. You then use the resulting errorlevel number to branch to the proper location in the batch file.

You also can set colors in the ASK statement. (Color options are described in the section "Using the SA Command" later in this chapter.) Including WHITE on BLUE in the BE ASK command line, for example, causes the prompt to appear as white letters on a blue background. The *color* selection is in effect only for the ASK prompt.

When you use the /DEBUG switch, the errorlevel of a command is displayed. This switch helps you figure out what the various errorlevel codes mean, because you cannot find out in DOS.

Using the BEEP Command

The BEEP command produces a tone or series of tones. This command can come in handy if you create a batch file that performs a long operation. You can use BEEP to tell you audibly that the batch file is finished or is at a certain stage of the process.

Note two versions of this command:

BE BEEP [*switches*]

BE BEEP [*filespec*] [/E]

If you include a *filespec* parameter, the file specified should contain a list of tones to be played. When used with *filespec*, the /E switch instructs the BE BEEP command to echo the text in the file to the screen.

If you do not include *filespec*, use switches to specify the tones to be played. The following switches are available for use with BE BEEP:

Switch	Description
/D*n*	Specifies the duration of a tone in measurements of 1/18 of a second. Thus, D3 specifies that the tone be sounded for 3/18 of a second.
/E	Echoes (displays) to the screen quoted text in comments in the BEEP script file.
/F*n*	Specifies the frequency of a tone, where *n* is hertz (Hz), or cycles per second. The switch /F440, for example, plays a tone at 440 Hz. The larger the value of *n*, the higher-pitched the tone.
/R*n*	Specifies that the tone be repeated *n* times.
/W*n*	Specifies a wait in durations of 1/18 of a second. The switch /W3, for example, causes a wait of 3/18 of a second. You usually use this switch to specify a pause between beeps.

The following command plays a tone at 440 Hz for one second (18/18), waits half a second (9/18), and then repeats the tone:

BE BEEP /F440 /D18 /R2 /W9

To place this command in a file named TONE, enter the following as the TONE file:

/F440 /D18 /R2 /W9

Note that when the tone information is in a file to be called by the BEEP subcommand, you do not place BE BEEP in front of the tone information.

Then enter the following command at the DOS prompt to sound the tone:

BE BEEP TONE

Using the BOX Command

The BOX command enables you to draw boxes on-screen. Boxes are helpful for emphasizing on-screen messages and for creating menus.

Here is the syntax of the BOX command:

BE BOX *top,left,bottom,right* [SINGLE|DOUBLE] [*color*]

The following parameters may be used with this command:

Parameter	Description
top	Specifies the row number of the top-left corner of the box
left	Specifies the column number of the top-left corner of the box
bottom	Specifies the row number of the bottom-right corner of the box
right	Specifies the column number of the bottom-right corner of the box
SINGLE	Produces a box with single lines (the default)
DOUBLE	Produces a box with double lines
color	Specifies color choices

The SINGLE or DOUBLE parameter specifies a single or double line around the box. The *color* parameter specifies color choices (see the section "Using the SA Command" later in this chapter).

Note this example:

BE BOX 2,10,10,70 SINGLE

This command draws a single-line box beginning at the 2nd row, 10th column of the screen and extending to the 10th row, 70th column.

Using the CLS Command

The purpose of the CLS command is to clear the screen. Optionally, you can use this command to set the screen color.

The CLS command has the following syntax:

BE CLS [*color*]

The *color* selections you can use are the same as those for the BE SA command. A list of color choices appears in the section "Using the SA Command" later in this chapter. The BE SA command has a /CLS switch option, so you can also use that command to set colors and clear the screen.

The following command clears the screen and displays characters in bold white on a blue background:

BE CLS BOLD WHITE ON BLUE

Using the DELAY Command

The DELAY command causes a batch file to suspend operation temporarily. Suppose that your batch file is displaying information on-screen. You may want to build in a delay so that you can read this information before other information appears on-screen.

The DELAY command has this syntax:

BE DELAY [*time*]

The *time* parameter is measured in 1/18 of a second. Thus, the following command causes a one-second delay:

BE DELAY 18

Using the EXIT Command

The EXIT command causes a script file to end. You can use this command, which has no options, to stop a script at any point.

Here is the syntax of the EXIT command:

BE EXIT

You should use this command only in a script file. The command has no meaning in a regular DOS batch file.

Using the GOTO Command

With the GOTO command, you can control the starting point of a script. You can use this command only in script files; it does not work in DOS batch files.

The GOTO command has the following syntax:

> BE *pathname* [[GOTO] *label*]

The *pathname* is a script file, and *label* is a label in the script file. As mentioned earlier, a label is a statement that begins with a colon. The following statement, for example, is a label:

> :THISISALABEL

Using the JUMP Command

With the JUMP command, you can perform conditional branching in a script. You can use this command only in script files; it does not work in DOS batch files.

Unlike GOTO, which always branches to a specified label, JUMP enables you to branch to one of several labels based on the current value of the exit code.

Note the syntax of the JUMP command:

> BE JUMP *label1*,[*label2*[,...*labeln*]] [/DEFAULT:*label*]

In this line, *label1* is the name of the label to which the flow of the script is sent if the exit code is 1, *label2* is the name of the label to which the flow is sent if the exit code is 2, and so on. If no label matches the exit code, the flow goes to the label specified by *label* in the /DEFAULT switch. If no match to an exit code and no default label exist, execution continues with the command following the JUMP command.

The following script file displays the day of the week:

```
BE CLS
BE WEEKDAY
BE JUMP SU,M,TU,W,TH,F,S
:SU
```

```
BE ROWCOL 1,1 "Today is Sunday"
BE JUMP /DEFAULT:LAST
:M
BE ROWCOL 1,1 "Today is Monday"
BE JUMP /DEFAULT:LAST
:TU
BE ROWCOL 1,1 "Today is Tuesday"
BE JUMP /DEFAULT:LAST
:W
BE ROWCOL 1,1 "Today is Wednesday"
BE JUMP /DEFAULT:LAST
:TH
BE ROWCOL 1,1 "Today is Thursday"
BE JUMP /DEFAULT:LAST
:F
BE ROWCOL 1,1 "Today is Friday"
BE JUMP /DEFAULT:LAST
:S
BE ROWCOL 1,1 "Today is Saturday"
:LAST
```

The BE CLS command clears the screen. The BE WEEKDAY command
returns 1, 2, 3, 4, 5, 6, or 7 (see the section "Using the WEEKDAY Command" later in this chapter). The BE JUMP command branches to the
correct day-of-week display, and the BE ROWCOL command prints the
message at the top of the screen. Then the JUMP /DEFAULT:LAST
command branches to the :LAST label and ends the program.

Using the MONTHDAY Command

The MONTHDAY command returns the day of the month as an exit
code, which you then can use in a JUMP command or an IF
ERRORLEVEL command.

The MONTHDAY command has the following syntax:

> BE MONTHDAY [/DEBUG]

The /DEBUG option causes the exit code to display on-screen.

The following example shows how you could use the BE MONTHDAY
command in a DOS batch file. The batch file clears the screen, and if
today is the first day of the month, an important message is displayed
on-screen:

```
ECHO OFF
CLS
```

```
BE MONTHDAY
IF ERRORLEVEL 1 GOTO FIRST
GOTO LAST
:FIRST
ECHO Today is the first day of the month!
ECHO Be sure to mail your house payment!
:LAST
```

Compare this example with the one in the preceding section to see the difference between writing a batch file and writing a script file. This example uses the DOS ERRORLEVEL command to branch, and the preceding section's example uses the Norton BE JUMP command to branch.

Using the PRINTCHAR Command

With the PRINTCHAR command, you can print a character a specified number of times. This command comes in handy if you are drawing images on-screen, perhaps to highlight a message or embellish a menu.

Here is the syntax of the PRINTCHAR command:

BE PRINTCHAR *character,repeats* [*color*]

The *character* parameter can be any ASCII character. You can specify any number of *repeats* up to 80. The *color* parameter is described in the section "Using the SA Command" later in this chapter.

T I P

In the BE PRINTCHAR command, you can use characters from the extended IBM character list—ASCII characters 128 to 255—if your program can access them. (Some editing programs, such as WordStar, may not be capable of accessing the IBM extended characters.) The ASCII codes for the extended character set are listed in the back of most DOS or BASIC manuals.

For example, to use the Greek letter beta (β) in the BE PRINTCHAR command, hold down the Alt key, type the ASCII code 225 on the numeric keypad, and release the Alt key. The letter β should appear on-screen.

To print the character 20 times, enter the following command:

BE PRINTCHAR β,20

Using the REBOOT Command

The REBOOT command enables you to perform a warm boot of the computer. REBOOT has the following syntax:

BE REBOOT [/VERIFY]

When you include the /VERIFY switch in the command, you are prompted to confirm whether the reboot should take place. This command may be useful if you change or replace your AUTOEXEC.BAT or CONFIG.SYS file within a batch file. Causing a reboot then resets your computer to the new values within these files.

Using the ROWCOL Command

You use the ROWCOL (Row Column) command to place the cursor somewhere on-screen before writing a message to the screen. With the ROWCOL command, you can place information anywhere on-screen and be creative in designing menus or messages.

Here is the syntax of the ROWCOL command:

BE ROWCOL *row,col*[,*text*] [*color*]

The *row* parameter represents the number of the on-screen row where you want the cursor to appear (usually 1 to 25). The *col* parameter is the number of the column on-screen (usually 1 to 80). The *text* parameter is a message, enclosed in quotation marks, that you want to display at the specified location. The *color* parameter is described in the next section.

Suppose that you are designing a menu screen and you want the text *ABC Company, Inc.* to appear on the top line of the screen. You can use the following command:

BE ROWCOL 1,33,"ABC Company, Inc."

In this command, 1 specifies the top line of the screen, and 33 specifies the 33rd column. This specification centers the message on-screen.

Using the SA Command

The SA (Screen Attributes) command enables you to specify colors and other screen features. With this command, you can design your screen by combining different colors, boldfaced text, normal text, and blinking text. You can use the SA command to call attention to messages on-screen or to make your menus more colorful.

You use one of the following versions of the SA command:

BE SA *main-setting* [*switches*]

BE SA [*intensity*] [*foreground*] [ON *background*] [*switches*]

The options for *main-setting* are NORMAL, REVERSE, and UNDERLINE. Choices for *intensity* are BRIGHT, BOLD, and BLINKING. (BRIGHT and BOLD are identical.) Choices for *foreground* and *background* colors are WHITE, BLACK, RED, MAGENTA, BLUE, GREEN, CYAN, and YELLOW.

Here are the available switches:

Switch	Description
/CLS	Clears the screen after setting the screen attributes; enables you to see the effects of the SA command on-screen immediately
/N	Instructs the SA command not to set a border color

The SA command is helpful not only as a command in Batch Enhancer but also directly in DOS. For example, to set your monitor to a blue background with white letters, use the following command:

BE SA WHITE ON BLUE

This sets the color for the screen and stays in effect until you use another command to change the setting.

The following is a list of color choices for SA:

Setting	Command
Intensity	BRIGHT or BOLD (these commands are identical) BLINKING
Main setting	NORMAL REVERSE UNDERLINE
Colors (either foreground or background)	WHITE BLACK RED MAGENTA BLUE GREEN CYAN YELLOW

Using the SHIFTSTATE Command

The SHIFTSTATE command reports the status of the Shift, Alt, and Ctrl keys. The command returns an exit code according to the state of the left Shift, right Shift, Alt, and Ctrl keys. You can then use the exit code to cause the script to branch with the JUMP command or DOS ERRORLEVEL command. Here is the syntax of SHIFTSTATE:

    BE SHIFTSTATE [/DEBUG]

The /DEBUG switch causes the exit code to display on-screen. SHIFTSTATE returns the following exit codes:

If Key Is in Shift State	Code Returned
Alt key (left or right)	8
Ctrl key (left or right)	4
Left Shift key	2
Right Shift key	1

For example, type **BE SHIFTSTATE /DEBUG** at the DOS prompt; then hold down the left Shift key and press Enter. The response will be the message ERRORLEVEL: 2. You can use SHIFTSTATE to create commands that perform different tasks according to which of these keys is being pressed when the command is invoked.

Using the TRIGGER Command

The TRIGGER command halts the execution of a script until a specified time. Suppose that you have a communications program set up to send data to a distant location. You can use this command to instruct the program to begin execution early in the morning, when telephone rates are lowest.

The TRIGGER command has the following syntax:

    BE TRIGGER *hh*:*mm* [AM] [PM]

The *hh*:*mm* parameter is the hours and minutes in military (24-hour clock) time. Thus, 14:00 is 2 p.m.

NOTE You can use the AM or PM designation in the command line to specify 12-hour clock time, as in 2:00 PM. In this designation, 12:00 AM is the same as 0:00 (midnight), and 12:00 PM is noon.

The following command causes the script to pause until 2 a.m. before continuing:

BE TRIGGER 2:00 AM

Using the WEEKDAY Command

The WEEKDAY command, which is similar to MONTHDAY, returns the day of the week as an exit code. You can use the WEEKDAY command in a JUMP command or an IF ERRORLEVEL command.

Note the syntax of the WEEKDAY command:

BE WEEKDAY [/DEBUG]

The /DEBUG switch causes the exit code to display on-screen.

For example, to cause a backup to be performed on the second day of the week (Monday), you can use the following commands:

BE WEEKDAY

BE JUMP NOBACKUP,BACKUP /DEFAULT:NOBACKUP

On the first day of the week, the command branches to NOBACKUP. On the second day of the week, the batch file goes to the label :BACKUP (which contains instructions for performing a backup). On other days, the flow of the script is to the :NOBACKUP label.

You can use the related command MONTHDAY in the same manner to design batch files that are sensitive to specific days of the month.

T I P

Using the WINDOW Command

Like the BOX command, the WINDOW command draws boxes on-screen. WINDOW, however, gives you the options of drawing the box with a shadow and of zooming the box onto the screen. You can use the WINDOW command to create menus or to highlight messages on-screen.

Here is the syntax of the WINDOW command:

BE WINDOW *top,left,bottom,right* [*color*] [SHADOW] [ZOOM]

The following parameters are available:

Parameter	Description
top	Specifies the row number of the top-left corner of the window
left	Specifies the column number of the top-left corner of the window
bottom	Specifies the row number of the bottom-right corner of the window
right	Specifies the column number of the bottom-right corner of the window
color	Determines color setting (see the section "Using the SA Command" earlier in this chapter)
SHADOW	Adds a shadow to the right and bottom edges of the window
ZOOM	Zooms the window onto the screen (the window starts as a small rectangle and grows to full size)

The following command draws a window with the top-left corner positioned two lines from the top and 10 columns from the left of the screen:

BE WINDOW 2,10,20,70 SHADOW ZOOM

The bottom-right corner of the window is 20 lines from the top and 70 columns from the left of the screen. The window, which has a shadow, zooms onto the screen. The main difference between the BOX and WINDOW commands is that BOX does not overwrite any text on-screen. WINDOW blanks out the window, erasing any text on-screen.

Combining DOS and Batch Enhancer Commands

By combining DOS batch commands and Norton Batch Enhancer commands, you can develop creative batch files. The following example is a batch file named MENU.BAT that uses DOS batch commands and several Batch Enhancer commands to create a menu system for your computer:

```
ECHO OFF
:BEGIN
CD\NU7
BE SA WHITE ON BLUE
CLS
BE WINDOW 2,10,12,65 WHITE ON RED SHADOW ZOOM
BE ROWCOL 3,30 "My Special Menu"
BE ROWCOL 5,16 "Exit to DOS.........................D"
BE ROWCOL 6,16 "Begin Norton Utilities.............N"
BE ROWCOL 7,16 "Begin WORDPERFECT..................W"
BE ROWCOL 8,16 "Begin KWIKSTAT.....................K"
BE ROWCOL 10,16
BE ASK "Choose an option letter:",dnwk default=D
IF ERRORLEVEL 4 GOTO KWIKSTAT
IF ERRORLEVEL 3 GOTO WORD
IF ERRORLEVEL 2 GOTO NORTON
IF ERRORLEVEL 1 GOTO THATSALL
:KWIKSTAT
CLS
CD\KWIKSTAT
KS
GOTO BEGIN
:WORD
CLS
CD\WP51
WP
GOTO BEGIN
:NORTON
CLS
CD\NU7
NORTON
GOTO BEGIN
:THATSALL
BE SA WHITE ON BLUE
CLS
```

After you create the batch file MENU.BAT and issue the MENU command from the DOS prompt, a screen like the one in figure 24.1 appears.

As you can see in lines 6 through 12 of the batch file, the batch file creates the menu by first drawing a box with the WINDOW command and then using the ROWCOL command to give the menu a heading and to locate the items for the menu. The ASK command captures the user's response, which the IF ERRORLEVEL commands evaluate. Each menu choice points to a label in the batch file, and at that label, the batch file begins a program or exits to DOS. If you choose a program by pressing

N, W, or K, the program associated with that selection begins. After the program returns to DOS, the batch file continues to operate and displays the menu again.

```
                    My Special Menu

Exit to DOS ...........................D
Begin Norton Utilities ................N
Begin WORDPERFECT .....................W
Begin KWIKSTAT ........................K

Choose an option letter:
```

The screen displayed by the batch file MENU.BAT.

The MENU.BAT program is created to run from the NU7 directory. Because the BE command is located in this directory, the program runs quickly. If you use a menu program like this one, be sure that you put the program in the directory that contains the Norton BE.EXE Batch Enhancer program. If you use the BE command in another directory, DOS searches the directories defined in your DOS path for the BE.EXE program. If the NU7 directory appears early in the path, the execution of the BE command goes faster than if the NU7 directory appears later in the path.

Summary

The Norton Batch Enhancer command enables you to create more useful batch files—programs that consist of a series of DOS and Batch Enhancer commands. This chapter described the commands you can use with the BE command and presented ways in which you can use these commands.

The next chapter shows you how to use Norton commands to find files by name and by content.

Finding Files

When it comes to managing your computer files, hard disks are both a blessing and a curse—a blessing because they can store thousands of files, and a curse because finding a file when you can't remember its name or location is frustrating. Norton Utilities provides not one, but three solutions to this problem.

The Text Search (TS) and File Locate (FL) commands, which relate to finding files, have been around since the early versions of Norton Utilities. Because they are command-line programs, you can enter them at the DOS prompt with switches and options, just as you would enter a DOS command. The third program, File Find, is a more recent development. Designed to be an interactive program, File Find enables you to choose options from information displayed in a dialog box. For many Norton Utilities users, the Text Search and File Locate commands are familiar, quick, and easy to use. If you prefer to see all the options on-screen and to choose them interactively, the File Find command is for you.

This chapter covers all the options of the File Find command, which includes the capability to find files and to set file attributes, dates, and times. The chapter also explains how to use the File Locate and Text Search commands.

Searching for Files

Two Norton commands enable you to locate files on disk by name. File Locate is designed to be used from the DOS prompt; File Find can be used to locate files interactively (that is, you choose search options in a dialog box).

If you created a file months ago but don't remember where you placed it on disk, File Find and File Locate can help. If you can remember the file's name—or even a part of the file name—you may be able to locate the file with one of these two commands. They also can help you find file duplicates or the most recent copy of a file on disk.

Using File Find To Locate a File

The File Find command displays a dialog box, where you provide information and select options.

To locate a file by name on the current drive with the File Find command, follow these steps:

1. Choose File Find from the Norton main screen or enter **FILEFIND** at the DOS prompt. The File Find dialog box appears (see fig. 25.1).

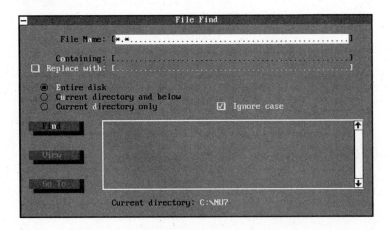

Fig. 25.1

The File Find dialog box.

2. In the File Name text box, enter the file name or a part of the file name (use the DOS wild-card characters * and ?). Do not type anything in the Containing field.

For example, to find all files with an XYX extension, type ***.XYX** in the File Name text box.

3. To select the portion of the disk to search, choose one of the following options: **E**ntire Disk, **C**urrent Directory and Below, or Current **D**irectory Only.

4. To start the search, choose Fi**n**d, which finds all files that match the criteria you specified. The Search Complete dialog box appears when the search finishes. Choose **OK**. A list of the matching files appears in the list box.

5. To view the contents of the list box, use the up- and down-arrow keys or the scroll bar to highlight the name of a file (or use the mouse to click the file name).

6. To view the contents of the highlighted file, choose Vie**w** or double-click the file name. The contents are displayed on-screen. To exit the view, press Esc or choose **C**lose.

To locate a file by name on multiple drives with the File Find command, follow these steps:

1. Choose File Find from the Norton main screen or enter **FILEFIND** at the DOS prompt.

2. In the File N**a**me text box, enter the file name or a part of the file name.

3. Choose **E**ntire Disk.

4. Choose the **S**earch Drives option from the **S**earch pull-down menu. The dialog box shown in figure 25.2 appears.

Fig. 25.2

The Drives To Search dialog box.

5. Choose **D**efault Drive (the default setting) to search only the current drive, choose **A**ll Drives to search all drives that appear in the Drives To Search dialog box, or choose **T**he Following Drives and then specify the drives to search.

6. Choose **S**ave to permanently save these drives for searching, or choose **OK** to save these drive specifications for the current File Find session only. To ignore your selections and return to the File Find dialog box, choose **C**ancel.

7. To start the search, choose Fi**n**d. When the search finishes, the Search Complete dialog box appears. Choose **OK**. A listing of matching files appears in the list box.

8. To view the contents of the list box, use the up- and down-arrow keys or the scroll bar to highlight the name of a file (or use the mouse to click the file name).

9. To view the contents of the file, choose Vie**w** or double-click the file name. The contents are displayed on-screen. To exit the view, press Esc or choose Cl**o**se.

To end File Find, choose **F**ile E**x**it.

Using the File Locate Command

The File Locate (FL) command is designed so that you can use it from the DOS prompt. FL has the following syntax:

FL [*filespec*] [*switches*]

The following switches are available:

Switch	Description
/A	Searches for files on all drives.
/F*n*	Finds the first *n* files that match the file specification. The default number of files to find is 1.
/P	Pauses after each screen.
/T	Searches the directories in the PATH statement only.
/W	Lists files in wide format on-screen.

To locate all files on all drives that match the file specification *.XYX, use the following command:

FL *.XYX /A

Norton then produces a listing of the locations where this file is found.

Searching for Information within Files

Two Norton commands enable you to search for information *within* files. The Text Search command is convenient to use from the DOS prompt, and the File Find command enables you to perform the search interactively.

When you look for a file that contains certain information, but you cannot remember the name of the file, you can perform a text search to help. You can even perform a search on erased files. The following sections show you how to search for text in files by using File Find and Text Search.

Using File Find To Locate Information

File Find locates a file that contains specified text in much the same way that the command locates a file, as discussed earlier in the chapter. When you locate a file with specified text, however, you place search criteria in the Containing field in the File Find dialog box and specify whether to ignore case.

The information you place in the Containing field specifies which files appear in the list box. Only those files that match the specified criteria in the Containing field will be listed. By default, the Ignore Case option is selected, which means that if you search for *QUE*, you also find occurrences of *Que*. To turn off the Ignore Case option, use the Tab key to highlight the option, and then press the space bar to deselect it (or point to the option with the mouse pointer and click).

Choose Find to begin the search; the matching files appear in the list box. End File Find by pressing Esc or choosing File Exit.

For information about viewing the files in the list box and searching multiple drives, see the section "Using File Find To Locate a File" earlier in this chapter.

Using Text Search To Locate Information

The Text Search (TS) command enables you to search for text in files anywhere on disk, including erased space. The command has the following syntax:

TS [*filespec*] [*string*] [*switches*]

The *filespec* variable specifies the files to be searched, such as *.BAT. If *filespec* is missing, all files are searched. The *string* is the text to be located, such as ALABAMA.

The following switches are available:

Switch	Description
/A	Automates the search (that is, ignores prompts).
/C*n*	Begins the search at the cluster specified by *n*.
/CS	Performs a case-sensitive search. If you specify the search string as *Alan*, it will not find *ALAN*.
/D	Searches the entire disk.
/E	Searches only the erased portions of the disk.
/EBCDIC	Specifies that files being searched are in EBCDIC format.
/LOG	Creates output suitable for a log file or printer.
/S	Searches subdirectories also.
/T	Sets the noninteractive summary total.
/WS	Specifies that files being searched are in WordStar format.

To find occurrences of *ALABAMA* in files with a TXT extension, use the following command:

TS *.TXT ALABAMA

To find all instances of ALABAMA in erased space on disk, enter this command:

TS *.TXT ALABAMA /E

The command displays the file name or location of a find and asks whether you want to continue the search (unless you have used the /A switch). Press Y to continue the search or press N to cancel the search.

Using File Find To Set File Dates and Times

The File Find command (like the File Date command discussed in Chapter 26) enables you to set the date and time stamp on a file. The date and time stamp usually contains information about when the file was created or last changed. This information is displayed when you use the DOS DIR command. You may want to reset the date and time stamp on a file, for example, to identify the release date or version number of a disk. If the release date for Version 1.3 of a program was 1-1-93, you could set the date of the files on the disk to 1-1-93 and the time to 1:30. Later, after the disk has been distributed, a support person can tell exactly what disk it is by looking at the date and time stamp.

To set the date and time of one or more files, follow these steps:

1. Choose File Find from the Norton main screen or enter **FILEFIND** at the DOS prompt.

2. Enter the file names to be affected in the File Name field. Do not enter anything in the Containing field.

   For example, to change all the dates and times for the files on drive A to 1-1-93 and 12:00, type **A:*.*** in the File Name field.

3. Make sure that the Entire Disk option is chosen. If it is not, choose this option.

4. Choose Find to start the search.

   In this example, choosing Find searches all files on drive A. The file names appear in the list box.

5. Choose the Set Date/Time option from the Commands pull-down menu.

6. The Set Date/Time dialog box appears (see fig. 25.3). This dialog box enables you to set the date and time for one file (the one currently highlighted in the list box) or for all files in the list. Choose the option you want.

Fig. 25.3

The Set Date/Time dialog box.

7. Select the Set Time To field and then press Tab to place the cursor in the time text box. In this example, type **12:00**.

8. Select the Set Date To field and press Tab again to place the cursor in the date text box. Type **1-1-93**.

9. Choose **OK**. The program changes the dates and times according to your selections. Press Esc or choose **Fi**le **Ex**it to end the File Find program.

The next chapter discusses the File Date (FD) command. The FD program is a command-line utility that also enables you to set file dates and times.

Using File Find To Set Attributes

You can use the File Find command to set attributes on files. When you create a file on disk, DOS stores the name of the file as well as other pieces of vital information. When you enter the DOS DIR command, you see some of this information—the size of the file, the date and time the file was created, and so on. DOS also stores four other pieces of information that you usually do not see.

With the File Attributes and File Find commands, you can control these attributes and protect important files from accidental changes or erasure. Chapter 9 covers ways to set these attributes.

Summary

When your hard disk accumulates files you created over several months or years, you may begin to lose track of which file is in what directory. When you need to search for a file by the file name, the extension, or the contents of the file, Norton Utilities provides two DOS command-line programs (File Locate and Text Search) and an interactive program (File Find) that enables you to search your disks for the file. This chapter described how to use the File Find, File Locate (FL), and Text Search (TS) commands.

Norton Utilities offers several other command-line utilities that can help you manage your computer's resources. Turn to the next chapter to learn about the File Date, Duplicate Disk, Line Print, File Size, and Directory Sort commands.

Using Norton Command-Line Utilities

Several Norton Utilities programs do not fit into the previous chapters. This chapter covers command-line utilities, which are utilities you use by entering a command at the DOS prompt. Except for the command that is new to Version 7 (DUPDISK), most of these programs have been part of Norton Utilities for many years. This chapter describes the following utilities:

- File Date (FD), which allows you to set the file data and time stamp for one or more files

- File Size (FS), which determines the size in bytes of a file or group of files

- Line Print (LP), which prints a text document to the printer

- Directory Sort (DS), which sorts a directory

- Duplicate Disk (DUPDISK), which duplicates disks

Directory Sort and Duplicate Disk can also be used interactively. This chapter explains how to use these programs and describes their command-line options. Other on-line utilities that have been described in previous chapters include Norton Cache (Chapter 21), File Attributes (Chapter 9), File Locate (Chapter 25), and Text Search (Chapter 25).

Using File Date (FD)

The File Date (FD) command enables you to change the date and time stamp on a disk file. When a file is created, DOS places the creation date and time in the file directory; when you issue the DOS DIR command, you see the date and time that the file was created or last changed. Usually, you cannot change the date and time stamp on a file. With the Norton File Date command, however, you can easily change this information. You use this syntax:

   FD [*filespec*] [*switches*]

The following command-line switches are available:

Switch	Description
/D[:]*date*	Sets date (*mm-dd-yy*)
/P	Pauses after each screen is displayed
/S	Also sets dates on files in subdirectories
/T[:]*time*	Sets time (*hh:mm:ss*)

To set all files on a disk to a date of 1-1-93 and a time of 12:00, use this command:

   FD *.* /D:1-1-93 /T:12:00

 NOTE   The File Find command, described in Chapters 9 and 25, can also be used to set the date and time stamp for files.

Using File Size (FS)

The File Size (FS) command enables you to list the size of a file or the total size of a group of files. You can, for example, find out how much room on your disk is taken up by files with the extension EXE.

File Size also lists the slack space associated with files. *Slack space* is space within a cluster that is allocated to a file but not actually used. If, for instance, a cluster is 512 bytes and the file stored in it is only 300 bytes, there are 212 bytes of unused slack space. This disk space is wasted because another file cannot use it. The only way that you can really control slack space is to control the size of your files so that their size is close to a multiple of the cluster size. That is hard to do, however. Another way to control slack space is to avoid having many small files by combining them into one large file.

You can use File Size to determine whether a target disk has enough space to receive a copy of a group of files. Because the size of clusters differs between hard disks and floppy disks, you cannot tell just by the size of files on your hard disk whether they will fit on a floppy disk. A floppy disk may have a 512-byte cluster, whereas a hard disk may have a 2,048-byte cluster. Thus, the 300-byte file on the floppy disk takes up one cluster (512 bytes), but the same file takes up 2,048 bytes on the hard disk. Even though you may have a group of files containing more than 360K on your hard disk, the files may fit on a 360K floppy disk. The File Size command tells you whether this fit is possible. Here is the syntax of the FS command:

FS [*filespec*] [*target drive:*] [*switches*]

The following switches may be used with FS:

Switch	Description
/P	Pauses after each screen
/S	Includes subdirectories in the file list
/T	Displays the total size for the specified files, not the size of individual files

To find out the size of all files in the current directory, use the command FS *.* or just FS. To find out whether there is room for these files to be copied onto drive A, use the command FS *.* A:.

Using Line Print (LP)

The Line Print (LP) command enables you to print a text file to the printer. This command is similar to the DOS PRINT command, but LP has a number of options not found in PRINT. Note the syntax of the LP command:

LP [*filespec*] [*output*] [*switches*]

The *output* parameter tells Line Print where to print the file. The default is PRN. Some common output designations are LPT1, LPT2, COM1, and COM2.

The following switches are available:

Switch	Description
/80	Sets page width at 80 columns.
/132	Sets page width at 132 columns.
/A	Appends the file to the specified output file. If an output file exists, the new information is added to the end of that file. Otherwise, LP creates a new file. This switch works only if you have specified an output file.
/B*n*	Sets bottom margin to *n* lines (default is 3).
/CONFIG:*file*	Prints *file* according to the information in the specified file. Use the NUCONFIG command to create this configuration file.
/EBCDIC	Tells Line Print that the original file is in EBCDIC format.
/HEADER*n*	Sets the type of header, where *n* is one of the following:
	0 = no header
	1 = header consisting of current date and time on line 1 (default)
	2 = header consisting of current date and time plus file date and time, on two lines
/HI*n*	Sets page height to *n* lines (default is 66).
/L*n*	Sets left margin to *n* spaces (default is 5).
/N	Turns on page numbering.
/PA*n*	Sets starting page number at *n* (default is 1).
/PR:*xx*	Tells LP what kind of printer you are using. Note the following options:
	TT = Teletype (TTY)
	GE = Generic (the default)
	EP = Epson dot matrix
	PR = Proprinter
	QU = Quietwriter
	TO = Toshiba
	LA = LaserJet
	PO = PostScript

Switch	Description
/R*n*	Sets right margin to *n* spaces (default is 5).
/SET:*filespec*	Tells Line Print that a printer setup string is in the specified file.
/SP*n*	Sets line spacing to *n* lines (default is 1).
/TAB*n*	Sets tab spacing to *n* spaces (default is 8).
/T*n*	Sets top margin to *n* lines (default is 3).
/W*n*	Sets page width to *n* spaces (default is 85).
/WS	Tells Line Print that the original file is in WordStar format.

For example, to print a file named REPORT.TXT (which was created with WordStar) to the printer, use this command:

    LP REPORT.TXT /WS

Using Directory Sort (DS)

Directory Sort (DS) enables you to sort one or more directories by name, extension, time, date, or size. You can use Directory Sort in command-line mode or interactively.

By sorting files, you can cause the file names to appear in a particular way when you use the DIR command. Sorting files makes it easier to find files with similar characteristics. If you sort by extension, you can easily locate all EXE files because they will appear together. If you want to look at the names of your most recently changed files, you can sort on date and time. Then the directory shows all the most recent files at the end of the directory list.

The following sections describe the Directory Sort options.

Using Directory Sort with Switches

Here is the syntax of the Directory Sort (DS) command:

    DS *sortkeys* [*directory*] [/S]

The *directory* option tells Directory Sort which directory to sort. If you do not include a directory, DS sorts the current directory. The *sortkeys* tell the utility how to sort the files in the directory. You can use the following sort keys:

Key	Meaning
D	Date
E	Extension
N	Name
S	Size
T	Time

You can include one or more keys in the command line. The sort progresses in the order in which the sort keys appear. If you use the keys EN, DS sorts on extension first, with names sorted within like extensions. If you place a minus sign after any key, the sort is in reverse order. For example, S sorts by size from smallest to largest, and S– sorts from largest to smallest.

The /S switch tells Directory Sort to sort the files in the current or specified directory and all subdirectories. For example, to sort files in the MYDIR directory and all subdirectories by date and time, use this command:

DS DT \MYDIR /S

Using Directory Sort in Interactive Mode

If you enter **DS** at the DOS prompt or choose Directory Sort from the Norton main screen, the Sorting dialog box appears (see fig. 26.1). In the left portion of this dialog box is a box containing a list of the files in the current directory, including the name, size, date, and time. In the right portion of the dialog box is the Sort Order box in which you specify the type of sort you want. To sort the file list according to the criteria in the Sort Order box, see the section "Specifying Sort Order" later in this chapter.

To end the program, press Esc or choose **Q**uit at the bottom of the dialog box. If you re-sort the directory and then choose **Q**uit, you are prompted with Write changes before quitting? If you choose **Yes**, the current sort is written to disk before the program ends. If you choose **No**, the program ends without saving the new sort order to disk. If you choose **Cancel**, you return to the Sorting dialog box.

The next two sections describe the options in the Sorting dialog box.

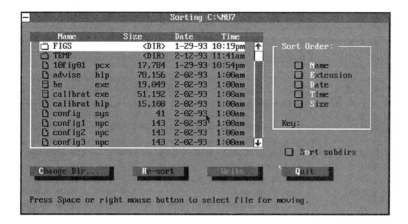

Fig. 26.1

The Sorting
dialog box.

Manually Rearranging Files

You can manually rearrange the files and directories in the list box in
the Sorting dialog box by moving a file from one position to another. To
move a file by using the arrow keys, follow these steps:

1. Use the up- and down-arrow keys to highlight a file or directory to
   move. Press the space bar to lock in your choice.

2. Use the up- and down-arrow keys to move the selected file or
   directory to a new location in the list.

3. Press the space bar or Enter to fix the selected file or directory in
   its new location.

To move a file or directory by using a mouse, follow these steps:

1. Point to the file you want to move with the mouse pointer.

2. Click and hold down the right mouse button to select the file to
   move.

3. While holding down the right mouse button, drag the file to a new
   location in the list. Release the mouse button to fix the file or
   directory in its new location.

To save this rearrangement to disk, choose **W**rite at the bottom of the
dialog box. To display files in another directory, choose **C**hange Dir and
then choose a directory from the list. Press Esc or choose **Q**uit to end
the program.

Specifying Sort Order

To specify the sort order, use the Sort Order box. Choose one or more of the sort items in the order in which you want the sort to take place. For example, to sort by extension first and then by name, choose Extension and then Name. A 1 appears beside your first choice, a 2 appears beside your second choice, and so on.

If you want to change the sort order, highlight the item and press the + or – key. A + or – appears to the right of the sort item to indicate the sort order. The sort key as you build it appears at the bottom of the Sort Order box.

Changing and Sorting Subdirectories

Below the Sort Order box is a check box named Sort Subdirs. If you check this box, the sort you perform affects the current directory and any subdirectories. To sort a directory other than the one containing the files in the list box, choose Change Dir. In the Change Directory dialog box, you are prompted to indicate the directory to use (see fig. 26.2). You can specify a new Path, select a new Drive, or choose a subdirectory from the Subdirectories list. After you make your selection, choose OK to return to the Sorting dialog box, or choose Cancel to exit the Change Directory dialog box without making a directory or drive change.

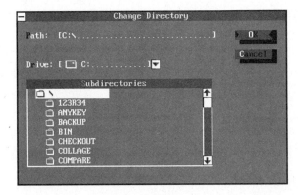

Fig. 26.2

The Change Directory dialog box.

Using Duplicate Disk (DUPDISK)

The Norton Duplicate Disk (DUPDISK) program is similar to the DOS DISKCOPY command, but DUPDISK has more features. Like DISKCOPY,

DUPDISK makes an exact duplicate of the contents of disks of the same size (such as 360K or 720K). You use the following syntax (*d:* is a disk drive):

>   DUPDISK *d:* [*d:*]

For example, to duplicate a disk from drive A to drive B, use this command:

>   DUPDISK A: B:

If you do not specify a second disk drive, DUPDISK assumes that the disk duplication will occur on the same disk.

Unlike DISKCOPY, DUPDISK enables you to make multiple copies of the same disk without having to reread the master (source) disk. If you are using a single floppy drive, DUPDISK usually asks you to swap disks only once during a copy instead of several times, as required by DISKCOPY.

DUPDISK and DISKCOPY create disks differently. When DOS formats a disk (beginning with DOS 4.0), it assigns the disk a unique volume serial number. (This number appears when you perform a directory listing of the disk.) Thus, when DOS runs DISKCOPY and formats the target disk, DOS gives that disk a serial number different from that of the original (source) disk. DUPDISK, however, makes an exact copy of the source disk to the target disk, including the serial number.

 NOTE Because DUPDISK is designed to copy disks of the same size, you cannot use DUPDISK to duplicate a 360K source disk on a 720K target disk. To copy disks of different sizes, use the DOS COPY command.

If you issue the DUPDISK command with no command-line prompts, a dialog box appears, enabling you to specify the source (**From**) and destination (**To**) drives for the copy (see fig. 26.3).

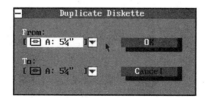

Fig. 26.3

The Duplicate Diskette dialog box.

Summary

This chapter described several command-line programs in Norton Utilities. These programs include File Date (FD), which allows you to change the date and time stamp on one or more files; File Size (FS), which determines the size in bytes of a file or group of files; Line Print (LP), which prints a text document to the printer; Directory Sort (DS), which sorts a directory; and Duplicate Disk (DUPDISK), which duplicates disks.

The next chapter describes the Norton Diagnostics (NDOS) program. With NDOS, you can run a thorough series of diagnostic tests on your computer.

Using Norton Diagnostics

In Chapter 18, "Using System Info," you were introduced to the concept of using your computer more efficiently. Before you can take advantage of the many features covered in that chapter, you need to understand where problems occur and when they occur. Like System Info, Norton Diagnostics (NDiags) can be viewed as taking an X-ray of the internal components of your system and then offering a diagnosis that can be treated appropriately.

NDiags provides a variety of diagnostic tests as well as the following access methods:

- You can select and run the tests individually from the pull-down menus.

- You can run the tests in a predefined sequence, presented at the time you begin NDiags.

- You can run the tests from within the Report component, where you can identify the areas to be tested as well as the report format for presenting the results.

Understanding the Diagnostic Tests

Norton Diagnostics can perform a variety of sophisticated diagnostics on the components that make up your computer system. NDiags can perform these diagnostics individually, by user-defined groups, or as a full group. The component checklist includes the following:

- System board
  DMA (Direct Memory Access) controller and registers
  DMA concurrency pertaining to hard disk transfers
  Interrupt controller responses
  Timer frequencies
  Real-time clock

- Serial ports
  Modem control and status
  Line control and status
  Interrupts
  Data
  Loop tests (requires a loopback plug)

- Parallel ports
  Control and data registers
  Interrupt test (requires a loopback plug)
  Data throughput (requires a loopback plug)

- CMOS status
  Hard and floppy disks
  Installed memory
  CMOS battery functionality
  CMOS time
  Fixed disk controller
  Memory and equipment configurations
  Checksum

- Base memory

- Extended memory

- Expanded memory

- Hard disks
  Sequential and random read tests
  Effective RPM

- Floppy drives
  - Sequential and random read tests
  - Disk change test
  - Write protect test
  - Rotation and speed test

- Video memory tests

- Video mode tests

- Video grid tests

- Video color tests

- Mouse test
  - Button press test
  - Movement test

- Speaker test

- Keyboard press test

- Keyboard light test
  - Num Lock, Caps Lock, and Scroll Lock status lights

By default, each test provides an introductory dialog box that describes the test. You can turn off the introductory dialog boxes, as explained in the section "Understanding the Information Dialog Boxes" later in this chapter.

When you begin Norton Diagnostics without using any of the available switches, you are immediately placed in a mode to begin testing all system components in the order given in the preceding list. This chapter explains how to do the following:

- Perform all tests in a predefined order

- Examine the results of the tests

- Run selected tests

- Prepare written documentation of the test results

Running Norton Diagnostics

You can access Norton Diagnostics in one of two ways. You can use Norton Diagnostics interactively by choosing Diagnostics from the Norton main screen (see fig. 27.1). You can also work from the DOS prompt by entering the following command:

NDIAGS [*switches*]

As illustrated in figure 27.1, you can enter switches in the text box containing the NDIAGS command. The switches in this figure run Norton Diagnostics in auto (automatic) mode with a screen pause of five seconds between tests.

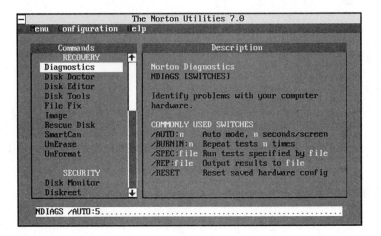

Fig. 27.1

The Norton
Utilities main
screen.

The following switches may be used with NDIAGS:

Switch	Description
/AUTO:*n*	Instructs the command to operate in automatic mode. The *n* parameter specifies a delay of *n* seconds between screens.
/BURNIN:*n*	Tells the command to perform the tests *n* number of times.
/SPEC:*file1*	Tells the command to generate a report with the parameters stored in *file1*. The section "Creating a Report" later in this chapter discusses this feature in greater detail.
/REP:*file2*	Tells the command to print a report to the file specified by *file2*.
/RESET	Tells the command to reset to the saved hardware configuration.

The **Help** option in the NDiags menu allows you to access Norton's Help feature, as described in Chapter 1 on the basics of Norton Utilities. When you are viewing a particular screen, you can choose **Help** or press F1 to display information about the currently displayed screen.

To exit the Norton Diagnostics program, press Esc, choose Exit from the File menu, or double-click the control box in the upper-left corner of the Norton Diagnostics dialog box.

Understanding the Information Dialog Boxes

Regardless of which method you choose for implementing Norton Diagnostics, until you elect to disable the messages that precede each test function, you are presented with an information dialog box describing the task(s) the test will perform. Figure 27.2 illustrates one of the information dialog boxes you encounter each time you access Norton Diagnostics. This particular message offers a comprehensive description of what NDiags does. To scroll through the entire message, press PgDn or click the scroll bar.

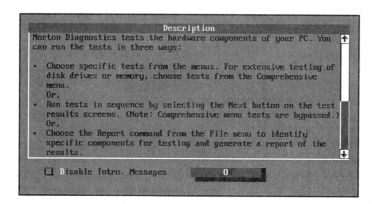

 Fig. 27.2

A description of Norton Diagnostics.

Notice the check box that allows you to disable the information messages. You should familiarize yourself with the diagnostic procedures before you disable this function. When this information is no longer useful and you feel comfortable with each test, select the **Disable Intro Messages** option.

NOTE If you disable the messages, you can reinstitute them by choosing **Options** from the File menu.

Listing the Hardware on Your System

If the introductory messages are still enabled, you see the System Information Description message, describing what test is about to be performed (see fig. 27.3). After you press PgDn or use the scroll bar to scroll through the Description message and then select **OK**, you are presented with a System Information Description message that describes the next function.

The System Information dialog box, shown in figure 27.4, provides a complete listing of the physical components that Norton Diagnostics has detected in your system. This information might be particularly useful if, for instance, you know that you have two serial ports installed in your computer but only one is detected by Norton Diagnostics. Such information might help you determine why a device (such as a printer, modem, or plotter) is not working.

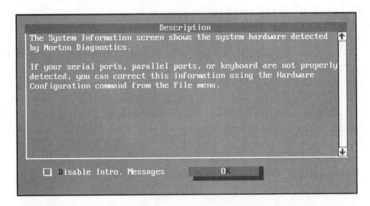

Fig. 27.3

The System Information Description message.

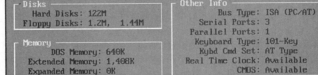

Fig. 27.4

The System Information dialog box.

As illustrated in figure 27.4, the system being tested here has AMI built-in BIOS, an 80386SX processor operating at 20 MHz, no math coprocessor, only 1 video adapter card (VGA), a serial mouse using IRQ 4 and mouse driver Version 6.24, a 122M hard drive, and 1.2M and 1.44M floppy drives. The Memory section shows 640K of DOS (base) memory, 1,408K of extended memory, and no expanded memory. The Other Info section indicates that this system's architecture (Bus Type) is ISA (PC/AT). The system has 3 serial ports and 1 parallel port; a 101-key, AT-type keyboard; and a real-time clock. CMOS is available. Examine this list closely to make sure that all components are present.

If you want to print your system configuration, choose **P**rint. As illustrated in figure 27.5, the printed report offers you a document worthy of filing for future reference.

```
                **************************
                *   System Information   *
                **************************

        --------------------- Computer ---------------------
          Built-in BIOS: AMI, Monday, April  9, 1990
          Main Processor: 80386SX, 20MHz
        Math Coprocessor: None
           Video Adapter: VGA,   Secondary: None
              Mouse Type: Serial Mouse,   Version: 6.24 IRQ: 4

        --------------------- Disks ---------------------
       Hard Disks: 122M
     Floppy Disks: 1.2M,   1.44M

        --------------------- Memory ---------------------
          DOS Memory: 640K
     Extended Memory: 1,408K
     Expanded Memory: 0K

        --------------------- Other Info ---------------------
            Bus Type: ISA (PC/AT)
         Serial Ports: 3
       Parallel Ports: 1
        Keyboard Type: 101-Key
         Kybd Cmd Set: AT Type
      Real Time Clock: Available
                 CMOS: Available
```

Fig. 27.5

The System Information report.

Starting the Diagnostic Tests

When you are ready to begin testing the components, choose Start Tests or press Enter.

After you choose Start **T**ests, the System Board Tests dialog box appears, offering information as to what is about to happen (if you have not disabled the introductory messages). Choose **OK** to begin testing the system board, or choose **S**kip to bypass this test. If you choose **OK**, the testing begins, and all components related to the system board are analyzed, with results presented in the format shown in figure 27.6.

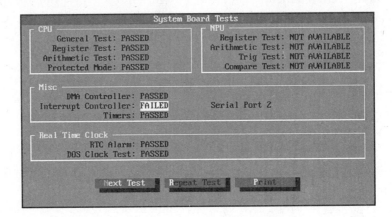

System Board Tests screen:

```
                          System Board Tests
  CPU                                 NPU
      General Test: PASSED             Register Test: NOT AVAILABLE
     Register Test: PASSED           Arithmetic Test: NOT AVAILABLE
   Arithmetic Test: PASSED                 Trig Test: NOT AVAILABLE
    Protected Mode: PASSED              Compare Test: NOT AVAILABLE

  Misc
          DMA Controller: PASSED
    Interrupt Controller: FAILED      Serial Port 2
                  Timers: PASSED

  Real Time Clock
            RTC Alarm: PASSED
       DOS Clock Test: PASSED

         Next Test      Repeat Test       Print
```

Fig. 27.6

The results of the System Board tests.

Note the following interpretation of the results:

Result	Meaning
All CPU tests PASSED	No problems were detected.
No NPU (numeric processing unit)	No test was performed.
Miscellaneous tests	A problem exists with the interrupt controller related to serial port 2.
Real Time Clock tests PASSED	No problems were detected.

After the completion of these tests and all those to follow, you may elect to choose Next Test, **R**epeat Test, or **P**rint. If the results are as expected, choose **N**ext Test. If components have failed the test, choose **R**epeat Test at least two more times to verify the failure. If you want to print a copy of the results, choose **P**rint.

Serial Port Tests

The Serial Port tests check all serial ports installed in your computer. Using the internal loopback inherent to your serial ports, NDiags tests the serial chip's registers. During this portion of the test, no data is actually transferred through the port; a loopback plug, which may be purchased from your local electronics store, provides for a more effective test of the serial port. The loopback plug will actually test data being sent to and received from the serial port at various speeds (300 baud to 115,200 baud). If you do not have a loopback plug, you can disable this particular test feature by canceling the test when informed that the test could not find a loopback plug (see fig. 27.7). Or you can disable the loopback feature by using **O**ptions from the **F**ile menu, as discussed later in this chapter.

After the serial port has been tested, the results are presented (see fig. 27.8). Had a loopback plug been available for this test, results would have been recorded in the appropriate place next to the baud rate(s) checked.

If any of the serial ports fails during the test, detach all devices connected to the serial port being tested and repeat the test. If the serial port continues to fail, you may have a defective serial port/card. You should also verify that your serial ports are not sharing the same IRQ with other devices used on your computer.

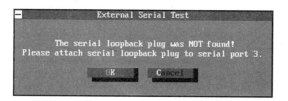

Fig. 27.7

A message indicating that the serial loopback plug was not found.

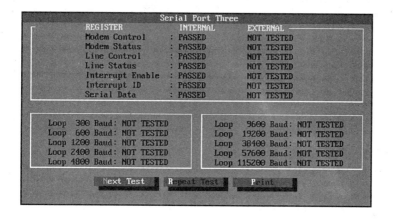

Fig. 27.8

The Serial Port Three test results.

If more than one serial port resides in your computer, each serial port is tested separately.

Parallel Port Tests

The Parallel Port tests operate in the same way as the serial port tests. A loopback plug offers a more thorough test, but again, if a loopback plug is not available, you may follow the preceding instructions for bypassing this part of the test. Figure 27.9 shows the results of the Parallel Port One test. Had a loopback plug been used, the EXTERNAL results would have indicated whether the port PASSED or FAILED.

As mentioned in the preceding section, if Norton Diagnostics indicates a problem, remove all devices attached to the parallel port that has failed and then run the test again. If the port fails after two more tests, you may have a defective parallel port/card.

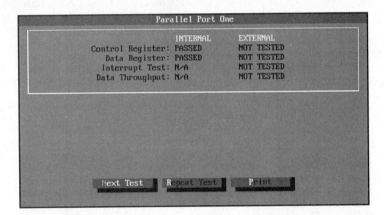

Fig. 27.9

The Parallel Port One test results.

CMOS Tests

The CMOS tests report the information derived from the internal CMOS table, as well as the POST (*power-on self-test*) results. The CMOS table includes the following information:

- Disk drive types and capacities

- Installed memory

- Functionality of the CMOS battery, CMOS time, fixed disk controller, memory and equipment configurations, and checksum

Figure 27.10 illustrates the results of the CMOS tests.

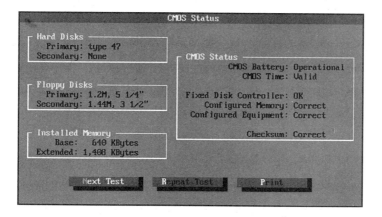

```
                        CMOS Status
 ┌─ Hard Disks ──────────────┐
 │   Primary: type 47        │
 │   Secondary: None         │  ┌─ CMOS Status ──────────────────────┐
 └───────────────────────────┘  │        CMOS Battery: Operational   │
                                 │           CMOS Time: Valid         │
 ┌─ Floppy Disks ────────────┐   │  Fixed Disk Controller: OK         │
 │   Primary: 1.2M, 5 1/4"   │   │     Configured Memory: Correct     │
 │   Secondary: 1.44M, 3 1/2"│   │  Configured Equipment: Correct     │
 └───────────────────────────┘   │                                    │
                                 │             Checksum: Correct      │
 ┌─ Installed Memory ────────┐   └────────────────────────────────────┘
 │     Base:   640 KBytes    │
 │ Extended: 1,408 KBytes    │
 └───────────────────────────┘

     [ Next Test ]      [ Repeat Test ]      [ Print ]
```

Fig. 27.10

The results of the CMOS tests.

The test results presented in figure 27.10 show that the system being tested has a hard disk present (type 47). The test has detected two floppy drives. Installed memory, both base and extended, has been detected. The CMOS is functioning properly, and the CMOS time is valid. The disk controller is functioning as it should, and the memory and system components are configured properly. Tests performed on the checksum have passed.

Failure of any CMOS component will require you to correct values. Information related to these values can be found in your hardware reference manuals.

WARNING: Altering the hard disk CMOS values may have disastrous consequences. Do not alter these settings unless you are absolutely sure of the exact CMOS values.

Base Memory Test

The Base Memory test tests memory, up to and including 640K, by sending information to the chips that make up the base memory and then testing to see whether the information was properly received by the chips. If a problem is detected, the memory address is displayed in the Failure List box (see fig. 27.11).

The test results indicate that information (1s and 0s) sent to the various memory blocks and bit locations was written and verified properly.

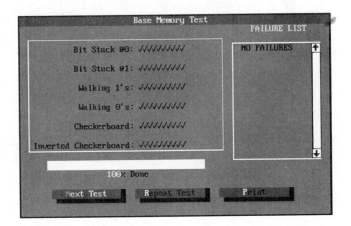

Fig. 27.11

The Base
Memory test
results.

If any of the test's patterns failed, immediately remove any terminate-and-stay-resident (TSR) programs from your AUTOEXEC.BAT file and remove all device drivers from your CONFIG.SYS file. Reboot your computer and repeat the Base Memory test again. Should you experience a failure again, run the Comprehensive Memory test, available from the Comprehensive menu. If this test fails, there is a high probability that a memory chip/module is defective.

Extended Memory Test

Much like the Base Memory test, the Extended Memory test sends information to extended memory and verifies that the information was received and manipulated properly. If an error occurs, the exact address of the problem appears in the Failure List box (see fig. 27.12).

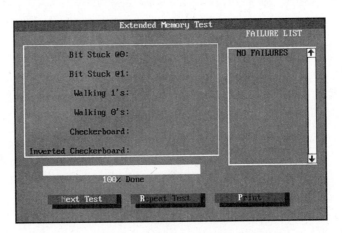

Fig. 27.12

The Extended
Memory test
results.

If any of the test's patterns failed, immediately remove any terminate-and-stay resident (TSR) programs from your AUTOEXEC.BAT file and remove all device drivers from your CONFIG.SYS file. Reboot your computer and repeat the Base Memory test again. If you experience a second failure, run the Comprehensive Memory test from the Comprehensive menu. If this test fails, there is a high probability that a memory chip/module is defective.

If you are using expanded memory, you must activate the memory manager. You may find it necessary to invoke the memory manager software, reboot the system so that it becomes active, and then perform this test. These steps are required if you want to test expanded memory.

Hard Disk Tests

The Hard Disk tests check the hard disk's read capabilities. The hard disk's rotation speed is also measured and reported. The Calibrate utility, discussed in Chapter 20, provides more in-depth information based on a more sophisticated testing routine. (Calibrate is not available here; it is a separate test procedure and is not part of the pre-defined test routine.) Figure 27.13 illustrates the tests in progress for Hard Disk 1, and figure 27.14 shows the results.

NOTE   This set of tests is nondestructive. The tests only read; no writes to the hard disk occur.

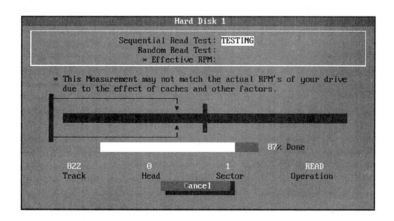

Fig. 27.13
The Hard Disk 1 tests in progress.

The Sequential and Random Read tests performed here show no signs of problems. The Effective RPM (revolutions per minute) is excessively high, which may be attributed to a hard drive caching controller.

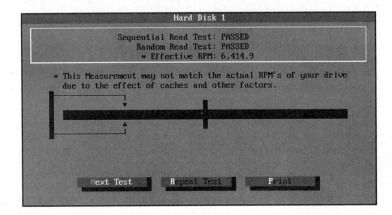

Fig. 27.14

The Hard Disk 1
test results.

NOTE Norton Diagnostics may give false results if your hard disk is
equipped with a caching controller. The average effective
RPM of most hard drives is around 3600 RPMs. The results
shown in figure 27.14 suggest that the hard disk being tested
here is equipped with such a caching controller.

If more than one hard disk was detected in your computer, the **Next
Test** option tests a second hard drive.

Floppy Drive Tests

As with the Hard Disk tests, the number of Floppy Drive tests performed depends on the number of floppy drives installed in your computer. Nearly identical tests to those for the hard disks are performed
here. The differences are in the tests that check whether a floppy disk
is write-protected or has been removed from the drive. Diagnostic
problems may be related not only to a defective disk drive but also to
defective disks. If an error is recorded during this test, try another disk.

The Floppy Drive tests require intervention on your part, and you will
need a formatted disk. Be sure that this disk contains no useful information because the information may be destroyed during the testing
procedure. A newly formatted disk is recommended. Concerning user
intervention, you will be prompted to remove the disk during the test,
enable write-protect, remove the disk again, and disable write-protect.
Figure 27.15 shows the first Floppy Drive test dialog box, prompting
you to insert a formatted floppy disk in drive x (x represents the floppy
drive about to be tested). In this example, the drive being tested is
drive A.

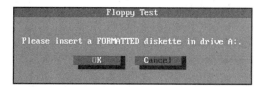

Fig. 27.15

Beginning a
Floppy Drive test.

After the Sequential and Random Read tests have been performed, you are prompted to remove the disk from the drive and then reinsert it. This Disk Change test checks your computer's capability to detect the removal and reinsertion of a disk.

After the Disk Change test is complete, you are prompted to remove the disk from the drive. Write-protect the disk and then reinsert it. This test is the last one performed on your floppy disk. Figure 27.16 shows sample results of testing drive B.

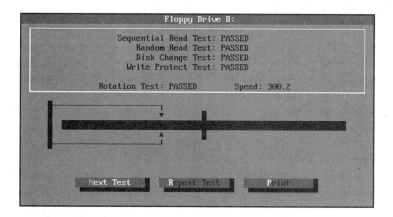

Fig. 27.16

Floppy Drive tests
of drive B.

Video Memory Tests

The Video RAM test is the first of a group of tests to be performed for your video card and display. This test, like many others, sends information to the memory of your video card and then verifies that the information was stored and manipulated properly. During this test, don't be alarmed if your screen goes blank or blinks several times. This is a normal part of the testing procedure. If everything is working OK, a dialog box like the one shown in figure 27.17 appears.

The Video Mode tests check the text and graphics capabilities of your video controller card. You will be asked several questions during this phase of testing. You respond by pressing Y if the display appears as it should, or N if the display is not acceptable. Figure 27.18 shows one of the test screens. Figure 27.19 illustrates the results of the Video Mode tests.

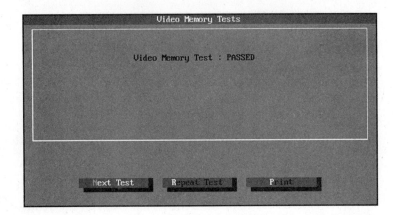

Fig. 27.17

The results of the
Video RAM test.

The various screens presented show the modes being tested and ask
you to press Y if the display reflects the appropriate mode, N if it is not
correct, and Esc if you want to cancel the test.

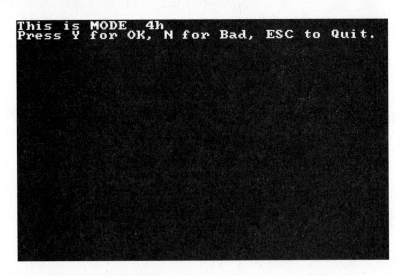

Fig. 27.18

A Video Mode
test in progress.

The Video Grid tests check each graphic capability available to your
video controller card. During this test, various grids are displayed on-
screen, and you are asked to verify the appearance of the grid. Press Y
if the grid appears to be OK, or press N if it is not acceptable. Press Esc
to cancel the Video Grid tests. Figure 27.20 shows the results of the
Video Grid tests.

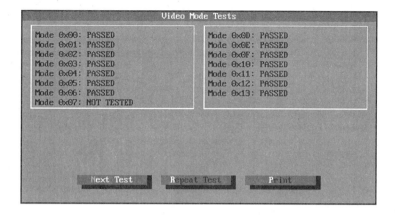

Fig. 27.19

The results of the
Video Mode
tests.

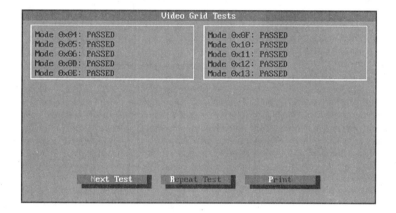

Fig. 27.20

The results of the
Video Grid tests.

The final video tests performed are the Video Color tests, which check
the appearance of all colors supported by your video controller card.
The three basic colors (red, green, and blue) are tested first. Then all
supported graphics modes are tested, using all colors supported by
the card. You must respond to the questions as they are asked.
Figure 27.21 shows the results of the Video Color tests.

Mouse Test

If you have a mouse connected to your computer and it has been detected by Norton Diagnostics, the Mouse test checks the functionality
of the mouse buttons and the movement of the mouse pointer. You are
presented with several prompts during this test—to press a button
or move the pointer, for example. Figure 27.22 illustrates one of the
prompts. Figure 27.23 shows the results of the six actions tested.

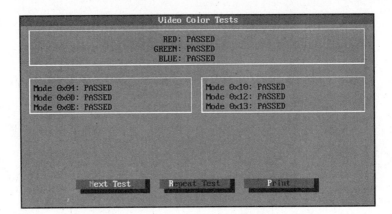

Fig. 27.21

The results of the Video Color tests.

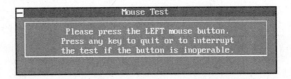

Fig. 27.22

A user prompt for testing the mouse functions.

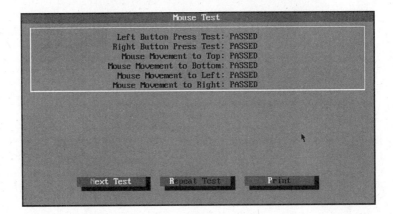

Fig. 27.23

The results of the Mouse test.

Speaker Test

The Speaker test checks the audibility of your speaker by sending a sequence of musical notes or a digitized voice message to the speaker. After the sounds are transmitted to the speaker, you are asked whether the sounds were audible. If they were, choose **Yes**; if they were not, choose **No**. Figure 27.24 illustrates a successful test.

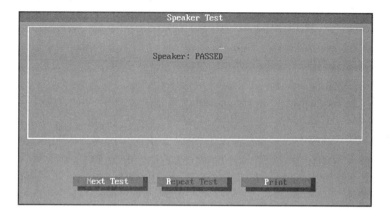

Fig. 27.24

The Speaker test results.

Keyboard Tests

The final two tests check the functionality of your keyboard. In the Keyboard Press test, you must press and release each key on your keyboard. This test is considered successful if Norton determines that all keys have been pressed. If you terminate the test by pressing any single key three times in succession, you are prompted to choose **P**assed if you are satisfied with the results, **F**ailed if you encountered a problem, **C**ancel if you want to stop, or **R**esume if you want to continue. As each key is pressed, its associated scan code is displayed in the Scan Code text box. Figure 27.25 illustrates a successful Keyboard Press test.

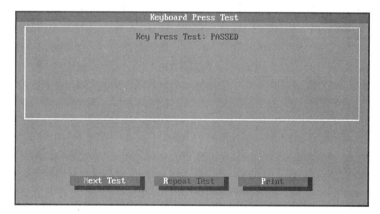

Fig. 27.25

The results of a successful Keyboard Press test.

The Keyboard Lights test is the last test to be performed in this default sequence of tests. It verifies that all keyboard lights (Num Lock, Caps Lock, and Scroll Lock) are performing correctly. Figure 27.26 shows the

Keyboard Status Light test in progress. Look at your keyboard lights.
For this example, if the Num Lock light is off, press Enter or press Y.
Continue this cycle until you have responded to all questions, after
which you are given the results of the test.

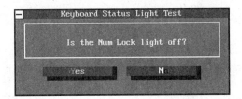

Fig. 27.26

The Keyboard
Status Light test
in progress.

Using Norton Diagnostics Menus

You can activate all the test functions described in the previous sections from the menu bar at the top of the Norton Diagnostics dialog
box. The options on the menu bar are **F**ile, **S**ystem, **M**emory, **D**isks,
Video, **O**ther, **C**omprehensive, and **H**elp. To open these pull-down
menus, press Alt plus the highlighted letter of the menu name; or press
F10, highlight the menu you want, and press Enter. Alternatively, you
can point to a menu with the mouse pointer and click. After you extend
the menu, you can use the right- and left-arrow keys to move from
menu to menu, and the up- and down-arrow keys to choose options
within the menus.

The **F**ile menu is shown in figure 27.27. From this menu, you can choose
Hardware Configuration, **O**ptions, **R**eport, and E**x**it.

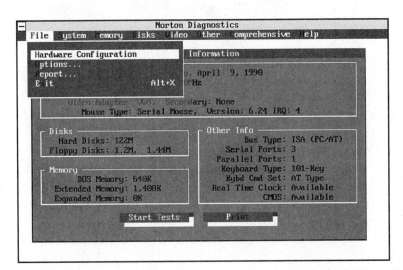

Fig. 27.27

The Norton
Diagnostics **F**ile
menu.

If an option is in parentheses or is grayed (dimmed), the option is not currently available.

Creating a Report

The previous sections discussed the various tests available in Norton Diagnostics. Each test that was run offered you the option to print a report containing the results of the individual test performed. By choosing **R**eport from the **F**ile menu, you can define which tests you want to run and then generate a comprehensive report based on your selections. When you choose the **R**eport option, a Report dialog box appears on-screen (see fig. 27.28).

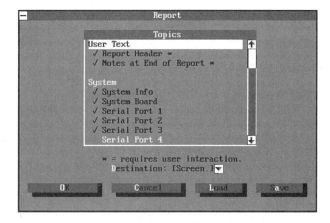

Fig. 27.28

A Report dialog box.

From this dialog box, you can choose which items you want to test and which items you want to appear in the report. These items correspond to the tests and reports discussed earlier in this chapter. Because each item is an independent part of the report, you can be selective about what items will be tested and printed in the report. When an item is selected to appear in the report, a check mark appears to the left of the item name. An asterisk to the right of an item name indicates that when the test is run, the user must provide or perform some sort of user input. (With the Keyboard Press test, for example, you must press the keyboard keys to complete the test.)

The two items under the User Test heading in the Topics list allow you to include your own information in the title (header) of the report and at the end of the report. Notice that the list is in a list box, which means that you can scroll the box by pressing the up- and down-arrow keys or clicking the scroll bars. The following report items appear in the list:

- **User Test**
  - Report Header
  - Notes at End of Report

- **System**
  - System Info
  - System Board
  - Serial Port 1
  - Serial Port 2
  - Serial Port 3
  - Serial Port 4
  - Parallel Port 1
  - Parallel Port 2
  - Parallel Port 3
  - Parallel Port 4
  - CMOS Status

- **Disks**
  - Hard Disk 1
  - Hard Disk 2
  - Floppy Disk A
  - Floppy Disk B

- **Memory**
  - Base
  - Extended
  - EMS

- **Video**
  - Memory
  - Mode
  - Grid
  - Color

- **Other**
  - Mouse
  - Speaker
  - Keyboard Press
  - Keyboard Lights

- **Comprehensive**
  - Floppy A
  - Floppy B
  - 16550 1
  - 16550 2
  - 16550 3
  - 16550 4

The 16550 1, 2, 3, and 4 tests check a special buffering chip used in serial communications. Your system may not be equipped with 16550 UART chips.

Some of the items in this list may appear in parentheses or grayed (dimmed), indicating that the item is not available for the report. If you have only one floppy disk drive, for example, the Floppy Drive B test will not be available.

When the report is created, only information from those items with a check mark will be placed in the report. To select items, use the arrow keys to highlight the item on the list, and press the space bar to select or deselect the item. Or just click the item. By default, all available items are checked (selected).

Option buttons at the bottom of the Report dialog box include **OK**, **Cancel**, **Load**, and **Save**. If you choose **OK**, the report is created with all the selected report parameters. Choosing **Cancel** closes the Report dialog box and returns you to the Norton main screen.

The **Load** and **Save** buttons enable you to save the current selections in the list box and load them back at a later time. For example, you could create and save several different selections: a short report (only disk drives are tested and reported on), a medium-sized report (only system board, output port, and disk drives are tested), and a comprehensive report. To save a group of topic selections, select the items you want tested and reported, and choose **Save**. You are prompted to enter the name of the file where you want to store the settings (see fig. 27.29). The file is stored with the extension NDR. If you enter the name **BOBBIE** as the file name, the file is stored on the disk as BOBBIE.NDR. After you specify the name, press Enter or choose **OK**.

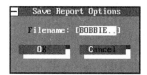

Fig. 27.29

The Save Report Options dialog box.

Later, when you use the NDiags **R**eport option again, you can choose **Load**. A list of previously defined report-options files will be listed (see fig. 27.30). Choose the name of the report-options file you want to use; then press Enter or choose **OK**. All selections in the Topics list in the Report dialog box will revert to the settings that were in effect when the report-options file was saved.

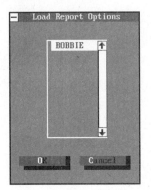

Fig. 27.30

The Load Report Options dialog box.

Below the Topics list in the Report dialog box is the **D**estination drop-down list box. From this box, you can choose to output the report to the printer, the screen, or a file. To change this setting, choose **D**estination, press PgDn to display the drop-down list, and choose the destination you want. Or click the triangle at the right of the box to display the drop-down list, and then click the destination. If you choose the File option, you are prompted to enter a file name to be assigned to the report, as shown in figure 27.31. The default report name is NDIAGS.RPT. To accept the default file name, select **O**K; if you want to quit without saving the report to a file, choose **C**ancel. If you want to assign another file name to the report, just begin typing the new name (remember to conform to DOS file-naming conventions) and then choose **O**K. You can use this name or enter your own file name. If you print to the screen, you use a scroll bar to move through the report.

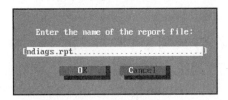

Fig. 27.31

Specifying the name of the report file.

If you chose the Report Header option from the Topics list, you are prompted to enter a single line of information to appear in the title of the report, as shown in figure 27.32. After you specify the name, press Enter or choose **O**K. The printed report is shown in figure 27.33. (This figure shows an abbreviated version of the full report.)

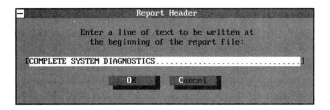

Fig. 27.32

Specifying the
report header.

```
                    Norton Diagnostics
            Tuesday, March  2, 1993 11:28pm
              COMPLETE SYSTEM DIAGNOSTICS

            ************************
            *  System Information  *
            ************************

    -------------------- Computer --------------------
     Built-in BIOS: AMI, Monday, April  9, 1990
    Main Processor: 80386SX, 20MHz
   Math Coprocessor: None
     Video Adapter: VGA,   Secondary: None
       Mouse Type: Serial Mouse,  Version: 6.24 IRQ: 4

    -------------------- Disks --------------------
    Hard Disks: 122M
   Floppy Disks: 1.2M,  1.44M

    -------------------- Memory --------------------
       DOS Memory: 640K
   Extended Memory: 1,408K
   Expanded Memory: 0K

    -------------------- Other Info --------------------
        Bus Type: ISA (PC/AT)
      Serial Ports: 3
    Parallel Ports: 1
    Keyboard Type: 101-Key
     Kybd Cmd Set: AT Type
   Real Time Clock: Available
             CMOS: Available



            ************************
            *  System Board Tests  *
            ************************

    -------------------- CPU --------------------
      General Test: PASSED
     Register Test: PASSED
   Arithmetic Test: PASSED
    Protected Mode: PASSED

    -------------------- NPU --------------------
     Register Test: NOT AVAILABLE
   Arithmetic Test: NOT AVAILABLE
        Trig Test: NOT AVAILABLE
     Compare Test: NOT AVAILABLE

    -------------------- Misc --------------------
     DMA Controller: PASSED
   Interrupt Controller: PASSED
            Timers: PASSED

    -------------------- Real Time Clock --------------------
         RTC Alarm: PASSED
   Test DOS's Clock: PASSED
```

Fig. 27.33

An abbreviated
report.

If you chose the Notes at End of Report option from the Topics list, a User Notes dialog box appears (see fig. 27.34). The end-of-report message can be up to 10 lines long. You might want to include such information as serial number of the computer, warranty information, or the physical location of the computer. After typing the information, press Enter or choose **OK**.

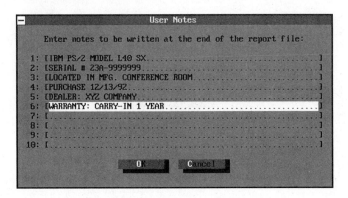

Fig. 27.34

Entering additional notes to be printed at the end of the report.

After you enter the Report Header and User Notes information, the tests are performed, and the report is printed to your printer or stored in a file according to the destination you have selected.

For purposes of comparison, upkeep, diagnostic, and support, it would be helpful to run this kind of report on all your computers and then file the information for future use.

Running Individual Tests from the Menus

The rest of the NDiags menu options allow you to choose individual tests and their associated reports. If you do not want to test multiple items as discussed previously, you have the option of accessing single tests. The following list shows the tests available in each menu:

- File

    Hardware Configuration Tests

- System

    Information, **System** Board Test, Serial Port **1**, Serial Port **2**, Serial Port **3**, Serial Port **4**, Parallel Port 1 (hot key **A**), Parallel Port 2 (hot key **B**), Parallel Port 3 (hot key **C**), Parallel Port 4 (hot key **D**), and CMOS Status

- ■ Memory

    Base Memory Test, Extended Memory Test, and Expanded
    Memory (EMS) Test

- ■ Disks

    Hard Disk **1** Test, Hard Disk **2** Test, Floppy Disk **A** Test, and
    Floppy Disk **B** Test

- ■ Video

    Memory, M**o**de, **G**rid, and **C**olor

- ■ Other

    Mouse, **S**peaker, **K**eyboard Press, and Keyboard **L**ights

- ■ Comprehensive

    Floppy **A**, Floppy **B**, **R**un CALIBRAT, **M**emory Test, 16550 **1**,
    16550 **2**, 16550 **3**, and 16550 **4**

The difference between the Floppy **A** and Floppy **B** tests on the Comprehensive menu and the previously discussed Floppy Drive tests is
the addition of the write tests. In the previous Floppy Drive tests, only
Sequential and Random Read tests were performed. During this sequence of Floppy **A** and Floppy **B** tests, read and write tests are performed. You will need a formatted floppy disk containing useless data.
Any data contained on the disk used during the test will be destroyed.

NOTE Chapter 20 offers a complete explanation of the Calibrate
program. Before running Calibrate, you should perform a
complete backup of your entire system. Calibrate runs a
low-level format procedure; although this procedure isn't
destructive, you should safeguard against unforeseen
problems.

Summary

This chapter covered the use of the Norton Diagnostics utility. This
portion of Norton Utilities 7 tests your system components and
produces appropriate reports about the success and failure of those
components. The reporting capabilities allow you to print individual
reports about specific components, or an all-encompassing report
about all components. These reports can be helpful in diagnosing
and correcting problems related to the successful operation of your
computer.

In the next chapter, you learn to use NDOS, a set of utilities that will
enhance your DOS capabilities.

Using NDOS, Norton Backup, and Norton Commander

Using NDOS

A file called COMMAND.COM contains the core of the commands used for DOS. When you use a command such as DIR or COPY at the DOS prompt, the COMMAND.COM program interprets that command and causes the computer to perform the request. Norton's NDOS program replaces the normal COMMAND.COM file because NDOS has all of COMMAND.COM's features—and more. With NDOS, you add a whole new set of "DOS" commands to use.

This chapter explains how to use NDOS commands. It was written with the assumption that you would already be familiar with commonly used DOS commands. If you need a refresher course in DOS commands, however, read Appendix A, "A DOS Review."

Installing NDOS

To try out NDOS at any time, begin the program by entering **NDOS** at the DOS prompt. If you like NDOS, place it in your CONFIG.SYS file so that NDOS is activated each time you boot your computer. The easiest way to install NDOS in your CONFIG.SYS file is with the Norton configuration program described in Chapter 2. When NDOS loads, you see the copyright screen. Otherwise, your DOS prompt looks the same as it does under normal DOS. If you enter **NDOS** at the DOS prompt to begin NDOS, entering **EXIT** returns you to the standard COMMAND.COM mode.

Using NDOS Command Enhancements

Before this chapter introduces specific NDOS commands, it describes a number of enhancements that NDOS provides beyond the normal DOS commands. These enhancements include on-line help, expanded command-line editing, command recall, more flexible use of wild-card characters, file descriptions, multiple commands per line, conditional commands, enhanced batch processing, and added redirection options.

Accessing On-Line Help

NDOS provides an on-line Help facility for all DOS and NDOS commands. Beginning with DOS 5, DOS also has a Help feature. To display a brief explanation about a command, you enter the command name at the DOS prompt followed by a /? switch. For example, if you enter the command

> CLS /?

at the DOS prompt, the information shown in figure 28.1 appears on-screen. In MS-DOS, only a one-line description appears for the CLS help; with NDOS, the Help information that appears is more extensive. Notice that the Help dialog box is the same as for other Norton commands (as described in Chapter 1).

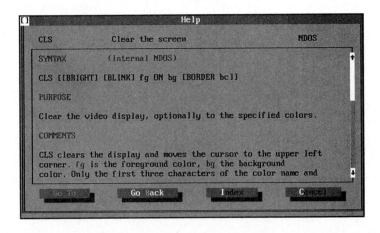

Fig. 28.1

The NDOS Help dialog box for the CLS command.

You also can get help for NDOS commands not found in DOS. For example, if you enter the command

DELAY /?

at the DOS prompt, the information shown in figure 28.2 appears.

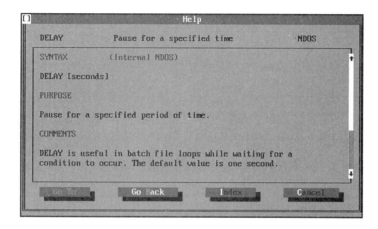

Fig. 28.2

The NDOS
Help dialog box
for the DELAY
command.

A second way to get help is to press the F1 key to bring up a menu of topics. You can then choose to display information about a particular command.

Another way to get help is to enter **HELP** at the DOS prompt. A Help menu similar to the one in figure 28.3 appears. From this menu, you can choose Help topics. See Chapter 1 for more information on the Help system options.

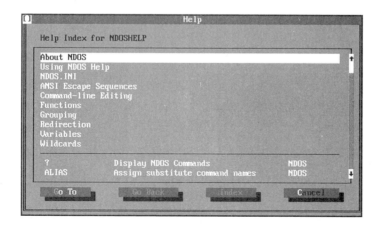

Fig. 28.3

An NDOS Help
menu.

Using Expanded Command-Line Editing Features

The normal DOS command line has limited editing features. If you type a long command and then notice that something is wrong, you must use the Backspace key to erase much of the command, and then retype the command. With NDOS, you get a basketful of editing options, including the capability to move the cursor on the command line and insert, change, and delete characters. Table 28.1 lists the available editing keys.

Table 28.1 Command-Line Editing Keys	
Key(s)	**Description**
←	Moves cursor one space to the left.
→	Moves cursor one space to the right.
↑	Recalls preceding command entered at DOS prompt.
↓	Recalls next command in the Commands list.
Ctrl+←	Moves cursor one word to the left.
Ctrl+→	Moves cursor one word to the right.
Home	Moves cursor to beginning of line.
Ctrl+Home	Deletes characters from beginning of line to character preceding cursor.
End	Moves cursor to end of line.
Ctrl+End	Deletes characters from cursor to end of line.
Ins	Toggles insert and overwrite modes.
Del	Deletes character at cursor.
Backspace	Deletes character to the left of cursor.
CR or LF (carriage return or line feed)	Executes command on command line.
Esc	Erases entire line.
Ctrl+L	Deletes word to the left of cursor.
Ctrl+R or Ctrl+Backspace	Deletes word to the right of cursor.

Key	Description
Ctrl+D	Deletes current command history entry (a previous command entered at the NDOS prompt), erases line, and displays preceding command history entry.
Ctrl+E	Displays last command history entry.
Ctrl+K	Saves current command history list and erases current line.
F1	Begins on-line help procedure.
F3	Repeats preceding command.
F8 or Shift+Tab	Enters on the command line a previously used file name displayed by F9.
F9 or Tab and F10	Looks at the file name or wild-card characters to the left of the cursor and replaces the file name with the first matching file name. Press F9 to replace with the next matching name. Press F10 to append the file name at cursor.
Alt+255	Tells NDOS to ignore a command character. Usually, if you enter an NDOS line-editing command (such as Ctrl+D) on the command line, NDOS performs the function associated with the command. In some cases, however, you may need to include a command character that you do not want to be seen by NDOS as a command on the command line. By pressing Alt+255 and entering the command character (Ctrl+D, for example), NDOS does not respond to Ctrl+D as a command. The computer just beeps when that command character is entered.
	For example, hold down the Alt key and type **255** from the numeric keypad. Release the Alt key and press Ctrl+D. Instead of NDOS recognizing Ctrl+D as a command, the Ctrl+D character (a diamond) appears on the command line.

Suppose that you want to view a file on-screen with the NDOS LIST command, but all you can remember is that the file has the extension TXT. Enter the following command and press the F9 key:

    LIST *.TXT

The first match of *.TXT is placed in the command line instead of *.TXT. If that file is not the one you want, press F9 again; the next matching file name appears. Keep pressing F9 until the file you want appears. Then press Enter to execute the command.

To recall a previous command, press the up-arrow key. The preceding command entered at the DOS prompt appears. You can press Enter to execute the command, or you can edit the command with the editing keys. Pressing the up-arrow key several times recalls commands in sequence so that you can recall a command you entered a number of commands ago. NDOS usually sets aside 1,024 bytes of memory to hold the history commands. You can change this size by using the SET command, described in the "SET" section in this chapter.

Using Multiple Commands on One Line

With DOS, you can enter only one command per line. With NDOS, you can enter several commands on one line. To enter more than one command on a line, separate the commands with a caret (^), which is Shift+6 on most keyboards. For example, to delete all BBB files and then display a directory, enter the following command at the DOS prompt:

    ERASE *.BBB^DIR

Using Conditional Commands

NDOS provides a way to execute a second command on a command line based on the outcome of the first command. When a DOS or NDOS command is executed, an exit code in the computer is set. This code explains the result of the command; it usually reports whether the command succeeds or not. All NDOS commands return an exit code of 0 if successful. If a command is not successful, the exit code is a number other than zero.

If two ampersands (&&) separate two commands, the second command is executed only if the first command returns an exit code of 0. If two commands are separated by vertical bars (||, meaning OR), the second command is executed only if the first command returns a nonzero exit code.

Suppose that you want to copy the files *.* to the disk in drive A. If the copy fails, you want the message ERROR IN COPY! to be displayed. You can have this message appear with the following command:

    COPY *.* A: || ECHO ERROR IN COPY!

Using Batch-to-Memory Files

DOS usually executes the commands in a batch file by reading one line at a time and executing the command in the current line before going to the next command. NDOS provides a faster way to execute the commands in a batch file with the batch-to-memory command. This command is designated by a BTM file rather than a BAT file. The batch-to-memory method of batch file execution is significantly faster than the normal DOS execution.

DOS batch files allow the use of variable names that correspond to information entered on the command line when the batch file name is entered at the DOS prompt. These variable names are %0 to %9. NDOS batch files use 128 variables (%0 to %127) instead of DOS's 10 variables (%0 to %9).

To convert a DOS batch file to a batch-to-memory file, you use the RENAME command to change the BAT extension to a BTM extension. To change a batch file named SETUP.BAT to a BTM file, use the following command:

        RENAME SETUP.BAT SETUP.BTM

You run the BTM file in the same way you run a normal BAT file. For example, entering **SETUP** at the DOS prompt executes the SETUP.BTM batch file.

Using Executable Extensions

With NDOS, you can specify a certain meaning for a file extension; then, when a file with that extension is entered as a command name, the appropriate program is executed. Suppose that you have many TXT files that you often want to read on-screen. You can tell NDOS that if you enter the name of a TXT file at the DOS prompt, that name should be viewed with the LIST command. Use the following command:

        SET .TXT=LIST

If you have a file named MARY.TXT, entering **MARY** at the DOS prompt causes the LIST program to execute and display the file MARY.TXT.

Using I/O Redirection

DOS allows the use of redirection commands to direct the output of a command to a file or device (other than the monitor), or to input information to a command from a source other than the keyboard. NDOS uses these standard DOS redirection commands:

> \>

> \>>

> <

> |

NDOS adds some new options, however. The following redirection commands are available:

Command	Description
< *filename*	Gets input from the specified file instead of the keyboard
> *filename*	Sends the output of a command to the specified file
>> *filename*	Appends the output of a command to the specified file
>! *filename*	Sends the output of a command to the specified file, overriding the NDOS NOCLOBBER setting that usually prevents a file from being replaced
>& *filename*	Sends the output and standard error messages to the specified file
>&> *filename*	Sends only standard error messages to the specified file
>&! *filename*	Sends output and standard error messages to the specified file, overriding the NDOS NOCLOBBER setting that usually prevents a file from being replaced
com1 | com2	Uses the output of the command COM1 as the input for the command COM2
com1 |& com2	Uses the standard output and standard error of COM1 as the input for COM2

The I/O commands help to redirect information into or from a command. To output the results of the DIR command to the printer (LPT1:), for example, use the following command:

DIR > LPT1:

To sort the information in a file called LIST.TXT and to output the results to a file called SORTED.TXT, use the following command:

SORT < LIST.TXT > SORTED.TXT

This command tells DOS to use the LIST.TXT file as input to the SORT command and to place the resulting output in the SORTED.TXT file.

These I/O commands also work with NDOS commands. For example, to send the output of the NDOS MEMORY command to the printer, use this command:

        MEMORY > LPT1:

Using Escape Sequences

NDOS has several character sequences that have special meanings. These sequences include an Escape character (not the ASCII Esc key) followed by a single letter. You produce the Escape character by pressing Ctrl+X, which appears as an up arrow on-screen. (See "SETDOS" later in this chapter to change the Esc key sequence.) The following single letters are available for use with the Escape character:

Escape Command	Description
b	Backspace
e	ASCII Esc character (ASCII 27)
f	Form feed
n	Line feed
r	Carriage return
t	Tab

For example, certain terminals and printers enable you to change characteristics by using Escape characters. If your computer has the ANSI.SYS device driver installed (in the CONFIG.SYS file) and you are using a color monitor, you can set the monitor default color with ANSI Escape sequences. The following command causes your monitor colors to be bright white on blue:

        ECHO ^Xe[1;37;44m

 NOTE The ^X (Ctrl+X) appears as an up arrow on-screen when you type the command.

For more information on ANSI codes, see Que's *Using MS-DOS 6,* Special Edition.

Using Norton NDOS Commands

Norton NDOS provides more than 90 commands, some of which are the same as those you use in DOS. Some commands are similar to DOS commands but have been enhanced with added features. NDOS also supports many commands supported by Norton Batch Enhancer (BE). More than 50 commands are new NDOS commands.

The following commands supported by NDOS are the same as DOS commands:

BREAK	DATE	TIME
CHCP	EXIT	VER
CTTY	GOTO	VERIFY

The following commands are similar to DOS commands but are enhanced under NDOS:

CALL	FOR	REN
CD (CHDIR)	IF	RENAME
CLS	MD (MKDIR)	RMDIR
COPY	PATH	SET
DEL	PAUSE	SHIFT
DIR	PROMPT	TYPE
ECHO	RD	VOL
ERASE	REM	

For a list of Batch Enhancer commands supported by NDOS, see the "BE" section later in this chapter. Chapter 24 describes the Norton Batch Enhancer commands.

The following sections discuss the enhanced DOS and NDOS commands. Many of the Norton NDOS commands have several options. In this book, the following conventions apply to those options:

- In the command syntax, items enclosed in [brackets] are optional.

- For words written in *italic*, substitute the appropriate word. For example, to use the DIR [*switches*] syntax, you type **DIR /W**, **DIR /P**, and so on.

- The [*d:*] option is a designation for the disk drive name, such as drive A:, B:, C:, or D:.

■ The [*filespec*] option is a designation for a file specification. Unless noted, this specification can include a path name. For example, the file specification for a file named MYFILE.TXT in the WP51 directory is \WP51\MYFILE.TXT. You can usually use DOS wild-card characters—the asterisk (*) and question mark (?)—in file specifications. For instance, *.TXT specifies all files with the TXT extension. When *filespec*... appears, you can include multiple file specifications.

■ The [*color*] option refers to a selection of colors. WHITE ON BLUE can be a color designation, for example. Chapter 24 describes how to use colors.

The following descriptions of NDOS commands do not cover all the NDOS options that duplicate those of DOS commands.

?

The NDOS ? command displays a list of available internal NDOS commands. This command has no options; simply enter **?** at the DOS prompt. A list of the NDOS commands appears on-screen.

ALIAS

With the NDOS ALIAS command, you can create a new command from another command. The ALIAS command has the following syntax:

> ALIAS [*switches*] [*name*=[*value*]]

The following switches are available for use with ALIAS:

Switch	Description
/P	Pauses after displaying a screenful of information
/R *filespec*	Tells the command to read an alias list from the specified file

Suppose that you want to create a new command called DD that performs a DIR /W command (wide directory). Enter one of the following commands:

> ALIAS DD DIR/W

> ALIAS DD=DIR/W

The equal sign (=) is optional. In this command, the DD is the new name assigned to the value DIR/W. Now, whenever you enter the command **DD** at the DOS prompt, a DIR /W command executes.

ATTRIB

The NDOS ATTRIB command, similar to the DOS ATTRIB command, displays or changes the attribute settings on files. The DOS version of ATTRIB, available only in DOS 3 or later, does not include the /D switch included in the NDOS version and does not enable you to set hidden or system attributes (available in DOS 5). ATTRIB has the following syntax:

ATTRIB [*switches*] [–|+[AHRS]] *filespec*...

If you enter **ATTRIB** with a path name and no options, the current attribute settings of the files appear.

The following switches may be used with ATTRIB:

Switch	Description
/D	Modifies directory attribute settings and file settings
/S	Modifies the attributes of matching files in subdirectories of the specified directory
/Q	Quiet mode; does not display file names whose attributes are being changed

The following options are available for use with the ATTRIB command. Here the vertical bar (|) means *or*. Thus, for the A option, you can place a plus or minus sign in front of the A (+A or –A).

Option	Description
[+|–]A	Sets/clears the archive attribute
[+|–]H	Sets/clears the hidden file attribute
[+|–]R	Sets/clears the read-only attribute
[+|–]S	Sets/clears the system file attribute

For each option, a plus sign (+) sets the attribute on, and a minus sign (–) sets it off. For example, the following command sets the attribute for the file named SECRET.FIL to read-only and hidden:

ATTRIB +RH SECRET.FIL

This command is similar in function to the Norton Utilities File Find and File Attributes commands, which are described in Chapters 25 and 9.

BE

The NDOS BE (Batch Enhancer) commands are similar to the BE commands in Norton Utilities (described in Chapter 24). The following BE commands are supported in NDOS:

ASK	MONTHDAY	SHIFTSTATE
BEEP	PRINTCHAR	TRIGGER
BOX	REBOOT	WEEKDAY
CLS	ROWCOL	WINDOW
DELAY	SA	

BEEP

The NDOS BEEP command, used to beep the computer's speaker, is similar to the BE BEEP command described in Chapter 24. However, this command is an internal NDOS command with a slightly different use. BEEP has the following format:

BEEP [*frequency duration*]

The *frequency* is the value in hertz (Hz). For example, 440 is the rate of A. The *duration* is the length of time for the sound in 1/18-second increments. To sound an A for a half second, for example, use this command:

BEEP 440 9

BREAK

The NDOS BREAK command, similar to the DOS BREAK command, enables, disables, or displays the Break key setting (Ctrl+Break or Ctrl+C). You use the following syntax:

BREAK [ON | OFF]

The OFF option tells DOS to check for a Ctrl+Break (or Ctrl+C) when information is entered into the computer through the keyboard, screen, serial port, or printer. The ON option tells DOS to check for a Ctrl+Break (or Ctrl+C) during any DOS operation. The ON option makes breaking out of a program easier. If the command doesn't include either option, the current status of BREAK is displayed.

CALL

The NDOS CALL command enables you to call one batch file from another batch file. CALL has the following syntax:

CALL *filespec*

The *filespec* parameter represents the name of a batch file. NDOS supports calling batch files within up to eight nested files. For example, if you are within one batch file, you enter the following command to call another batch file named SECOND:

CALL SECOND

After the SECOND batch file finishes, control returns to the original batch file.

CANCEL

The NDOS CANCEL command ends a batch file. You use the following command:

CANCEL

No options are available. CANCEL enables you to end a batch file within any nested (called) batch file and return to DOS. For more information, see the "CALL" and "QUIT" sections in this chapter.

CD or CHDIR

You use the NDOS CD or CHDIR command (like the DOS CD or CHDIR command) to change directories. The NDOS version also displays the name of the current directory. This command has the following syntax:

CD [*d*:][*path*]

The *d*: designation is the name of the disk drive to access, and *path* is the name of the directory. CD changes to the directory designated by the path. The drive is not changed. Using CD with no options causes the command to display the name of the current directory. As in DOS, entering the following command makes the root directory the default:

CD \

Entering the following command changes to the parent directory, making it the current directory:

CD..

NDOS adds a new feature. Entering the following command changes to the directory one higher than the parent directory:

CD...

Thus, if you are in the directory \MYDIR\YOURDIR\OURDIR and enter CD..., you change to the \MYDIR directory.

CDD

The NDOS CDD command is similar to the CD command except that NDOS CDD also changes the default drive and directory. CDD has the following syntax:

CDD [*d:*][*path*]

If you are in the drive and directory C:\MYDIR, you can enter the following command:

CDD D:\YOURDIR

This command changes the default drive to drive D and the default directory to \YOURDIR. Otherwise, CDD operates just like the NDOS CD command.

CHCP

Like the DOS CHCP command, the NDOS CHCP command displays or changes the current system code page. A *system code page* controls which language character set DOS uses. The CHCP command requires that you load the COUNTRY.SYS information file in the CONFIG.SYS file, run the DOS NLSFUNC (National Language Support) command, and specify code pages with the DOS MODE *device* CODEPAGE PREPARE command. (See your DOS manual for information on how to use the NLSFUNC and MODE commands.) CHCP has the following syntax:

CHCP [*nnn*]

Here *nnn* is the number of the code page to set. Consult your current DOS manual for a list of the code pages supported by your version of DOS. If you issue the CHCP command without options, the current code page is displayed.

CLS

The NDOS CLS command is similar to the DOS CLS command, but NDOS CLS also contains the capability to change your monitor's colors. This command has the following syntax:

CLS [[BRIGHT] [BLINK] *foreground* ON *background*]

Entering CLS with no options clears the screen. The colors available for *foreground* and *background* are BLACK, BLUE, YELLOW, GREEN, RED, MAGENTA, CYAN, YELLOW, and WHITE. For example, to clear the screen and switch to a bright white foreground with a blue background, use the following command:

CLS BRIGHT WHITE ON BLUE

The BLINK option makes the entire screen blink in the selected colors. You can use this option to create, for example, an eye-catching warning screen in a batch file.

COLOR

The NDOS COLOR command sets the foreground and background colors for your monitor without clearing the screen as CLS does. You use the following syntax:

COLOR [BRIGHT] [BLINK] *foreground* ON *background*

The colors available for *foreground* and *background* are BLACK, BLUE, YELLOW, GREEN, RED, MAGENTA, CYAN, YELLOW, and WHITE. To set your monitor to use white letters on a blue background, for example, use this command:

COLOR WHITE ON BLUE

For more information, see the "SCRPUT" section later in this chapter.

COPY

Similar to the DOS COPY command, the NDOS COPY command enables you to use a list of files to copy. Here is the syntax for the COPY command (the optional plus sign [+] concatenates the files, as in a DOS command):

COPY [*switches*] *filespec* [+]...[/A] [/B] *filespec* [/A] [/B]

The following switches are available for use with COPY:

Switch	Description
/A	Treats the file as ASCII text (default).
/B	Treats the file as binary text.
/M (Modified)	Copies only files with the archive bit set. The archive bit (the archive attribute discussed in Chapter 9) is retained on the copy.
/P	Prompts you to confirm each copy.
/Q (Quiet)	Suppresses the display of the names of files being copied.
/R (Replace)	Prompts you before overwriting an existing file.
/U (Update)	Copies only files that are newer than the matching target files.
/V	Verifies that copy is OK.
/C	Copies changed files only.
/H	Copies hidden files only.
/N	Performs all actions as if the copy were performed, but does not actually do the copy. You can use this switch to see what the results of the command would be before actually performing it.
/S	Copies subdirectory trees.

You use the /A, /B, and /V switches and the + key with the NDOS COPY command as you would use them with DOS COPY. In the NDOS version of COPY, you can copy more than one file to a destination. To copy the files *.WK1 and *.DBF to the disk in drive A, use the following command:

COPY *.WK1 *.DBF A:

To copy all files from drive A to drive C and to avoid overwriting any existing files on drive C that have the same name on both drives, use this command:

COPY /R A:*.* C:

You are prompted to confirm the copy before any file from drive A overwrites a file with the same name on drive C. For more information, see the "MOVE" section later in this chapter.

CTTY

The NDOS CTTY command, which is similar to DOS CTTY, changes the default I/O console device. This device is usually the keyboard (called the console). CTTY has the following syntax:

CTTY *device*

The possible devices to use include AUX, COM1, COM2, COM3, COM4, and CON (console). To be used by NDOS, the device must support all standard DOS I/O functions, including DOS internal commands (with the exception of the DRAWBOX, DRAWHLINE, LIST, SCREEN, SCRPUT, and SELECT commands, as well as all the BE commands). To change the CTTY device to a device connected to the first COM port, use the following command:

CTTY COM1:

Now the device (usually a terminal) on the COM1 port assumes control of all command input and output for your system.

To change back to the standard use of the keyboard and display, use this command:

CTTY CON:

DATE

The NDOS DATE command is similar to the DOS DATE command. The DATE command has the following syntax:

DATE [*mm-dd-yy*]

If you issue the DATE command with no option, you are prompted to enter a new date.

DEL and ERASE

The NDOS DEL and ERASE commands are similar to the DOS DEL and ERASE commands. However, with the NDOS versions, you can specify a list of files to delete. DEL and ERASE are the same command. You use one of the following forms:

DEL [*switches*] *filespec*...

ERASE [*switches*] *filespec*...

These switches are available for use with DEL and ERASE:

Switch	Description
/P	Prompts for a confirmation before deleting a file.
/Q (Quiet)	Suppresses the display of file names being deleted.
/Y (Yes)	Assumes that all responses are yes, including responses to the command DEL *.* or ERASE *.*.
/Z (Zap)	Deletes hidden, system, and read-only files (overrides the NDOS EXCEPT command; see "EXCEPT" later in this chapter).
/N	Performs all actions as if the deletion were performed, but doesn't actually do the deletion. You can use this switch to see what the results of the command would be before actually performing it.

To erase the files that match the file specifications *.WK1 and *.DBF, use one of the following commands:

    ERASE *.WK1 *.DBF

    DEL *.WK1 *.DBF

To erase files but be prompted before each deletion, use one of these commands:

    ERASE /P *.WK1 *.DBF

    DEL /P *.WK1 *.DBF

DELAY

The NDOS DELAY command causes the computer to pause for a few seconds before resuming operation. This command is most often used in a batch file. DELAY has the following syntax:

    DELAY [*seconds*]

To cause the computer to wait five seconds before resuming operation, use this command:

    DELAY 5

The default is one second.

DESCRIBE

The NDOS DESCRIBE command creates, modifies, or deletes file and subdirectory descriptions. With the DESCRIBE command, you can write a description for a file or subdirectory so that when you issue a DIR command, the description appears on-screen. DESCRIBE has the following syntax:

DESCRIBE *filespec* ["*description*"]

To add a description to the file MARY.TXT, use the following command:

DESCRIBE MARY.TXT "Mary had a little lamb poem."

When you perform a DIR command, the description appears next to the file name in the directory listing. If you enter the DESCRIBE command with a file name but no description, you are prompted to enter a description. To delete a description, enter a blank description.

To delete the description for MARY.TXT, enter the following command:

DESCRIBE MARY.TXT ""

DIR

Like the DOS DIR command, the NDOS DIR command displays file information. Unlike DOS's DIR command, however, NDOS DIR displays any descriptions you have defined for file names. With NDOS DIR, you can place more than one file specification on the command line. File names appear in lowercase, and directory names appear in uppercase, making it easier to tell them apart at a glance. The NDOS DIR command has the following syntax:

DIR [/A:[*attributes*]] [/O[:][*sortorder*]] [*switches*] [*filespec*]

When you use the /A option, DIR displays only those files that have the requested attribute or attributes set (or are not part of a particular set if a minus sign precedes the attribute name).

The following attributes are available for use with DIR:

Attribute	Description
h	Hidden file
r	Read-only file
s	System file

Attribute	Description
d	Directory
a	Archived file

To list the names of all the read-only files, use this command:

DIR /A:r

To list all files that are *not* archived, use this command:

DIR /A:–a

With the following *sortorder* options, you can sort the directory list. Placing a minus sign (–) before a sort order causes the sort to be in descending order rather than ascending order (the default).

Option	Sort Order
d	Date and time
e	File extension
i	NDOS file description
n	Name
s	Size
g	Directories first in the list (default)
u	Unsorted (same as normal DOS DIR)

To list the files in name and extension order, use this command:

DIR /O:ne

Other switches can help you customize the way the DIR command lists the files. The following switches may be used:

Switch	Description
/1	Displays files in a single-column list
/2	Displays files in a double-column list
/4	Displays files in a four-column list
/A	Displays files with a particular attribute
/B	Suppresses the header line and summary information

continues

Switch	Description
/C	Displays compression specifications for file names
/E	Displays file names in uppercase
/F	Displays the full path for each file name
/J	Justifies file names as in the DOS DIR command
/K	Suppresses the display of the volume label and path name information
/L	Displays file names in lowercase
/M	Omits the display of total bytes
/N	Resets the DIR command to its default values
/O:n	Displays files in a requested sort order, where n is one of the sort order options
/P	Pauses after each screen of information is displayed
/S	Displays files in the directory and all subdirectories
/T	Displays only the file attributes
/U	Displays only the summary information
/V	Displays the file names sorted vertically rather than horizontally (use with the /2, /4, or /W option)
/W	Displays the files names in wide five-column mode (same as DOS /W)

To display a directory of files with the WK1 extension from the MYFILE directory and all its subdirectories, use this command:

DIR /S \MYFILE*.WK1

If you want the DIR command to display files in a certain way all the time, you can set the defaults for the command in your AUTOEXEC.BAT file. To set the command always to display files in sorted order by name (/O:n), use the following command (n represents one of the sort order options):

SET DIRCMD=/O:n

The DIRCMD is a DOS environment variable that enables you to preset DIR command parameters and switches. Refer to your DOS documentation for more information on DIRCMD.

DIRS

The NDOS DIRS command displays the current directory stack. The PUSHD and POPD commands, however, create and recall a directory stack. Suppose that you are in the root directory. When you enter the PUSHD C:\MYDIR command, the root directory (C:\) is placed in the directory stack, and your default directory is changed to \MYDIR. Then you enter the command PUSHD C:\TMP; the C\MYDIR directory is placed in the stack, and you are changed to the \TMP directory. If you then enter the command DIRS, the following listing is displayed:

```
C:\MYDIR
C:\
```

This listing means that the first (or top) directory in the stack is C:\MYDIR and that the previous directory is C:\ (root). For more information, see the "POPD" and "PUSHD" sections in this chapter.

DRAWBOX

The NDOS DRAWBOX command draws a box on-screen. This command is similar to the Norton BE BOX command. However, some differences exist. If you draw overlapping boxes by using DRAWBOX, the command detects other boxes on-screen and draws appropriate connecting characters when possible. DRAWBOX also has a Fill option, which is not available in BE BOX. (BE BOX is discussed in Chapter 24.) DRAWBOX has this syntax:

DRAWBOX *ulrow ulcol lrrow lrcol style* [BRIGHT] [BLINK]
foreground ON *background* [FILL *backgroundfill*] [SHADOW]

The *ulrow* variable specifies the position of the upper-left row of the box. Similarly, the *ulcol*, *lrrow*, and *lrcol* variables specify the upper-left column, lower-right row, and lower-right column. On a standard 25-line-by-80-row screen, the valid rows are 0 to 24, and the valid columns are 0 to 79. The BRIGHT option displays the box in a bright (high-intensity) version of the color, and BLINK causes the box to blink on-screen. The SHADOW option causes the box to be displayed with a shadow.

The *style* variable refers to the style of box to be drawn. You can choose from the following style options:

Option	Description
0	Borderless
1	Single line

continues

Option	Description
2	Double line
3	Single lines on the top and bottom, and double lines on the sides
4	Double lines on the top and bottom, and single lines on the sides

The *foreground*, *background*, and *backgroundfill* variables are colors. You can choose from the options BLACK, BLUE, GREEN, RED, MAGENTA, CYAN, YELLOW, and WHITE.

To draw a single-line box with a bright white foreground and a red background, use this command:

DRAWBOX 10 10 20 20 1 BRIGHT WHITE ON RED

DRAWHLINE

With the NDOS DRAWHLINE command, you can draw a horizontal line on-screen. You use the following syntax:

DRAWHLINE *row col len style* [BRIGHT] [BLINK] *foreground* ON *background*

The *row* and *col* variables specify where the line begins on-screen. The *len* variable specifies the length, and *style* refers to style 1 (single line) or style 2 (double line). The *foreground* and *background* colors are BLACK, BLUE, GREEN, RED, MAGENTA, CYAN, YELLOW, and WHITE. On a standard 25-line-by-80-row screen, the valid rows are 0 to 24, and the valid columns are 0 to 79. The BRIGHT option displays the line in a bright (high-intensity) version of the color, and BLINK causes the line to blink on-screen.

To draw a single white line with a blue background across the middle of the screen, use this command:

DRAWHLINE 10 0 79 1 WHITE ON BLUE

DRAWVLINE

The NDOS DRAWVLINE command is similar to the DRAWHLINE command except that DRAWVLINE draws a vertical line on-screen. DRAWVLINE has the following syntax:

DRAWVLINE *row col len style* [BRIGHT] [BLINK] *foreground* ON *background*

To draw a single white line with a magenta background down the middle of the screen, use the following command:

DRAWVLINE 12 0 24 1 WHITE ON MAGENTA

ECHO

The NDOS ECHO command is similar to the DOS ECHO command. The main advantage is that NDOS ECHO enables you to use the NDOS redirection symbols (see the section "Using I/O Redirection" earlier in this chapter) and to include multiple commands per line (see the earlier section "Using Multiple Commands on One Line"). The NDOS ECHO command has the following syntax:

ECHO [ON | OFF | *message*]

In NDOS, the default is ECHO ON for batch files and ECHO OFF for keyboard commands. If you enter ECHO ON at the keyboard, NDOS displays fully parsed and expanded commands (including aliases and variables) before the command is executed. If no arguments are included, ECHO displays its current state (OFF or ON).

For example, look at the following three lines in a batch file:

ECHO OFF
REM This is a comment—not displayed
ECHO This is displayed

This file causes ECHO to be turned off (first line), which causes the REM (remark) *not* to be echoed (second line). The third line *is* displayed on-screen. When entering the ECHO OFF or ECHO ON command, you may precede the command with the *at* symbol (@) to suppress the ECHO command from being displayed on-screen. For example, this command is *not* displayed on-screen:

@ECHO OFF

The following command is displayed:

ECHO OFF

ECHOS

The NDOS ECHOS command is similar to the ECHO command except that when a message is displayed, the cursor is not automatically sent to the next line (no carriage return is performed). This command enables you to echo another message that begins where the previous message left off.

ENDLOCAL

The NDOS ENDLOCAL command restores the computer to a previously saved (with a SETLOCAL command) disk drive, directory, environment variable, or alias. ENDLOCAL, which has no options, is useful in a batch file when you temporarily change directories (using the CD command) or disk drives to execute a procedure, and you then want to change back to your current settings.

The following example uses the SETLOCAL command to save your current settings. Some changes are made, and then the previous settings are restored by the ENDLOCAL command:

```
SETLOCAL
C:
CD \MYDIR
SET PATH = C:\KWIKSTAT
KS
ENDLOCAL
```

In this example, suppose that your current drive is A and your directory is \. The batch file changes to drive C and the \MYDIR directory, and then executes the SET and KS commands. At this point, if the batch file ended, your current drive and directory would be C:\MYDIR. However, the ENDLOCAL command automatically switches you back to your original state (captured by the previous SETLOCAL command). Thus, your current drive and directory are set back to A:\. See the "SETLOCAL" section for more information.

ESET

The NDOS ESET command edits environment variables and aliases. Environment variables are used to customize how DOS operates. Aliases are substitute names for commands (see the "ALIAS" section in this chapter). ESET has the following syntax:

ESET [*switches*] *varname*

The following switches are available for use with ESET:

Switch	Description
/A	Assumes that the *varname* is an alias, which allows you to edit an alias that has the same name as an environment variable
/M	Edits an environment variable in the master environment

You can list more than one environment variable in the *varname* list; separate the names with a blank space.

To edit the file search path, for example, enter this command:

ESET PATH

The current path is displayed on-screen. Then you can use the NDOS command-line editing keys to edit the path (refer to table 28.1).

EXCEPT

The NDOS EXCEPT command enables you to perform a command and specify the files that should be excluded from that command. EXCEPT has the following syntax:

EXCEPT (*filespec...*) *command*

The following DOS command displays all files with a WK1 extension:

DIR *.WK1

The following command displays all files *except* the ones with the WK1 extension:

EXCEPT (*.WK1) DIR

EXCEPT recognizes all NDOS internal commands, aliases, external commands (including DOS external commands), and batch files. EXCEPT does not work with the DEL or ERASE command if you use the /Z switch on those commands.

EXIT

You use the NDOS EXIT command to return from a secondary command processor. The EXIT command has this syntax:

EXIT [*n*]

Here *n* is an errorlevel value you have selected. This value returns you to the calling command processor. If *n* is not included, the errorlevel is the one returned by the last external program. EXIT is usually used when a program "shells" temporarily to DOS to enable you to enter a DOS command. When you enter **EXIT** at the DOS prompt, you are returned to the original program. If you began NDOS from the DOS command line, EXIT ends NDOS, and you return to the DOS prompt. For information about how to use errorlevel values, see Chapter 24 on Batch Enhancer.

You choose the errorlevel you want. Otherwise, for some Norton commands, the /DEBUG option displays the errorlevel (exit code) returned. In general, 0 means that the program exited with no problems, and NOT 0 usually means that the program ended in error. See the discussion of the BE ASK command in Chapter 24 for more information on using an errorlevel.

FOR

The NDOS FOR command, like the DOS FOR command, repeats several times a command defined by a set of files. You use the following syntax:

FOR [/A[[:] [–]rhsda]] %*variable* IN (*set*) [DO] *command*

FOR repeats the command and replaces the variable in the command with the information in *set*. Commands recognized by the NDOS FOR command are internal DOS commands or aliases, external commands, or batch files. The /A switch followed by a list of attribute letters causes the command to retrieve only those files that match the attribute list. Here are the meanings of the attributes:

Attribute	Description
h	Hidden file
r	Read-only file
s	System file
d	Directory
a	Archived file

The colon [:] after the /A is optional (for appearance only). For example, the switch /A:rh retrieves only files that have the read-only and hidden switches set. If a minus sign appears before the attribute list (as in /A:–rh), the FOR command excludes those files that match the attribute list.

The DOS FOR command requires the variable name to be only one character in length (such as A), but NDOS allows variable names of up to 80 characters (for example, *%variablename*). The DO is optional in NDOS but is required in the DOS command.

Look at the following example:

FOR %a IN (*.DOC *.TXT) DO LP %a

This command causes all DOC files to be printed with the LP command followed by all TXT files. In other words, this command translates into the following two commands:

LP *.DOC

LP *.TXT

FREE

The NDOS FREE command displays the total disk space available, total bytes used, and total bytes free on disk. FREE has the following syntax:

FREE [*d:*]...

To get this information for drives A and C, for example, enter this command:

FREE A: C:

If you do not specify a drive, information for the default drive is displayed.

GLOBAL

The NDOS GLOBAL command executes a command in the current directory and its subdirectories. GLOBAL has the following syntax:

GLOBAL [*switches*] *command*

The following switches are available for use with GLOBAL:

Switch	Description
/H	Looks for hidden directories.
/I	Ignores nonzero exit codes. GLOBAL usually ends if a nonzero exit code is returned.
/P	Prompts for excution of the command in each directory.
/Q	Suppresses the display of each directory name.

To erase all BK files in the TEXT directory (assuming that is the current default directory) and all its subdirectories, use this command:

GLOBAL ERASE *.BK

GOSUB

The NDOS GOSUB command calls a subroutine in a batch file. A *subroutine* in a batch file is a series of commands that begins with a label and ends with the command RETURN. GOSUB has the following syntax:

GOSUB *label*

Suppose that you have a subroutine in your batch file with the following commands:

:MYSUB
ERASE *.BAK
RETURN

To execute this subroutine, use the following command:

GOSUB MYSUB

The command in the subroutine executes, and the flow of the batch file returns to the line following the GOSUB command.

GOTO

Like the DOS GOTO command, the NDOS GOTO command branches the flow of a batch file to a specified label. This command has the following syntax:

GOTO [/I] *label*

In this line, *label* is a standard DOS batch file label, which must begin with a colon (:) on the label line (for example, :ENDBATCH). However, when you reference the label in the GOTO command line, do not include the colon in the label name. This practice is standard for referencing labels in DOS.

For example, the following command transfers control of the batch file to the label :ENDBATCH in the batch file:

GOTO ENDBATCH

GOTO is often used with the IF command. Suppose that you want to check for the existence of a file and then go to a label depending on whether that file exists. The command

IF EXIST EDIT.EXE GOTO ITSTHERE

causes the flow of the batch file to go to the label :ITSTHERE if the file EDIT.EXE is on disk. If EDIT.EXE does not exist, the flow of the batch file continues with the command following the IF command.

You may use the GOTO statement to exit an IFF block (see the "IF" and "IFF" sections in this chapter). Note that if you use a GOTO within an IFF block, the statement must branch entirely outside the block. The /I switch tells GOTO not to cancel any IIF statements.

HELP

The NDOS HELP command is similar to the DOS (Versions 5 and 6) HELP command. HELP has the following syntax:

HELP [*topic*] [*switches*]

Using HELP with no switches displays a list of topics. From this list, you can pick a specific topic for which help is available.

You can use these switches with the HELP command:

Switch	Description
/BW	Displays information in black and white
/HERC	Displays information using Hercules Graphics
/M	Displays information in monochrome display mode
/G0	Disables the graphic mouse pointer and graphics symbols (for EGA or VGA monitors)
/G1	Disables the graphic mouse pointer only (for EGA and VGA monitors)
/G2	Disables the use of graphic dialog boxes
/LCD	Displays information using colors appropriate for an LCD (usually a laptop) monitor

To display help on the command HISTORY in black-and-white mode, for example, enter the following command:

HELP HISTORY /BW

Figure 28.4 illustrates the Help dialog box for the HISTORY command. From this dialog box, you can choose Go **T**o to go to the next topic (commands are in alphabetical order), Go **B**ack to go to the preceding topic, **Index** to display a list of topics, or **Cancel** to end Help and return to the DOS prompt. You can also use the mouse pointer to choose these options.

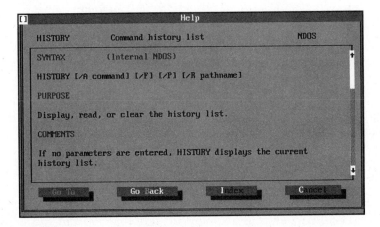

HISTORY

The NDOS HISTORY command displays, clears, or reads a list of previously entered commands. HISTORY has the following syntax:

HISTORY [*switches*]

These switches are available for use with HISTORY:

Switch	Description
/A	Adds a command to the history list
/F (Frees)	Clears the history list
/P	Tells the command to pause after displaying a screenful of information
/R *filespec*	Tells the command to load a command history from the file specified by *filespec*

To save the output of the HISTORY command to a file, use the redirection option (>). To save the current history information to a file named HISTORY.TXT, enter this command:

HISTORY > HISTORY.TXT

Using the HISTORY command with no options causes the command to display the current contents of the history list. Each time you enter a command at the DOS prompt, that command is added to the history list. When the history list gets full (the SETDOS command specifies its size), older commands are dropped to make room for new commands.

IF

The NDOS IF command, like the DOS IF command, is used in batch processing to transfer the flow of the batch file to a label. This transfer depends on a condition. The list of conditions recognized by the NDOS IF command is more extensive than the conditions recognized by the DOS IF command. The NDOS IF command has the following syntax:

IF [NOT] *condition command*

NDOS evaluates the *condition*. If the *condition* is true, NDOS executes the *command*. If the NOT option is used, the *command* is executed only if the *condition* is false. The *condition* can use one of the following forms:

Condition	Description
string1==*string2* or *string1* EQ *string2*	True if *string1* is equal to *string2*
string1 NE *string2*	True if *string1* is not equal to *string2*
string1 LT *string2*	True if *string1* is less than *string2*
string1 LE *string2*	True if *string1* is less than or equal to *string2*
string1 GT *string2*	True if *string1* is greater than *string2*
string1 GE *string2*	True if *string1* is greater than or equal to *string2*
ERRORLEVEL [*condition*] *n*	Errorlevel tested to the number *n* (for *condition*, use ==, EQ, and so on)
EXIST *filespec*	True if file names by *filespec* are found on disk
ISALIAS *aliasname*	True if the specified name is an alias
ISDIR *dirname*	True if the directory named exists

NOTE   The designation *string* refers to a group of characters.

When using EQ, NE, LT, LE, GT, and GE comparisons, IF performs a numeric comparison if both strings begin with numeric digits. The comparison otherwise is an ASCII comparison (case differences are ignored). For example, the following test performs a DIR command because ALAN is less than BAKER:

    IF "ALAN" LE "BAKER" DIR

(The letter A appears before B in the alphabet.) A variable is usually used in an IF statement of this sort. If the command line variable %1 is to be compared with BAKER, for example, use this command:

    IF %1 LE "BAKER" DIR

You can also use the IF statement with the NDOS INPUT command, which enables you to input a variable. The following example inputs the name of a directory to print:

    :NEXTDIR
    INPUT "Enter directory to print or END to End:" %%CHOICE
    IF %%CHOICE == "END" THEN GOTO THATSALL
    DIR %%CHOICE >LPT1:
    GOTO NEXTDIR
    :THATSALL

If you enter END, the procedure stops. Otherwise, the DIR command is performed, and the output is sent to the printer (LPT1:).

See also the "INPUT" section in this chapter.

IFF

The NDOS IFF command, although similar to the IF command, adds an ELSE clause. You use the following syntax:

    IFF [NOT] *condition1* THEN *command1* ELSE [IFF[NOT]]
    condition2 THEN *command2* ENDIFF

The conditions are the same as those used in the IF command. NDOS tests *condition1*. If *condition1* is true, *command1* is executed. If *condition1* is false, the ELSE *condition2* is checked. If the ELSE *condition2* is true, *command2* is executed. Consider the following example:

    IFF EXIST KS.EXE THEN ^ GOTO ISTHERE ^ ELSE GOTO
    NOTTHERE
    :ISTHERE
    ...*commands*
    :NOTTHERE
    ...*commands*

This example tests to see whether the file KS.EXE exists. If the file exists, the flow of the batch file is sent to the label :ISTHERE. If the file KS.EXE does not exist, the flow of the batch file is sent to the label :NOTTHERE.

INKEY

The NDOS INKEY command displays a prompt and waits for single-keystroke input from the user. Then you can assign this input to a variable name. INKEY has the following syntax:

INKEY [/K"..." /W*n*] [*text*] %%*varname*

The /K"..." option enables you to specify a list of allowable keystrokes. For example, /K"ABCD" causes the command to recognize only the keystroke A, B, C, or D. The /W*n* switch causes a wait of *n* seconds for an input to be entered. If no keystroke is entered in the specified time, the value of %%*varname* is unchanged. If you use /W0, the buffer is checked immediately for an entry and returns that value to the %%*varname* if a keystroke exists.

The *text* option enables you to display a message on-screen.

The %%*varname* parameter is a variable name where the input is stored. The double percent sign (%%) tells NDOS that this name is a variable name. (Do not confuse %%*varname* with %*varname*.) Keystrokes are stored as ASCII values. The uppercase letter A, for example, is 65. Keystrokes that are extended characters are stored in the variable as an *at* symbol (@) plus a number. The Home key, for example, is @71.

You can use %%*varname* in IF statements. Consider the following example:

INKEY Enter a drive name: %%CHOICE
IF %%CHOICE == "C" THEN GOTO HARDDRIVE
...*batch file code continues*...
:HARDDRIVE

In this case, the name of a directory (a single character) is requested. If the value of %%CHOICE is equal to C, the batch file branches to the label :HARDDRIVE.

INPUT

The NDOS INPUT command enables you to enter a variable. You use the following syntax:

INPUT [/W*n*] [*text*] %%*varname*

The /W*n* switch causes a wait of *n* seconds for an input to be entered. If no keystroke is entered in the specified time, the value of %%*varname* is unchanged. If you use /W0, the buffer is checked immediately for an entry and returns that value to the %%*varname* if a keystroke exists.

The *text* option enables you to display a message on-screen. The %%*varname* parameter is a variable where the input is stored. You can also use INPUT with an IF command. For more information, see the "IF" section in this chapter.

KEYSTACK

You use the NDOS KEYSTACK command to send keystrokes to a program from a batch file. KEYSTACK has the following syntax:

KEYSTACK ["*text*"] [*nn*] [*key*] [@*nn*] [!] [/W*n*]

The *text* option is input that is sent as characters to the program. The *nn* values are ASCII codes. For example, 65 sends an uppercase A to the program. The @*nn* values are extended codes. The optional ! clears all pending keystrokes in the KEYSTACK buffer and the keyboard buffer. The optional /W*n* switch specifies an *n*-second pause while waiting for a response.

Suppose that you want to create a batch file that changes one string to another string by using the EDLIN editor. (EDLIN is an editor provided with DOS. See your DOS manual for more information on EDLIN.) To create such a file (called CHANGE.BAT), you use the following commands:

KEYSTACK "1,999R%2" @64 "%3" 13 "Exit" 13
EDLIN %1

Suppose that you then want to change all occurrences (from line 1 to line 999) of the word *lamb* to *sheep* in the ASCII text file MARY.TXT. Use this command:

CHANGE MARY.TXT lamb sheep

The KEYSTACK command in the batch file then enters the following command (in EDLIN):

> 1,999RlambF6sheepCR
> ExitCR

F6 is the F6 function key, and CR is the Enter key (carriage return). Notice that the KEYSTACK is defined before the application (EDLIN, in this case) is called. For keystack to work, you must have the device driver KEYSTACK.SYS defined in your CONFIG.SYS file.

LIST

The NDOS LIST command displays a file with forward and backward scrolling. LIST has the following syntax:

> LIST [*switches*] [*filespec*]...

The following switches are available for use with LIST:

Switch	Description
/H	Strips the high bit from each character before displaying it. This process is necessary for displaying some non-ASCII files created by some word processors.
/S	Reads from the standard input rather than from a file. With this switch, you can read the output from commands, such as DIR, as a list file.
/W	Wraps the text at the right margin.

When viewing a file, you can scroll by using the following keys:

Command	Description
Home	Displays first page of the file
End	Displays last page of the file
Esc	Exits current file and goes to the next file in the file specification list (if one exists)
Ctrl+C	Quits list
↑	Scrolls up 1 line
↓	Scrolls down 1 line

continues

Command	Description
←	Scrolls left 8 columns
→	Scrolls right 8 columns
Ctrl+←	Scrolls left 40 columns
Ctrl+→	Scrolls right 40 columns
F1	Calls on-line help
F	Prompts and searches for a string
N	Finds the next matching string
P	Prints file to LPT1

To examine a file called KS.DOC, enter the following command:

LIST KS.DOC

To redirect the output of the DIR command to a list file, use this command:

DIR | LIST /S

LOADBTM

The NDOS LOADBTM command is used in batch files to switch a running batch file from or to the BTM (batch-to-memory) mode. Batch files run faster in BTM mode because all commands are read at once; normal batch files, however, read a command from disk when needed. LOADBTM has this syntax:

LOADBTM [ON | OFF]

For example, placing the command

LOADBTM ON

in your batch file causes the contents of the batch file to be read into memory and executed. The following lines are a small batch file. The LOADBTM command causes the commands beginning with COPY to be read into memory and executed:

```
REM switch to BTM mode
LOADBTM ON
COPY *.* A:
DIR A:
```

LOADBTM ON tells NDOS to read the batch file lines into memory to the end of the batch file or until a LOADBTM OFF command appears.

LOADHIGH or LH

Like the DOS LOADHIGH or LH command, the NDOS LOADHIGH or LH command causes a program to be loaded into high DOS memory. This command can give you more conventional memory, enabling you to run larger programs on your computer. You must use DOS 5 or later to use this command; you must also be operating on a 286 (or higher) system with suitable software and have the command DOS=UMB in your CONFIG.SYS file.

Note the following forms of the LOADHIGH command:

LOADHIGH [*filespec*]...

LH [*filespec*]...

To load the program MYPROG.COM into high memory, use this command:

LOADHIGH MYPROG.COM

If not enough memory is available in the 640K or 1M range to load the program, the program is loaded into conventional memory.

LOG

You use the NDOS LOG command to save a log of the commands entered at the DOS prompt. LOG has the following syntax:

LOG [/W *filespec*|ON|OFF|*text*]

The /W switch causes the command to be stored in the file specified by *filespec*. The ON option tells the command to begin logging commands; OFF stops the saving of commands. The *text* option enables you to insert a header or other text into the log file. Using LOG with no options causes the command to report whether the log is on or off. To save a command to a file named MYLOG.TXT, use this command:

LOG /W C:\MYLOG.TXT

MD or MKDIR

The NDOS MD or MKDIR command operates the same as the DOS MD or MKDIR command. With the NDOS version, however, you can have multiple commands per line. You use the following syntax:

MD [*drive*]*path*...

To create a subdirectory called WP51 from the root directory, for example, use this command:

MD /WP51

To create two directories at once (\WP51 and \KS), use this command:

MD \WP51^MD \KS

Remember that the caret (^) is a separator between two commands.

MEMORY

The NDOS MEMORY command, like DOS MEMORY, displays the amount of memory available, including total RAM, number of bytes free, total EMS memory and bytes free, XMS memory, size of the total environment and bytes free, size of the alias space and bytes free, and size of the history buffer. No options are available.

MOVE

The NDOS MOVE command moves files to other directories or drives. MOVE has the following syntax (similar to the COPY command syntax):

MOVE [*switches*] *filespec... filespec*

The following switches may be used with COPY:

Switch	Description
/C	Moves changed files
/D	Requires a directory as the target *filespec*
/H	Moves hidden files
/N	Tests and displays the results of the move without making the changes
/P	Prompts for confirmation before each move
/Q	Turns off the display of file names as they are moved
/R	Prompts for confirmation before each move that replaces an existing file
/S	Moves files from the current directory and any subdirectories
/U	Moves the designated file only if a file with that name exists in the target location and the target file is older

To move files with a WK1 extension from the C:\MYDIR directory to the D:\YOURDIR directory, use the following command:

MOVE C:\MYDIR*.WK1 D:\YOURDIR

PATH

The NDOS PATH command, similar to DOS PATH, tells DOS where to look for executable files and batch files when they are not in the current default directory. The main difference in the NDOS version of PATH is that PATH also looks for BTM, COM, EXE, and BAT files. The NDOS PATH command has the following syntax:

PATH [*path*/[;*path2*]...]

Using PATH with no options causes the command to display the current path on-screen. Using PATH with a single semicolon clears the path. To tell NDOS to search the NU, DOS, and KWIKSTAT directories (all on drive C) when a command is not in the current directory, use this command:

PATH C:\NU;C:\DOS;C:\KWIKSTAT

PAUSE

Like DOS PAUSE, the NDOS PAUSE command suspends the processing of a batch program until you press any key (except Ctrl+Break or Ctrl+C). With the NDOS version, you can place more than one command on the command line. PAUSE has the following syntax:

PAUSE [*message*]

Consider this example:

PAUSE Press a key to continue with this batch file...

When this command is encountered, the following message appears on-screen:

```
Press a key to continue with this batch file...
```

The batch file does not continue to the next command until a key is pressed. This command is often useful for pausing after displaying information on-screen so that the information does not scroll off the screen before the user has a chance to read the message.

POPD

Use the NDOS POPD command to recall a command from the top of the directory stack. POPD has the following syntax:

POPD [*]

If the * option is included, the directory stack is cleared without changing the current drive and directory.

For more information, see the "PUSHD" section, which describes how to create directory stacks, and the "DIRS" section, which displays the current directory stack.

Suppose that you are in the root directory on drive A. When you enter the PUSHD C:\MYDIR command, the root directory (C:\) is placed in the directory stack, and your default drive and directory change to C:\MYDIR. Then, after you enter **PUSHD D:\TMP**, the C:\MYDIR directory is placed in the stack, and you are changed to the D:\TMP directory and drive. If you enter the command

POPD

you are switched back to the first drive and directory entry on the stack (C:\MYDIR).

PROMPT

The NDOS PROMPT command, similar to the DOS PROMPT command, changes the prompt used by DOS. You use the following syntax:

PROMPT [*text*]

The DOS prompt usually consists of the current disk name followed by >. For example, if you are logged on to drive A, the default prompt is A>.

The *text* option enables you to specify what appears on the prompt line by listing a series of commands; each command is preceded by a dollar sign ($). Text that is not a command preceded by a dollar sign is displayed verbatim. The following commands are available:

Command	Description
$b	| character.
$c	Opening parenthesis (NDOS only).
$d	Current date, *WWW MMM DD, YYYY* (day of week, month, date, and year). An example is Thu Oct 17, 1993.

Command	Description
$e	Esc character (ASCII 27).
$f	Closing parenthesis (NDOS only).
$g	> character.
$h	Backspace character. (You can use this command to display characters. For example, dhhhhh$h causes the last six characters in the date ($d) to be erased from the prompt so that it appears as Thu Oct 17.)
$l	< character.
$n	Default drive letter.
$P	Current disk and directory in uppercase. (In DOS, $P is always displayed in uppercase.)
$p	Current disk and directory in lowercase (NDOS only).
$q	= character.
$s	Space character.
$t	Current time (in hours, minutes, and seconds).
$v	DOS version number.
$X[$]d:	Current disk and directory in uppercase, where d: is the drive specification (NDOS only).
$x[$]d:	Current disk and directory in lowercase, where d: is the drive specification (NDOS only).
$z	Current NDOS nesting level (NDOS only).
$$	Dollar sign.
$_	CR/LF (go to next line).

Those options marked as "NDOS only" are available only in the NDOS version of the PROMPT command, not in the PC DOS or MS-DOS version of PROMPT. To cause the prompt to appear as the name of the disk drive and the name of the current directory, use either of the following commands:

    PROMPT Pg

    PROMPT Xc:

The optional dollar sign, when included in the second version of the PROMPT command, causes the ending colon to appear in the prompt.

When you are in drive C and in the \MYDIR directory, these two commands cause the DOS prompt to be the following:

```
C:\MYDIR>

C:\MYDIR:
```

PUSHD

The NDOS PUSHD command places a disk drive and directory in the directory stack. PUSHD has the following syntax:

PUSHD [[*d:*]*path*]

For more information, see the "POPD" section, which tells you how to recall a directory stack, and the "DIRS" section, which discusses displaying the current directory stack.

Suppose that you are in the root directory of drive A. When you enter the command

PUSHD C:\MYDIR

the root directory (C:\) is placed in the directory stack and your default drive and directory changes to C:\MYDIR. Then you enter the following command:

PUSHD D:\TMP

This places the C:\MYDIR directory in the stack and changes to the D:\TMP directory and drive. If you enter the command POPD, you are switched back to the last drive and directory entry (C:\MYDIR).

QUIT

You use the NDOS QUIT command to end the processing of a batch file at any point. No command-line options are available. If you quit one batch file that has been called from a previous batch file, you return to that previous batch file.

RD or RMDIR

The NDOS RD or RMDIR command, used to remove directories, is similar to the DOS RD or RMDIR command. Unlike the DOS version, however, this version enables you to list several directories to delete at once. You use one of the following forms:

RD [*drive*:]*path*...

RMDIR [*drive*:]*path*...

To delete the directories \MYDIR and \YOURDIR, use the following command:

RD \MYDIR \YOURDIR

Before removing a directory, you must delete all files in that directory. See the "MD or MKDIR" and "CD or CHDIR" sections for more information.

REM

The NDOS REM command, like the DOS REM command, places a comment in a batch file. For example, the following command is ignored when the batch file commands are being processed:

REM This is a comment in a batch file

Programmers usually use REM lines to document the actions of the batch file for purposes of maintaining the file.

REN or RENAME

The NDOS REN or RENAME command, like the DOS REN or RENAME command, renames a file or subdirectory. You use one of these forms:

REN [*switches*] *filespec*...*filespec*

REN [*switches*] *path*...*path*

The following switches may be used with REN:

Switch	Description
/N	Displays the projected results of the command—without changing any files
/P	Prompts you to confirm each rename
/Q	Suppresses display of the names of the files as they are being renamed
/S	Renames subdirectories with a wild-card specification

To rename a file named MYFILE.TXT to YOURFILE.TXT, use this command:

REN MYFILE.TXT YOURFILE.TXT

Unlike DOS, you can rename files to a different directory (but not a different drive). Consider the following command:

REN \WP51\MYFILE.TXT \TMP\YOURFILE.TXT

This command renames the file in the WP51 directory to the TMP directory. You can rename directories also. For example, the following command renames the directory MYDIR to YOURDIR:

REN \MYDIR \YOURDIR

RETURN

The NDOS command RETURN ends a subroutine in a batch file. This command has no command-line options. Suppose that in your batch file you have a subroutine with the following commands:

```
:MYSUB
ERASE *.BAK
RETURN
```

To execute this subroutine, use the following command:

GOSUB MYSUB

The subroutine is executed up to the command RETURN. The flow of the batch file then returns to the line following the GOSUB command.

SCREEN

The NDOS SCREEN command positions the cursor on-screen and optionally displays a message. You use the following syntax:

SCREEN *row column* [*message*]

To locate the cursor at the 10th row and 4th column and to display the message Here I am, use this command:

SCREEN 10 4 Here I am

SCRPUT

The NDOS SCRPUT command displays text in color. SCRPUT has the following syntax:

SCRPUT *row column* [BRIGHT] [BLINK] *foreground* ON *background text*

The colors available for *foreground* and *background* are BLACK, BLUE, YELLOW, GREEN, RED, MAGENTA, CYAN, YELLOW, and WHITE. For example, to place the text This is a message on-screen with bright white letters and a cyan background 10 rows down from the top and 12 columns over from the left, use this command:

SCRPUT 10 12 BRIGHT WHITE ON CYAN This is a message

SELECT

The NDOS SELECT command enables you to choose command-line file arguments from a full-screen menu by using the arrow keys or mouse pointer. After you make your selections, the command is executed on the selected files. You use the following syntax:

SELECT [/A:*attributes*] [/C] [/D] [/O:*sortorder*] *command* (*filespec...*)

The /A switch causes files with certain attributes to appear in the select list, and the /O switch causes files in the select list to be displayed in a sorted order. The /C switch causes the list to be displayed in upper-case; the /D switch disables directory colorization.

When the /A option is used, SELECT displays only those commands that have the requested attributes set (or commands that do not have the requested attribute set if a minus sign precedes the attribute name). The following attributes are available:

Attribute	Description
h	Hidden file
r	Read-only file
s	System file
d	Directory
a	Archived file

To use SELECT to copy a list of all archived files to drive A, enter this command:

SELECT /A:a COPY (*.*) A:\

To copy all files that are *not* archived, use /A:–a instead of /A:a.

The *sortorder* parameter enables you to sort the select list. The following sort order options are available. Placing a minus (–) before a sort order causes the sort to be in descending order rather than ascending order (the default).

Option	Sort Order
d	Date and time
e	File extension
i	NDOS file description
n	Name
s	Size
g	Directories first in the list
u	Unsorted (same as normal DOS DIR)

When you enter the SELECT command, a file list appears on-screen. If, for example, you enter the following command, you see a screen similar to the one in figure 28.5:

SELECT COPY (*.EXE) B:

Use the up- and down-arrow keys to move the highlight from line to line. To select a file to be copied, press the space bar (or the plus key). Selected files have a small triangle to the left of their names. If a file already is selected, pressing the space bar (or the minus key) unselects the file. Pressing the asterisk (*) key selects all files. After you select the files you want to copy, press Enter to initiate the COPY command.

SET

The NDOS SET command, like the DOS SET command, displays, creates, modifies, or deletes environment variables. SET has the following syntax:

SET [/M] [/P] [/R *filespec*...] [*variable*[=] [*value*]]

```
 33 chars | ↑ or ↓ Selects | + Marks  - Unmarks | ENTER to run | Page  1 of  2
copy (*.exe) b:                               Marked:      0 files       OK
 brt71efr.exe    87248    2-24-93   3:34a
 epson.exe        1499    2-24-93   3:34a
 herclj.exe       2688    2-24-93   3:34a
 ks3.exe         35707    2-24-93   1:09p
 ks3aov1.exe     36395    2-24-93   9:20p
 ks3aov2.exe     40731    2-25-93   3:34a
 ks3cros.exe     37947    2-25-93  10:40a
 ks3entry.exe    33723    2-25-93   1:02p
 ks3life.exe     30491    2-24-93   9:38p
 ks3nonp.exe     31819    2-25-93  10:40a
 ks3plot1.exe    35195    1-04-93   6:36p
 ks3reg.exe      35419    2-25-93  10:40a
 ks3simu.exe     26939    1-04-93   6:34p
 ks3stat.exe     37387    2-25-93  10:40a
 ks3test.exe     33090    1-04-93   3:33a
 ks3tfor.exe     38486    1-04-93   3:33a
 ks3time.exe     38811    2-25-93   3:34a
 ks3trans.exe    26683    2-22-93   2:51p
 ks3tww.exe      34074    1-04-93   3:33a
 ks3util.exe     38859    2-25-93  10:40a
 ksetup.exe      15819    2-25-93  12:54p
 laserjet.exe     2688    2-24-93   3:34a
 mark.exe          571    2-24-93   3:34a
```

Fig. 28.5

Picking file names from a SELECT command list.

The /M switch tells the command to display or modify the master environment rather than the local copy of the environment. The /P option tells the command to pause after displaying a page of entries. The /R *filespec* option tells the command to load a list of environment variables from the file specified by *filespec*. To create a file that contains environment variables, you can redirect the output of the SET command to a file name. For example, use the following command:

SET > ENVIRON.LST

This command creates a file named ENVIRON.LST containing the current environment settings. Then you can use the /R option to read these same settings back.

Using the command SET with no options lists the current settings on-screen. To add a variable, use this form:

SET *varname=value*

To set the value of the variable MYVAR to the path C:\MYDIR, use the following command:

SET MYVAR=C:\MYDIR

To erase the variable MYVAR from the list of variables, use the following command:

SET MYVAR

To edit an environment variable, use the NDOS command ESET, described earlier in the chapter.

Using the SET command, you can tell NDOS that a file with a particular extension should be used for a specific program. Suppose, for example, that you have many TXT files that you often want to display on-screen to read. You can tell NDOS that you want to use the LIST command to view any TXT file entered at the DOS prompt. Here is the command for this procedure:

SET .TXT=LIST

If you have a file named MARY.TXT, entering **MARY** at the DOS prompt causes the LIST program to execute and display the file MARY.TXT.

SETDOS

The NDOS SETDOS command displays or sets the NDOS configuration variables. With this command, you can customize NDOS for your personal use. SETDOS has this syntax:

SETDOS [*switches*]

The following switches are available for use with SETDOS:

Switch	Description
/A*n*	Determines whether NDOS tries to use ANSI Escape sequences. With /A0, NDOS can determine whether an ANSI driver is installed. /A1 forces NDOS to assume that an ANSI driver is installed. /A2 forces NDOS to assume that an ANSI driver is not installed.
/C*n*	Tells the command what compound character to use for separating multiple commands on the same line. The default is ^ (caret). You cannot use the following characters: | < > = , ; To use the tilde (~) as the compound character, use the option /C~.
/E*h*	Sets the character to be used as the Escape character (see the earlier section "Using Escape Sequences"). The default is ^X (Ctrl+X), which appears as an up arrow. You cannot use the following characters: | < > = , ;
/F0	Tells the command to turn on file name truncation. (This switch is the default.) /F1 uses full file names. When truncation is on, a file with a long path may appear in command output with the path \..\.

Switch	Description
/H*nnn*	Determines the minimum command size to save to the history list. /H0 saves all command lines (the default). /H256 disables history saves.
/I[+|-]	Enables or disables the specified internal NDOS command. For example, /I-LIST disables the LIST command; /I+LIST enables the command.
/L*n*	Determines whether you can edit the command line. /L0 (the default) enables NDOS command-line editing, and /L1 reverts to the standard DOS line input.
/M*n*	Determines the line-editing mode. /M0 (the default) sets line editing to overwrite mode. /M1 sets line editing to insert mode.
/N*n*	Enables or disables overwrite mode. /N0 (the default) sets NOCLOBBER to off, which enables files to be overwritten by output redirection (>). /N1 prevents files from being overwritten and requires that a file exist for the >> redirection command to work.
/R*n*	Sets the number of screen rows used by the video display. For example, /R20 sets the rows to 20. This switch is useful for nonstandard monitors with less than 25 lines.
/S*s:e*	Determines the shape of the NDOS cursor. The format is /S*s:e*, with *s* representing the starting scan line and *e* representing the ending scan line. For more information on placing the cursor on-screen, see Chapter 24.
/U*n*	Determines whether file names are displayed in upper- or lowercase. /U0 (the default) displays the file names in commands, such as DIR and COPY, in lowercase. /U1 displays the file names in uppercase.
/V*n*	Determines whether commands are echoed to the screen. /V1 (the default) echoes commands from a batch file (verbose). /V0 suppresses command echoing.

To change the compound character to @, for example, use this command:

    SETDOS /C@

To suppress the display of commands in batch files, use the following command:

    SETDOS /V0

SETLOCAL

The NDOS command, SETLOCAL, saves the names of the current disk drive, directory, environment variables, and aliases. The NDOS ENDLOCAL command restores the computer to previously saved names. SETLOCAL, which has no options, is useful in a batch file when, after you change from a directory or disk drive temporarily to execute a procedure, you want to change back to your current settings.

The following example uses the SETLOCAL command to save your current settings. Some changes are made in order to run the KS program (which requires the new PATH setting C:\KWIKSTAT). When that program is finished, the previous settings are then restored by the ENDLOCAL command:

```
SETLOCAL
C:
CD \MYDIR
SET PATH = C:\KWIKSTAT
KS
ENDLOCAL
```

For more information, see the "ENDLOCAL" section in this chapter.

SHIFT

The NDOS SHIFT command, similar to DOS SHIFT, enables you to use more variables in a batch file. In DOS, you can usually use the variables %0 to %9 (10 variables in all) in a batch file. NDOS supports the variables %0 to %127. Otherwise, SHIFT works the same as the DOS SHIFT command.

SWAPPING

With the NDOS SWAPPING command, you can display, enable, or disable the NDOS swapping state. The swapping state controls how NDOS swaps its transient portion when other programs run. Setting swapping off usually means that small programs run faster, but the amount of DOS conventional memory is temporarily reduced by as much as 80K.

If swapping is on, you have more memory available to run programs.

The SWAPPING command has the following syntax:

```
SWAPPING [ON|OFF]
```

When you use SWAPPING with no options, the current swapping state (on or off) is reported. To set swapping on, use the following command:

> SWAPPING ON

To set swapping off, use this command:

> SWAPPING OFF

TEE

The NDOS TEE command copies a file to the standard output device (usually the monitor) and meanwhile saves a copy of the output to a file or files. You use the following syntax:

> TEE [/A] *path name...*

The /A switch causes output to be appended to the specified file instead of replacing the file.

TEE often is used to capture the intermediate piped output of a command. Suppose that you want to search the file REPORT.TXT for lines containing *CREDIT*, copy the matching lines to C.DAT, sort the lines, and write them to the output file CREDIT.DAT. Use this command:

> FIND "CREDIT" REPORT.TXT | TEE C.DAT | SORT > CREDIT.DAT

TEXT and ENDTEXT

Use the NDOS TEXT and ENDTEXT commands to display a block of text in a batch file. TEXT has the following syntax:

> TEXT
> *lines of*
> *output text*
> ENDTEXT

For example, the following lines cause the poem "Mary Had a Little Lamb" to be output to the screen from within a batch file:

> TEXT
> Mary had a little lamb
> Its fleece was white as snow
> And everywhere that Mary went
> The lamb was sure to go.
> ENDTEXT

This method of displaying text is often more convenient than using the ECHO command on every output line.

TIME

Similar to DOS TIME, the NDOS TIME command enables you to display or set the current system time. You use the following syntax:

TIME [*hh*[:*mm*[:*ss*]] [A|P]]

To set the system time to 1:30 p.m., enter either of the following commands:

TIME 1:30 P

TIME 13:30

 When you do not use the A or P option, the line is in 24-hour format.

TIMER

You use the NDOS TIMER command to turn the NDOS system stopwatch on and off. This command has the following syntax:

TIMER [ON] [/S] [/1] [/2] [/3]

To start the timer, enter **TIMER** with no options. To display the current time, leaving the timer running, use this command:

TIMER /S

When a timer is running, the TIMER command with no options turns the timer off. The current clock time and elapsed time are then displayed. To force the timer's stopwatch to restart, use the ON option. The /1, /2, and /3 options refer to three different timers. The default is 1. Thus, you can operate three separate timers independently.

TRUENAME

The NDOS TRUENAME option finds and displays the full, true path and file name for each file. TRUENAME has the following syntax:

TRUENAME *filename*

The *filename* is the name of a file whose true path you want to know. The TRUENAME command displays the actual name of a file even if the name is disguised by the use of DOS JOIN or SUBST.

TYPE

The NDOS TYPE command, which is similar to the DOS TYPE command, displays the contents of a text file on-screen. The DOS version does not have the /L and /P switches. You use the following syntax:

TYPE [*switches*] *filespec*...

The following switches are available for use with TYPE:

Switch	Description
/L	Precedes each output line with a line number
/P	Pauses after a page of text has been displayed on-screen

To display the contents of the files REPORT.TXT and BUDGET.TXT on-screen and pause at each screen of information, use the following command:

TYPE /P REPORT.TXT BUDGET.TXT

UNALIAS

The NDOS UNALIAS command removes an alias from the list. You can use either of these forms:

UNALIAS *alias*...

UNALIAS *

If you use the * version, all aliases are deleted.

You can specify one or more aliases to delete from the list. To delete the aliases D and DDD from the list, use this command:

UNALIAS D DDD

For more information, see the "ALIAS" section in this chapter.

UNSET

The NDOS UNSET command removes variables from the environment list. You can use one of these forms:

UNSET *name*...

UNSET [/M]*

The /M switch removes the master environment variables. If you use the second version (with the .*), all environment variables are deleted. Use this version with caution.

You may specify one or more names to delete from the environment list. To delete the names MYENV and YOURENV, for example, use this command:

UNSET MYENV YOURENV

See the "SET" section for more information.

VER

The NDOS VER command, like the DOS VER command, displays the current DOS version numbers for NDOS and DOS. VER has the following syntax:

VER [/R]

In DOS 5.0 or later, you can use the /R switch to display the DOS revision level and the location of the DOS kernel.

VERIFY

With the NDOS VERIFY command, which is similar to DOS VERIFY, you can enable or disable the capability to display the current setting of write verification. DOS uses the verification process to check that no write error occurs when information is written to disk. You use the following syntax:

VERIFY [ON|OFF]

If the command is given with no options, the current state of VERIFY is displayed. To enable write verification, enter the following command:

VERIFY ON

To disable write verification, enter this command:

VERIFY OFF

The default setting for VERIFY is OFF.

VOL

Similar to DOS VOL, the NDOS VOL command is used to display the disk volume label. This command has the following syntax:

VOL [*d:*]...

Entering VOL with no options displays the volume label for the current disk. You can request the volume label for one or more disks at once. To display the volume label for drives A and C, enter this command:

VOL A: C:

VSCRPUT

The NDOS VSCRPUT command enables you to display text vertically on-screen. VSCRPUT has the following syntax:

VSCRPUT *row column* [BRIGHT] [BLINK] *foreground* ON *background text*

The options are similar to the SCRPUT command described earlier, except that the text is displayed vertically rather than horizontally.

Y

The NDOS Y command copies standard input to standard output while copying specified files to the standard output. You use the following syntax:

Y *filespec*...

Suppose that you want to enter information from the keyboard (standard input), append the file MARY.TXT to the information, append to that information a file named HUMPTY.TXT, and output the three sources to one file named RHYMES.TXT. Use the following command:

Y MARY.TXT HUMPTY.TXT > RHYMES.TXT

This command results in the file RHYMES.TXT, which includes input from the keyboard, the contents of MARY.TXT, and the contents of HUMPTY.TXT.

When you use the Y command to enter information from the keyboard, you must signal an end to the input by entering ^Z (Ctrl+Z) and then pressing Enter.

Summary

The NDOS commands provide you with a much richer operating system than the normal DOS commands provide. With NDOS, you retain all the features you are already comfortable with in DOS, you gain more flexibility for the commands you already know, and you gain a whole new repertoire of handy, DOS-like commands. Some of the benefits of NDOS are its capability to read more than one line on a command line, extended editing features on the command line, and the capability to bring up previously entered commands to reexecute.

Backing Up and Restoring Files with Norton Backup

Norton Backup is a powerful tool that helps protect the one thing you cannot replace: your data. Many threats to your data exist—hard disk failure, accidental erasure, and viruses. With Norton Backup, you can protect your data from potential hazards and perform a variety of other tasks. For all the power that Norton Backup offers, however, it remains a program you can easily master.

In this chapter, you learn the basic terminology of Norton Backup, as well as ways to use the Backup, Restore, and Compare features. This chapter also introduces the Backup Scheduler, which enables you to automatically perform backups at regular intervals. Along the way, you should discover ways to customize Norton Backup so that it runs most efficiently for you.

Menu	Description
Tape Tools	Contains six tools that assist users who back up files to a tape drive:
	Identify displays a directory of the contents of the tape in the drive.
	Erase erases files on tape (similar to deleting a file from a disk).
	Security Erase erases files on tape and then overwrites the files to ensure that the files cannot be undeleted.
	Format formats the tape in the drive for use.
	Delete Volumes enables you to delete one or more volumes from the tape.
	Retension winds the tape to the end and rewinds it back to the beginning. Use this tool if you're having difficulty writing to or reading from a tape.
Help	Contains on-line help for all aspects of the Norton Backup program.

The Norton Backup main screen also displays the following options in the Norton Backup 2.0 dialog box:

- **B**ackup enables you to set up and run backups tailored to your individual needs. For more information, see the next section, "Backing Up Files."

- Backup **S**cheduler helps you maintain a consistent backup strategy by automatically running all types of backups on the days and times you specify. See the section "Using the Backup Scheduler" for more details.

- **R**estore enables you to return backup files to a hard disk in cases of hard disk data loss. You also use this option to transport data from one computer to another. See the section "Restoring Backup Files" for more information.

- **C**ompare compares backup files to originals to ensure data integrity. See the section "Using Compare" later in this chapter.

- Co**n**figure displays a dialog box that contains the default setup determined by the data Norton Backup used in the initial system configuration tests. You change the default settings through this dialog box. See the later section "Reconfiguring Norton Backup" for more information.

- **Q**uit exits Norton Backup.

The following sections examine the options in the Norton Backup main screen.

Backing Up Files

When you choose the **B**ackup option from the Norton Backup main screen, the Norton Backup dialog box appears (see fig. 29.2). Through this dialog box, you can choose to back up any number of drives and files. You can back up a complete drive or just a few files. You can choose the destination—a floppy drive or tape drive—for the backed-up files.

NOTE If you use the Basic program level, the dialog box shown in figure 29.2 displays the heading Norton Basic Backup, the Advanced program level displays Norton Advanced Backup, and the Preset program level displays Norton Preset Backup. You set these levels during the configuration process when you first start Norton Backup.

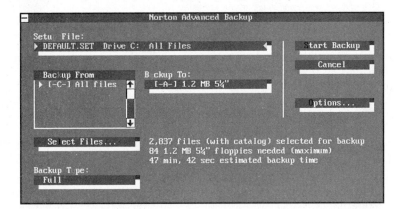

Fig. 29.2

The Norton Advanced Backup dialog box.

This section takes you through the steps for making a backup of drive C. After you have a basic understanding of the procedure, the various steps are explained so that you understand the different types of backups that exist. You also learn about selecting files and options such as data verification and compression, which make Norton Backup conform to your needs as it helps you protect your data.

Making a Quick Backup

The following exercise creates a backup of drive C. This exercise should help familiarize you with the backup process. Follow these steps:

1. From the Norton Backup main screen, choose **B**ackup. The Norton Backup dialog box appears (refer to fig. 29.2).

2. Choose the Setu**p** File option. A list of setup files appears. These files are backup routines that have been saved. You learn how to create your own setup files in the section "Working with Setup Files" later in this chapter.

3. From the list of setup files, choose the file named DEFAULT.SET, using the arrow keys or the mouse.

   After you choose DEFAULT.SET, all other selections are made for you. Check each selection to make sure that it's correct. Look at the Backup **T**ype to see that a full backup is selected. Check the B**a**ckup To box and make sure that the correct disk or tape drive is chosen for your system.

NOTE The Norton Backup dialog box also gives you information for the backup you select. Figure 29.2, for example, shows that drive C contains 2,837 files to back up. The operation requires 84 1.2M 5 1/4-inch floppy disks and takes about 47 minutes and 42 seconds to complete. The information on your screen may be different.

4. Choose the **S**tart Backup option to begin the backup.

Norton Backup prompts you to place new disks or tapes in your drive. Be sure to number your disks or tapes so that you know the correct order.

You may not want to take the time to back up your hard drive now. If you don't, choose **C**ancel or press Esc. If you decide to continue with the backup, make sure that you have an adequate number of disks.

Understanding Backup Types

You can perform several types of backups, each with its own purpose. In the Norton Backup dialog box, choose the Backup **T**ype option to bring up the Backup Type dialog box, which displays a list of backup types (see fig. 29.3).

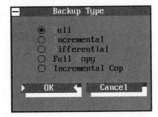

Fig. 29.3

The Backup Type
dialog box.

The following list describes the backup types available:

■ **Full** provides a complete backup that backs up all selected files—
whether or not you changed the files since the last backup. After
backup, archive flags are set to off. A full backup doesn't require
backing up the entire hard disk. You can choose a full backup of a
subdirectory or a few files.

NOTE DOS uses an *archive flag* to indicate whether a file has
been changed since it was last backed up. After a file is
changed or created, DOS sets the archive flag to on,
signaling that the file hasn't been backed up.

T I P To have a complete set of all data on the disk, begin backing up files
with a full backup of the entire hard disk.

■ **Incremental** provides a partial backup that backs up only those
files changed or created since the last full or incremental backup.
An incremental backup looks only for files with the archive flag
on. After backup, it sets the flag to off. To maintain complete protection, use this type of backup with a full backup.

NOTE Do not use the same incremental backup disks more
than once. You also must keep all sets of incremental
backup disks between full backups. If you reuse the
disks before you perform a full backup, you overwrite
previous data with new data.

■ **Differential** also provides a partial backup. Unlike the incremental
backup, a differential backup backs up files that have changed

since the last full backup. After a differential backup finishes, the archive flag is left on. With each subsequent differential backup, the files backed up in the first differential backup are backed up again, so you don't need to maintain several sets of differential backups. You can reuse the same set of disks each time. You need only the full backup set and a differential backup set.

NOTE If the same disks are used, a differential backup overwrites previous differential backups. This feature isn't usually a problem because a differential backup continues to back up the same files. For people who want to maintain older file versions, however, a problem develops. If you need to keep older file versions, use the incremental backup as described earlier.

■ Full Copy provides a full backup, but it doesn't reset the archive flag. You can use Full Copy to copy your files without disrupting your backup cycle. This option enables you to transfer files or the contents of your hard drive to another computer.

■ Incremental Copy enables you to copy selected files that have changed without changing the archive flag. You can use this option to keep a remote computer up-to-date with your current work.

Now that you understand the various types of backups available, you can choose the appropriate type for your needs. Then choose **OK** to accept your choice and return to the Norton Backup dialog box. The Backup Type option reflects the backup type you chose.

Selecting Files To Back Up

You may not want to back up your entire hard drive each time you use Norton Backup. Sometimes you may want to back up only files you have been working on that day. If you are working on a special project, for example, you may want to back up only project files. Norton Backup provides an easy method to select the drives, directories, subdirectories, and files you want to back up.

Choose the Select Files option from the Norton Backup dialog box to begin selecting files to back up. The Select Backup Files dialog box appears (see fig. 29.4).

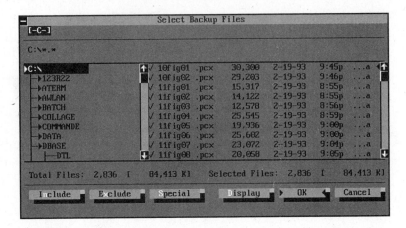

Fig. 29.4

The Select
Backup Files
dialog box.

The drive list at the top of the dialog box (just below the title bar) shows the drives you can select to back up. Notice that the dialog box in figure 29.4 shows only one available hard drive. If you have more than one hard drive (for example, C and D), both appear as available options. Simply press Tab and then Enter to select the hard drive you want, or click the drive.

On the left side of the dialog box is a directory tree, which lists all directories and subdirectories for the currently selected hard drive. To the right of the directory tree is the file list, which lists the files in a selected directory or subdirectory. To scroll through the items in the directory tree and file list, use the arrow keys or the scroll bars.

To make a selection in one of these areas, click the area or press Tab until the highlight moves to the area. Next select the drive, directory, or file by double-clicking or highlighting the one you want. Then press the space bar.

If you use the Advanced backup configuration, you can also make selections with the **In**clude option at the bottom of the Select Backup Files dialog box. Choose this command to display a dialog box that you can use to include or exclude all subdirectories. The default setting is to include—that is, to back up—all subdirectories of the selected directory. An **Ex**clude option, which removes a file from the backup list, is also available.

After you make a selection, an arrow appears, indicating the selected directory or subdirectory, and a check mark appears before selected files in the file list (refer to fig. 29.4). As you select files for back up, a message showing the total number of files on the hard drive and the number of files selected for backup appears in the dialog box.

T I P

If you do an Advanced backup, you can select files by date created as well as by name. The **S**pecial option displays the Special Selections dialog box. In this dialog box, you can fill in the **F**rom and **T**o text boxes to select all files in a certain date range. The program selects all files that fall between the two dates. (Note that you must choose the option **A**pply Date Range.) You can back up all files created or modified in a specified day, week, month, or year. The Special Selections dialog box also enables you to exclude from the files selected within the date range any files that are copy-protected, read-only, system, or hidden.

The **D**isplay option can help you select files. This option calls up the Display Options dialog box, from which you can control the way the files are displayed in the Select Backup Files dialog box (see fig. 29.5).

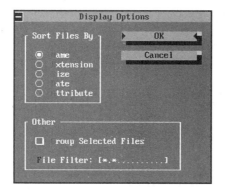

Fig. 29.5

The Display
Options
dialog box.

From the Display Options dialog box, you can choose to sort the files by **N**ame (the default setting), **E**xtension, **S**ize, **D**ate, or **A**ttribute. You can also create a filter to display only certain files or all selected files as a group. This filter is useful when you try to find and back up specific file types. If, for example, you want to back up only dBASE IV files, you specify *.DBF as the filter. By doing so, you eliminate all files that have an extension other than DBF.

Working with Setup Files

Because everyone has different backup needs, Norton Backup enables you to create a customized file called a *setup file*. A setup file is needed when you back up and restore files. You used a setup file named DEFAULT.SET in the section "Making a Quick Backup" earlier in this chapter.

Using Norton Backup

If you have already used Norton Backup and configured it to suit your needs, you can start the program from the DOS prompt. Be certain that you are in the subdirectory containing NBACKUP, or that you have established a path to the subdirectory. Then type **NBACKUP** and press Enter. The Norton Backup main screen appears (see fig. 29.1).

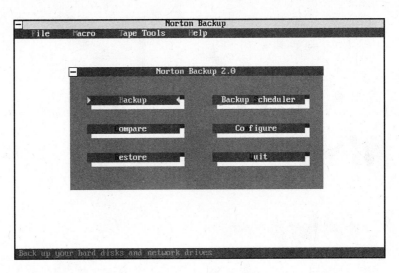

Fig. 29.1

The Norton Backup main screen.

On the menu bar at the top of the screen, the four menus—**F**ile, **M**acro, **T**ape Tools, and **H**elp—provide additional options to use with Norton Backup. Table 29.1 gives an overview of each menu.

Table 29.1 Norton Backup Menus

Menu	Description
File	Provides options that enable you to open, save, delete, and print setup files (SET extension) used in Norton Backup.
Macro	Enables you to record keystrokes for a macro and play macros. (A *macro* enables you to record a sequence of often-used keystrokes and replay them by pressing only one or two keys.) Each setup file can contain one macro. When the setup file is loaded, the macro for that setup file is also loaded.

To create setup files, you must be in the Advanced level of operation. If you are now using the Basic level of operation, you can use already created setup files, but you cannot create them. To change the program level, see the section "Reconfiguring Norton Backup" at the end of this chapter.

From the Norton Advanced Backup dialog box (refer to fig. 29.2), you have many choices that enable you to customize the way you back up files. You can choose the backup type you want to perform, the drives and files you want to back up, and where to send the backed-up files (floppy disk or tape drive). More than likely, you want to make different types of backups at different times. You probably don't want to do a full backup every time you back up; perhaps you want to back up only the files that have changed since your last full backup.

To create a setup file, you can select different backup options and then save these options. You can open the setup file the next time you want to perform the same type of backup.

Creating a setup file is simple. Follow these steps:

1. From the Norton Advanced Backup dialog box, make the following selections:

   ■ Use the Backup From list box and the Select Files option to select the drive, directories, and files to back up.

   ■ Use the Backup Type option to choose the type of backup to perform.

   ■ Use the Backup To option to choose the drive to back up to.

 You also can choose Options in the Norton Advanced Backup dialog box to select the various data-compression and error-correction choices available. See the next section, "Choosing Backup Options."

2. From the File menu at the top of the screen, choose Save Setup As. The Save Setup File dialog box appears (see fig. 29.6).

 If you choose Save Setup instead of Save Setup As, all your selections are saved in the setup file now in use.

3. In the Save Setup File dialog box, type a new file name for your selections in the File Name text box. Remember to leave the file extension SET that Backup provides.

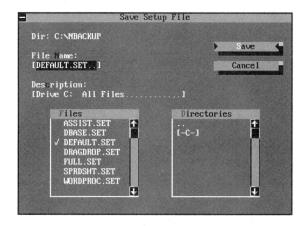

Fig. 29.6

The Save Setup
File dialog box.

To overwrite an existing setup file, choose the setup file's name
from the Files list box.

4. Type a description of the setup in the Description text box.

5. Choose the location in which to store the setup file from the
Directories list box. You usually store the setup file in the default
directory with your other setup files.

6. Choose Save to save your setup file.

You successfully saved a new setup file. The setup file is now ready for
you to use.

Choosing Backup Options

You can choose a number of options with Norton Backup. For example,
you can customize the speed of the backup, password-protect the
backed-up data, and test your hard disk before you start the backup.

To set the options, choose Backup in the Norton Backup dialog box.
Choose Options to bring up one of two dialog boxes. If you back up to
disks, the Disk Backup Options dialog box appears (see fig. 29.7). If you
back up to tape, the Tape Backup Options dialog box appears. Both
dialog boxes contain the same basic options; you can switch from one
menu to the other through the Disk Options or Tape Options option in
each dialog box.

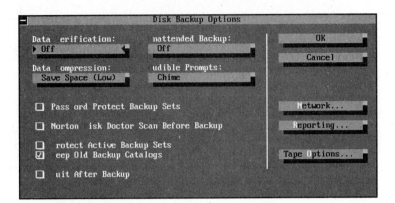

Fig. 29.7

The Disk
Backup Options
dialog box.

Using Data Verification

The first option in the Disk Backup Options dialog box is Data Verification. This option enables you to activate or deactivate the program's data verification feature. You choose the option to ensure the integrity of your backed-up data.

You can choose one of the following levels of data verification:

- **Off** performs no data verification.

- **S**ample Only randomly checks sections of the backed-up data to see whether it matches the original data.

- Read and **C**ompare checks all backed-up data against the original (the most thorough method of verification).

 The term *data verification* describes the process of checking the backed-up data to see whether it matches the original. Any discrepancies found in the data are corrected to match the original.

If you use any type of data verification, the backup process slows. Read and **C**ompare, for example, decreases backup speed by approximately 50 percent. The increased integrity of your data justifies this decrease in speed, however.

For your first full backup, use the **S**ample Only verification or even Read and **C**ompare. For incremental backups, choose **O**ff (not using verification). If you have been using disks for some time, choose Read and **C**ompare when you perform a full backup.

NOTE When you use the Read and Compare verification option, Norton Backup prompts you if you need to replace a disk with questionable data integrity.

Compressing Backup Data

Data compression enables Norton Backup to compress your data onto fewer disks or less tape. If you choose the Data Compression option in the Disk Backup Options dialog box, the Data Compression dialog box appears. This dialog box enables you to choose whether to compress the data you are backing up.

NOTE On some older computers, choosing to compress data increases the amount of time that backing up takes.

You can choose from the following compression options:

- **Off** doesn't compress data.

- **Save Time** uses computer time that is not being used for reading or writing data to compress data read from the hard disk.

- Save Space (**Low**) compresses as much data as possible with as little effect on backup speed as possible.

- Save Space (**High**) performs the most compression at the cost of backup speed.

If time is a concern, choose the Save Time option, which compresses data the least. For most users, especially those who back up to floppy disks, space is more important than time. Choose Save Space (Low), which compresses data significantly; or, to save the maximum amount of disk or tape space, choose Save Space (High) for full compression of the data.

> The Save Time option is best for the widest range of computers. The Save Space (Low) option is best for higher-performance computers, such as those with 80386 or 80486 CPUs.

T I P

The best data compression option depends a great deal on the computer you use. To determine the best option for your computer, perform a sample backup of about 1M of data, using each compression option. (Be sure to include COM and EXE files in the sample backup as well as data files.) After each backup, record the time the backup took, the amount of data per second backed up, and the compression ratio. This information appears each time you back up. Select the compression with the best overall specifications.

A 12 MHz 80286 computer, for example, may give the following backup statistics for the compression options covered earlier:

	Off	Save Time	Save Space (Low)	Save Space (High)
Backup Time (Seconds)	31	19	21	41
Bytes/Second	2045K	3337K	3020K	1546K
Compression Ratio	0	1.7	2.3	2.4

Save Time or Save Space (Low) is a good choice for this computer. If the computer contains 50M of data to back up, however, the Save Space (Low) option costs only about two more minutes and saves about five disks. Remember, however, that backup time is the time the computer spends backing up data—not the time you spend changing disks. If you choose Save Time rather than Save Space (Low), you actually can use the two minutes saved changing the additional five disks.

 NOTE   You don't have to do anything special to compressed backup data before you restore it. When you restore the data, the program expands the files, returning them to normal size. For more information, see the section "Restoring Backup Files" later in this chapter.

Performing an Unattended Backup

During the backup process, you must respond to prompts to continue the process. Norton Backup prompts you to insert new disks. After you place a new disk in the drive, you press a key or click to tell Norton Backup to continue. By using the Unattended Backup option in the Disk Backup Options dialog box, you can have Norton Backup answer the prompts and avoid answering the prompts yourself.

 NOTE   If you are not able to change disks during an unattended backup, the backup process stops.

You can choose from the following options for an unattended backup:

Option	Description
Off	You must respond to all prompts.
On, **No** Delay option	Norton Backup responds to a prompt immediately with a predetermined response.
On, **5** Second Delay	Norton Backup waits 5 seconds for you to respond and then uses a predetermined response.
On, **15** Second Delay	Norton Backup waits 15 seconds for a response.
On, **60** Second Delay	Norton Backup waits 60 seconds for a response.

When you first start using Norton Backup, you should set Unattended Backup to **Off**. After you feel comfortable with Norton Backup, you can select one of the On settings.

Setting Audible Prompts

When Norton Backup requires you to respond to a prompt, the program doesn't rely just on a visual prompt. An alarm also sounds to draw your attention to the computer. When you choose the Audible Prompts option from the Disk Backup Options dialog box, three different settings for the alarm are available (besides turning off the alarm):

Option	Description
Off	No alarm
Low Tone	Low-pitched buzz
High Tone	High-pitched beep
Chime	Four tones that simulate an alarm clock

In an office environment, you may want to choose the **Off** setting because an audible tone may bother your colleagues.

T I P

Password-Protecting Backup Sets

Files that you keep on your computer may contain sensitive data. Just because the data is backed up, however, doesn't make the data less sensitive. If you include a password with your backup, the information cannot be restored without the password.

To include a password with the backup set, choose the Password Protect Backup Sets option from the Disk Backup Options dialog box. When you choose this option, Norton Backup prompts you to type the password twice (see fig. 29.8). Asterisks appear each time you type the password. After you enter the password the second time to ensure that you correctly entered it, choose **OK** to save the password.

Passwords can be from one to eight characters long and are case-sensitive. If you create the password *WiLkey*, for example, you must remember to use uppercase *W* and *L* and lowercase *key*.

CAUTION: Password protection is case-sensitive, and there is no way to disable the case-sensitivity. Be certain that you remember the exact way you entered your password. If you forget your password and its associated case-sensitivity, there is no way to restore your backup files.

If the Password Protect Backup Sets option has a check mark in the Disk Backup Options dialog box, you cannot restore the backed-up files unless you correctly enter the password.

Scanning with Norton Disk Doctor

Problems with files on your hard disk can affect a backup. Nothing is worse than nearing the end of a backup, only to find that a problem with a file on the hard disk kept you from having a sound backup.

The Norton **D**isk Doctor Scan Before Backup option tests the integrity of your hard disk and its files before the backup begins. If an error is found, you can correct it before you continue with the backup. (For more information, see Chapter 12, "Diagnosing and Treating Disks with Disk Doctor.")

Protecting Backup Sets

After you back up your data, Norton Backup creates a *catalog file*. The catalog contains information about the backup, such as the names of the files you backed up. When you restore backup files, catalog files are useful. A user must load the catalog file that corresponds to the backed-up data in order to restore it. The section "Restoring Backup Files" later in this chapter has more information on catalog files.

Two check boxes in the Disk Backup Options dialog box deal with catalogs:

- **Protect Active Backup Sets.** If you choose this option, Norton Backup warns you when a backup disk contains information from a different backup set. This warning keeps you from accidentally destroying data on a backup disk from another backup set.

- **Keep Old Backup Catalogs.** If you choose this option, information from previous backups is maintained in the master catalog. Keeping previous catalogs enables you to restore an earlier version of a file, if necessary. You must have the backup disks that correspond to the previous catalog, however.

Setting Network Options

You can use Norton Backup to back up files from a Novell-based network server, but you must make special considerations. If someone on the network accesses a file, for example, you cannot back up the file. Instead of skipping a file, set the network options so that you can accomplish a full backup without missing any files.

After you choose the Network option from the Disk Backup Options dialog box, the Network Options dialog box appears (see fig. 29.9). From this dialog box, you can select how to back up files in use and whether to send a message to a user.

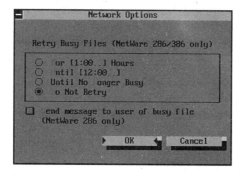

Fig. 29.9

The Network Options dialog box.

To back up files in use, you can choose from the following options:

■ The For [ ] Hours option specifies the length of time that Norton Backup tries to back up a file in use. Norton Backup continues to try to back up the file until the time expires.

■ The Until [ ] option specifies the time of day (in 12-hour format) that Norton Backup stops trying to back up the file.

■ The Until No Longer Busy option specifies that Norton Backup continues to try to back up the file until it is no longer in use.

■ The Do Not Retry option instructs Norton Backup to ignore backing up any file in use.

The other option in the Network Options dialog box is only for users of NetWare 286. If you choose the Send Message to User of Busy File option, Norton Backup sends a message to any user of a busy file that the file will be closed so that it can be backed up.

Creating a Backup Progress Report

Norton Backup can automatically create a report after it completes a backup. If you choose the Reporting option in the Disk Backup Options dialog box, you see the Reporting Options dialog box (see fig. 29.10). You use this dialog box to save the report to disk in the directory that contains Norton Backup. The report file name is the name of the setup file, but with the extension RPT. If you back up using the DEFAULT setup file, for example, a file called DEFAULT.RPT contains the report.

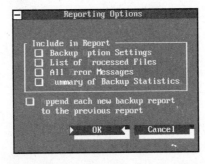

Fig. 29.10

The Reporting Options dialog box.

Two types of information are in the report: data you cannot change and information you can choose to include. The following information always appears in the report:

■ The starting date and time of the backup

■ The setup file name and description

■ The catalog name

You can choose to include the following information:

- Backup **O**ption Settings includes all backup option settings.

- List of **P**rocessed Files lists all backed-up files, including file name, size, date, time, attributes, and number of backup tapes or disks.

- All **E**rror Messages lists errors that occurred during backup and files that cannot be backed up.

- **S**ummary of Backup Statistics includes the same information listed in the Backup Progress dialog box, which appears after a backup.

You may not find this information useful other than for documentation when you watch the backup. For unattended backups, however, the information in this report is very valuable.

The final option that you can choose from the Reporting Options dialog box is **A**ppend Each New Backup Report to the Previous Report. If you don't choose this option, each report is replaced by the successive report.

Quitting When Finished

If you choose the **Q**uit After Backup option from the Disk Backup Options dialog box, Norton Backup automatically quits after the backup is complete. Generally, you choose **Q**uit from the Norton Backup dialog box. If you run Norton Backup from a batch file or with the Backup Scheduler, however, choose the **Q**uit After Backup option.

 For more information about batch files, see Chapter 24.

Using the Backup Scheduler

The Backup Scheduler is a program that enables you to run Norton Backup at regular intervals and specific times. Use the Backup Scheduler even if you work in another DOS program. When the designated time for a backup arrives, the Backup Scheduler asks whether you want to run the backup.

NOTE The Backup Scheduler depends on another program, NSCHED.COM, which is a terminate-and-stay-resident (TSR) program. After you load the TSR, NSCHED.COM remains active in the computer's memory. Norton Backup shares this TSR with Scheduler.

When you install Norton Backup, you can choose whether to load NSCHED.COM each time you start your computer. This method is best, especially if you want to run backups on a regular schedule, because scheduled backups cannot take place without NSCHED.COM.

If you didn't have the AUTOEXEC.BAT file changed to run NSCHED.COM at computer startup, you can load NSCHED.COM manually. Enter **NSCHED** at the DOS prompt before you start Norton Backup. NSCHED.COM must be the last TSR loaded in order to operate correctly.

Start the Backup Scheduler from the Norton Backup main screen (refer to fig. 29.1). The Backup Scheduler dialog box, shown in figure 29.11, displays a calendar and an information box that lists scheduled backups. From the Backup Scheduler dialog box, you can add, delete, and edit scheduled backups.

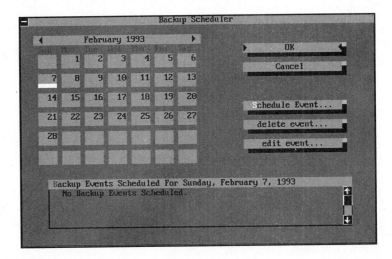

Fig. 29.11

The Backup
Scheduler
dialog box.

To schedule a backup, choose the **S**chedule Event option. The Schedule Backup Event dialog box appears (see fig. 29.12). From this dialog box, you can set the following information:

- **S**etup enables you to choose the setup file to use for the scheduled backup.

- **F**requency enables you to set how often to run the scheduled backup. Choose from the options **O**nce (one time only), Wee**k**days (Monday through Friday only), **D**aily, **W**eekly (once a week), **M**onthly, and **C**ustom (specified days).

- With **B**ackup Type, you can set the type of backup from the Backup Type dialog box. Choose **F**ull, **I**ncremental, **D**ifferential, Full **C**opy, or Incremental Cop**y**.

- Start **D**ate enables you to set the first date (*mm-dd-yy*) to perform the backup.

- With Start **T**ime, you can set the time of day to perform the backup; you can use 12-hour or 24-hour (military) time format.

Make the changes you want; then choose OK. The backup now is scheduled to start on the date you select. The calendar shows the days that backups are scheduled (see fig. 29.13).

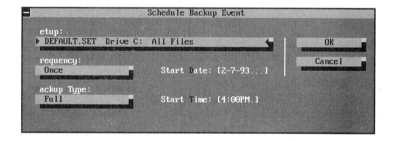

Fig. 29.12

The Schedule Backup Event dialog box.

The calendar in the Backup Scheduler displays any backups you scheduled. A check mark appears by the day that any backup is scheduled. The window at the bottom of the dialog box displays any backup information for the current day. If a backup is scheduled for that day, the window displays the setup file that controls the backup, the type of backup, the frequency of the backup, and the time the backup will occur.

The following sections enable you to begin hands-on work with the Backup Scheduler. The sections take you through the process of scheduling an actual backup and then editing or changing a backup that you already scheduled.

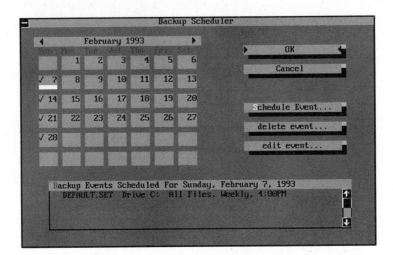

Fig. 29.13

Scheduling
a weekly
backup begin-
ning Sunday,
February 7,
1993.

Scheduling a Backup

Now that you understand the basics of the Backup Scheduler, you may
find the following exercise helpful. It takes you through scheduling a
weekly backup of drive C. Follow these steps:

1. In the Backup Scheduler dialog box, choose **S**chedule Event.

2. In the Schedule Backup Event dialog box, choose **S**etup, which
   displays a list of active files with the SET extension. From that list,
   select DEFAULT.SET. The Setup command button now displays
   DEFAULT.SET.

3. Choose **F**requency, which displays a list of frequency options. To
   back up drive C every week, choose **W**eekly.

4. To select the type of backup to perform every week, choose
   Backup Type. From the list, choose **F**ull.

5. In the Start **D**ate and Start **T**ime text boxes, type the start date and
   time of the backup. If you want the backup performed every Friday, type the date of the upcoming Friday. Type **4:00pm** in the
   Start Time text box to schedule the backup for 4 p.m.

6. Choose OK to save the scheduled backup.

You have successfully scheduled a backup. Regardless of the program
in which you are working, each Friday at 4 p.m., you are asked whether
you want to back up your hard disk.

Changing Scheduled Backups

After you schedule backups, you can edit or delete them to fit your changing needs. From the Backup Scheduler dialog box, select the scheduled backup that you want to change from the Backup Events list at the bottom of the dialog box. Highlight the scheduled backup and press the space bar to select it, or just double-click it.

To edit the scheduled backup, choose the Edit Event option to display the Edit Backup Event dialog box. This dialog box works just like the one you used to schedule the backup initially. Make the appropriate changes and choose OK.

Deleting a scheduled backup is even easier. After you select the backup to be deleted and choose **D**elete Event, Norton Backup asks you to verify that you want to delete the backup. To delete the backup, choose OK from the warning box.

Restoring Backup Files

Though the similarity may not be obvious at first, backing up your data and buying health or life insurance have much in common. When you buy insurance, you want the best policy that fits your needs for the least cost, but you never want to have to use the policy. Similarly, you want the best backup that fits your needs for the least cost in disks, tapes, and time. And you never want to have to use your backup disks. Just as people file health and life insurance claims daily, however, people restore backup disks daily.

The **R**estore option in the Norton Backup dialog box places your backed-up files onto your hard disk. After you choose **R**estore, the Norton Restore dialog box appears (see fig. 29.14).

 NOTE Different levels of Restore exist, just as different levels of Backup exist. The levels are Basic, Advanced, and Preset. Depending on the level of Norton Backup, the actual name of the Norton Restore dialog box changes to include the program level. Figure 29.14 shows the Norton Advanced Restore dialog box.

Catalog files are very important to the backup and restore process. The following section describes catalog files so that you can better understand their purpose and the way you work them. You also learn how to read the information in the name of a catalog file. With that understanding, the process of restoring a backup is easier to master. All restore options also are explained to enable you to make the restore process work more efficiently for you.

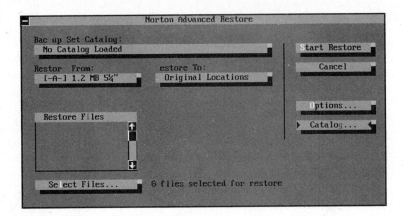

Fig. 29.14

The Norton
Advanced
Restore
dialog box.

Using Catalogs with Restore

After you complete a backup, Norton Backup creates a catalog file for
the backup. Norton Backup stores these catalog files in two places: in
the Norton Backup directory and on the last disk of the actual backup.

The *selections* catalogs and the *master* catalogs are the two types of
catalog files. Selections catalogs, which are usually referred to as just
catalogs, contain the names of all the backed-up files and the directory
structure from which the files originated.

Selections catalogs have the extensions FUL, INC, DIF, and CPY. The
extensions correspond to the various backups you can perform: full,
incremental, differential, and copy (see "Understanding Backup Types"
earlier in the chapter). These types of files are the ones that Norton
Backup looks for when you initiate the **R**estore command.

Understanding how a selections catalog file is named is important so
that you can later determine the file's contents. When you look at the
catalog list, you see file names like CD20221A.FUL. Here are the meanings of the characters in the file name:

Character	Meaning
C	Stands for the first drive backed up in the file. In this case, the first drive backed up was drive C.
D	Indicates the last drive backed up in the file (in this case, drive D). If you have only one drive, this letter is the same as the first letter.
2	Denotes the last digit of the year in which the backup was performed—for this file, 1992.

Character	Meaning
02	Corresponds to the month the backup was performed—for this file, February.
21	Indicates the day the backup was performed. Combining this information with the preceding year and month information tells you that the backup was performed on February 21, 1992.
A	A sequence letter that distinguishes between catalogs of the same name. Because this file is the first file created under this name, the next file has the letter B, the file after that has the letter C, and so on, through the letter Z.
FUL	An extension that tells you the type of backup performed.

The other catalog type, the master catalog, coordinates the information when you restore files to the hard drive. The master catalog, stored in the Norton Backup directory, maintains a list of the catalog files. A master catalog takes the same file name as the setup file, except that a CAT extension is used (see the earlier section "Working with Setup Files" in this chapter).

Restoring Data

Now that you understand the two types of catalogs, you can get to know the Norton Restore dialog box better (refer to fig. 29.14). Although this dialog box looks similar to the Norton Backup dialog box shown in figure 29.2, the options are different. The Norton Restore dialog box provides the following options:

- Backup Set Catalog displays a list of catalogs containing files you can restore.

- Restore From selects the drive that contains the backup disks.

- Restore To selects the destination on the hard drive to which you want to restore. You can choose from a number of destinations. The Original Locations option restores the files to the location from which the files were backed up. Choosing Other Drives restores files to a different drive, and Other Directories restores to a different directory. Single Directory places all files in one directory, even if they originally resided in different directories.

- Restore Files displays the name of the drive as supplied by the catalog file.

■ Select Files chooses specific files to restore from the catalog.

■ Options selects advanced restore options (described in the next section).

■ Catalog loads, finds, or rebuilds a catalog.

Restoring is similar to backing up. The difference is that you move information from backup disks back to the hard drive. Selecting the catalog to use is like selecting the setup file to use when backing up. Selecting files to restore is exactly the same as selecting files to back up.

After you set all your restore parameters in the Norton Restore dialog box, choose the Start Restore option. Norton Backup restores the files to the drive and directory you selected.

T I P You generally restore files to their original locations, but not always. Suppose that you store spreadsheet files in your hard disk at C:\SHEETS. Your colleague wants to copy those files to drive D, in the directory SSHTS. Use Norton Backup to back up all the spreadsheets. On the other computer, choose Restore from the Norton Backup dialog box and choose Restore To from the Norton Restore dialog box. From the Restore To dialog box, choose Single Directory and then choose OK. Because you chose Single Directory, a text box appears below the Restore To command button. In that box, specify the directory to which you want to restore; for this example, type **D:\SSHTS**.

Using the backup/restore process to move files from one PC to another is more efficient than simply copying files to a disk with DOS for two reasons:

■ With Norton, you can select all files to be transferred at once. This way, you save time—you don't need to enter the COPY command for every file or subdirectory.

■ You can compress the data being transferred. This way, you can put more files on less disk or tape space. You may not want to use Norton for a few files, but if you transfer many files, this way is more efficient.

Setting Restore Options

You can customize the restore process by using the Options option, which displays the Disk Restore Options dialog box. The dialog box, shown in figure 29.15, lists all the options you can change for Restore.

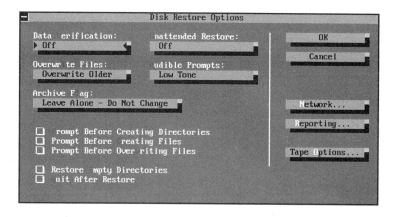

Fig. 29.15

The Disk
Restore Options
dialog box.

The options in the Disk Restore Options dialog box are the same
whether you restore from disk or from tape. The options are self-
explanatory or similar to their backup counterparts (see the earlier
section "Choosing Backup Options" for more details). Here are the
available options:

Option	Description
Data **V**erification	Verifies data before restoring it. Choose **O**ff (the default), **S**ample Only, or Read and **C**ompare.
Overw**ri**te Files	Specifies what to do if a file that is being restored already exists on the hard drive. Choose **N**ever Overwrite Files, **O**verwrite Older Files Only (the default), or **A**lways Overwrite Files.
Archive F**l**ag	Shows whether a file is new or changed. Choose **L**eave Alone—Do Not Change (the default), **C**lear—Mark as Backed Up, or **S**et—Mark as Not Backed Up.
Unattended Restore	Enables Restore to respond to prompts. Choose **O**ff (the default); On, **N**o Delay; or specify a 5-, 16-, or 60-second delay.
Audible Prompts	Specifies the type of audible tone to use when prompting for user specifications. Choose **O**ff, **L**ow Tone (the default), **H**igh Tone, or **C**hime.
Prompt Before Creating Directories	Prompts the user before a directory is created.

continues

Option	Description
Prompt Before Creating Files	Prompts the user before a file is created.
Prompt Before Overwriting Files	Prompts the user before an existing file is overwritten.
Restore Empty Directories	Creates directories even though no files are stored in them.
Quit After Restore	Immediately quits Norton Backup after a restore procedure is completed.

 NOTE   To access the options for tape drives, choose the Tape Options option. Likewise, in the Tape Restore Options dialog box, choose Disk Options to access options for disk drives.

Restoring to a Network

When you restore to a network, you face the same potential problem you had when you back up from a network: files that you want to restore may be in use. You cannot back up from or restore to a file in use; however, you can specify that Restore retry files in use.

The Network option in the Disk Restore Options dialog box works exactly the same as in the Disk Backup Options dialog box. You can specify how long to continue retrying to restore a file in use, when to stop retrying to restore the file, or to skip a file in use. You can also send messages to users on a NetWare 286 network that files in use will be closed for a restoration. Make whatever settings are appropriate for your type of network and choose OK.

See the section "Setting Network Options" earlier in the chapter for more information.

Creating a Restoration Report

As with Backup, you can generate a report by choosing the Reporting option from the Disk Restore Options dialog box. You can specify that the report contain such information as the option settings used for the restoration, a list of processed files, the restoration statistics, and a list of any error messages.

Generating a report that includes any of these options is a good idea because it provides tangible and ready information for future reference and use. For more information on generating reports, see the section "Creating a Backup Progress Report" earlier in the chapter.

Using Compare

The **C**ompare option in the Norton Backup dialog box matches backed-up files with the originals to ensure that the backup is an exact duplicate. After you choose **C**ompare, you see the Norton Compare dialog box (see fig. 29.16).

NOTE The actual name of the Norton Compare dialog box reflects the level of Norton Backup in use (Basic, Advanced, or Preset). Figure 29.16 shows the Norton Advanced Compare dialog box.

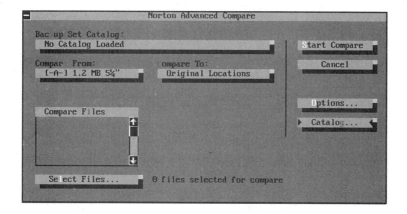

Fig. 29.16

The Norton Advanced Compare dialog box.

You may notice that the Compare dialog box is nearly identical to the Restore dialog box discussed earlier. The process of using the command is also the same.

First use the Bac**k**up Set Catalog option to choose the catalog that corresponds to the files you want to compare. If you are not sure which catalog you want, choose the Catalo**g** option to list the available catalogs. Through the Catalog list, you can search for files, retrieve files from floppy disks or the hard drive, load other catalogs from floppy disk, and delete entire catalogs.

If you cannot remember which catalog contains a certain file, you can choose the Select Files option. This option prompts you for the name of the file and provides you with a list of all the catalogs that contain that specific file.

T I P

After you find the catalog that contains the files you want to compare, double-check the Compare From and Compare To options to make sure that the source and destination of the files are correct. Then select the files to compare.

The Options option in the Compare dialog box enables you to choose the Unattended Compare and Audible Prompts options in the same way as the Restore and Backup commands. You also can choose how to handle network options and the type of report to create. (See the earlier section "Restoring Backup Files" for more on these options.) Choosing Start Compare in the Compare dialog box activates your selections and begins comparing your backed-up files to the hard drive.

Reconfiguring Norton Backup

To look at or change Norton Backup's configuration settings, Norton Backup provides a simple way to review these settings through the Configure option in the Norton Backup dialog box. Choosing this option displays the Configure dialog box, as shown in figure 29.17.

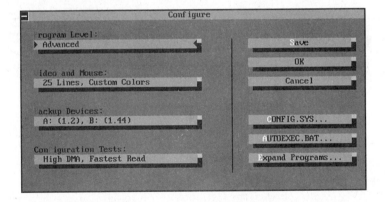

Fig. 29.17

The Configure dialog box.

The Configure dialog box enables you to adjust all the settings that Norton Backup determined for you when you first started the program. The first setting, Program Level, enables you to choose the Basic, Advanced, or Preset level of operation.

T I P   At the Advanced level, you can create and save your own setup files, as discussed in the earlier section "Working With Setup Files."

With the Video and Mouse option, you can customize the way your screen and mouse work. If you choose this option, you see the Video and Mouse Configuration dialog box, which enables you to access six additional dialog boxes (three for video and three for the mouse). The options in this dialog box work similarly to those in the Norton Utilities Configuration dialog box (see Chapter 2 for details).

The Backup Devices option displays a dialog box that lists two floppy drives and a tape drive (if a tape drive is installed). Because Norton Backup determines the types of drives you have in your system, you simply need to choose the backup drive you want. You can change drives by selecting the appropriate drive from this list, and you can choose Auto Config so that Norton Backup checks your system and reinstalls all drives. The Auto Config option is best for users who add a tape drive to their system.

With the Configuration Tests option in the Configure dialog box, you can check the settings that Norton Backup's initial tests determined were most efficient for your system (displayed on the Configuration Tests button). The Direct Memory Access (DMA) and Compatibility tests are the two basic tests. For more information on these tests, see Appendix C on installing Norton programs.

> **CAUTION:** During the DMA test, your computer may *hang*, or stop working. If the message Testing DMA appears for more than 30 seconds, your computer has hung. If this problem occurs, re-start your computer and Norton Backup. The DMA now is set to Low Speed. Don't try to set it to High Speed. (The Low Speed and High Speed options in the Configuration Tests dialog box determine the rate at which data can be transferred.)

In the lower-right corner of the Configure dialog box, notice the options AUTOEXEC.BAT and CONFIG.SYS. During the Norton Backup initial testing and installation, you had the choice to change these two files. If you chose to change them, Norton Backup changed CONFIG.SYS so that it had 30 BUFFERS and 30 FILES. Norton Backup also was added to your AUTOEXEC.BAT file's PATH statement, as were the Norton Backup environment variable and NSCHED.COM (the Backup Scheduler TSR program). If you didn't choose to change the files, you can use these two options to do so at any time. Choose either option and the proposed changes appear, along with OK and Cancel options. To accept the changes, choose OK.

The last option in the Configure dialog box is **E**xpand Programs. Choosing this option displays a dialog box explaining the process of expanding archived files and asking whether you want to proceed. Norton Backup keeps some files compressed and, when those files are needed, expands them. It recompresses them again when through.

 **NOTE** If Norton Backup seems to take a long time to execute, the delay may mean that your system works better with the files expanded at all times rather than expanded only when needed. Choosing OK expands the files. Remember that after these files are expanded this way, you cannot compress them again.

After you make all the configuration changes you want, you can choose to make the changes permanent or leave them active only for the current session. If you choose **S**ave, all changes are saved as your regular configuration setup. If you choose OK, the changes are effective until you exit from Norton Backup. Choosing Cancel ignores any changes made and returns you to the original setup configuration.

Summary

In this chapter, you became familiar with Norton Backup's dialog boxes, enabling you to harness the power of the program. Whether you want to back up a small number of regularly used files or a complete hard disk, a few mouse clicks or keystrokes can assure you that the data you worked so hard to create is protected and secure.

The next chapter explores another powerful Norton program, Norton Commander.

Using Norton Commander

Norton Commander 3 is a program that enables you to perform a variety of tasks on your computer in a menulike environment rather than from the DOS command line. Instead of having to remember the syntax of the DOS COPY command, for example, you can follow a series of menus and prompts through the Commander copy process. Commander automates commands through its menu structure, making the "driving" of the computer easier for you. Commander is particularly helpful for beginning users who have not memorized DOS and Norton commands.

Commander is not just a substitute for some DOS commands, however; it also has several features that are not available in DOS. You can use Commander, for example, to view the contents of a variety of database, spreadsheet, and word processing files without having to use the respective programs. Commander also enables you to execute several Norton Utilities commands, such as those that display a sorted directory, set file attributes, find files, and set an EGA monitor to display more than 25 lines.

Using Norton Commander is like adding a "power package" to a plain automobile. DOS is that plain automobile that generally gets you where you want to go. With Commander added to DOS, however, you have power windows (pull-down menus), extra horsepower (commands that can do more than DOS commands), a car phone (MCI Mail), and more. Commander makes using your computer more fun, and the program's array of features also can make you more productive.

This chapter introduces the basics of using Norton Commander. The chapter is arranged according to how you normally would use Norton Commander, not necessarily by the order of the options in the on-screen menus. You first learn how to display and access the various Commander menus. Most of the action takes place in the Commander's left and right panels, so the contents of the panels and the options that control these panels are discussed early in the chapter.

After giving a preliminary description of how Commander works, the chapter explains how to manage and manipulate your directories and files; look at files from spreadsheet, database, and word processing programs; use the Commander editor to edit ASCII files; and customize Commander.

NOTE In this chapter, it is assumed that you already have installed Norton Commander on your hard disk. If not, see Appendix C for installation instructions. Be sure that you choose to place the NC directory name in the PATH statement in your AUTOEXEC.BAT file (an option during installation). If you already have installed Commander but did not place NC in your PATH statement, see Appendix A for information on how to use the DOS PATH command and edit an AUTOEXEC.BAT file.

Understanding Norton Commander Basics

To begin the Norton Commander program, type **NC** and press Enter at the DOS prompt. A screen similar to the one shown in figure 30.1 appears.

Under normal installation, the initial Commander screen consists of a directory panel on the right half of the screen and a function key bar at the bottom of the screen. As you learn later in this chapter, however, you can customize the way that Commander looks on your screen. Generally, the screen includes four areas of interest: a right panel, a left panel (not visible in fig. 30.1), a menu of function key commands at the bottom of the screen, and a menu bar at the top of the screen (not visible in fig. 30.1). Notice that the normal DOS prompt appears just above the function key menu.